TRAVELER'S
CHINA
COMPANION

The 1998–1999 Traveler's Companions

ARGENTINA • AUSTRALIA • BALI • CALIFORNIA • CANADA • CHINA • COSTA RICA • CUBA •
EASTERN CANADA • ECUADOR • FLORIDA • HAWAII • HONG KONG • INDIA • INDONESIA • JAPAN •
KENYA • MALAYSIA & SINGAPORE • MEDITERRANEAN FRANCE • MEXICO • NEPAL • NEW ENGLAND •
NEW ZEALAND • PERU • PHILIPPINES • PORTUGAL • RUSSIA • SPAIN • THAILAND • TURKEY •
VENEZUELA • VIETNAM, LAOS AND CAMBODIA • WESTERN CANADA

Traveler's CHINA Companion

First Published 1998
World Leisure Marketing Limited
9 Downing Road, West Meadows Industrial Estate
Derby, DE21 6HA, England
Web Site: http://www.map-world.co.uk

ISBN: 1-84006-053-0

By arrangement with Kümmerly+Frey AG, Switzerland
© 1998 Kümmerly+Frey AG, Switzerland

Created, edited and produced by Allan Amsel Publishing
53, rue Beaudouin, 27700 Les Andelys, France
E-mail: Allan.Amsel@wanadoo.fr
Editor in Chief: Allan Amsel
Editor: Fiona Nichols
Original design concept: Hon Bing-wah
Picture editors and designers: David Henry and Laura Purdom

Printed by Samhwa Printing Company Limited, Seoul, Korea

TRAVELER'S CHINA COMPANION

by Derek Maitland and Chris Taylor

photographed by Adrian Bradshaw and Nik Wheeler

Contents

TOP SPOTS

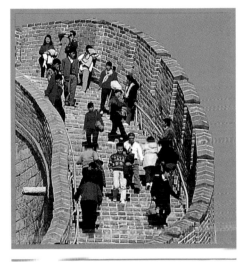

The Great Wall

IT'S THE SYMBOL OF CHINA, AND NOT TO CLIMB IT AT SOME POINT IN YOUR CHINA TRIP WOULD BE A PITY. It's not until you get up onto its fortified ramparts and watch it snaking away over the pale green hills into the horizon, both before you and after you, that you realize, "this *is* a great wall." As Richard Nixon said: "This is a great wall, and only a people with a great past could have such a great wall." He was, like many visitors, at a loss for words.

Like any compelling historical attraction the Great Wall yields up its secrets reluctantly. Academics have been heard to wonder aloud about when it came into being, the Qin dynasty original of 2,000 years ago probably being a much more modest undertaking than the monster that is visible from the moon today. Which brings us to the question: Is it really visible from the moon? Some say, no. What about its length? Nearly every reference will give you a conflicting answer. The Chinese themselves call it formally the *wanli changcheng*, or the "10,000 *li*-long wall," a *li* being a Chinese measurement of length that equals around half a kilometer, making the wall 5,000 km (3,100 miles) long. But you'll hear anything from 3,500 km to 6,000 km from other sources. And for that matter, how "great" was it, anyway? As far as Genghis Khan was concerned, only as great as "the courage of those who defend it." Marco Polo didn't even bother mentioning it. And to top it off, it didn't fulfull its purpose: Invaders swept across it, and the Europeans and Japanese approached from the wrong side.

All the more reason to make that pilgrimage from Beijing to **Badaling**, where the Coca Cola brigade clamor for your small change and the approach swarms with hawkers of "I Climbed the Great Wall" T-shirts. It's all part of the fun. You might even pop into the 360° Great Wall Circle Vision Theatre and watch a 15-minute promotional video. But once you've had your Coke, bought your T-shirt, seen the movie, it's time to shrug off the crowds. Ignore the lines for the cable car, and climb up under your own steam. Turn left on top and head north. It's surprising how quickly the

OPPOSITE and ABOVE: The Great Wall — contrasting views of serenity and activity.

crowds start to thin, and if you're feeling energetic, before long you'll have the wall to yourself. Within a mile the new, reconstructed section of the wall ends and you'll be amongst the ruins.

It's here that the greatness of this wall forces itself upon you. Look at it climbing and descending through this lonely landscape. Imagine the soldiers patrolling it, one eye nervously on the barbaric wastes to the west, the other longingly on hearth and home to the east. The soldiers were conscripts more likely than not, as were the wall's builders. Nobody knows how many tens of thousands perished building, defending and attacking this edifice. It's a disturbing thought, but one that slips away as you trudge back to the shops and restaurants and souvenir shops, and get on the bus that takes you back to your hotel in Beijing and perhaps a duck dinner, content in the knowledge that you've climbed the Great Wall. You'll have the T-shirt to prove it.

Tread in the Footsteps of the Celestial Emperor

WHAT CAN POSSIBLY BE MORE INVITING THAN THE FORBIDDEN? Off limits to the masses for 500 years, the gilded nest of 24 Ming and Qing dynasty emperors, their concubines, princesses and scheming eunuchs, is now open to anyone who can afford the price of an admission ticket.

Founded in 1420, the Forbidden City awes and astounds. For a start it's big — 720,000 sq m (over two million square feet) to be precise: More than 900 rooms (an auspicious 999 according to legend) are hidden away in the buildings that overlook its sweeping courtyards, gardens and squares. The palace walls are 10 m (33 ft) high and stretch for 3.4 km (2.2 miles). Surrounding all this is a 52-m (170-ft)-wide moat. Then there's the uniquely Chinese poetry of the names: the Hall of Terrestrial Tranquillity, the Hall of Celestial Purity, the Hall of Supreme Harmony, the Hall of Literary

Glory, the Hall of Military Prowess. The "Purple Forbidden City" is what it's called in Chinese, a reference to the purple palace of the Emperor of Heaven, whose home is in the faraway reaches of space, near the North Star. The Forbidden City is truly an attempt to duplicate all the glory of the heavens.

It's easy to be swept away by the vast grandeur of it all and miss the details: the carved marble carriageways underfoot, the haughty expressions of stylized fury on the faces of the sculpted lions (the male with the pomegranate symbol of power in his right paw, the female with a cub beneath her left), the gold filigree depicting dragons and other mythological creatures. You cannot pause to savor such moments of observation for long; there's too much to see.

Entry is via the **Meridian Gate** in the southern walls of the city. Built in 1420, this is the grand main gate, the largest of all the many gates in the city, and in times past ceremonial drums would sound from the gates to announce important occasions. The gate opens out into an expanse of courtyard. Try to imagine the scenes of vast pomp and splendor — the emperor accompanied by an imperial guard that included Burmese elephants in its ranks — that once graced its flagstones. Today it bustles with tourists, many of them lingering on the five marble bridges that symbolize the five Confucian virtues. Don't forget to

turn and look back at the Meridian Gate: It looks best from inside the walls.

This is the Outer Palace. The "Great Within," as it was referred to, is approached by the **Gate of Supreme Harmony**, which lies ahead. This gate in turn takes you into another vast courtyard, so big that at special ceremonies it could accommodate the entirety of the imperial court, which at its height numbered upwards of 100,000.

At the end of the courtyard is the first and the most magnificent of the palace halls, the **Hall of Supreme Harmony**, where only the most important affairs of

Light blanket of snow softens imperial architecture and mood of the Ming dynasty's most dramatic legacy, the Forbidden City, in Beijing.

state were performed. Ahead lies the **Hall of Middle Harmony**, where the visiting heads of faraway vassal states might be ushered to kowtow before the emperor, and ahead again lies the **Hall of Preserving Harmony**, where the empire's best and brightest scholars took examinations for positions as mandarins in the exalted imperial service.

You are, if you haven't realized it yet, approaching the inner sanctum of the Celestial Empire in stages as you walk northwards: The emperor faced the outside world from the Meridian Gate; he addressed his court from the Gate of Supreme Harmony; he disposed of state affairs in the Hall of Middle Harmony; he appointed the inner core of his administration in the Hall of Preserving Harmony; and beyond all this was the imperial living quarters, which were the preserve of the emperor, his concubines and an army of court eunuchs.

Today you can stroll through the living quarters and try to imagine the life of the "Son of Heaven," the man who sat at the center of an empire that for many centuries believed itself the center of the world. And if your imagination stretches this far, spare a thought for Pu Yi, the last of the Manchu emperors, cast down from such glory and ending his days as a municipal gardener in Beijing. It seems a long way to fall.

Witness the Reawakening of a Great City

HUANGPU PARK IS A GOOD PLACE TO START YOUR SHANGHAI TOUR. AHEAD IS THE BUND. When travelers arrived by boat, back in the old days, this was their first glimpse of the city. As for the park, formerly the British Public Gardens, it is remembered as the site of that notorious sign: "No dogs or Chinese!" Today there are knots of people promenading, taking photographs — you might see a local

walking a dog. There's a wistful statue of Mao nearby and a café selling gourmet coffee. Get here early enough and you'll see middle-aged couples rehearsing ballroom dancing, the elderly going through sinuous t'ai chi routines.

It's a far cry from the dowdy city of the mid-1980s. Back then, Nanjing Road, once the commercial hub of the Far East, had fallen into sad neglect, a windswept boulevard lined with near empty stores. Shoppers — uniformly dressed in blue Mao suits — had the grim look of people going about dull but unavoidable chores. Shop clerks scowled and blew scornfully into jam jars of tea. The cafés habitually "ran out" of milk, cream and sugar. A geriatric jazz band at the Peace Hotel

OPPOSITE: The Bund, Shanghai's unforgettable waterfront skyline. ABOVE: The crowds on Shanghai's Nanjing Road are not for the faint-hearted. RIGHT: A tranquil escape from China's most hustle-bustle city at the Yuyuan Gardens.

(formerly The Cathay) that played pedestrian hits from the 1930s was all that was left of Shanghai's once infamous nightlife. The city was like a museum that had been invaded by listlessly unimaginative squatters: Colonial villas had been converted into kindergartens, banks into obscure government ministries, the once famous Wing On Department Store had become the drab Nº 10 Department Store.

What a difference a decade or so can make. Shanghai has been busy dusting off the cobwebs, tunneling subways, erecting expressways and relearning the art of window dressing. There are vacationing crowds on the Bund — Chinese families dressed to the nines, munching on snacks, squinting at maps and pointing out historical sites. The shoppers on Nanjing Road bustle in and out of refurbished department stores, boutiques and restaurants. Skyscrapers pop up almost before your very eyes on the other side of the river. The Nº 10 Department Store been once again rechristened as the Hua Lien Department Store.

And Shanghai, China's definitively modern city, is reclaiming its style too. You can see it on The Bund. The Peace Hotel is a wonderful piece of *fin de siècle* elegance. Back when it was The Cathay, Noel Coward wrote *Private Lives* ensconced in a suite here. The Long Bar in the Tung Feng Hotel, once home to the most exclusive club in the Far East, is now ironically home to a branch of an American fastfood outlet, but the bar has been recreated in Shanghai style up in the Shanghai Centre on Nanjing Road.

But while that thirties retro look is popular (there's money in it), Shanghai has a sharp eye to the future. Indeed, the pace of change tempts you to reach for words such as "dizzying." Even locals despair of keeping up with it. Someone guides you around the corner to a renowned restaurant only to find a fast-food centre or a boutique specializing in Yves Saint Laurent and Guy Laroche. "That's funny," they say, rubbing their chin with a look of troubled dislocation. "It was here last week, I'm sure of it."

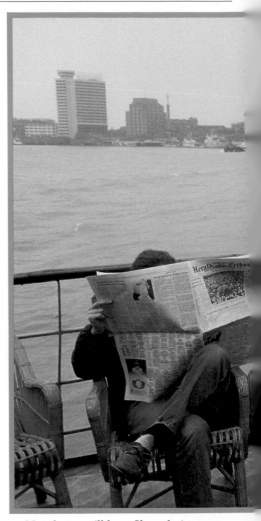

Not that you'll hear Shanghainese complaining. This sudden invasion of the twenty-first century is nothing more than their birthright. True, the city may have nodded off for a few decades, but it was always the brashest, brightest, biggest city in China, one of the biggest in the world (13.4 million people at last count), and all Chinese agree that the Shanghainese have a street savvy matched by no one.

See the high-rollers stalking their way into brightly lit banquet restaurants and red-carpet karaoke parlors — you can spend US$300 or more on a bottle of XO brandy in one of these places if you like; many customers do. The Rolexes and the suits come from the massive

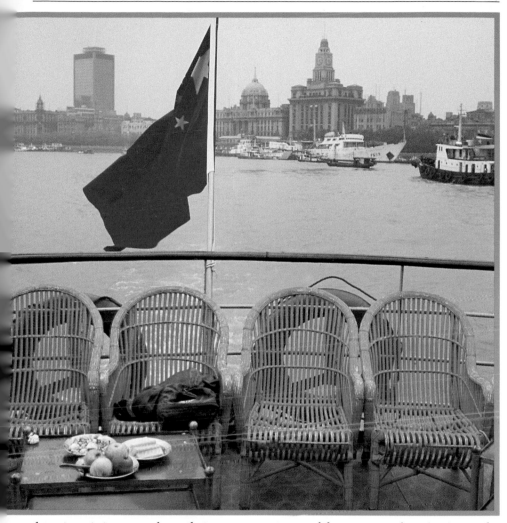

department store complexes that Japanese investment has brought to town — Isetan and Yaohan to name two. There are late-night queues and eagle-eyed door staff at dance clubs such as New York New York and LA Café. Just north of Suzhou Creek is a crackling neon entertainment enclave that looks for all the world like it's been plucked from downtown Tokyo.

This new Shanghai is in a hurry to catch up. As you stroll around town there is an infectious sense of urgency about the place — "I've got to see what I can because it may not be here tomorrow," you find yourself thinking. So you desert fashionable Huaihai Road, where the commercial instinct is rapidly driving all

traces of the past towards extinction, and head off down a quiet side street. Washing hangs from poles in the windows, old men sit on collapsible stools playing dominoes, a woman wobbles past on a bicycle laden with groceries. And there, up ahead, is a narrow building where the first National Congress of the Communist Party was held. Not far away, on what was once the rue Molière, is a former residence of Sun Yatsen, China's Quixotic revolutionary father. In the northwest of town is the Jade Buddha Temple, home of a 1,000 kg (2,200 lb) jewel-encrusted Buddha statue brought from Myanmar.

Ferry provides moment to catch up on news on Huangpu River cruise along the skyline of Shanghai's famous waterfront, The Bund.

It's a relief to find these historical sites still standing. Others are long gone: The Shanghai Racecourse is now the People's Park and People's Square. Others have been transformed: The Yuyuan Gardens and Bazaar, on the northern edge of the old Chinese quarter, may date from sixteenth century Ming China, but today it's more theme park than monument. Beijing is the city with the sights. The Shanghainese are too busy making money, eating, getting on with things, to worry much about tourist attractions: You go to Shanghai because it is Shanghai; and if that's where you come from, nowhere else really counts.

Into the Sea of Clouds

CHINA'S SACRED PEAKS ARE SCATTERED THE LENGTH AND BREADTH OF THE COUNTRY; pilgrims have toiled up their slopes and artists sought inspiration in their views for centuries. Most peaks are either Buddhist or Daoist: Emeishan in Sichuan, for example, is Buddhist, while Taishan in Shandong province is Daoist; but a few peaks — such as Huangshan in Anhui province — have been sanctified by their beauty alone.

Whether Buddhist, Daoist or simply beautiful, climbing one of China's sacred mountains is like slipping through some magical backdoor into the world of the Chinese watercolor. Those fluted rocks surmounted by a lone pine, roiling clouds lapping at gnarled roots really do exist. The catch is that getting up to the elevations required for such views invariably demands serious exertions.

At Anhui province's **Huangshan**, perhaps the most gorgeous of all China's sacred mountains, the path up into the clouds is long and arduous, and — as the song goes — "with many a winding turn." The scenic western approach, which includes precipitous steps hewn out of rock faces, and a vertiginous approach up to the **Heavenly Capital Peak**, is a full 15 km (10 miles) of climbing. Even if you're in good shape, you can be sure you'll have some aches and pains the next day. I could barely walk for two days after visiting Huangshan, and all I'd done was the western *descent*. (Don't underestimate the effort involved in going down.)

Of course — and there are those who will resent such modern encroachments — the inevitable has happened, and at the most popular sacred mountains a cable car will be waiting to whisk you to the summit. In the case of Huangshan, the cable car does the trip in just eight minutes. Contrast this with the quickest walking route — the eastern approach — which takes a minimum of three grueling hours, and the temptation to do the ascent sitting down becomes difficult to resist. Unless you're in Olympic condition or have oodles of time on your hands, I recommend the cable car one way, and a foot slog the other. Up or down, take your pick; it's hard either way, but at least you have momentum and gravity on your side on the descent. If you find yourself regretting the endeavor half way up or down, spare a thought for the famed Chinese artist Liu

ABOVE: Scaling the heights at Huangshan.
OPPOSITE: Huangshan's watercolor landscapes have inspired artists for centuries.

Haisu, who climbed Huangshan for the tenth time in 1988… at the age of 93! He stayed on the mountain for two months and knocked off 46 paintings.

At Huangshan, like other peaks, the chief attraction at the summit is what the Chinese poetically call *yunhai* — the "sea of clouds." With the advent of mass tourism in China, heaving crowds of oohing and aahing Chinese can be guaranteed at the most popular mountains. Strike off on the side trails, however, and you will soon leave the crowds behind. It's usually still possible to find some quiet corner where the clouds roll lazily against the rocky shore far below your feet and you can commune with the poets and brush-masters of times past.

For the true pilgrim experience, Buddhist **Emeishan**, in Sichuan province, is the most accessible. Even here there's a short cut, by way of a minibus service that takes you to the Jieyin Hall, where there is now a cable car that whisks latter-day pilgrims to the summit in minutes. But the real attraction of Emeishan is the opportunity to slowly scale the heights, stopping at Buddhist monasteries and temples with the Chinese pilgrims (armed with staves that double as walking sticks and monkey-deterrents) overnight. One night is enough to get up the mountain and down again, but if you can afford the time, give it two nights. Some of the temple and monastery hotels, such as the one at **Wannian Temple**, are eight centuries or more old. A night spent in circumstances of such antiquity is a rare privilege indeed in the new China.

Cormorants, Caves and Limestone Peaks

IF YOU TIRE OF BEING BUSSED FROM ONE FIVE-STAR HOTEL TO ANOTHER AND START GETTING THE SNEAKING FEELING THAT YOU'RE MISSING OUT ON THE REAL CHINA, escape to **Yangshuo**, Guilin's small-town rival. The cruise boats from Guilin glide downriver

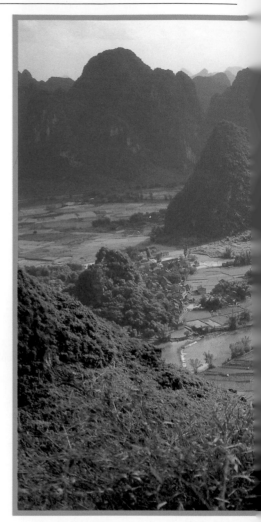

past the hulking limestone monoliths that the region is famous for and stop in Yangshuo, where tourists are taken back to Guilin in tour buses. Skip the bus and spend a night in Yangshuo instead.

Backpackers discovered this charming village 15 years ago, and despite the fact that the restaurants and hotels continue to grow in number, Yangshuo is far from being overrun. Strike off into the backstreets and you'll find feisty traders presiding over piles of cabbages and fruit, clumps of talkative retirees squatting on wicker stools, and noisy mahjong games in progress. Head out of town on a bicycle and within 10 minutes you'll have paddy fields on either side.

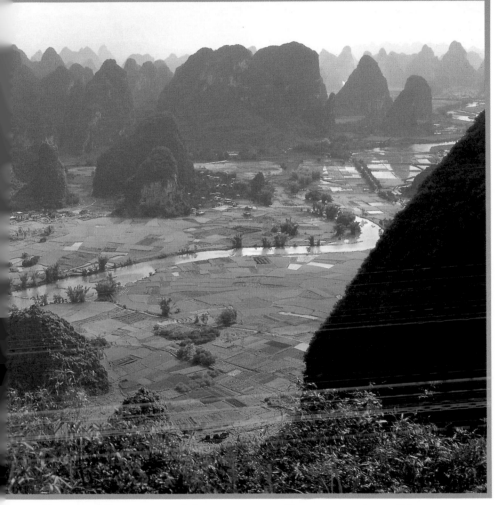

You can while away a week in Yangshuo doing very little but taking in the scenery. The bicycle ride to nearby **Moon Hill** is a veritable rite of passage. From a huge natural arch in one of the limestone peaks you can gaze out across the patchwork of paddy fields, the karst monsters marching away into the horizon. Bring some lunch and make a picnic of it. In the afternoon you might take a trip down into the recently discovered **Black Buddha** and **Black Dragon** caves. These cave systems are still being explored, but in the meantime enterprising locals will guide you on tried and tested routes into the caves. Don't wear your best clothes, and expect to get wet.

If caves are not your thing, an afternoon splash in the river might be. Hiring inner tubes and lazily drifting with the current has become a surprisingly popular pastime in Yangshuo, and it is a good way to get a closeup look at the local village life. If you get a hankering to jump on one of those boats that putter past every now and again crowded with locals going home from market or from work, don't forget to take your bicycle. A boat journey to the rural village of **Xingping** takes a couple of hours, and about the same to return by bicycle, a popular round trip.

The eerie karst landscape surrounding Yangshuo, as seen from Moon Hill.

And just as evening is looming and you think you've run out of things to do, you see a sign in the village advertising **cormorant fishing**. Don't pass it up. For a small fee, locals will take you out onto the river at dusk where you can see the fishermen plying an age-old trade with the help of trained cormorants. A halter around the cormorant's neck prevents the bird from swallowing the fish, but the fisherman allows the bird to guzzle one down every now and again. It's an atmospheric scene: The birds lined up on the prow of a small punt in the flickering light of an oil lantern, the last light of the day etched in searing red into the western sky.

Don't worry about missing dinner. The village main street is packed with restaurants, many of them open until late. Order an inexpensive bottle of the local brew, Guilin beer, as you contemplate your meal — fish perhaps.

Silk Dreams

THOSE GREAT TRADING ROUTES OF AGES PAST EXCITE OUR MODERN MINDS. Imagine if the cans and jars we so casually toss into our baskets at supermarkets had traversed canals in junks, crossed deserts on camel back, survived marauding bandits and Mediterranean pirates. (There probably wouldn't be a great deal in the supermarkets.)

The most intriguing of the ancient trade routes is without a doubt the Silk Road, that artery of trade, ideas and culture between the East and the West that survived from around 100 BC until the thirteenth century AD. It's difficult for us now to comprehend how valuable silk was, or why it so captivated the Romans when they first encountered it in the banners of their enemies in Central Asia. Nobody in Europe knew how the material was produced and the Chinese guarded the secrets of its production under the pain of death. Such was the popularity of silk in Rome that massive imports built up an imbalance of trade and threatened the Roman economy.

The route started in Chang'an, the ancient Tang dynasty capital now known as Xi'an, and it's perfectly possible nowadays to follow part of the old Silk Road and witness scenes that have changed very little in the centuries that have passed since the route fell into disuse (shipping and the discovery of sericulture in Europe brought about the road's demise). For today's China travelers the ultimate Silk Road destination is Kashgar, but in times past this five-month journey was just the first stage of the long road west.

The five-month journey can be done in a couple of weeks now, though it is an arduous trip: From Xi'an travel by train to Lanzhou, and from there take an Urumqi-bound train to Liuyuan. Liuyuan is a 130-km (80-mile) bus journey from the first of the great Silk Road oasis towns, Dunhuang, where you can see some of China's most impressive Buddhist cave art and stay in a town surrounded by rolling sand dunes.

From Dunhuang you can either carry on by bus to Hami, another oasis town, famed for its melons, or return to Liuyuan and continue to Turpan by train. Turpan lies at the edge of the feared Taklamakan Desert, and for Silk Road traders marked the start of one of the most arduous sections of the entire route. A series of Buddhist cities once

lay between Turpan and faraway Kashgar, but today they are ruins. Some of the ruins can be visited from Turpan. In the summer months they simmer under a ferocious sun, so hot that your guides will undoubtedly claim proudly that you can cook an egg on the broken doorstops and tumbledown walls. Even if the heat seems unbearable, try and linger a couple of days in Turpan. The local markets are fascinating and the grapes delicious.

The old towns of Kuqa and Aqsu, once important stops on the Silk Road, are now mere shadows of their former

A baker and his wares in Turpan, Xinjiang Province, an oasis town on China's legendary Silk Road.

glory and can easily be skipped if you wish to save yourself the hardship of a long bus journey. In this case, fly from Urumqi to Kashgar; but, whatever you do, try not to miss Kashgar. Said to be the farthest town from the sea in the world, this city of mosques and kebabs and Middle Eastern fabrics is the quintessential Silk Road destination.

A Night at the Opera

A NIGHT AT THE OPERA IS NOT TO BE MISSED IN CHINA. It's noisy — ear-piercingly so at times — you won't have a clue as to what's going on, the stage is more often a bewildering blur of leaping figures clothed in impractical suits and fitted with hats that on close inspection are bordering on plain silly, but what a spectacle it all is. Like Japanese *kabuki* and Thai *lakhon*, Beijing opera and the various regional operas found across China are a stylized dance drama accompanied by a boom-crash orchestra of startling sounds and a chorus of octave-leaping vocal effects.

Beijing is the famous place for opera, and it's certainly worth catching a performance while you're there, but for a more intimate look at this theatrical tradition watch a performance of Sichuan opera in Chengdu. Unlike in Beijing, you can arrange to arrive early and have that rarest of treats, a visit backstage to watch the actors applying their makeup. There was a time when all roles, including female parts, were undertaken by male actors; nowadays, both men and women perform, though the occasional bit of cross-dressing may still turn up in a performance for comic effect. The makeup can take a long time to apply; essentially, the performer is creating a mask of his or her face with greasepaint and a startling array of different sized brushes.

Backstage is a hive of activity, the performers hunched over mirrors, busily dusting and brushing away at their faces, while the stars of the show are hustled through their makeup routines by teams of fussing helpers, the people who take care of the elaborate costumes and the hairstyles. The result of all this work is that performers emerge godlike, reminiscent of the mythological figures who adorn Chinese temples, which is indeed the intention.

When it comes time to watch the performance, resist the impulse to make too much sense of the proceedings. Instead watch the way the actors interact with each other, and let a plot of sorts emerge in your imagination. Betrayal and revenge, mistaken

The Opera — OPPOSITE: The splendid pomp of Beijing opera. ABOVE: Beijing opera performer dons vibrant traditional makeup. RIGHT: A detail of a fan, one of the many stylized props used in Sichuan opera.

identities and unrequited love, the great dramatic themes, all make an appearance. Because there are no props at all on an opera stage, every gesture and action must speak its object loudly, much in the way that mime does. An actor with a whip in his hand galloping around the stage is obviously riding a horse, the young beauty bashfully simpering behind a sleeve is obviously embarrassed.

There's little fear of boredom. Performances are usually a medley of high points from the best of the opera tradition. Moments of high drama collide with swashbuckling action, where the stage comes alive with whirling, leaping fighters armed with spears and swords. There's something joyous about these noisy, acrobatic, dazzling events, so that even those who came prepared for the worst end up thundering their applause as the performance draws to a close.

An Army in Stone

WITH SEVERAL THOUSAND YEARS OF HISTORY BEHIND IT, TODAY'S CHINA MUST BE A TREASURE TROVE OF YET UNDISCOVERED ARCHEOLOGICAL DIGS. The most famous discovery this century came about in 1974, when some Shaanxi peasants digging a hole for a well to provide much-needed water uncovered a huge underground vault. The vault was found to contain over 1,000 life-size terracotta figures, with an estimated further 7,000 figures still awaiting excavation.

Unwittingly the well-digging peasants had stumbled upon a vast stone army grouped in defense of the mausoleum of Qin Shihuang who, in 221 BC, became the first leader of a unified China. Qin Shihuang achieved much, standardizing the written language and weights and measures, but the stone army you can see today near Xi'an says everything about his methods. China's first emperor, the man who started work on the Great Wall, has passed into history as a tyrant, and is remembered more for his decrees that all books not written to the glory of the Qin dynasty be destroyed than for his success in bringing the squabbling states of the time under a unified leadership.

The terracotta warriors, as Qin Shihuang's army has come to be known, is at its most impressive in **Vault 1**. The warriors are *in situ* and in battle formation, protected from the elements by a huge hangar. The only pity is that their hands — which once held real weapons — are now empty, most of the wooden sections of spears and bows having long ago rotted away. As you stroll along the elevated walkways that take you through the military ranks, you'll be struck by the expressions and features of the faces. Some scholars have theorized that the faces may have been modeled on actual members of the imperial guard, an astounding thought when you consider that there are believed to be a total of 10,000 soldiers (including the groups in two other vaults). Each soldier's rank is displayed and the uniforms of knee-length protective tunics and armored tunics were once brightly colored. Note the soldiers' hair, which is tied up in buns.

It's worth making several swoops around the Vault 1 hangar, picking up more details as you go. The other two vaults are smaller. **Vault 2** comprises archers and charioteers, some of which are superbly executed. **Vault 3** is speculated to have been the guard of honor, perhaps the leadership core of Qin Shihuang's army, leading the 10,000 into battle. Nowadays they are witness to daily skirmishes between the army staff and visiting tourists determined to surreptitiously break the no-photographs rule. Snapping from the waist, nonchalantly reeling off a couple of shots from within a crowd, the tourists sneak their photographs in, while the museum staff stand by in thwarted vigilance. The army in stone seem oblivious; their job is to defend an empire, after all.

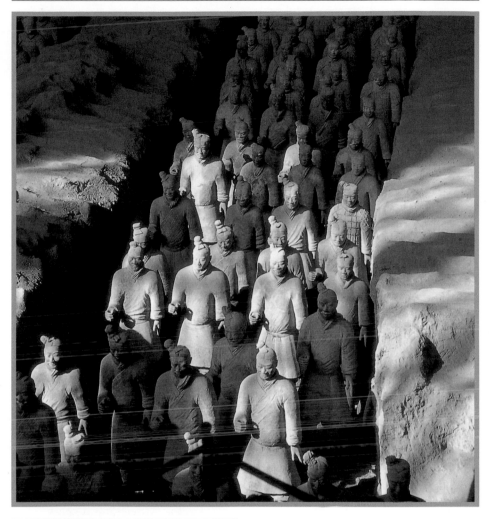

All Roads Lead to Lhasa

THE TIBETAN PLATEAU, AN AREA THE SIZE OF WESTERN EUROPE, with altitudes that average around 3,600 m (11,800 ft), is a place of nomads, villages and just one city worth the name, Lhasa. Tibetans in faraway Qinghai and Gansu provinces whisper the city's name with reverence. Villagers from hundreds of miles distant make that once in a lifetime pilgrimage to Lhasa on their bellies — measuring themselves on the ground every second step — and arrive months later, dusty, mantra-muttering, to prostrate their way around the city's holiest of holies, the **Jokhang Temple**.

The pilgrim circuit (*kora*) around the Jokhang is known as the **Barkhor**, and starts at Barkhor Square. With its magnificent views of the entrance to the Jokhang and its bustling market for pilgrim accessories (prayer wheels, prayer flags, leather padding for your knees and elbows, amulets and the like), it's easy to while an hour or so away here before joining the clockwise flow of faith around the temple. Note the alleys that disappear into markets selling yak cheeses and yak yogurt, the alfresco pool tables surrounded by proud Tibetan nomads, dressed to the nines in felt capes and

The serried ranks of Xi'an's famous terracotta warriors.

sturdy boots, the muted colors of Tibetan carpets hung up against whitewashed walls. The tableau is medieval (apart from the pool tables), and in that sedately moving crowd of the faithful, a pilgrim several steps ahead climbing wearily to his feet from the cobblestones, you find yourself wondering how such a place could continue to survive to the very dawn of the twenty-first century.

When you finish your Barkhor *kora* and find yourself back in front of the Jokhang, it's time to enter. Everything about this ancient temple (it dates back to the seventh century) is otherworldly. In the forecourt a steady stream of pilgrims prostrate themselves in front of the heavy curtains draped over the entrance. Inside you will see the four Guardian Gods, two on each side. Immediately the smell that belongs uniquely to Tibetan temples strikes you. It is the smell of yak butter candles, an oily, sweet and sour odor so strong that, as your eyes adjust to the darkness, you will wonder if you haven't been plunged into another realm where the sense of smell reigns over that of sight.

In the ghostly candlelight follow the murmuring crowds (they're all muttering that holiest of mantras: *Om mani padme hum*) as they make a clockwise circuit of the Jokhang's many chapels, each enshrining a sacred image. Directly to the rear of the temple is Tibet's holiest sanctuary: a small chapel that houses Jowo Sakyamuni, the Lord Buddha aged 12. Stand back from the pilgrims and watch them filing in. They are each of them absorbed with devotion, their lips flickering repetitively, their fingers kneading at strings of prayer beads. They touch their foreheads to the leg of the boy Buddha and depart. This is as close to the heart of Lhasa as you can get.

Later, continue your exploration of the Jokhang to the roof, where you will find monks' quarters, soaring gilded eaves, walls painted in the muted reds and browns of Tibetan design. There, over the entrance, you have a sweeping view, the

Prayer flags flutter at the base of Lhasa's Potala Palace, former residence of the Dalai Lama.

prostrating pilgrims directly beneath you, and beyond them Barkhor Square, and beyond the square, dominating the middle ground between the city and the distant snow capped mountains, the Potala, the palace of the Dalai Lamas.

All roads lead to Lhasa. And as you stand with this scene spread before you, there is no doubting the reason.

Across the Water to the Peak

THE CHINESE WORD FOR SCENERY IS SHANSHUI — LITERALLY "MOUNTAIN-WATER" — AND IT'S CUSTOMARY TO HAVE A PREFERENCE: "do you like mountains or water?" a Chinese will ask. If you happen to like both, nowhere in China do the two meet so spectacularly as in Hong Kong.

Start your journey at the **Star Ferry Terminal** in Tsimshatsui. Started in 1898, this is one of Asia's most venerable ferry services. The ferries themselves look like they have been chugging across the harbor since day one of operations, and all sport heavenly names such as *Celestial Star* and *Twinkling Star*. As everyone will tell you, get first-class tickets (at HK$2 it will be the cheapest first-class boat trip of your life), and sit back to gawk at Asia's most stunning skyline, that sky-scraping testimonial to Hong Kong's rags-to-riches glory.

From the Star Ferry Terminal in Central it's a 20-minute walk to the **Peak Tram**. The walk takes you through Statue Square, the Legislative Council Building on one side, the soaring Hong Kong Bank (formerly known as the Hong Kong and Shanghai Bank) building ahead. Bear right through Chater Garden, exit on the south side of the small park and stroll up Garden Road, past St. John's Cathedral to the Peak Tram Terminus.

Back in 1885, the very idea of a tramway to the top of Victoria Peak — the exclusive residential area for colonial Brits — was met with ridicule. How could you possibly engineer a tram to trundle up a steep and forested 554-m (1,817-ft)-high mountain? Sedan chairs were obviously the only viable means of ascent to this elite aerie. Three years later, the plan became reality

and a tram (strictly speaking, it's a funicular railway) started creaking and groaning up the Peak, starting from Garden Road and finishing 373 m (1,223 ft) higher, just below the summit.

It has been going strong ever since (though today's carriages date from 1989 and both terminals have been repeatedly renovated, the one at the top most recently in 1996). Fundamentally, the operating system and the route itself haven't changed. And the only times the tram has stopped service are during World War II and during a ferocious 1966 typhoon which washed away some of the hillside. Today's passengers are mostly tourists. (Peak residents tend to prefer their chauffeur-driven limousines.)

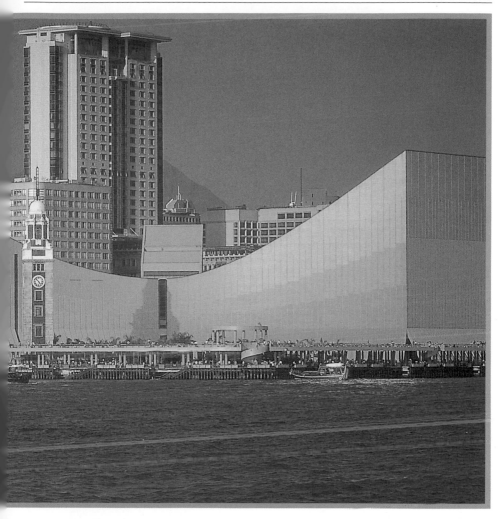

The eight-minute journey provides views of the tower blocks of Central and Mid-levels far below, the rooftop penthouses and swimming pools, and the stunning harbor beyond. Nearby, almost close enough to touch, the untamed greenery and banyan creepers are full of chittering birds. Keep an eye out at the start for some of Hong Kong's older buildings — the whitewashed Helena May boarding house and St. Paul's Church. As the gradient increases, the buildings below seem to tilt and you'll find yourself anxiously clutching the handrail in front of you.

At the top, you'll be greeted by the stunning new Peak Tower, a seven-story extravaganza which opened in 1997. It incorporates not only the Tram Terminus but also shops, restaurants and a motion-simulated ride called the Peak Explorer and a dark computer-operated ride, the Rise of the Dragon, which takes you through the history of Hong Kong.

Leave these busy attractions behind and set off on a walk. Within moments you'll know why you came, as you gaze down the mountain, past the bristling commercial strip of Central to Quarry Bay, across the harbor to Kowloon, and out to sea: the island-studded water.

The Star Ferry, perhaps the world's cheapest cross-harbor cruise; the new wing of The Peninsula hotel rises in the background.

YOUR CHOICE

The Great Outdoors

Few countries are as geographically diverse as China, the world's third largest nation. In the northwest are deserts, in the southwest the towering Tibetan plateau, and in the north grassland plains. Most of China's vast population are crowded into the lush coastal provinces in the east.

Although it's the remote areas of China that offer the best opportunities to strike out into the great outdoors, the crowded east coast provinces are not without some beautiful regions in which hiking and climbing are popular recreational activities. The most famous of these without a doubt is **Guilin** and its surrounding villages, in particular

Yangshuo, which backpackers have made into a budget holiday resort. Guilin is famed for its limestone karst scenery. Poets and painters have celebrated the area's beauty for centuries, and from the moment you arrive you understand why. There are few sights in China that compare with these marching rows of limestone pinnacles, a patchwork of fields and the wandering threads of the Li River at their feet.

But for the Chinese the countryside occupies a very different cultural space than it does for Westerners. Scenes that we might find nostalgically bucolic the Chinese are likely to see as simply poor and undeveloped. When they embrace nature it is usually in aesthetic terms that have historical precedent or are authenticated by religious impulses. Nowhere is this more so than in China's sacred mountains. Guilin, which is the subject of misty watercolors hung in hotel lobbies the length and breadth of the land, is no exception to this rule, but equally famous is **Huangshan** in Jiangxi province, not far from Shanghai. An overnight stay on the mountain, with a day of hiking on either side, surrounded by hordes of toiling latter-day pilgrims is one of the highlights of any China journey.

Scenes of rural Yunnan Province — OPPOSITE: The terraced hills of China's deep south. ABOVE: Fields of rape provide a brilliant contrast in rolling farmland.

Farther west in Yunnan province, the **Stone Forest (Shilin)**, a popular day trip from Kunming, the provincial capital, is akin to a high-density version of Guilin, where limestone pillars jostle together in a scene that is immediately suggestive of the area's poetic name. Elsewhere in Yunnan, the Dai minority town of **Dali** offers the prospect of boat trips on **Erhai Lake** and extended hikes into the surrounding countryside. If hiking is not to your taste, don't fail to hire a bicycle and strike off for a day of relaxed pedaling with the turquoise lake on one side and the vertiginous face of the snow-capped Cangshan Mountains on the other. **Lijiang**, home of the matriarchal Naxi tribe and a day's bus journey to the north of Dali, is another popular hiking region, though mainly with backpacking travelers.

North of here, Sichuan province is another region with scope for exploration in the outdoors. With the exception of the Buddhist sacred mountain, **Emeishan**, however, most of Sichuan is remote and seldom visited. **Jiuzhaigou**, in the mountainous deep north of the province, is held to be one of the most stunning destinations in all China, but accommodation — mostly Tibetan — is primitive and access by road is dangerous. Sichuan is also one of the last places where pandas still roam wild. The **Wolong Nature Reserve**, around 150 km (93 miles) northwest of Chengdu, is difficult to reach unless you join a tour; in addition, pandas are notoriously shy creatures, and sightings are rare.

It's out beyond the Great Wall that China becomes a land of open spaces. In Inner Mongolia tours are operated from **Hohhot** to the grasslands, from whence the Mongol tribes once swept down on China and claimed the Celestial Throne as their own. Summer is the time to visit, if you want the grasslands to be the color of grass — in winter the plains turn a frostbitten brown. Today you can venture out into these regions and stay in the Mongolian's traditional *yurt* dwellings.

In Xinjiang province, the Chinese Turkestan of yore, through which the Silk

Road passed, you can travel to the edge of the feared Taklamakan desert and stay at **Turpan**. From Turpan it is possible to hire jeeps and journey out to ruined Silk Road cities, the remnants of a Buddhist civilization that disappeared centuries ago. For those with more time, the road continues farther to **Kashgar**, the fabled oasis town at the far western extreme of the Chinese Silk Road. Continue on from here and you are on the Karakorum Highway destined for Islamabad in Pakistan, a route only for the most intrepid and hardy of travellers.

A similarly demanding trail is the high road to **Lhasa** in Tibet. There are flights from Chengdu in Sichuan province, but for the adventurous traveler the road leads from Xi'an to Lanzhou and from there by train to Xining and Golmud. At Golmud a 30-hour bus journey to the roof of the world awaits. The train journey between Xining and Golmud itself is worth all the hardship of the journey, Qinghai Lake a

OPPOSITE: Remarkable Stone Forest (Shilin) was formed by massive upheaval and erosion of limestone. A giant panda ABOVE at Xi'an Zoo. Rare and protected, they are indigenous to Western China.

ribbon of blue in the foreground, the Maqen mountain ranges behind it, and occasionally the pinprick suggestion of a camel train wending its way through the intervening dunes.

Perhaps China, unlike neighboring Nepal, is not the first place that comes to mind when you want to commune with nature, but all the same it is a country where the great outdoors is never far away, whether it be scenes of farmers toiling with oxen in fields, or whether it be in the seemingly endless deserts of the far west.

Sporting Spree

China is many things, but a compelling sporting destination it is not. Recreational sports with snob appeal such as golf are gaining headway in China, but for most other sports you will be at the mercy of your hotel facilities.

GOLF
Following the lead of Japan, Taiwan and the other booming Asian economies, golf is popular amongst China's growing executive class. The sport is in its early days, however, and as you would expect the best greens are in Hong Kong.

The **Royal Hong Kong Golf Club Fanling** ((852) 2670-1211 FAX (852) 2679-5183, New Territories, is one of Asia's first, established in 1908. It has three courses: the Old Course, the New Course, and the Eden Course, each with 18 holes. The Old Course is the easiest of the three.

The **Royal Hong Kong Golf Club Deepwater Bay** ((852) 2812-7979 FAX (852) 2812-7111, Hong Kong, is a par 28 course, measuring 1,650 yards, part of which overlap.

The **Kau Sai Chau Public Golf Course** ((852) 2791-3388 FAX (852) 2792-0982, is as the name suggests a public course, but in order to play you will have to produce a handicap certificate or take part in a beginner's clinic.

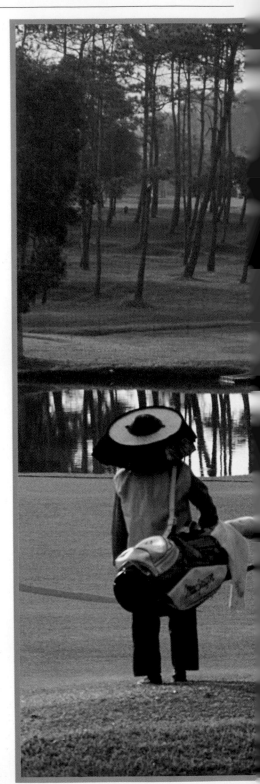

The Hong Kong Golf Club Fanling, New Territories.

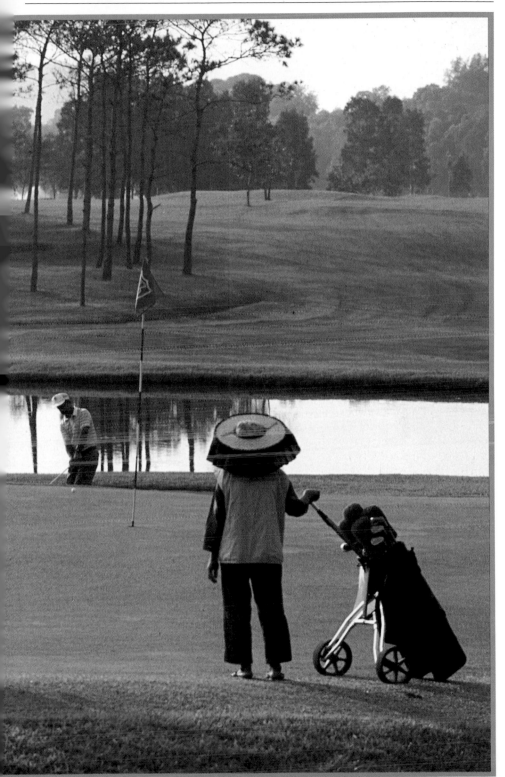

Some of the best courses outside Hong Kong are in neighboring Guangdong province. **Sand River Golf Club** ((755) 660-9270, in Shenzhen Bay, Shenzhen, is a 27-hole Gary Player designed course. The **Shenzhen Golf Club** ((755) 330-8888 FAX (755) 330-4992, is one of the China's oldest.

WATER SPORTS

Despite its long eastern coastline, China has little in the way of water sports, or indeed anywhere for **swimming**.

Sanya and **Yalong Bay** are beach resorts on **Hainan Island**, where swimming and sunbathing (still not popular with the Chinese, for whom fair skin is considered an asset) is the main attraction. SCUBA diving and snorkeling are also available at Sanya. Other popular beach resorts can be found at **Qingdao**, in Shandong province, and at **Beidaihe**, 300 km (187 miles) east of Beijing — the latter having been for many years the off-limits preserve of exalted cadres.

In Hong Kong swimming is popular through the summer months, but pollution and sharks are both concerns. Shark nets have been installed in popular beaches and pollution levels are closely monitored — check with the **Hong Kong Tourist Association** ((852) 2807-6177 for details. At weekends and on public holidays during the official swimming season (April 1 to October 31) the most popular beaches (e.g., at Stanley on Hong Kong Island) are packed with swimmers and sunbathers. There are good facilities at these major beaches — lifeguards, warning flags for rough seas, changing rooms and toilets and sometimes even beachside cafés or snack stalls. The biggest and most glorious stretch of beach in Hong Kong is Cheung Sha on Lantau; there are facilities at both ends of the beach, with a couple of Chinese restaurants at its easternmost end (Lower Cheung Sha).

CYCLING

With more motorized traffic taking to the roads with each passing day, China is not the cyclist's dream that it was when the entire country got around on two wheels. But touring China (or at least parts of it) by bicycle is still an attractive proposition.

Some keen cyclists bike over the border from Hong Kong or even from Kathmandu (you have a long uphill slog ahead of you if you take this route) and tour across China solo. While this is certainly not impossible, it is not easy. A less arduous way to see China by bicycle is to join a specialized tour. Alternatively, take your bike with you and bundle it on to the roof of buses or into the goods vans of trains for the long sectors, and leave your cycling for the parts of China where touring is rewarded by breathtaking views.

Backroads ((800) 462-2848 FAX (510) 527-1444, 801 Cedar Street, Berkeley, CA 94710, USA, is tour organizer that specializes in adventure and cycling tours. **Himalayan Travel** ((800) 225-2380 FAX (203) 359-3669, 112 Prospect Street Stamford, CT 06901, USA, is another operator with cycling tours to China. In London **Imaginative Traveller** ((181) 742-8612 FAX (181) 742-3113, 14 Barley Mow Passage, London W4 4PH, UK, has trekking and cycling tours in China.

The Open Road

Only in the last decade has China begun to grapple with the huge task of bringing its roads up to scratch. Add to this the fact that increasing numbers of inexperienced drivers are taking to the roads armed only with a horn and a dim understanding of traffic rules, and most visitors will agree that the sensible thing is to leave your international license at home.

Car rental is available in China, and the car will usually come with a driver. There are very few roads that foreigners are permitted to drive themselves — the Shenzhen-Guangzhou superhighway is one; the highway between Beijing and

A typical rural street scene in the environs of historic Xi'an.

Tianjin is another. Car hire is available in major cities but driving permits are only valid within the city limits.

Cycling on a hired bicycle is as close as most travelers will come to experiencing the joys of the open road in China. In rural areas such as **Yangshuo** in Guangxi province and **Dali** in Yunnan province, cycling can still be a joy. In many of the larger cities, where once bicycles were the only mode of transport besides buses, there are now armies of honking cars and trucks. Always take a good look at traffic conditions before launching off on a pedal-power journey of discovery in a new town.

Backpacking

THE BACKPACKING TRAILS

When China first opened up to individual travelers in the early 1980s, adventurous backpackers flooded in. Travel was demanding in those days, but meals, accommodation and transportation were bargains, providing that magical combination of low costs and hardship that the backpacking spirit thrives on. Two and a half decades later, China is both less challenging and more expensive. But this doesn't mean that it's no longer an attractive destination for the budget voyager.

Travelers bent on keeping costs down should minimize their time in booming eastern China — from Beijing all the way south to Hainan Island. Of course, skipping the east altogether means that you miss out on some of China's premiere attractions — Shanghai (now bouncing back with a vengeance), Suzhou (famed for its gardens and canals), Hangzhou (famed for its West Lake), Xiamen and Qingdao (both of which have retained some of their Old World charm), not to mention bustling Guangzhou, and Beijing, the capital. But in most of these destinations accommodation costs have skyrocketed in the last decade, and old backpacker standbys have been renovated to attract a "better class" of guest.

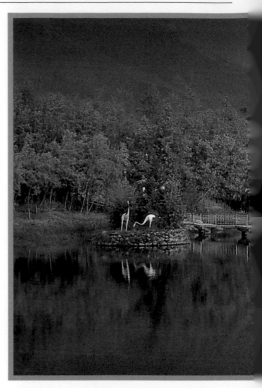

The key is to plan your itinerary on the east coast carefully, and be prepared to go through your money much more quickly there. In Beijing, for example, finding a double room (or even a single room for that matter) for under US$30 is possible but rarely easy, particularly at peak holiday periods. Entry fees to attractions around Beijing are high (the Forbidden City is over US$10 these days) and if you drop into a bar in the evening for a drink you may well find yourself paying Hong Kong prices.

The solution for many young travelers is to do whirlwind tours of the historical sights of **Beijing** and then head west or southwest. Few budget travelers bother with the east coast at all, though some stop in **Shanghai**, which has direct rail connections with Kunming and Guilin, backpacker meccas.

From Hong Kong, the route of choice is a boat or a train to **Guangzhou**, and from there a combination of boat (to Wuzhou) and bus to **Yangshuo**, with its stunning limestone karst scenery. Yangshuo's cafés are renowned and rooms are available for around US$5. From Yangshuo most travelers continue westwards to **Kunming**, the capital of subtropical, minority rich Yunnan.

Although Kunming has witnessed something of a tourist boom in recent years, by the time you are this deep into the southwest of China, day-to-day expenses begin to plummet. In the border regions of **Xishuangbanna** and **Dehong**, it is possible to get by on less than US$20, staying in budget hostels, hiring bicycles and cycling out to minority villages by day, and in the evenings enjoying the superb local cuisine cooked family-style. The route from here runs up to **Dali**, an old walled town by the exquisite **Erhai Lake**, and on to Lijiang, home of the matriarchal Naxi tribe. North of here — and accessible by a combination of bus and train — lies the Buddhist sacred mountain of **Emeishan**, **Leshan** with its Grand Buddha (bigger than the one on Hong Kong's Lantau Island, and around 1,250 years older), and the large cities of **Chengdu** and **Chongqing**. The remote — and largely Tibetan — northwest of

Sichuan is a magnet for intrepid backpackers, and routes have sprung up from Chengdu to **Xining** in Qinghai province, **Lanzhou** in Gansu province, from either of which it is possible to travel by bus to destinations such as **Turpan**, **Urumqi** and **Kashgar** in **Xinjiang**, to **Lhasa** in Tibet (via Golmud) or to **Xi'an**, home of the Terracotta Warriors and a city where expenses can still be kept to a reasonable level.

GETTING AROUND
The cheapest way to get around China is by bus. Travel this way tends to be slow, crowded and often dangerous — some drivers appear to be relative newcomers to their vocation. Nevertheless, in many of the remoter destinations in China, bus or minibus will be the only way to get around. In Yunnan, for example, trains link the capital Kunming with Chengdu in Sichuan and Guilin in Guangxi, but elsewhere around the province — to Dali

Dali's fabulous Three Pagodas, mirrored in the placid waters of Erhai Lake.

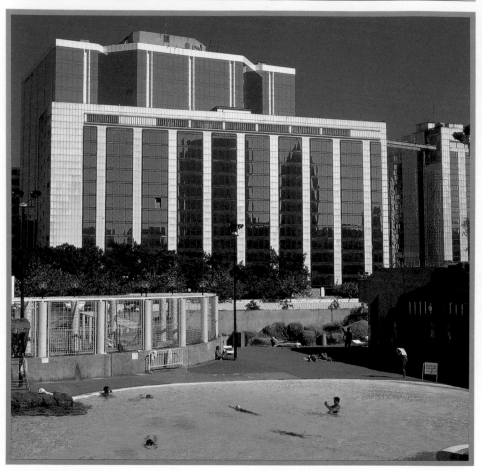

and Xishuangbanna, say — you either take a bus or settle for a relatively expensive flight.

Trains are rarely a bargain in China, but if you're prepared to rough it, there is always the "hard seat" option. Hard seat is the equivalent of third-class, though there are few places in the world where third-class is such a rough and tumble proposition. With hard-seat prices weighing in at roughly a quarter the cost of a soft sleeper (first class) ticket, and half the price of a hard sleeper (second class) ticket, many budget travelers find the savings irresistible. Those who travel long distances this way often come away with nightmarish horror stories; few do it again.

The open-air swimming pool at Kowloon Park.

WHERE TO STAY

In the early days of China travel, the only kind of hotel foreigners could stay in (with the exception of the rare joint venture) was a *binguan*, or guesthouse. These were usually sprawling, institutional setups that were built to house visiting "foreign experts" and cadres on the move. When individual budget travelers started to arrive in China in the early 1980s, a lot of these guesthouses were discovered to have inexpensive dormitory accommodation, though staff were rarely willing to admit to it. Before long, hapless Chinese guesthouse staff, who had no training for such an onslaught, were dealing with a daily deluge of belligerent foreigners in search of value for their *yuan*.

Things have changed enormously since those days. Most of the old guesthouses have been renovated, some beyond recognition into three-, four- or even five-star hotels, and dormitory accommodation is difficult to find. Indeed, in the coastal provinces virtually no dormitory accommodation is available for foreigners. But where budget accommodation is available, and most of western and southwestern China falls into this category, getting a dormitory bed or a budget room is still very straightforward.

The best place to seek out inexpensive accommodation is around the main bus or train station. If it's a dormitory bed you're looking for, don't forget that essential word: *sushe*, pronounced "sooshir".

Living It Up

The toiling masses dream of just one thing nowadays, and it's not Mao's collectivized society, it's Deng's dream of being gloriously rich. You can live like a king in the new China, if that's what you wish, though high flyers will find that China's best is no less expensive than the best anywhere else in the world.

EXCEPTIONAL HOTELS
China's top hotels are where you would expect them to be, in Hong Kong and in Beijing. Nevertheless, Shanghai gives the capital a run for its money, and Guangzhou is not without some minor-league contenders.

Hong Kong, of course, has some of the world's most luxurious accommodation. Top of the list are the **Mandarin Oriental** in Central and **The Peninsula** in Tsimshatsui, where you can expect the very best in service, luxury down to the finest detail, and room rates soaring to around US$450 a night.

The palatial **Beijing Hotel** was the first international style hotel to be built in the capital, and it commands pole position in the heart of the old city, overlooking the Forbidden City. Next door to the Beijing Hotel, the **Grand Hotel** is the new kid on the block. With

similar views and levels of luxury, it's an alternative to staying at the Beijing, where service standards come in for some criticism.

Shanghai lacks a truly luxurious hotel on The Bund, which is a pity. The best this historically significant part of town can offer is the Peace Hotel, which was formerly known as the Cathay, when it shared a prestige rating that equaled the Peninsula in Hong Kong, the Stanley Raffles in Singapore and the Taj in Bombay. Take one of the suites — perhaps it will be the same one in which Noel Coward wrote *Private Lives*.

For Shanghai at its best, the **Portman Shangri-La Hotel** is not only an opulent taste of the future that Shanghai is building for itself, it also offers the utmost in convenience, being in Shanghai Centre, where you will also find most of Shanghai's foreign airlines, consulates and business representatives.

In Guangzhou, **White Swan Hotel** was one of the pioneering joint venture hotels in the early days of China tourism. Unlike some, who have fallen by the wayside, the White Swan has managed to keep apace of rising standards, and whatever happens it will always have its delightful location on Shamian Island, the most charming corner of the city. In the northern commercial part of town the **Garden Hotel** has long been the first choice of business travellers, and is a vast place with excellent amenities and some of the city's best dining.

The Shangri-La chain is well represented in China, but it's hard to beat the **Shangri-La Hangzhou**, which has a fabulous setting, overlooking the northern section of Hangzhou's famous West Lake. The Hyatt group, who set consistently high standards throughout China, is superbly represented inside the city walls of ancient Xi'an at the **Hyatt Regency Xi'an**.

The Holiday Inn group also have hotels all over China, including excellent choices in Beijing, Urumqi and Xiamen, but full marks go to their hotel on the roof of the world, the **Holiday Inn Lhasa**, which manages, against all odds, to bring the high life to a part of the world that until now has always had the "high" but not the "life" to go with it.

EXCEPTIONAL RESTAURANTS

Given the beating that China's restaurant culture got during the Communist era, not to mention the Cultural Revolution, by which time one of the world's great cuisines was in danger of devolving into greasy spoon canteen slop, it's remarkable to see the renaissance in dining out that is taking place all over China. It will still be some time before China is able to offer the diversity that is on offer in, for example, Hong Kong and Taipei, which between them arguably command center stage in the haute cuisine stakes. Still, Hong Kong *is* China these days, so if its exceptional restaurants you want in China, look to Hong Kong first.

The Grand Hyatt's **One Harbour Road** Cantonese restaurant and the Island Shangri-La's **Summer Palace** are two of the best hotel restaurants that Hong Kong has to offer. Out on the streets, **Fook Lam Moon Restaurant** has long been noted as one of the best in town and is famous for its (very) pricey shark fin dishes, which appear on the first page of a menu designed to shock (if you're paying) and impress (if you're the guest). Remember too that it is not just Chinese cuisine that Hong Kong is celebrated for, but everything from Vietnamese to Mexican (see HONG KONG pages 128-133 for a representative selection).

Over the "border" in China everything changes. For a start, you generally pay far less for your meals than in Hong Kong. To be sure, standards are not as high, but you certainly get value for your money. At famous restaurants such as **Beijing's Qianmen Quanjude Roast Duck** you can sample the capital's famous duck dish in sumptuous surroundings for around $20, and outside the five-star hotels this is generally about as expensive as dining out in China gets.

Guangzhou has been an open city for some time now, and its proximity to Hong Kong has allowed some famous old restaurants to flourish. The best of these include **Taotaoju Restaurant**, a delightful place that started life as an academy of learning in the seventeenth century, the **North Garden Restaurant**, which has an inner garden courtyard, and the **Panxi Restaurant**, which lays on the old China theme as thickly as you're likely to ever experience it.

In general it is still the case that the best in Chinese cuisine is sponsored by the five-star hotels in Beijing, Shanghai and Guangzhou. Although quality is improving elsewhere, it will still be some time before restaurants that do justice to China's culinary traditions are commonplace even in the major cities.

NIGHTLIFE

The affluent youth of China are marching to a different drummer than that of their parents. Out are the non-differentiating Mao suits and the puritanical mistrust of boys and girls brought together in anything other than revolutionary zeal, and in are Parisian fashions and the London beat.

Mind you, for most of China a night out means a meal in a restaurant and a sing-along at a karaoke parlor — look for the neon signs ending in the English letters "OK." Karaoke, which originated in Japan and involves singing along to popular hits minus the vocals, is fun to try, but for most foreigners it is of limited appeal, particularly given that the average Chinese is enormously ungifted with a microphone. Add to this the fact that most karaoke "menus" only sport one or two English songs, and after one or two experiences most Westerners retreat to a Western-style bar for a quiet drink.

In the remoter parts of China, you will only find bars in the top hotels, but as you get closer to the major cities, nightlife becomes increasingly diverse, and by the time you arrive in Beijing, Shanghai or Guangzhou it is positively frenetic. In each of the big three you will find branches of international staples such as the **Hard Rock Café**, and more imitators than anyone would care to list.

In Shanghai, **Shanghai Sally's** was a pioneer in the British pub trend that is now becoming popular in China. Beijing's British pub, **Poachers Inn**, is a far more adventurous institution, with live music and late night dancing.

Don't pass up an opportunity to visit one of Beijing's or Shanghai's happening dance clubs. In Shanghai **New York New York**, in an old French theater, is the place to be, and in Beijing the warehouse, **JJ's** ((10) 6607-9601 packs in thousands of sweaty bodies on the weekends.

Family Fun

Nobody spoils their children the way the Chinese do. If China is at times a trying destination for a family with children to tackle, this open-heartedness of the Chinese is a major compensation.

As is the case elsewhere in Asia, there are some practical concerns if you are planning a family vacation in China. Firstly, have your children had all their vaccinations? Although China is more hygienic than, say, India or Nepal, it is still a poor country and in many regions medical facilities are primitive: ensuring your children remain healthy throughout the trip is the first step towards a successful trip.

Some of the major cities, in particular Shanghai and Guangzhou, are extremely crowded. If you have small children, a baby carrier that straps on to your back or chest is a far better way to get them from point A to point B than in a stroller. This is true in many rural areas as well, where you're unlikely to find sidewalks and where the roads are often rutted and potholed.

On a more positive note, the Chinese are remarkably tolerant of children's antics. Parents dining in restaurants will let their children run wild with little regard for other diners (admittedly Chinese diners don't seem to mind), and this means that you can relax somewhat when dining out.

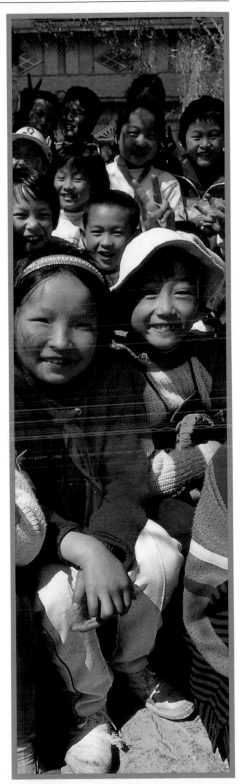

Smiles all round on a school outing in Kunming.

Around the major cities there are amusement parks for children, and in the smaller cities there will always be a central People's Park (*renmin gongyuan*), where you will often find climbing rails and so on. But mostly, outside the big coastal cities, Western children may be bored by Chinese game areas and cultural attractions. Think ahead and bring games and toys that will keep your children amused. This is particularly true if you are going to be taking long train journeys. Buses are best avoided in China if you are traveling with children.

All things considered, China is a better destination for older children who are able to appreciate the grand adventure of visiting this populous and ancient nation. For the tiny tots, other Asian destinations such as Thailand and Bali, where there are beaches and hotels that are used to dealing with children, are probably much more practical propositions.

Cultural Kicks

There are any number of ways to appreciate a country as vast as China. In the big cities you might spend your nights in bars and dance clubs and your days sleeping off the effects. In the country there are sacred mountains to be climbed, otherworldly landscapes such as Guilin to be explored. In the far west, deserts sprawl under a cruel sun, and in Tibet the mountains touch the sky. But for most visitors, the overwhelming attraction is China's cultural tradition, whose lineage, as the Chinese themselves will proudly pronounce, stretches back through 5,000 years of history.

There's more than a touch of hyperbole in this 5,000-years claim, but the great are frequently forgiven their small vanities, and many commentators are happy to go along with this one; however, there's very little in China of cultural value that dates back 5,000 years. That anything older than two or three hundred years has lingered into the present, given the turbulence of the last few centuries, is miraculous. Some visitors come away from China disappointed at how "modern" the country is, and complaining that there was so little of historical significance to see. This is true to a certain extent. China has no Venice, no Naples, no Rome, no

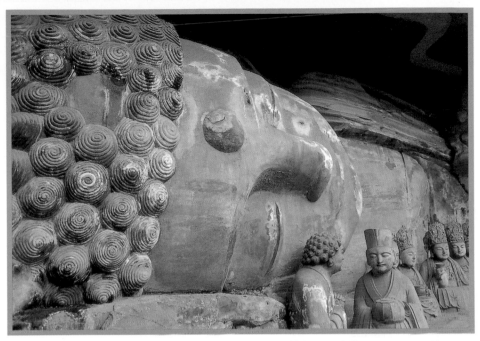

Paris; the best preserved Chinese cities are largely ugly growths of factories and faceless housing estates.

If you feel a twinge of disappointment, remind yourself that China's transition into the modern world has been a painful, troubled one, that has involved a great deal of disgust with all that went before. In the Western hemisphere we lived through the sixties, which we have mythologized as a ferment of discontent and youth rebellion. In the Chinese sixties, during the Great Proletarian Cultural Revolution, the young literally tore the country apart.

Yet China's past survives. You'll find it everywhere you look, if you take the time to slow down. The Cantonese opera burbling out from speakers in a Guangzhou park. The serried ranks of oblivious oldsters performing the dawn ritual of catlike t'ai chi routines. The roar and sizzle of the roadside stir-fry. The rural street performers and local opera troupes. Then of course, there's the Great Wall, the Buddhist grotto art, the temples coming back to life, the Forbidden City, the artists splashing ink onto paper before limestone landscapes draped in mist... .

THE ARCHITECTURAL LEGACY

China's architectural legacy is scattered the length and breadth of the country, but the place for an overview of Chinese architecture at its best is Beijing. The **Forbidden City** is rightly the first stop for most visitors. Heart of the empire through the Ming and Qing dynasties, the remarkable point about the Forbidden City is the way it maintains such elegant detail over such a vast canvas. If the Forbidden City is unforgettable, it is also overwhelmingly large, so that unless you have plenty of time and can make repeat visits it tends to remain a jumble in your memories after you leave. For a more focussed glimpse of Ming dynasty design, Beijing's **Tiantan** (Temple of Heaven) is undoubtedly Beijing's superlative architectural attraction.

Northeast of Beijing is some of China's finest surviving imperial architecture at **Chengde**. By Chinese standards, the temples and palaces of Chengde are

The China every traveler dreams of is still much in evidence in Beijing; OPPOSITE is the Yonghegong Lama Temple. ABOVE: The Reclining Buddha of Dazu, Sichuan Province, sprawls like a sleeping giant.

recent arrivals, the earliest of them being constructed in the first years of the eighteenth century. Indeed, Chengde was the site of a frenzy of building that culminated the construction of a replica of the Potala in Lhasa.

Beijing's city walls are long gone, but **Xi'an**, in Shaanxi province, has a well preserved city wall. Xi'an is the former Tang dynasty capital and has a wealth of other historical attractions. On the architectural front, the Dayan (**Big Wild Goose) Pagoda** is a 52-m (210-ft) pagoda, that was originally founded in 652 AD.

For those on an architectural pilgrimage, there can be few more fascinating destinations than **Qufu**, the home of Confucius in Shandong province. The Kong clan lived in a maze of over 450 rooms, but it is the adjacent **Confucius Temple**, over a kilometer (at least a half mile) in length — which grew to its enormous size from humble beginnings in the fifth century BC — that is the main attraction. It is one of China's most important classical architectural relics.

Kunming, in the southwest of China, capital of Yunnan province, is not an obvious destination for architecture buffs, but for those who make it this far west, Kunming (and also some more remote destinations in Yunnan not covered in this book such as Baoshan and Tengchong) has some picturesque wooden street architecture that is long gone elsewhere in China. Nearby is the breathtaking **Golden Temple**.

For the intrepid traveler **Tibet** is a destination with architectural sights you will remember for the rest of your life. The **Potala**, former residence of the exiled Dalai Lama, and the **Jokhang**, spiritual heart of the holy city of Lhasa, alone make Tibet worth a visit.

Ironically, some of China's most imposing architecture reposes in the buildings constructed by the Western imperial powers in the late nineteenth century. The **Bund** in Shanghai is undoubtedly the most famous of these, a skyline that famously evokes Manhattan and dockyard Liverpool by turns. **Tianjin** is another city with some

fascinating colonial architecture. More low-key but not without interest is **Shamian Island** in Guangzhou and the delightful island of **Gulangyu**, just off Xiamen, in Fujian province. Xiamen is also home to the 1,000-year-old **Nanputuo Temple**.

MUSEUMS

China is full of museums. Every provincial capital has one, and most historically significant counties have one too. Unfortunately, they're rarely well maintained, English is almost never featured in the labeling, and the displays have a tendency to shoot off on wild tangents, so that you might move through several thousand years of history in the space of several steps.

The current generation of Chinese museums is best exemplified by the new **Shanghai Museum**, where meticulous attention has been given to labeling, presentation and lighting, making a tour of the museum's displays of ancient artifacts, notably the bronzes, a joy.

In Beijing, the palace area of the **Forbidden City** is in fact a museum, and the constant inward flood of tourist ticket money and ongoing restoration work means that the displays — and indeed the palace — are in the best shape they've been in for over a century. The **Museum of Chinese History** on Tiananmen Square doesn't live up to its promise, but is not without interest. The drawback is the absence of English labeling.

Xi'an, the ancient Tang dynasty capital of Chang'an, has two excellent museums. The **Shaanxi Provincial Museum** is a high-quality version of the typical provincial museum, with little in the way of English explanations, but nevertheless a fascinating collection of Buddhist images and over 1,000 steles. The **Shaanxi History Museum** is a more recent arrival (opened in 1992), tracing the evolution of civilization in Shaanxi province through thoughtfully displayed

Snow frosts the simple elegance of Beijing's famous Temple of Heaven.

and clearly labeled exhibits. Along with the Shanghai Museum it is probably the best in the country.

PERFORMANCES

China isn't as rich in performance as you might hope, but for those coming in on a whirlwind tour of the main Chinese tourist attractions, there will probably be something to see every night.

Beijing is the place for opera, and nightly performances are held, though mostly for the benefit of tourists. Check the listings magazine, *Beijing Scene*, for performances of the real thing — whether traditional or avant garde. Be warned, however, a real performance of Beijing opera is a nonstop actionfest of acrobatics, eardrum-piercing wails, gong clanging and choreographed fight scenes.

Beijing is famous for its opera, but regional operas can also be found throughout the country. In **Guangzhou** you will probably see small opera ensembles performing in the parks around town; such performances are informal, with everyone dressed casually in flip-flops and T-shirts. Sichuan is one of the few provinces that is actually working to keep its operatic traditions alive, and in **Chengdu** you can enjoy fascinating short opera performances and even backstage visits afterwards.

Shanghai is the place for acrobatics, and if you've never seen Chinese acrobatics don't fail to get tickets for one of the evening performances.

Shop till You Drop

The major tourist destinations of China are superb for shopping. There's no need, as in the old days, to seek out the nearest "Friendship Store." These days you'll find most things you need and souvenirs for home in department stores and in street markets.

BARGAINING

Bargaining in China is not the way of life it is in some parts of Asia. In most shops prices are marked, and marked prices mean what they say. Out on the streets, it's a different matter. When market shopping, for example, prices quoted, particularly for tourist souvenirs, are likely to be inflated, sometimes grossly.

The first trick is to hang back. Never rush into purchases at the beginning of your trip. It's highly unlikely that a souvenir that has caught your eye will not be available in other places (unless it's an original work, of course). As your China trip progresses, you will find yourself becoming more familiar with how things work and bolder at making counter offers. The second trick is to never look too "hungry." Maintain an engaged but disinterested smile, offer what you feel is the value of the object, and if you think the price is not right walk away. Walking away can often by a very effective strategy for getting a last-minute discount. Never lose your temper when bargaining.

ANTIQUES

Unless you really know what you're doing, China is not a good place to buy genuine antiques. The quality of imitation antiques is simply too good for the average collector to discern the difference. On the other hand, this is good news to those shoppers who are happy buying attractive Chinese articles and don't require the cachet of a genuine antique.

Start your antique hunt at the Friendship Stores. The branches in Beijing and Xi'an are particularly good, and in theory, if you buy a genuine antique from one of the Friendship branches you will receive a letter of authentication. The Friendship stores will at least give you a good overview of the kinds of antiques that are available, and most of them have shipping facilities.

Like the Friendship Stores, Chinese museums will often have imitations of prize exhibits for sale. These can often be large and expensive, but it's always worth taking a look at the souvenirs

Modern shopping district on Tianjin's fashionable Heping Road.

section of museum. Travelers with a keen interest in antiques who make it to Beijing should be sure to make a detour to the neighboring city of **Tianjin**, where the huge Antique Market is said to be slowly selling off antiques that were confiscated during the Cultural Revolution.

Hong Kong is an excellent place to shop for antiques, though prices can be staggering. The place to go is the area in Central starting from the upper end of Wyndham Street, continuing all the way along Hollywood Road until you reach "Cat Street," just by the Man Mo Temple. Don't imagine for a moment that all the items displayed in the antique boutiques of this area are Chinese: Chinese and Thai carved Buddhas, Indonesian masks and batiks, Persian and Indian carpets, rosewood furniture, Himalayan artwork and a fascinating array of snuff bottles, porcelain, silver jewelry, Korean and Japanese wooden chests and traditional Chinese silk paintings and scrolls are all on offer.

In Hong Kong, always look out for the Hong Kong Tourist Association (HKTA) membership sign on shop doors, and don't forget to pick up a copy of HKTA's *Official Shopping Guide*. This handy little booklet is packed with information on where to go and who to trust on your shopping spree, and it offers the added guarantee of its own membership system — every retail outlet in the book has the HKTA stamp of approval. If you have any complaints or queries about a member, you can contact the HKTA Hotline ((852) 2807-6177. (There is no equivalent system elsewhere in China.)

ART
You needn't be a connoisseur and you needn't be fabulously wealthy to shop for art in China. Admittedly, a Tang dynasty scroll may be out of the question, but there are legions of artists in China producing exciting art in a variety of media.

At the bottom of the range are inexpensive wall hangings, usually traditional-style watercolor landscapes. The cheaper ones can be as little as $20 or $30, and can be found anywhere in China where there are tourists. The better works will cost at least $100.

Most tourist-class hotels sell Chinese art in their souvenir shops, but the best places to buy are always in the small, privately run studios you'll find in art centers such as **Suzhou**, **Hangzhou** and **Guilin**. In **Kunming** it is common to come across the work of painters whose work — some in watercolors, some in oils — depicts scenes from minority villages. Generally the prices marked on paintings are optimistic, and there is some latitude for bargaining in studios.

CLOTHES
The Chinese become more fashion conscious with every passing day, but it's still not a wildly exciting place to shop for clothes except, perhaps, in some of the large open-air markets in Beijing where there are a number of bargains, especially in winter clothing and basic silk items, to be had. Outside the major cities, choice is limited and quality is poor. If new clothes are part of your plans, be sure to allocate some time for Hong Kong.

For a quick overview of Hong Kong's shopping possibilities you might start in **Central District**. Take a look at the high-class boutiques in **Swire House** and the **Mandarin Hotel** and, via pedestrian crossovers, the **Prince's Building, The Landmark** and the elegant **Galleria**, an area bristling with names such as Gucci, Chanel, Christian Dior, Lanvin, Hermes, Giorgio Armani, Nina Ricci, Issey Miyake and Salvatore Ferragamo. Close by are more affordable options such as **Marks & Spencer's**, on the corner of Wyndham Street. **Lane Crawford** on Queen's Road Central, is the traditional home of Harrod's-style upper-drawer British shopping.

Causeway Bay is a better area for bargains, though the accent changes from Western to Japanese high fashion and luxury accessories in the giant Tokyo-style department stores, **Mitsukoshi, Daimaru, Matsuzakaya** and **Sogo**. Just around the corner from Mitsukoshi, between Russell and Sharp streets, you'll find the spectacular **Times Square**, which has virtually everything you could possibly need.

On the other side of the harbor, in Tsimshatsui and Tsimshatsui East, is a city of interconnected shopping complexes: **Star House, Harbour City (Ocean Terminal, Ocean Centre** and **Ocean Galleries)** and **China Hong Kong City**. An information desk in the Ocean Terminal, staffed by English-speaking guides, will provide you with maps and even a computer printout of suitable shops to help you find your way through the retail maze.

ELECTRONICS

China may not be famous for its electronics bargains, but Hong Kong certainly is. The electronics shopping districts are mostly on Kowloon side, but you can shop in Central too. Stanley Street, in Central, is the place for photographic goods. **Photo Scientific Appliances** ((852) 2522-1903, 6 Stanley Street, Central, is recommended. Prices are unlikely to be higher here than in Tsimshatsui, and service will probably be much better. For other electrical items, try the two Sony Service Centre's **Chung Yuen Electrical Co. Shop** ((852) 2524-8066, 104–105 Prince's Building, Chater Road, in Central; and ((852) 2890-2998, 2/F In Square, Windsor House, 311 Gloucester Road, in Causeway Bay.

The so-called "Golden Mile" of Tsimshatsui's **Nathan Road** is Hong Kong's famous tourist shopping district. Prices are not usually marked (they are in the non-tourist parts of town), and some of the salespeople operating out of these shops are very unscrupulous. Take care. **Crown Photo Supplies** ((852) 2376-1836, 27 Hankow Road, and the **Camera Shop** ((852) 2730-9227, Shop 121, Ocean Terminal, can be recommended for photographic needs.

For computers, **Silvercord**, 30 Canton Road, and **Star Computer City**, 2/F Star House, 3 Salisbury Road are two complexes where you can shop around

for the latest software and hardware. The **Golden Shopping Arcade** in Shamshuipo is famous for providing software at unbeatable prices. Some legitimate shops also operate out of this maze of computer dens.

Short Breaks

China is such a formidably huge place that — for anyone with on brief vacation or a stopover in Hong Kong, Shanghai or Beijing — coming up with a manageable and sensibly conceived itinerary for some out-of-town sightseeing can be daunting. The trick is not to attempt too much: The last thing you want to do is spend so much time getting to where you're going that you're too tired to enjoy it.

HONG KONG

Transport connections between Hong Kong and the rest of China have improved to the extent that "popping over the border" for a day or two is perfectly reasonable. The obvious destination — it's closest — is **Shenzhen**. Shenzhen, it must be said, is not the most exciting place in China, nor is it endowed with cultural riches. It is, however, a fascinating lesson in what a difference a few hundred meters can make: enter Shenzhen and you instantly feel very far

Chinese silk is a good buy in Hong Kong.

from Hong Kong. Shenzhen has several theme parks, such as **Window on the World** (see SHENZHEN, page 135).

A far more worthy China excursion is a trip to **Guangzhou**. Long looked down on as Hong Kong's poor nephew, Guangdong's provincial capital has acquired an air of vibrancy in recent years. Visitors from Hong Kong find the dining cheaper, the people friendlier, the room rates vastly lower, and if the roads are chaotic, it lends some adventure to the trip. Guangzhou also has enough sightseeing to keep you busy for a couple of days.

The easy option (and, if you are pushed for time, the best) is a tour, such as the two-day package from CITS (see TAKING A TOUR, page 66) costing around HK$2,000, which starts in Hong Kong and includes a quick visit to Guangzhou, Foshan (famous for its pottery and temples), Zhongshan and Macau.

Macau, that tiny Portuguese enclave, makes a rewarding day trip in itself (it's only an hour by boat from Central), but for those with time, an overnight stay in Macau is time well spent: Not only will you be able to see most of the cultural sights but you'll also be able to catch Macau's Portuguese flavor most enjoyably by lingering over meals in typical Portuguese style — that means several hours spent over a three-course lunch that naturally includes aperitifs (a dry white port, perhaps), wine and a vintage port with your coffee. Sightseeing after such lunches is invariably a strain — so it's best to follow the Portuguese way and have a quick siesta back at your hotel.

BEIJING

The area around Beijing is blessed with some of China's best attractions. The crowd-pleaser is the **Great Wall**. Most people climb the wall at **Badaling**, which is around 70 km (43 miles) northeast of Beijing, and an easy day trip from the capital, but if you're looking to escape

Repulse Bay and its high cost condominiums which overlook Hong Kong's most popular beach.

the crowds (and at Badaling, they're not be underestimated), **Simatai**, which is 110 km (68 miles) from Beijing is a far more relaxing spot to enjoy the wall. The **Ming Tombs** tend to get tagged onto some Great Wall tours, but are only worth a visit if you've absolutely exhausted Beijing and its environs.

Just 80 km (50 miles) east of Beijing, **Tianjin** gets overlooked by many China travelers. This is a pity. A vibrant port city, Tianjin has some superb colonial architecture, a legacy of its concession days, and probably the best antique market in all China. It takes about two and a half hours by bus or train from Beijing to get to Tianjin, making it a long, but worthwhile day trip.

An interesting option is to spend a morning sightseeing in Tianjin, and then catch an afternoon train to **Beidaihe** or **Shanhaiguan**, two beach resorts around three hours north of Tianjin. Beidaihe got its start as a European beach resort, but its visitors today are overwhelmingly Chinese. Shanhaiguan is the more interesting destination, as it is here that the Great Wall descends into the sea. It's a charming town, and some mid-range accommodation is starting to materialize here as tourists arrive in greater numbers. A train back to Beijing takes four to five hours.

Chengde, around four hours northeast of Beijing by train, has some of China's most splendid imperial architecture. However, there's far too much to see to attempt it as a day trip from Beijing. It's far better to spend a night in Chengde, get up early, join a sightseeing tour, and then head back to Beijing in the late afternoon.

SHANGHAI

Shanghai is something of a bottleneck when it comes to transportation, so you should always plan ahead for excursions out of town. But do make a point of getting out of town if you can. Shanghai is surrounded by prime attractions, including two of China's most highly rated destinations: **Suzhou** and **Hangzhou**.

Suzhou is well worth overnighting in, though it's just an hour from Shanghai by train and an easy day outing. After Shanghai, Suzhou's canals and alleys lined with souvenir shops and restaurants will seem village-like. But it's the traditional gardens that are the city's main drawing card.

Hangzhou's main attraction is West Lake, which is the model for hundreds of other West Lakes in China, such is its fame. The lake tends to get swamped with tourists, but if you can manage an overnight stay, things tend to quiet down in the late afternoon. Trains from Shanghai take around three hours to get to Hangzhou.

Festive Flings

As anyone who's spent any time in Taiwan will know, the Chinese celebrate a myriad of festivals. Unfortunately in China most of them have been swept away and will probably never be celebrated again. Nowadays the minority regions of China, such as southern Yunnan, are the best places to see colorful festivals, but as these vary from group to group, listing them would require years of research. The most famous minority festival is the Dai **Water Splashing Festival**, which is held in mid-April.

SPRING

The one festival that everyone has heard of is **Chinese New Year**, known in Chinese as *chunjie*, or Spring Festival. It lasts for the first two weeks of the first lunar month, which usually places it in late January or early February. This is a time for Chinese to be with their families, so it's not realistic to expect a great deal of festive activity on the streets. You may see the occasional lion dance and hear the explosions of fire crackers going off. Sensible China travelers avoid being in China for Chinese New Year because the transport infrastructure comes under enormous pressure at this time of year (getting a

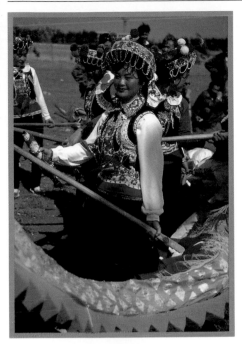

SUMMER

The big Chinese summer festival is the **Dragonboat Festival**. This is one festival that can be quite thrilling, with teams of rowers taking to the water in "dragonboats." *Zongzi*, the packets of rice and pork steamed in lotus leaves, is the traditional festival snack. Hong Kong is a good place to see dragonboat races, as is Yueyang in Hunan province and Nanning in Guangxi province.

AUTUMN

The seventh lunar month is **Ghost Month**, an inauspicious time for new business ventures, exams, and buying important things such as a house or a car. For the most part, life goes on as usual, but look for special celebrations at Daoist temples, particularly in Hong Kong. In Tibet, **Shotun**, or the Yoghurt Festival, is celebrated in the first week of the seventh lunar month, with picnics, dances and operas held in Lhasa.

On the fifteenth day of the eighth lunar month is the **Moon Festival**, also known as Mid-Autumn Festival. Like New Year, this is a time for family reunions (more traffic jams), though some street activity is to be expected, with firecrackers and lantern displays. The traditional festival snack is the *yuebing*, or moon cake, a pastry with a soft filling that is made from lotus seeds and sugar — there are hundreds of rival recipes for moon cake fillings.

September 28 is **Confucius' Birthday**. Celebrations are held in Confucius temples all over China, but particularly in Qufu, the Great Sage's hometown.

WINTER

The cold winter months are a lean time for festivals in China. Christmas has little significance outside China's small Christian flocks, but it is usually treated as an excuse for a night out and a big meal, as it is in other countries in the East.

flight or a seat on a train is nearly impossible at short notice). In addition, much of the country shuts down.

Despite the cold, Chinese New Year is a good time to be in Lhasa, as the Tibetans celebrate **Lhosar**, or the Tibetan New Year, with dances, performances and ritual observances. On the fifteenth day of the first lunar month, the **Lantern Festival** is held in Lhasa, with huge yak butter candles gracing the holy Barkhor circuit. A similar Lantern Festival is celebrated on the same day throughout China; it marks the end of New Year and is celebrated by hanging paper lanterns in the street.

In late March or Early April, **Guanyin**, the Buddhist goddess of mercy, has her birthday. Although a Buddhist deity, she gets the most colorful parties at Daoist temples. Also in early April is the national festival and holiday, **Qing Ming**, or Tomb Sweeping Day. This is the day one's thoughts turns to one's ancestors, and respect is shown by a visit to their graves, which are tidied up. Like Chinese New Year, Qing Ming is not the time to be traveling in China, as transportation gets booked up.

Near Kunming, colorful dancers keep minority traditions alive.

Galloping Gourmets

Food is never far from the thoughts of the average Chinese. A common greeting amongst friends is "Chi fanle, meiyou?" or, "Have you eaten?" Complete strangers on trains can fall into long, rapturous conversations about the regional delicacies of the towns they grew up. Indeed, it wouldn't be far from the truth to say that the Chinese are obsessed by food. The world can be thankful for this, for from it springs a cuisine that ranges adventurously across the entire spectrum of tastes and flavors.

If your experience of Chinese food is limited to sweet and sour pork from the local take-out joint, you are in for a big surprise. Chinese cuisine is far more complex than many people imagine, owing to different regional styles of preparation and tastes. Most of the Chinese food you find outside China is in fact Cantonese, with a definite Hong Kong influence and usually adulterated to conform with what Chinese imagine to be Western tastes.

Like China's many dialects, the food changes as you travel through the country. For convenience it's reasonable to divide China's cuisines broadly into **Northern** (Beijing and Shandong), **Eastern** (Shanghai and Zhejiang), **Southern** (Chaozhou and Cantonese) and **Sichuan**.

NORTHERN

One of the first things you notice in the north of China is that thick noodles and steamed breads are the staples of the local diet. Even in Beijing's most famous imperial culinary legacy, Beijing (Peking) duck, the bird is wrapped in *chepati*-like pancakes, not eaten with a bowl of rice.

On the streets look for typical northern treats like *congyoubing*, a griddle-fried pancake stuffed with leeks — it's a snack that has to be eaten hot.

For the Cantonese, a fondue cooked over charcoal braziers is a favorite dish in winter months.

Lamian, literally "pulled noodles," made from wheat have a slightly chewy texture to them when served correctly, and come in a steaming bowl of broth mixed with fresh leeks, chilis and perhaps some pork. Other northern specialties include the famous *jiaozi,* or dumplings, which if they're good can constitute an entire meal. The basic form of *jiaozi* is chopped pork and chives wrapped in dough and boiled. Dipping sauces are created by the diners themselves with a combination of vinegar, sesame oil, soy sauce and chili.

It's the imperial dishes that pull in the crowds. Along with the famous duck, dishes like beggar's chicken — in which a chicken is wrapped in lotus leaves and cooked in a mud pack (it was originally cooked underground), imparting a curious but intriguing taste to the chicken — are famous.

Beijing's meaty barbecue dishes stem from the days of the Mongol Khans and later from the Manchus. If you're in Beijing in the winter, a Mongolian barbecue is obligatory. It should be accompanied with a Mongolian hotpot, in which vegetables are simmered in a spicy broth.

SOUTHERN

While northern cuisine is heavy and dark — both in its tastes and constituents — the food of the south, Guangdong (Canton) in particular, is light and clear. Unlike the northerners, who have grown used to making it through the long cold winters with pickled vegetables, the southern Chinese are able to cook with fresh ingredients all year round. Indeed the Cantonese take this obsession with freshness to the extremes of displaying their ingredients live and kicking: fish, eels and lobsters swimming around tanks of water, live mammals incarcerated miserably in cages.

When it comes to vegetables it's difficult to think of a better approach than the Cantonese way, which is to stir-fry them quickly at super-hot temperatures; touches of garlic and salt add flavor.

Not everything is stir-fried. Steaming is the preferred option for seafood dishes and *dim sum.* Roasting is employed to great effect on duck and pork, the latter in the famous *chashao.* Cantonese casseroles (*bao*) are another not-to-be-missed specialty. The casseroles are actually sealed up before being heated, allowing the ingredients inside to simmer, with delicious results.

EASTERN

One of the famous qualities of eastern cuisine is the way salty and sweet tastes combine. Wuxi spareribs, from the town of the same name, is a dish in which the ribs are simmered in a red soy sauce broth with sugar. As in the south, rice is the staple, and fish is a favored dish: The Jiangsu and Zhejiang region are referred to by the Chinese as the *yumi zhixiang,* literally the "land of fish and rice," but with the meaning of "land of plenty," or as we might put it, the "land of milk and honey."

Eastern cuisine frequently gets overlooked by foreigners. The Shanghainese, for example, have their own range of tasty tea snacks, or *dianxin,* to rival the *dim sum* of the south, though typically they tend to be sweeter. Try Shanghai's *xiaolongbao,* a steamed dumpling that you will recognize in shape from the dumplings you had in Beijing and in Guangzhou, but in this case filled with a hot, sweet and salty soup. They're quite delicious, if you don't mind the soup dribbling down your chin.

SICHUAN

Sichuan is the fiery cuisine from the west. Little can prepare you for the extremes of heat the Sichuanese will put up with, and enjoy, in their food. You might even think you like hot food until you try a Chongqing-style *mala huoguo,* literally a "numb-hot" hotpot. The culprit is not just chili, and you'll see plenty of it swimming around in your food, but little peppercorns called *huajiao,* or "flower peppers."

The famous spicy dishes from Sichuan are *gongbao jiding,* stir-fried chicken with peanuts and *mapo doufu,*

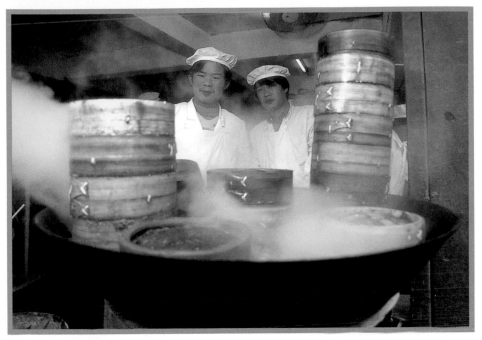

bean curd cooked in a sauce made of ground pork, spring onions, chili and garlic.

Despite the reputation for spices, Sichuan cuisine reaches out in a variety of directions. Few foreigners can resist the tasty novelty of *guobu roupian*, pork in a soupy stir-fry that is dumped on a bed of crispy rice crusts. Sichuan's sauces too are famed throughout China. Fish-flavored sauce may not taste a much like fish, but it's still very tasty and is featured in dishes of national renown, such as *yuxiang qiezi*, fish-flavored eggplant. Sichuan's smoked duck is a dish you should sample if you make it to Chengdu or Chongqing — at its best, it rates favorably with China's other famous duck dish.

DRINKS

China's number one drink is tea. There are hundreds of varieties, grown at varying altitudes, in different climates, picked in different seasons, but the basic varieties you'll encounter in restaurants are jasmine, flower and wulong (also known as Oolong). When you sit down in a restaurant in China, you will usually be served a pot of tea, for which there is a small charge. If you like, you can forego the tea and ask for China's number two drink: beer.

How beer got to be so popular in China would make an interesting tale; it got its start at Qingdao, in Shandong province, under the Germans, who had a concession there in the late nineteenth century. Tsingtao is still China's top beer and is widely available, but there will always be a cheaper local brew. Try the local beers; they are usually very good, and, as the joke in China runs, cheaper than bottled water.

Other Chinese alcoholic drinks are rarely appreciated by non-Chinese. Syrupy liqueurs distilled from flowers and fruits are the norm; these, or near-lethal spirits, such as Maotai, which is strictly for toasting your host into oblivion and not the thing for a quiet tipple. Foreign wines and prestigous alcoholic drinks such as brandy are making significant inroads into the Chinese market nowadays.

Avoid drinking tap water in China. Bottled water is available everywhere nowadays and costs very little. Hotel

Steaming dumplings, a common street scene, Nanjing, Jiangsu Province.

rooms are always supplied with a thermos of hot water; if yours is empty or your room doesn't have one, notify your floor staff with a shout of "*kaishui!*"

If you can't do without Coca Cola, Pepsi, Sprite and company, rest assured you'll find them in the remotest of destinations in China. Trudge to the top of a sacred mountain, and there will probably be someone waiting for you at the top with a can of Coke.

Special Interests

China is not an easy place to pursue special interests in. If you are keen, it's feasible, say, to enroll in a course in watercolor painting at a university in Suzhou or Hangzhou, but you will probably have to learn Mandarin first. You might conceivably study martial arts at Shaolin Temple (some foreigners do), but again some Mandarin would help and it would be unrealistic to expect that applications and even the study program itself will go smoothly.

Before committing yourself to a study program in China always look into the alternatives in Hong Kong and Taiwan. Taiwan is an especially good place to learn Mandarin.

COOKERY CLASSES

Hong Kong is the place for cookery classes. Try contacting one of the following: **Chopsticks Cooking Centre** ((852) 2336-8433, G/F 108 Boundary Street, Kowloon; **Oriental Culinary Institute** ((852) 2881-5528 FAX 2822-3333, 12/F, 22 Yee Woo Street, Causeway Bay; **Hong Kong Electric Company (Home Management Centre)** ((852) 2510-2828, 10/F Electric Centre, 28 City Garden Road, North Point; **Towngas Centre** ((852) 2576-1535, Basement, Leighton Centre, 77 Leighton Road, Causeway Bay.

LANGUAGE COURSES

If you want to speak Mandarin with a prestigious northern burr, the place to go is Beijing. Full degree programs as well as short courses for all levels are available at the **Beijing Language and Culture University**, 15 Xueyuan Road, Haidian District Beijing, 100083, and at the **Beijing Second Institute of Foreign Languages**, Dingfuzhuang, Chaoyang District, Beijing, 100024. Other courses are available in many of China's provincial capitals, but if you're going to be studying Mandarin in China, you may as well do it in Beijing.

For those who don't fancy a long stint in Beijing, the **Yale in China Language Program** at the Chinese University of Hong Kong, Shatin, New Territories ((852) 2609-6727 FAX (852) 2603-5004, is recommended.

The best place in the world to study Mandarin is probably Taipei. Contact the **Mandarin Training Centre** (Taiwan), National Taiwan Normal University, 129-1 Hoping East Road, Section 1, Taipei.

Taking a Tour

For visitors who choose the mainstream or organized tour trail, there's a wide variety of package tours and luxury expeditions offered by the leading tour operators and specialized "trailblazer" agencies of Britain, Europe, the United States and Australia. They'll put you on a train in London and deliver you to Beijing via the memorable Trans-Siberian Railway. They'll fly you directly from London, San Francisco, New York, Seattle, Vancouver, Paris, Frankfurt, Geneva or Sydney to Beijing, Shanghai or Guangzhou or to the main staging point for many China tours, Hong Kong. You can take an ocean cruise from Sydney Harbour and call in on Shanghai and Guangzhou, or you can arrive triumphantly in Kashgar or Lhasa aboard a luxury bus.

Travel to China can be less expensive as an individual traveler, but organized group tours are the most comfortable, convenient and predictable way to do it — you have the advantage of being able

A practitioner of China's ancient art of *qigong*, oblivious to his surroundings in Lu Xun Park, Qingdao.

to roll along with your group knowing that you don't have to lift a finger on your own behalf except to eat, drink and buy souvenirs. Most of the big established operators provide escorts with a sound experience of China travel and Chinese culture, and they also take care of everything from visas to a very welcome short stopover in Hong Kong at the end of the trip. Their prices generally include international travel to and from China, all internal travel, full accommodation and meals, cultural excursions, Chinese interpreters and guides and airport taxes.

TOUR OPERATORS
BRITAIN

Voyages Jules Verne is probably Europe's biggest and most experienced China tour operator, with its own office in Beijing to help smooth out accommodation and itinerary problems. The company has a wide range of tours to China and Tibet that can also takes in North Korea, the Republic of Mongolia and Russia. It also conducts several tours on the Trans-Siberian/China rail route (see THE TRANS-SIBERIAN RAILWAY, below). For brochures and detailed information their London office is:
Travel Promotions Ltd. ((44 171) 616-1000 FAX (44 171) 723-8629 E-MAIL sales@vjv.co.uk, 21 Dorset Square, London NW1 6QJ.

For other reputable operators offering mainstream package tours contact:
Abercrombie & Kent Ltd. ((44 171) 730-9600 FAX (44 171) 730-9376, Sloane Square House, Holbein Place, London SW1W 8NS.
Far East Travel Centre ((44 171) 414-8844 FAX (44 171) 414-8848, 33 Maddox Street, London W1R 9LD.
Hayes and Jarvis (Travel) Ltd. ((44 181) 741-9932 FAX (44 181) 741-0299, Hayes House, 152 King Street, London W6 0QU.
P&O Travel Ltd. ((44 171) 800-2222 FAX (44 171) 831-1410, 77 New Oxford Street, London, WC1A 1PP.
Premier Holidays ((44 1223) 516516 FAX (44 1223) 516615, Westbrook, Milton Road, Cambridge CB4 1YQ.

Swan Hellenic ((44 171) 800-2200 FAX (44 171) 831-1280, 77 New Oxford Street, London WC1A 1PP, which offers a 17-day art treasure tour of China.
Thomas Cook Ltd. ((44 171) 499-4000 FAX (44 171) 408-4299, (Worldwide Office), 45 Berkeley Street, London W1A 1EB.
World Expeditions ((44 1628) 74174 FAX (44 1628) 74312, 7 North Road, Maidenhead, Berks, SL6 1PL.

CONTINENTAL EUROPE

Swiss-based **Kuoni Travel** has tours of all kinds. They have many offices around the region, including one in the UK:
Kuoni ((44 1306) 740500 FAX (44 1306) 744222, Kuoni House, Dorking, Surrey, RH5 4AZ, England.
Voyages Kuoni ((33 1) 42 85 71 22 FAX (33 1) 40 23 06 26, 95, rue d'Amsterdam, F-75008 Paris, France.
Reiseburo Kuoni ((49 89) 2311-1630 FAX (49 89) 2311-1650, Furstenfelderstrasse 7, D-80331 Munich, Germany.
Kuoni Travel (Head Office) ((41 1) 277-4444 FAX (41 1) 272-0071, Neue Hard Nº7, CH-8037 Zurich, Switzerland.

UNITED STATES

Abercrombie & Kent International ((1 630) 954-2944 TOLL-FREE (800) 323-7308 FAX (1 630) 954-3324 E-MAIL info@abercrombiekent.com, 1520 Kensington Road, Oak Brook, IL 60523.
China Voyages ((1 415) 398-2244 FAX (1 415) 399-0827 582 Market Street, Suite 605, San Francisco, CA 94104.
Himalayan Travel, Inc. ((1 203) 359-3711 TOLL-FREE (800) 225-2380 FAX (1 203) 359-3669 E-MAIL worldadv@netaxis.com, 112 Prospect Street, Stamford, CT 06901.
Mountain Travel ((1 510) 527-8100 FAX (1 510) 525-7710, 6420 Fairmount Avenue, El Cerrito, CA 94530.
Pacific Delight ((1 212) 684-7707 TOLL-FREE (800) 221-7179 FAX (1 212) 532-3406, 132 Madison Avenue, New York, NY 10016.

A riot of neon competes for attention along Nathan Road, Kowloon.

CANADA
Pacific Rim Travel Corporation
((1 250) 380-4888 FAX (1 250) 380-2638
E-MAIL pacrimtc@pinc.com, 419–1207
Douglas Street, Victoria, BC V8W 2E7.

AUSTRALIA
**Flight Centres International —
Sydney** ((61 2) 133133 Level 11,
33 Berry Street, North Sydney 2090;
Melbourne ((61 3) 9600-0799
TOLL-FREE 1800-679943, Level 7, 343 Little
Collins Street, Melbourne 3000; **Brisbane**
((61 7) 3229 5917 TOLL-FREE 1800-500204 ,
Level 13, 157 Ann Street, Brisbane 4000.
STA Travel — Melbourne (1300-360960,
256 Flinders Street, Melbourne 3000;
Sydney ((61 2) 9212-1255, 855 George
Street, Sydney 2000; **Brisbane** ((61 7)
3221-3722, Shop 25-26, 111-117 Adelaide
Street, Brisbane 4000.

HONG KONG
An alternative to taking a package tour
directly from your home country is to
fly to Hong Kong, enjoy a few days of
leisurely shopping and sightseeing, and
then take advantage of China trips
organized and operated from there.
From Hong Kong, tours ranging from
a one-day hop over the border to two-
to three-week grand tours are offered
by China International Travel Service
(CITS), China Travel Service (CTS) as
well as many other travel and tour
agencies:
CITS (Head Office) Kowloon ((852)
2732-5888 FAX (852) 2721-7154, 13/F,
Tower A, New Mandarin Plaza, 14
Science Museum Road, Tsimshatsui
East; Branch Office ((852) 2810-4282,
Room 1807, Wing On House, 71 Des
Vœux Road, Central.
CTS (Head Office) ((852) 2853-3888
FAX (852) 2851-0642, CTS House, 78–83
Connaught Road Central, Hong Kong;
Hong Kong Branch Office ((852) 2521-
7163 FAX (852) 877-2033, China Travel
Building, 77 Queen's Road Central;
Kowloon Branch Office Tsimshatsui
((852) 2721-1331, 1st Floor; Alpha
House, 27–33 Nathan Road, Hong
Kong.

OTHER AGENCIES (HONG KONG ISLAND):
Abercrombie & Kent ((852) 865-7818
FAX (852) 2866-0556
E-MAIL akhkg@attmail.com, 19th Floor
Gitic Centre, 28 Queen's Road East,
Wanchai.
CAAC Holidays Ltd. ((852) 2922-1028
FAX (852) 2865-1143
E-MAIL caacholi@hkstar.com, Unit 34C,
United Centre, 95 Queensway Road,
Quarry Bay.
Concorde Air-Sea Services Ltd. ((852)
2524-5121 FAX (852) 2877-2160
E-MAIL concorde@netvigator.com 1/F &
7/F Galuxe Building, 8–10 On Lan Street,
Central.
Forceten Ltd. Central ((852) 2526-0336
FAX (852) 2537-6223
E-MAIL forceten@netvigator.com Room
403 Tung Ming Building, 40–42 Des
Vœux Road.
Thomas Cook Travel Services (HK) Ltd.
((852) 2853-9888 FAX (852) 2545-7477
E-MAIL infobox@thomascook.com.hk
18/F, Vicwood Plaza, 199 Des Vœux
Road, Central.
Wallem Travel Ltd. ((852) 2876-8220
FAX (852) 2876-1220 E-MAIL wtlhk@
wallem.com, 46th Floor; Hopewell
Centre, 183 Queen's Road East, Wanchai.
Other Agencies (Kowloon):
Phoenix Services ((852) 2722-7378
FAX (852) 2369-8884, Room B, 6th Floor;
Milton Mansion, 96 Nathan Road,
Tsimshatsui.
P&O Travel Ltd. ((852) 2956-6888
FAX (852) 2956-6789
E-MAIL inbl@pandotravel.com. Suite 1701,
Tower II, The Gateway, Harbour City,
Canton Road, Tsimshatsui, Kowloon.
Sunflower Travel Service Ltd. ((852)
2369-0283 FAX (852) 2721-8035, 2/F, Alpha
House, 27–33 Nathan Road, Tsimshatsui,
Kowloon.

THE CHINA CONNECTION
Information on China International
Travel Service (CITS) and China Travel
Service (CTS) tours and other China
travel matters can also be obtained by
contacting their overseas branches or
agents — or you can get in touch with

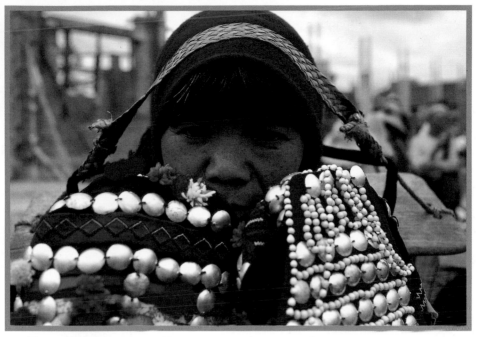

the China National Tourist Office (CNTO) (see page 308).

Australia ((61 2) 9211 2633 FAX (61 2) 9281-3595, Ground floor; 757–759 George Street, Sydney, NSW 2000.

Canada ((1 604) 872-8787 FAX (1 604) 873-2823, 556 West Broadway, Vancouver, BC V5Z 1E9.

France ((33) 142 86 88 66 FAX (33) 142 86 88 61, 30, rue Gramont, 75002 Paris.

Germany ((49 69) 250515 or 250516 FAX (49 69) 232324, China Travel & Trading, Dusseldorferstrasse 14, 60329 Frankfurt am Main 1.

Japan ((81 3) 3273-5512 FAX (81 3) 3273-2667, Nihombashi-Settsu Building, Chuo-Ku, Tokyo.

Singapore ((65) 224-0550 FAX (65) 224-5009, Ground Floor, SIA Building, 77 Robinson Road, 0106.

United Kingdom ((44 171) 836-9911 FAX (44 71) 836-3121, 24 Cambridge Circus, London WC2H 8HD.

United States ((1 415) 398-6627 FAX (1 415) 398-6669, 2nd Floor, 212 Sutter Street, CA 94108.

THE TRANS-SIBERIAN RAILWAY

This grand rail journey from London to Hong Kong, crossing Europe, the

former Soviet Union and China, has been turned into a series of adventure tours since the Trans-Siberian Railway joined the mainstream tourism trail a few years ago.

One of the leading operators is UK-based Voyages Jules Verne with a selection of tours ranging from the 21-day London to Hong Kong epic to a 13-day Silk Road adventure from Samarkand in Central Asia to Shanghai on luxury trains. For more details contact: **Travel Promotions Ltd. (** (44 171) 616-1000.

A less expensive tour operator that specializes in tailor-made Trans-Siberian journeys is **One Europe Travel (** (44 181) 566-9424, in London. In addition, most of the travel agents listed above will have information on Trans-Siberian tours.

At a market in Xishuangbanna, Yunnan Province, a minority woman in Menghun displays locally produced handicrafts.

The Middle Kingdom

A TOUR OF CHINA is more than just a tour, it is a grand pilgrimage through a civilization that has endured for thousands of years. Its cultural heritage is so vast, and its monuments, relics and other wonders stir the imagination so evocatively, that it is one of the most fascinating and rewarding travel experiences on earth.

Not that China is all exotic tradition. During the last 10 years China's open-door policy and free-market economic policies have brought about immense changes: People are more affluent; high-rises litter the urban landscape; and foreign tourists enjoying the sights are outnumbered by Chinese tourists these days. The foreign traveler in modern China can enjoy high service standards, excellent cuisine and hotel comforts that travelers not more than half a decade ago could only dream about.

For those who find such modern encroachments off-putting, China's cultural attractions remain every bit as astonishing as the textbooks and tour literature would have us believe. For Westerners, its modern society is as strange, as interesting and even as bizarre as one would expect of a people who have triumphed over resounding social collapse, terrible warfare and civil conflict, violent revolution, and almost complete isolation for more than three decades from the rest of the world. In a certain sense, it is this society that is China's biggest wonder; and the heart of a China tour is a pilgrimage to the soul of its people.

The good news is that it is easier to meet those people. Not long ago China was a challenge: not only physically huge — the third largest country in the world — but poorly serviced by road and air. Nowadays express highways are slashing travel times, and flights to even the remotest destinations are abundant. The road from Mao to Mammon has created a new, brighter China in which it's easier to get around, and the people you meet are more open and friendly.

This is obviously a boon to visitors, who are now in a much better position to travel individually. Officially, there is still a definite preference for organized group tours, allowing foreigners in, but in tightly controlled circumstances, on strict itineraries and largely segregated from the ordinary people. But the growing hordes of business travelers involved in foreign investment and the modernization program have triggered a boom in international-class hotels and a major improvement in the standards of older properties, and authorities have practically given up trying to steer travelers into tours. Nobody's complaining: While the organized tour means comfort and convenience and protection from the more arduous and less attractive aspects of the society, it is at the price of open contact with the masses.

At the other end of the travel spectrum lies tight-budget backpacking, but this can mean the misery of being too close to the society's bottom rungs — dingy and even squalid hostels and guesthouse dormitories, a continual competition for the cheapest seats on trains, a struggle in the awful crush that occurs on the overcrowded and often dilapidated public buses, and bad food in unhygienic conditions. Such hardship does little to enhance the grand physical and cultural panorama of China.

THE MIDDLE WAY

In between these two extremes there is a compromise, the Middle Way — a path that the new legions of individual business travelers have found. It offers comfort when you most need it, the freedom to rough it when circumstances call for it, and,

OPPOSITE: Old woman of Tibet. ABOVE: "One country, two systems" — neon signs will continue to advertise Hong Kong's capitalist style, for 50 years after 1997.

most importantly, complete immersion in Chinese society.

Don't expect your trip to always be easy. Few things in China are. Take one billion energetic, industrious people and an infrastructure — transport, accommodation and communication — that was seriously neglected in the decade of violent social upheaval called the Great Proletarian Cultural Revolution, kick the whole lot into a fast-track program of modernization, and not surprisingly, you get a system that blips from time to time. A group tour will remove you from it, a threadbare backpacker's existence could make you a begrudging victim of it. The Middle Way will throw you into the heart of it, but on terms that are your own.

In the final analysis, anyone's chosen form of travel in China is going to be decided on personal and financial grounds — age, stamina and the amount of money available for the trip. To any elderly person or anyone who doesn't feel up to the rigors of individual travel, a package tour is recommended, and again, on the principle that the paramount consideration on any visit to China should be to enjoy it, not endure it.

For those brave enough to strike off and go it alone, China's secrets yield themselves far more readily than for those trapped in a group tour. You will meet fellow travelers on trains who share their food and — as far as the language barrier permits — their thoughts. You will encounter unexpected kindnesses and smiles. There will be hardships to be sure, but if the Middle Way allows you to rough it, you can be comforted by the thought that you have enough money to treat yourself to a bit of luxury when you need it — a clean, warm bed, a good bath, a good meal and a chance to have your clothes laundered and feel reasonably human again.

Xuanwu Park is a world apart from the bustle of downtown Nanjing, Jiangsu Province.

The Country and Its People

THE SWEEPING EAVES

Just as China is physically vast, it is also a land of vividly contrasting terrain and climate. It is the third largest country on earth after Russia and Canada, its territory covering seven percent of the world's total land surface, an area of nearly 10 million sq km (3.8 million square miles) including Tibet. It stretches 5,500 km (3,410 miles) from its northern to southern borders and almost the same distance from east to west.

Dotted around its 14,000-km (8,680-mile) eastern and southern coastline are nearly 5,000 islands, some of them, such as Hainan off the southern coast, large enough to support substantial farming and fishing communities. The island of Taiwan, where the Nationalist Guomindang forces fled in the revolution of 1949, is considered by the Beijing leadership to be part of China and pressure mounts on the island to come back into the mainland fold. The tiny Portuguese-administered enclave of Macau will return to China in 1999. And of course, as nobody could have failed to have heard, such was the media coverage, the former British colonial possession of Hong Kong—that remarkable capitalist industrial and trading center which has thrived and fattened over the years as the communist giant's principal source of foreign exchange—returned to full Chinese sovereignty on July 1, 1997.

The terrain within all this territory is so variable and contrasting that, for the relatively casual visitor, it needs to be approached in its simplest terms. In one sense it has the same basic architecture as its traditional man-made temples and pavilions with their sweeping, multitiered eaves. If you take Tibet in the far west as the tip of the roof (and Tibet is, in fact, popularly termed the "Roof of the World"), the rest of the terrain sweeps and falls away to the east in a series of descending plateaus and plains, arriving finally at sea level along the eastern seaboard.

The landscape is dominated by two great river systems, the Yellow River in the north and the mighty Yangtze to the central southwest. Both originate in the upper reaches of the Tibet–Qinghai Plateau and surge downhill toward the eastern coast, and both have

acted as the landscape's principal sculptors. Over many thousands of years the Yellow River has deposited and then carved its way through a vast plain of soft loess soil, creating a dramatic and sometimes bizarre pattern of winding canyons, rounded bluffs and strangely shaped outcroppings where harder soil and rock have resisted its knife. To the south, the Yangtze has carved the narrow, precipitous Yangtze gorges of Sichuan province, and beyond that its southern tributaries have rushed and seeped through a wide belt of limestone to form a similarly dramatic

landscape of karst — geological formations in which erosion has left pinnacles, underground caverns and abruptly shaped mounds and hills that have given the city of Guilin and its Guangxi-Zhuangzu autonomous region its fairyland character.

These river systems have been both life-giving and death-dealing over the many centuries of recorded Chinese history. Both have periodically unleashed terrible floods which have destroyed croplands and wiped out whole communities, killing countless numbers of people. The Yellow River, known

OPPOSITE: Picturesque Sky Lake lies in the Tian Range near Urumqi — revered as heaven by ancient Xiongnü nomads. ABOVE: Turkic-speaking merchant from Urumqi.

in the past as "China's Sorrow," has breached its banks and dikes more than 1,000 times, changed its course on at least 20 occasions, and during the 2,000 years from the Han to Qing dynasties, the Yangtze has gone on the rampage in more than 200 disastrous floods.

Elsewhere, the landscape sprawls and soars through climates that range from frigid-temperate with permafrost in the far north to temperate, subtropical and tropical as it sweeps south. In winter the far northern reaches, lashed by bitter winds from the Siberian steppes, are bleak and forbidding,

either dry and frozen or, as one of Mao Zedong's many poems depicted them, "a thousand miles sealed with ice, 10,000 miles of swirling snows." Meanwhile, in the far south, the sun beats down upon lush rainforests, bamboo groves and rice paddies below the Tropic of Cancer. In summer the entire country boils in the south and bakes in the drier north, with the temperature at a national average of 25°C (77°F).

The western mountains of Yunnan, Sichuan and Qinghai provinces rise majestically to heights of 7,000 m (23,000 ft) or more to form the foothills of the awesome Himalayas; the deserts and dust bowls, including the dreaded Taklamakan and the harsh Turpan Depression — more than 150 m

(500 ft) below sea level, one of the lowest land surfaces on earth — are moonscapes of relentlessly shifting sands under which the houses, temples and bones of the fabled Silk Road and the frontiers of Chinese civilization lie buried. And in between these stark contrasts there lies a wide diversity of prairies, jungles, "green seas" of bamboo, spectacular rivers — some 1,500 of them — 370 large lakes, gentle streams and jagged coastlines.

GAZELLES AND GINGKOS

Despite its huge land space, only about 15% of China is suitable for agriculture and extensive human settlement, and this means that in some areas there is an abundance and similar diversity of vegetation and wildlife. In all, China claims to have some 32,000 species of higher plants and more than 4,500 species of animals and birds, including more than 400 species of mammals, or 10% of the world total.

Some of this natural heritage, including the giant panda and the gingko tree of Sichuan province, is native only to China. And as the near-arctic forest wildernesses of the north give way to sweeping grasslands and the lush tropical river plains of the south, there are tigers, bears, moose, deer and gazelle, wild horses and camels, wolves and foxes, snow leopards, yaks, antelopes, monkeys, civet cats and even elephants.

However, that's not to say that the country is one vast and flourishing natural habitat. The giant panda hasn't been adopted as the emblem of the World Wildlife Fund for Nature just for its cuddly features and striking colors — hunting, land clearance and centuries of deforestation of many areas have reduced the giant panda population, and many other animal species in China, to crisis point.

Industrialization has also taken its toll, and so have the immense pressure for food and the wholesale slaughter of wildlife for ingredients for traditional Chinese medicine; and if you climb Mount Emei in Sichuan, for example, you'll come across a far less illustrious symbol of Chinese conservation — skeletal dried monkey carcasses set up on stalls to advertise herbal and animal medicines.

THE PEOPLE PRESSURE

The most stunning feature of China, however, is its population of over one billion people, a quarter of the human race, packed into 15% of its land surface. It has created a stark contrast of its own — teeming eastern and southern cities, with Shanghai and its municipal zone, crammed with no less than 13 million people, and comparatively deserted wildernesses in parts of the north and in the northwest. It has also created a society

years of Chinese history, it is more important to consider how this economic nightmare has been tackled over the past 40 years, and how the struggle stands today.

The communist revolution sought, among other things, to slay the economic dragon and rebuild, out of chaos and collapse, a new, prospering, self-governing and self-sufficient China. For all the mistakes, misguided idealism and subsequent chaos that are nowadays being blamed on the Maoist era, some tremendous achievements were made. Simply figuring out how to feed

whose entire character is governed by one phenomenon — a furious competition for all the most basic necessities of life.

It is this unremitting human struggle that is the most challenging, and yet the most fascinating, aspect of a visit to China. If you're not shielded from it on an official tour you are, in many respects, competing with a billion people for services and amenities. But it is this struggle that makes the Chinese who they are, and a China tour so unlike most other travel experiences.

Arriving in China you encounter a society that is the definition of economics taken to its extreme — vast, unlimited demands, severely limited resources. Leaving aside the implications that this has had through 5,000

a population of a billion was an achievement. They also rebuilt an industrial base and an infrastructure — transport, public housing and communications — which lifted the nation out of the hopelessness and grinding poverty of the violent pre-revolutionary years. On top of that, they instituted a crucial form of national effort and discipline, based on a mass campaign and a code of individual and group responsibility that is still expressed here and there today with the phrase "to be of service to the people." But then, something went wrong. While the

OPPOSITE: Industrialization and intense people pressure have led to the construction of huge public housing projects in the major cities. ABOVE: Youth sporting Western fashions in Beijing.

people were encouraged to exist in a Utopian mood of cooperation and communal responsibility, power struggles went on in the leadership; and in the most crucial high-level political struggle of all, on the direction in which the development of China should be guided, the embattled Chairman Mao unleashed the Great Proletarian Cultural Revolution. It got out of hand. The principle of self-sufficiency was taken to an idealistic extreme, the society turned in on itself and the clock of progress stopped while, for almost a decade, another wave of violence and chaos swept the land.

THE NEW CHINA

Today, it's hard to imagine the China of 10 years ago, a place still reeling under the legacy of a broken main spring, an infrastructure that had fallen into disrepair. The Chinese modernization

program has been more successful than even its most optimistic backers could have hoped. The new China is booming, bringing high-class international hotels and modern travel services to the big cities — hotels with four- and five-star accommodation, IDD telephone services in all rooms, business centers and quality Chinese and international restaurants. The deluxe Palace Hotel and China World Trade Centre in Beijing, the Hilton and Portman Shangri-La in Shanghai and the Holiday Inn Downtown and Garden hotels in Guangzhou are among the new properties which reflect this general upgrading throughout China.

This top end boom has had the effect of inspiring mid-range and even budget hotels to refurbish and train their staff in the basics of the hotel industry. Still, improved though standards may be, it's likely that in the mid-range and certainly in the budget hotels you will still come across toilets and showers that don't work, hot water that never materializes, creaky plumbing, idiosyncratic heating, threadbare carpeting and all the other discomforts sent to plague the traveler.

TRANSPORTATION

Nothing better reflects China's giddy push for the future than the improvements that are taking place in the transport infrastructure. Roads are being upgraded everywhere you look. New trains are being brought into service. And the restructuring of the national aviation administration, CAAC (Air China), into a flurry of localized domestic airlines has replaced old Russian Tupolevs with modern Boeing, McDonnell Douglas and Airbus jets. Airports too are being upgraded, although more remote destinations are still subject to delays, cancellations and poor passenger service.

The rail system, like the rest of the infrastructure, is under tremendous people pressure. On any day most railway stations throughout China have up to 2,000 people and their baggage camped outside them waiting for tickets or trains. Others fill the booking halls, struggling and sometimes fighting to get to the ticket windows. The simple process of checking through the ticket gates to get to the trains can turn into a mob scramble, sometimes policed but sometimes uncontrolled, which can leave you breathless, angered and even bruised. The best way to avoid such scenes is to travel "soft sleeper," the Chinese equivalent of first class, which will not only provide you with a comfortable berth but should also provide you with a first-class waiting room away from the pandemonium elsewhere in the station.

Yet for all this, the trains do run strictly on time. They are also reasonably comfortable, and they can stir the imagination. Whenever time permits, choose the train for travel across China — few experiences compare with the sight of paddy fields flashing past, seen from the inside of a train.

There is little romance, however, about the public buses. Inner city buses are always cheap, but they are often ludicrously overcrowded and sometimes the haunt of pickpockets. Long-distance services are not much better. The trend these days is towards "sleeper buses". If there are two of you, this form of transport is fine for an overnight trip, but if you are on your own you will probably find yourself squeezed into the equivalent of a single bed with a complete stranger. On obscure long-distance routes the general practice is to cram as many passengers in as possible and then putter along at an average of around 25 kph (15 mph).

Travel in China can be frustrating beyond words. Yet, like almost everything else in China, there's another side to the coin of discomfort. You may find yourself pressed against the inside wall of a bus, fighting claustrophobia, and someone will get up and offer you a seat and insist that you take it, despite your protests, because you are a foreign guest. Such gestures of comradeship and hospitality happen often in China, and they tend to happen at the most crucial moments, when the three most vital qualities that every visitor to China must have — patience, understanding and peace of mind — are wearing dangerously thin. They prove, time and time again, the admirable strength of the ordinary Chinese people, their ability to put up with the most grueling, derelict conditions, day after day, and still retain a sense of humor and generosity. It's merciful that it does happen, because even the most equable Western temperament can reach breaking point in the pitfalls and surprises of this bewildering society.

THE MILLIONAIRE SYNDROME

China's long period of cultural isolation manifestly affects the way in which the Chinese regard foreigners. Many of them believe all Westerners are millionaires. Certainly, when you compare the standard of living that Western tourists exhibit in China with the level at which they live, particularly in the working-class districts of major cities

China's national rail network is one of the last in the world to operate steam locomotives alongside modern diesels.

and the poorer rural areas, foreigners look as though they've got money to burn. (Not all Chinese regard foreigners as rich: The rise of the Chinese capitalists, particularly the new wave of entrepreneurs and joint-venture factory czars of Shanghai and the burgeoning Pearl River Delta in Guangdong province, has already created an elite level of wealth beyond anything that the average Westerner can imagine.)

For a long time this perception of foreigners as fabulously wealthy justified the institutionalization of special "tourist prices,"

which might range from 75 to as much as 300% more than the local prices. This policy has been abandoned, but travelers are still likely to encounter vestiges of it around China. In some of the down-market hotels, desk clerks may try to put you into the most expensive rooms, telling you these are the only rooms available, and you have to be prepared to take a firm, patient stand and negotiate.

At some of the major tourist attractions, particularly the Great Wall at Badaling near Beijing, the terracotta army in Xi'an and the Stone Forest in Yunnan province, the hustle for tourist money has become so fierce that you encounter packs of souvenir hawkers more frenzied than any you're likely to see

outside, say, Kuta Beach in Bali. At Xi'an they're so persistent that they've had to be confined to fixed areas outside the terracotta tomb because visitors were unable to view the soldiers for their sales clamor inside.

THE MAIN ATTRACTION

The foreigner in China is the oddest of things: affluent, privileged, free to travel, fashionable and curious in appearance. Chinese feelings about us are complex. In the leadup to the handover of Hong Kong, for example, a film called *The Opium Wars* vilified the British for their role as "merchants of death" in the last century, but at the same time a BBC production of *Pride and Prejudice* had Chinese glued to their television sets.

In short, we are every bit as strange to them as they are to us. For better or worse, we're showing them what to wear, how to wear it, what accessories and gadgets to own, when to use them, how the up-to-date human being generally behaves in a modern up-to-date world — all very materialistic, but the only practical way, aside from television, that they have of gaining a window on a world that has been a mystery to them for decades.

This intense fascination has ebbed somewhat over the last decade, so that in the big cities most Chinese won't bat an eyelid at the sight of a foreign face. But leave for the provinces and when you walk the streets you are under constant public scrutiny. On the trains it sometimes reaches the point where you can hardly bear to move for the attention and excitement that it can generate up and down the carriage. Wherever you go, you become the main attraction; and while it is generally a nice thing to be, it can also be tiring.

But what you get in return is attention. The Chinese not only want to study you, they want to be involved in some way with you. So, if you lose your bearings in the streets someone will inevitably help. If you're at a loss in the railway booking halls, someone will show you where to get your ticket. People will invite you to eat with them, to take pictures of them and their children. With what little they have, they'll offer you cigarettes, fruit, sweets, biscuits, sunflower seeds, nuts and other modest but touching gifts aboard the trains and buses. On an individual tour, you'll feel at times as though the Chinese people are almost handing you from one to another right across China.

CAN I HELP YOU?

Even in the most fraught situations, when the language barrier threatens to overwhelm you, an angel will usually appear with the greeting, "Hello. Can I help you?" This is the opening gambit of another cultural exchange that foreign visitors are called upon to take part in throughout China. It comes from young students, and there are many thousands of them, who are striving to learn English to "better ourselves" and who have very little opportunity to test their vocabulary and pronunciation.

They must seize upon any foreigner they see, and you have to be completely insensitive to resent it. Most of them are earnest and friendly and, in return for a little conversational practice, will go to great lengths to help with ticketing and other information. If their English is good enough you can also break through the official jargon of China and get some sense of the deeper impulses and attitudes of the society.

Although the English students are far more likely to be working part time jobs or busy in the classroom than lurking in the train station these days, it's still difficult at times not to feel that you are carrying an imaginary sign which says "teacher." Impromptu English-language sessions can be so frequent that some China travelers burn out and hide behind a few words of another language altogether when approached by the student of English. Just watch out that you don't end up becoming the recipient of an English lesson yourself if you do this.

THE CHANGING SCENE

China is changing at such breakneck speed that even the Chinese themselves find it difficult to keep up. Where just a decade ago there were exhortatory slogans, there are now billboards advertising Remy Martin, Marlboro and Coca Cola. Where everyone dressed in near identical Mao suits, they now deck themselves out in fashionable outfits from chains like Giordano and Bossini. Where once the streets teemed with Flying Pigeon bicycles, they now buzz with Hondas.

This burgeoning affluence and the promise of riches to come is making China a more confident place. The handover of Hong Kong on midnight June 30, 1997 was a grand event marked by five days of celebrations in Hong Kong. It ends what many Chinese consider a humiliating chapter in their history — the ceding of territory to opium peddling foreigners. And while there has been much ado in the foreign press about Hong Kong's fu-

ture prospects now that it is back in China's hands, astute observers have been heard to point out that influence is a two-way street: Over the last decade China has become increasingly like Hong Kong, not vice versa.

Perhaps this new China is not quite the country many of us imagine before we go, but it is no less interesting for it. The familiar emblems of the modern world take on new nuances of meaning in a Chinese context. China can never lose its power to surprise and astound. And with 5,000 years of history behind it, how could it be any other way?

OPPOSITE: One of 50,000 Buddha images in the 53 Yungang Grottoes west of Datong, Shanxi Province. ABOVE: An enthusiastic young stallholder displays his wares in a small clothes market in Beijing.

5,000 YEARS OF HISTORY

THE CULTURAL SAFE-DEPOSIT

A short visit to China is a fleeting encounter with one of the most complex cultures on earth, touching the tiny tip of an immense and almost limitless cultural iceberg. An extensive tour is a route-march through the cultural heritage of 4,000 to 5,000 years of recorded Chinese history, and at the end of the march it is still as complex and elusive as

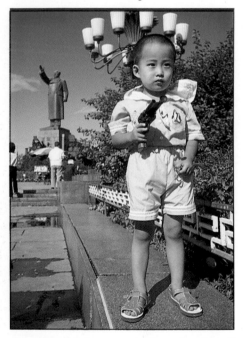

ever. You come away feeling that for all you've seen, and all the distance you've traveled, you've done little more than lightly scratch the surface. In one respect this is all that anyone can do, for the vast bulk of China's history lies buried in the ground. It's estimated that its current array of temples and monasteries, grottoes and statues, relics and artifacts and great monuments is only about 10 to 20% of that which may some day be available to see — the rest of it languishing in a kind of cultural safe-deposit, awaiting the archaeologist's key.

The history that it represents covers such a long and tumultuous span of time and events that no guidebook could ever do it justice, and no visitor other than the lifelong

China scholar could really set foot on Chinese soil with anything but the vaguest idea of what it's all about. The best that can be done in any one book, in fact, is to put it into a reasonably understandable perspective. As with its geography, Chinese history must be approached in its simplest form.

THE DISTANT DAWNING

The approach begins with the evidence that protohuman life existed in China at least 600,000 years ago. The most vivid testimonial lies in a museum and excavated cave at Zhoukoudian, about 50 km (31 miles) southwest of Beijing, where two teeth and a skull were discovered in the 1920s, provided the physical profile of one of the most celebrated archaeological finds of all time — the apelike Peking Man.

As long ago as 5000 BC, Peking Man's more human descendants were farming the rich alluvial valleys and plains of the Yellow, the Yangtze and other river networks in China's southeast region. For evidence of this you go to the culturally strategical city of Xi'an where, 40 km (25 miles) to the east, you'll find the Banpo Museum, a tacky tourist attraction which has an old-fashioned museum section featuring bones, pottery, stone tools, a covered excavation of a settlement of that distant Neolithic period and an interesting reconstruction of the circular earthen-walled and mud-roofed dwellings of that age.

Although a lot of China's early history lies in legend, and is attributed to legendary rulers, it is now firmly established that by about 1700 BC the various tribal settlements of eastern China, between what are now Shanghai and Tianjin, had been pulled together under the rule of one monarch to form the state of Shang — China's first dynasty. The first steps were taken toward a sophisticated level of civilization during the subsequent six centuries of Shang rule. The first written records appeared, inscribed on bamboo strips and on oracle bones and tortoise shells used in the first stirrings of institutional religion, including the tradition of divine rule. Also the huge pharmacopoeia of Chinese

Cadre's son ABOVE with toy in Shenyang.
RIGHT: The awesome Grand Buddha of Leshan.

herbal medicine began to form. In the later stages of Shang rule the royal capital was based at what is now Anyang in the far north of Henan province, where Shang tombs, ruins and writings have been excavated, and in the now strategic rail junction city of Zhengzhou.

The eventual collapse of the Shang reign in around 1027 BC weakened the tradition of centralized rule, and power was spread among independent regional warlords who jostled for supremacy but nonetheless owed allegiance to a titular ruler, the duke of Zhou. They were a wealthy, lavishly indulged bunch, as can be appreciated today in the small Hubei Provincial Museum in Wuhan where you can view some of the 10,000 treasures and relics unearthed in 1978 from the tomb of one of the prominent nobles of that time, the Marquis Yi of Zeng. The exhibition is evidence not only of wealth and refinement but another important step at that time along the road to civilization — it features a huge bronze musical bell chime, 65 bells in all and each with two different pitches. It is such a sophisticated instrument that its frequencies are close to those of today's modern music.

Inevitably these rival lords fell out with each other and the society stumbled into more than two centuries of almost constant warfare known as the Warring States period. Chinese civilization now came up against its first important crossroad. Wracked by intrigue and bloodshed, it could only hope for a supremely powerful state and an iron-fisted ruler to put it back on the civilized path and save it from continuing barbarism.

THE IRON EMPEROR

The immense power of the strongman who ultimately strode into the breach and saved the society at that crucial time, in 221 BC, can be imagined today when you stand and study one of China's most astonishing historic monuments — the eerie, half-excavated terracotta army of Qinshi Huangdi, the first emperor of Qin, outside Xi'an. This Darth Vader of Chinese history ruthlessly smashed and subjugated his rival warlords and then set about to impose his rule on much of the rest of China.

Although he paid posthumously for his iron reign, his "dynasty" collapsing in a vengeful popular uprising after his death, Emperor Qinshi Huangdi established two conventions which have dictated the impetus and attitude of Chinese society ever since: He gave the Chinese race its first real unity, and he began work on a magnificent protective barrier that would shield this unified civilization from outside threat, the Great Wall. He also reestablished the Shang dynasty's pyramidal social structure, the peasant masses at the base and the various succeeding levels of merchants, military, scholars and aristocracy reaching upward to the divine authority of one supreme ruler; this structure of power not only stayed in place for many dynasties to come but was

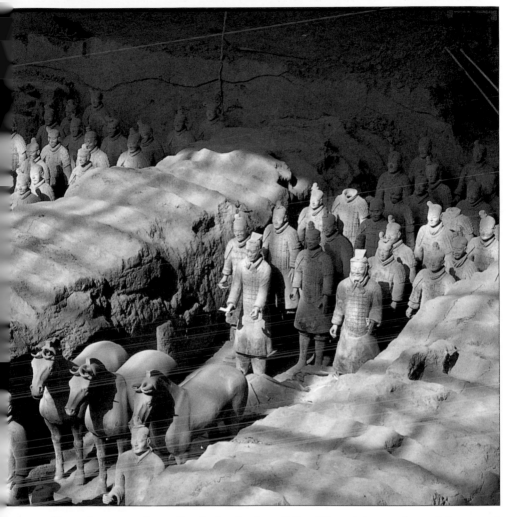

reaffirmed as recently as the "reign" of Chairman Mao Zedong.

THE AGE OF THE HAN

After the brief 11-year reign of Qinshi Huangdi, the first of the great dynasties arose, the Han. During its epic 400-year rule it strengthened the political and social pillars that Emperor Qinshi Huangdi had set in place, and so much so that its name has since been synonymous with membership in the Chinese race, the vast bulk of the society being referred to as Han Chinese. It also codified the teachings of a very learned, if ultraconservative, scholar of a previous age, Confucius (551–487 BC), to provide this society with a set of ethics and responsibilities by which all the different classes of people knew and appreciated their place.

The Han reign is remarkable, though, for its main preoccupation, protecting Chinese unity and civilization. While military expeditions were sent to the south to try to conquer resistant tribal groups and bring them into the Han "family," armies were also marched north to the harsh deserts of the northwest frontier, beyond the reach of Qinshi Huangdi's then-primitive Great Wall, to try to contain and crush the civilization's main enemies, the Xiongnü, or Huns, a fierce confederation of nomadic slave-trading tribes of Central Asia.

The legacy of Qinshi Huangdi, the ruthless "father" of Chinese unity, his terracotta army stands vigil near Xi'an.

One campaign after another was waged against these northern "barbarians," the modern-day descendants of whom can be seen among the strangely alien Turkic-speaking minorities of northern Gansu province and the cities of Hami, Turpan, Urumqi and Kashi (Kashgar) in the Xinjiang Uygur autonomous region. Under Han rule the die of the Chinese imperative was cast — it pitted membership of a select and civilized society against the barbarism that rode the wilds without; and so vital was this imperative that the cost of constant warfare with the Xiongnü eventually exhausted the dynasty and, in the second century AD, brought it to its knees.

Blind Man's Bluff

But not before another imperative had been introduced to the Chinese experience — the cultural imperative. The wars against the Xiongnü were waged not only to keep the Han nation intact but also to keep open and free of Xiongnü harassment the society's main link with the outside world — or rather, its link with mysterious lands that lay somewhere far beyond the barbarian domains.

This rather tenuous thread was the fabled Silk Road, the long and often perilous overland trading route that began near what is now the port of Sur in Lebanon and snaked across northern Persia and Afghanistan, northern India and part of the rugged territory now known as Tajikistan and Kyrgyzstan, and entered China at a point near Kashgar on the western border of present-day Xinjiang. From there the trail split into two to skirt the Taklamakan Desert and Turpan Basin, to pass close to Dunhuang and then through the fortified trading city of Yumenguan (Jade Gate Pass) and to continue southeast through Lanzhou to terminate at Xi'an.

With middlemen handling the business, two great civilizations, the Roman and the Chinese, traded with each other via the Silk Road like blind men exchanging gifts, neither setting eyes on the other. Huge camel trains carried Chinese silks, pottery and medicines along the Silk Road to the west, and back the other way came exotic animals and birds, plants, precious metals, precious stones, and products and artifacts of the Roman Empire. Along with them, around the year 65 AD, came an invading force that

no Great Wall or mighty army could hope to stop — Buddhism, destined to flourish alongside Confucianism and another already established Chinese belief, Daoism, as one of the Three Teachings of Chinese society.

So while the Han dynasty kept faith with the essential conventions of Chinese society — unity, protection of the civilization and the pyramidal social order — it introduced another convention which has dictated Chinese action and attitude ever since. Down through the centuries the Chinese response to foreign ideas or influence has tended to be an alternating pattern of acceptance or invitation followed in many cases by abrupt and even violent rejection when that influence has been deemed troublesome enough to threaten the three pillars of unity, civilization and social order. And this "open closing door" syndrome explains a great deal about the Chinese society that we are dealing with today.

Though Buddhism itself later had its own share of suppression and rejection, it was certainly invited into China in the Han reign. It is said that in 64 AD the Han emperor Ming had a dream in which a golden Buddha materialized before him. He saw this as a spiritual message and sent two emissaries to India to learn more about the religion. Two Indian monks were also invited to visit China, and they traveled in along the Silk Road bringing volumes of sutras, or religious texts, packed on white horses.

The emperor ordered the construction of the White Horse Monastery to commemorate the event, and you can stand and ponder the significance of Buddhism in China at this, the country's oldest Buddhist institution, set into a soaring hillside 13 km (eight miles) north of Luoyang, which at one point became the Han capital.

CHAOS AND THE CANAL

With the collapse of the Han dynasty in the year 220, the pillars of Chinese sovereignty tumbled with it. Confusion and warfare reigned as various triumphant northern tribes fought to take advantage of the power

China's Muslim minority of Xinjiang Province remain distinct in dress and custom from their Han Chinese counterparts.

vacuum, and for more than 270 years, from 304 to 580 AD, no fewer than 20 dynasties rose and fell. Most of them were non-Chinese, headed or manipulated by the Xiongnü, the Tibetans and other "barbarian" groups from beyond the northern and western frontiers.

Foreign influence, in the form of Buddhism, rushed to fill the void too, and during the most successful dynasty of that time, headed by the Toba, a nomadic cattle-raising tribe, it was adopted as the official religion, and the emperor was declared the reincarnation of Buddha himself.

The Toba court was based first in Datong, west of what is now Beijing and close to the present Inner Mongolia border, and later Luoyang, and today we can thank this "barbarian" dynasty and its religious fervor for its three most magnificent artistic contributions to Chinese culture—the huge Buddhist grottoes and their many murals at Mogao near Dunhuang in Gansu, Yungang near Datong and Longmen on the banks of the Yi River, 16 km (10 miles) south of Luoyang.

Significantly, it was the continuing barbarian threat from the north that enabled the Han Chinese to regain power for themselves. In the face of attacks by Turkic tribes in the northwest the Chinese and their Toba masters joined forces to defend the state, and the Chinese were able to take advantage of the pact to eventually drive the weakening Toba dynasty from the throne.

Sui grasped the reins of power, and although it was very short-lived, lasting only 37 years from 581 to 618, it quickly rebuilt the pillars of Chinese civilization and sovereignty. Unity was restored and even strengthened, the Sui rulers conquering the south and bringing it under their control and starting work on the single most unifying link between the southern and northern provinces, the Grand Canal.

It's estimated that close to five million peasant laborers were put to work on the canal, which eventually connected four great river systems — the Yangtze, Huang (Yellow), Huai and Qiantang — and made it possible to ship merchandise, men and military supplies from Hangzhou to the Sui court in Luoyang and then west to Xi'an. Extended even further in later reigns, the canal has since been celebrated as the longest man-made waterway on earth, and its importance to Chinese society can be appreciated even today as you stand on the bridges of Suzhou and Wuxi, the most colorful canal cities, and watch flat-hulled cargo boats and long convoys of tethered, loaded barges plying their way along waterways teeming with launches, tugs, sampans and other small vessels.

While the Sui dynasty strengthened and reinvigorated the Han Chinese society it also poured more conscripted labor and costly materials into new work on the Great Wall to keep the society intact. This protection of the civilization again became the paramount task of the dynastic order that swept the Sui from power in the year 618 and ushered in the "golden age" of the Tang.

THE GOLDEN TANG

The Tang dynasty (618–906) is noted for its grand cultural contribution to Chinese history. Under its auspices the arts flourished, poetry and literature reached celebrated levels of sophistication and the develop-

On the Grand Canal at Suzhou, patched and battered mainsail powers sampan ABOVE while OPPOSITE cargo barges snake along in convoy.

ment of porcelain, to name but one innovation of that era, thrust the technology of China well ahead of anything else in the world.

But the Tang reign is also significant for the constant dilemma that it faced as regards the world beyond its borders. As in the age of Han rule, it was cut off from all direct contact with the mysterious lands of the West, this time by the rise of Islam in the Middle East. But this was still an era of greatly expanded trade via the Silk Road and by sea, and the "open door" also allowed a growing stream of foreign influence to seep into the society — Nestorian Christianity from Syria and Persia; Manichaeism, also from Persia and driven east by Christian persecutors; Hinduism from India; Zoroastrians and even Jews, along with foreign merchants, mainly Moslem, whose Silk Road caravans were the vehicle of this new cultural invasion.

Buddhism also continued to spread throughout the society and in fact reached one of its artistic zeniths during the early Tang years. Huge monasteries, temples and stupas sprang up along the Silk Road and elsewhere, extravagant Buddhist festivals took their place in the Chinese peasantry's calendar of largely agricultural events and observances. Buddhism and the native "Chinese" Daoism — an older religious philosophy, with many deities, based on the relationship between man and nature — began a kind of cultural exchange in which the gods of one became the incarnates of the other. The Tang emperors themselves added their imperial splendor to the Buddhist grottoes at Dunhuang, Luoyang and Datong, commissioning the taller and more magnificent Buddha statues that make these cliff galleries and caves the tourist drawing card that they are today. The magnificent Grand Buddha of Leshan is another legacy of the Tang reign, along with a few dramatic hillside sculptures at Dazu in Sichuan province.

At the same time the Tang rulers had the continuing barbarian threat in the north with which to contend. Large military campaigns were fought not only against the persistent Turks of the northwest but the Tibetans to the west. And then there were increasingly dangerous challenges by the "Golden

Horde" Tartars, or Khitans, who rode the same arid steppes and desert basins as the Turkic tribes.

Tang armies were posted on permanent patrol of the frontier regions, operating from fortified garrisons, and at one point they managed to rout the Turkic warriors and bring what is now the Xinjiang autonomous region under Chinese control. In China today you can see all around you one of the most common symbols of the Tang dynasty's frontier wars — ceramic, bronze and iron "Tang horses" which have been popular works of art for centuries. These powerful "heavenly" war horses from the wilds of Central Asia were obtained by force of arms in the Han dynasty's punitive expeditions to replace the smaller, weaker steeds that the Chinese cavalries rode up until that time. They proved so successful that Han and Tang sculptors and artists immortalized them, and today some of the original sculptures and block prints can be found in the major museums of China — notably the Shaanxi Provincial Museum in Xi'an — and the National Palace Museum in Taiwan. Elsewhere, cheap mass-produced copies pack the shelves of souvenir shops and art and crafts centers.

But the constant struggle against the barbarians led to a great deal of damaging intrigue and power-play within the Tang hierarchy, weakening the dynasty. At the same time its authority came under growing challenge and pressure from Buddhism and other influences that had traveled with it down the Silk Road. The three pillars of the Chinese civilization began to shake again, and in 845 the Tang emperor of the day launched a violent reprisal to put things right.

"In the cities, in the mountains, there are nothing but (Buddhist) priests of both sexes," his imperial edict raged. "The number of monasteries grows daily. A great deal of gold is wasted on embellishing them. People forget their traditional rulers in order to serve under a master priest. Could anything more pernicious be imagined?"

The "Open Closing Door"

In the ensuing crackdown, all foreign religions were banned from China and foreigners were barred from all ports. And in the case of Buddhism, more than 4,500 monasteries were destroyed, and a quarter of a million monks and priests thrown out into open society. Confucianism was restored as the omnipotent national belief. Although trade was allowed to continue along the Silk Road, the Chinese door was firmly closed for some time on all cultural influence from the West, and the pattern of the "open closing door" came into being.

Inevitably, the Tang dynasty collapsed into chaos, uprising and constant power struggles that saw no fewer than five northern "dynasties" and 10 southern kingdoms rise and fall between the years 906 and 960. China's social pillars swayed and crumbled, and the power and prosperity of the Silk Road disintegrated with them, beginning an era in which China was almost completely isolated from everything beyond its western borders.

THE AGE OF ART

The collapse continued even with the rise to power of another great dynasty, the Song (960–1279). Although the Song rulers fought to buttress the main conventions of the society — the Confucian ethics of natural order and hierarchy were rigidly imposed, for instance, to shore up the society's pyramidal authority — they had considerably less success with the defense of the Han realm. The Khitans finally broke through in the north to establish their own Liao dynasty based at Shenyang, only to be supplanted in turn by another barbarian power, the Jurchens. An alliance of Turks and Tibetans established another dynastic power-base in the northwest — with the result that the Song dynasty was actually driven south where, for 150 years, it ruled from Hangzhou.

Nonetheless, the Song era is remembered as another great cultural benchmark in Chinese history. It was an age of refinement that added new luster to the arts with its particular developments in landscape painting, and it introduced the willowy green-glazed celadon ware to the growing showcase of Chinese ceramic techniques. It was also the age of the poet, one in which these romantic men and women of letters were elevated to the rank of social heroes — and none more so than the renowned Su Shih, better known as Su Dongpo, the product of a talented literary family who was also governor of Hangzhou for two years before it became the Southern Song capital.

You can see impressive statues of Su Dongpo, his father and brother, and study their literary works and stele rubbings of their calligraphy, at the Temple of the Three Sus built on the site of their family home at Meishan, 90 km (56 miles) west of Chengdu.

THE WRATH OF KHAN

Preoccupied as it was with the arts and civilized living, and confined within the southern-central region of China, the Song dynasty was in no shape or position to defend the territory or the integrity of the civilization when, around the year 1206, it faced the most terrible barbarian challenge of all time. In that year a huge confederation of nomadic tribes gathered in the wilderness beyond the northern frontiers and, under the banner of the ruthless warlord whose name has since been a byword for horrific violence and pillage, Genghis Khan's Mongol hordes thundered down through the boundless grasslands to put China to the sword.

The swift and brutal Mongol cavalries made short work of the Tibetan-Turkic stronghold to the west, and within a short time were ready to crush the Jin dynasty of the Jurchens ruling northern China from present-day Beijing. Only one thing stopped, or rather delayed them, the Great Wall, and it actually took Genghis Khan two years of procrastination beyond the immense barrier to arrive at the conclusion that it could be breached only by massive human-wave attack. He finally hurled the bulk of his armies at it, and despite a courageous stand by its Jin defenders and savage battles that left thousands dead on both sides, his warriors finally smashed their way through and descended upon Beijing in a flood-tide of murder and rapine.

When, after a short siege, the Mongols poured into the Jin capital, they went on a horrific month-long rampage in which almost the entire population was put to death and the city sacked of all its treasures. Then it was razed to the ground. From there, the Mongols turned their attention to the Song dynastic stronghold to the south.

At this, the most perilous point in Chinese history, it seemed as though the civilization faced complete destruction. The three pillars upon which it stood — unity, protection and social order — lay in ruins. Above the smoke and carnage stood a half-savage bandit chief whose lustful, simplistic outlook on life had been expressed in these bleak terms: "The greatest joy is to conquer one's enemies, to pursue them, to seize their property, to see their families in tears, to ride their horses, and to possess their daughters and wives."

Khan the Builder

But then a kind of miracle happened. With the initial conquest achieved, it was left to Genghis Khan's grandson, Kublai, to rule northern China and defeat and subjugate the Southern Song. Kublai Khan happened to have intelligence and a certain vision — he saw himself as the supreme ruler of a vast Eurasian empire, and for that he needed the help of experienced administrators; and, obviously, the only skilled people capable of administering China were the Chinese themselves. So, at the very brink of ruin, the Chinese bureaucracy reassembled and thus survived, and the Chinese civilization set about civilizing its conqueror.

In 1271 Kublai Khan proclaimed himself emperor of China and established a new dynasty, the Yuan. Eight years later he completed the conquest of virtually the entire country and immediately began doing what no nomadic brigand had ever done before — he began to build. First he constructed an entirely new imperial capital from the ruins of the Jin court, now Beijing. From the ashes of mass pillage a new imperial tradition emerged, an empire greater than anything the Chinese had ever seen. And when the intrepid Venetian business explorer, Marco Polo, journeyed along the route of the Silk Road to spend some 20 years in the court of the Great Khan, arriving in the year of Kublai's ascension to the imperial throne, the Chinese civilization was reaching toward the zenith of its power and prestige.

Its pyramidal structure had been restored, the society ascending class upon class to the absolute rule of the Great Khan, the new Son of Heaven. It was well protected, forming the lavish centerpiece of the vast Mongol

empire and nothing less in Chinese eyes than the very "center of the universe." It was also technologically about 900 years ahead of the Western world, as Marco Polo himself recorded, marveling over such inventions as gunpowder, paper, printing, canal lock-gates, the compass and the great four-masted sailing junks that carried him home in 1292.

The Chinese civilization had survived by absorbing and civilizing its conquerors, and after the death of Kublai Khan this process of absorption continued through the reigns of eight succeeding Mongol emperors. It was aided by the fact that, after the Great Khan, the Yuan leadership became inept, the settled Mongol armies became flaccid, the taste for lavish living of the succeeding Sons of Heaven forced increasingly heavy tax bur-

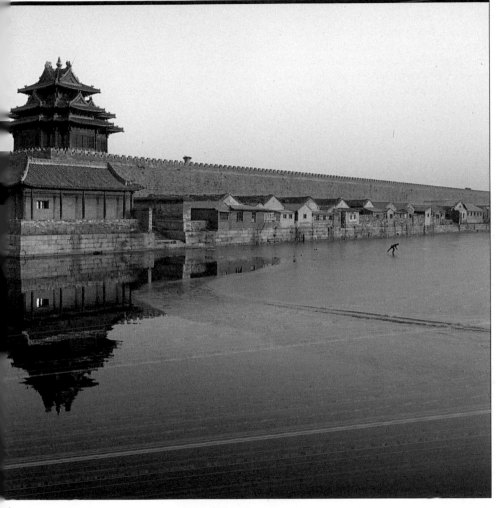

dens onto the peasantry, with traditional consequences.

THE GLORY OF THE MING

With the Mongol authority weakening and the peasantry reaching breaking point, the Chinese rose up in open revolt in 1352 and within 16 years had wrested back the reins of power and sovereignty, establishing the glorious Ming dynasty. The dissipated remnants of the great Mongol empire were driven back into the wilds beyond China's northern frontier.

Chinese ethnic unity was restored, along with the two other essential social pillars; and, to make sure that they could never be shaken or toppled again, one of the first major tasks

that the Ming dynasty undertook was a massive, complete restructuring and strengthening of the Great Wall — a project that took many millions of laborers no less than a whole century to complete.

The strengthening of the Great Wall was more than just a move to keep the retreating Mongols and other barbarians out, it was symbolic of the overriding Ming attitude to the rest of the world. While this era is noted as an age of Chinese exploration, with the eunuch admiral Zheng He leading large oceanic expeditions to parts of Asia, Arabia and Africa, it was also a time in which China again shut the door on contact with the West.

Wide moat and watchtowers made the Forbidden City both sanctuary and virtual prison of the emperors.

The nation's vision of itself as the Middle Kingdom, the center of all things, became more entrenched. The lands beyond Admiral He's junks had nothing that China needed or did not already possess.

The Silk Road, already in decline since its heyday during the Tang dynasty, was completely abandoned, and by the fifteenth century Islam had replaced Buddhism as the driving spiritual force along the old silk routes as far east as the Taklamakan region of Xinjiang, brought there by Arab imperial ventures in the wake of the Mongol collapse. Today, Islam is as strong as ever in China's northwestern region, with large Moslem minorities living side-by-side with Han Chinese in an area ranging north from Xi'an and Lanzhou through the Ningxia autonomous region to the Inner Mongolia border and west as far as the boundary of Xinjiang.

Within the Wall

With the rest of the world shut out, the Chinese set about virtually reconstructing their nation during the Ming reign. Beijing, destroyed by Ming forces in the struggle to unseat the last Mongol ruler, was completely rebuilt and firmly established, for its strategic position guarding the north, as the nerve-center of Chinese rule; and much of its present-day historic splendor, such as the Forbidden City and Temple of Heaven, is a legacy of the Ming architects and builders.

The Great Wall was transformed into the monolithic heavily defended structure which can be viewed today at places like Badaling, 75 km (46 miles) north of Beijing, and at Shanhaiguan at its eastern extremity, overlooking the Bo Sea. Ming engineers built double walls of massive stone blocks and filled the interior with packed earth and rock to form what is, in effect, an elevated roadway with defensive turrets on either side, along which troops and supplies could be rushed in event of an enemy threat. Some 25,000 fortified watchtowers and garrison towers were built along the huge barrier, linked by a communications system of fires, flags, drums and rockets. The Ming Tombs, another of today's cultural drawing cards, dotting the plain of Shisanling, 50 km (31 miles) northwest of Beijing, testify to the living power and posthumous glory of the Ming emperors.

In many respects the Ming dynasty recalled the "golden age" of the Tang reign. It was an era of prosperity, and of population growth, both of which provided a fertile seed bed for new advances in the arts. Porcelain and ceramics reached their highest level of craftsmanship and creativity; intricate cloisonnée, which can be seen in a myriad of latter-day forms all over China today, became a celebrated artform; novelists replaced poets as the society's literary lions. But in the midst of all this social fattening and refinement the Ming court

began rotting at the core — and the Forbidden City bears testament to the failure of the dynasty.

While the Forbidden City represents the grandeur of the Ming reign it also symbolizes the hollowness of Ming authority. Within its heavily guarded walls and courts, beyond which the common people ventured only at pain of immediate death, the later Ming emperors became corrupt pleasure-seeking imperial recluses, isolated completely from the society. Their power was usurped by conniving court eunuchs who virtually ruled the nation behind their backs and amassed huge personal fortunes at the expense of the people. Once again, the three social pillars began to sway.

The moral and political bankruptcy of the waning Ming dynasty was compounded by a famine spreading across the far northern provinces, triggering peasant uprisings. It was ultimately bankrupted altogether by betrayal — its eunuch overlords treacherously opening the gates of power to a rebel army backed and manipulated by a new invading force from beyond the Great Wall, the Manchus. The glorious age of the Ming finally ended in 1644 in an awful night of madness and murder: The last Ming emperor, besieged by rebels, hacked his closest fam-

it left China in the throes of something which, for all its turmoil and upheaval over so many centuries, it had never experienced before: revolution.

As with the preceding Ming, the early Qing emperors were vigorous builders, and many of China's monasteries, temples and cultural monuments owe their survival to renovations and expansion in their reigns.

These early rulers wielded enough personal authority to keep the social pyramid intact, and this gave China a new period of stability and prosperity. It also caused an-

ily members to death and then hanged himself on Coal Hill (Mei Shan, also known as Jing Shan), an mound built by his more illustrious predecessors out of the earth excavated from the moat around the Forbidden City.

THE LAST DYNASTY

The Manchu Qing dynasty, formed from an alliance of tribes with no real cultural distinction to the north and northeast of the Great Wall, was the last to rule China. Although it remained in power from 1644 to 1911 it presided over the total disintegration of the three vital pillars of society — unity, protection of the civilization and strict pyramidal authority — and when it finally sank into oblivion

other upswing in the population, but this time the country's food production didn't keep pace, so famine and unrest broke out again. More significantly, China had not kept pace with the rising scientific and technological power of the Western world. Confronted with this power, the later Manchu rulers retreated into hidebound conservatism, clinging to an illusion of Chinese cultural supremacy, and in doing this they slammed the China door shut again behind them. It was this retreat that destroyed the 4,500-year-old dynastic order.

OPPOSITE: Old Silk Road gateway near the Great Wall. ABOVE: Decorated doorway opens onto courtyards and palace quarters and the distant vista of Coal Hill (Mei San) in the Forbidden City, Beijing.

The Western Challenge

To be fair, the Manchu had inherited a society that the Ming dynasty had already allowed to slip far behind the technological development of the West. Whereas Chinese invention and science had been nearly a thousand years ahead of the West during the Yuan dynasty, by the time of the Manchu rule they were obsolete and virtually helpless in the face of modern Western naval firepower and maritime strength, military weaponry and the corresponding fierce drive for trade and colonial expansion by the major European powers.

Instead of modernizing to counter this new threat, the Manchu response was the imperious dismissal of anything that it could have gained from the Western world; and nothing sums up the Qing dynasty's insular attitude more bluntly than the imperial reply to Britain's demand for a free two-way exchange of trade. "I set no value on strange or ingenious objects," the emperor informed Great Britain's King George III, "and have no use for your country's manufactures."

It was probably the most fateful declaration that any Chinese ruler had ever made, for it set into motion a trade struggle, which was followed by open armed conflict, and which ultimately tore apart Chinese sovereignty.

The British, following on the heels of the Portuguese and Dutch, had actually been trading with China for years, but their traders were strictly confined to segregated enclaves in Guangzhou (Canton) and Macau. And the trade itself was very much a one-way deal — the British could buy all the teas and silks they wanted but could not interest the Chinese in anything worthwhile in return. The British were forced to pay for their tea, in particular, with silver bullion, and they bought so much of the stuff — trying to keep pace with a growing national craving for it back home — that at one point the nation's silver reserves sank so low that the Exchequer was almost bankrupted. To try to wrest some of the bullion back, they cast about for anything they could find that would provoke a similar fierce demand in China. And they found the ideal commodity — opium from Bengal.

The Opium Wars

The struggle that followed the wholesale introduction of opium to China can be described in modern-day hindsight as one of the most sordid of history's episodes. In 1839, when opium smuggling and addiction had reached the point of crisis in China, the Qing administration blockaded the Guangzhou trading depot, confiscated the British traders' opium stocks and burnt it all in front of them. The British retaliated with naval attacks, and in a decisive battle off the southeast coast the advanced guns and rockets of an iron-hulled steam-paddle warship, the *Nemesis*, smashed and sank the Qing navy's main fleet of antique junks. And the pillars of society went down with them.

From that point on, China was at the mercy of the Europeans and the one rival Asian power which was modernizing rapidly to meet the Western challenge, Japan. China became the victim of its own imperial arrogance, ruthless Western expansion and what seems today to be one of history's most bitter ironies — the spectacular Great Wall, costing many thousands of lives to build, standing in permanent vigil against the threat from the north, while the most perilous threat of all came from the south, from the seas and from the "round-eyes" of distant Europe.

In the ensuing Opium Wars, Britain grabbed Hong Kong as a colonial trading post and forced open the China door, establishing Treaty Ports such as Shanghai, Hankou, Amoy (Xiamen) and Nanjing. From that point on the Europeans, including Russians, and Japanese rushed to carve up the country into commercial "spheres of interest." In 1870 Japan took Taiwan, then annexed Korea and then, in 1895, secured parts of southern Manchuria. Much of the rest of Manchuria was acquired by Russia as a concession four years later. In 1905 the Japanese defeated the Russians in an historic naval battle, grabbed the Russian Manchurian concession as booty and began what was to become a progressive and bloody campaign to subjugate and colonize all of China. In the south, the French acquired the Indochina Peninsula — Vietnam, Laos and Cambodia. In the east, the Germans forced their way into Shandong province, establishing Qingdao (Tsingtao) as their own Treaty Port.

The Iron Empress

Apologists for this era of foreign intervention in China often point to the fact that the occupying powers did, after all, build China's first modern infrastructure — factories, roads, railways, telegraph systems. Those who condemn it point to the sole reason why that infrastructure was laid down — to extract the resources that the Europeans were after and distribute the export products from their own countries that they wanted the Chinese to buy.

No matter how one views it, the overall picture of that time is certainly not of a backward nation enjoying the white man's benefits. There were dreadful famines and just as dreadful uprisings — including the violent Taiping and Boxer Rebellions, both of them ruthlessly crushed — against the alien rule and the impotence of the Manchu, against corruption, against injustice and against the Western presence.

When it finally became clear that only modernization, by the Chinese for the Chinese, could enable them to resist and possibly drive out the Europeans, another of the bitter ironies of Chinese history came to pass. The stubborn and scheming Empress Dowager, the last effective imperial ruler of China, turned around and fought to restore and strengthen the traditional pillars of autocracy and conservatism that had ruled Chinese society for 4,000 years before her. In doing so she quashed all attempts around her to reform and modernize society and its armed forces — even imprisoning the heir-apparent, Guangxu, when he came of age and ascended to the throne, for suggesting change.

Her last-ditch stand on behalf of the China of her imperial ancestors was not only imprudent but also in vain. In the south of China particularly, contact with the foreign communities and the growing practice of many "modern" Chinese families of sending their sons and daughters to study in Britain and other European countries had led to an upsurge of modern ideas. The seeds of revolution began sprouting, nurtured and closely watched from exile in Japan and elsewhere by a fervent young reformist from Guangdong province, Sun Yatsen.

As the battle lines of conservatism and reform hardened, so China approached the second most crucial crossroads of its long history. But to give the Ci Xi her due, she held out to the end — even arranging the murder of her politically "wet" emperor charge just before she died in 1908.

Of all the evidence that remains of the Empress Dowager's bizarre but decisive reign, nothing alludes more to its style and character than the extravagant Summer Palace she built herself in 1888, about 12 km (7.5 miles) northwest of Beijing. It cost a fortune, about 24 million taels (42.3 million ounces) of silver — and she appropriated the money from funds set up to modernize the Chinese navy.

THE REPUBLICAN FAILURE

When the Empress Dowager died, the dynastic tradition died with her. She left another emperor on the throne, (Henry) Pu Yi, but he was eminently unqualified for the job: He was only two years old. A constitutional government, already established in the Iron Empress's fading years, moved swiftly to take the reins of power. In 1910 China's first National Assembly was held, and a year later Sun Yatsen returned from exile to become president of a provisional government based in Nanjing, where Sun Yatsen Tomb is now one of the main tourist landmarks. For the first time in nearly 5,000 years, China was having its first taste of democracy. Largely for this reason, the Chinese Republic, the first of the nation's two great modern-day revolutions, was destined from the very beginning to fail.

From today's vantage point it is little wonder that a society structured for such a vast length of time on a strict autocratic pyramidal rule, and faithful for most of that time to the social order laid down by Confucianism, should find the principles of democracy alien and unworkable. As it was, the period from 1911 right up until the 1930s was one of social and political chaos, with regional warlords vying for power, Sun Yatsen unable to build enough personal authority to institute effective national rule, the government in Beiping (now Beijing) too weak to run the country properly and the Japanese and the European powers playing one rival faction off against the other to promote their own interests.

Again, there were devastating famines in the north, peasant revolts, trade union strikes and demonstrations that were dealt with violently by the authorities. Out of all this turmoil there emerged the rival, bitterly competing political movements that were to decide the future structure and course of the Chinese society — the nationalists led by Chiang Kaishek and the communists under a revolutionary leadership that was eventually dominated by Mao Zedong.

THE REVOLUTIONARY STRUGGLE

Backed by the European "allies" and the United States, Chiang Kaishek attempted to secure the mandate of the old emperors by establishing himself as the head of a fascist-style military dictatorship. Hardly a government, it nonetheless held power for 20 years, during which time Chiang concentrated his main energies on a campaign to purge the communists from society. He was so obsessed with this that his forces virtually stood by and allowed Japan to expand its occupation of the north.

By 1935 the Japanese had virtually colonized Manchuria and set up the puppet state of Manzhouguo (Manchukuo) with the ousted Qing emperor, Henry Pu Yi, as its king. They had also occupied Hebei province and Inner Mongolia. Two years later, Japanese planes, tanks and infantry smashed their way down through the heart of China, occupying the country as far south as Guangzhou and forcing Chiang Kaishek and his nationalists to retreat to a western enclave in Chongqing.

The communists stayed in the hills and behind the Japanese lines in Shandong province and the northeast, and from there they conducted guerrilla warfare against the occupation army — aided by the local peasant population — that not only helped defeat the Japanese but also shaped the character and outcome of the communist struggle for power after World War II had ended.

To understand the immediate postwar cataclysm in China, it has to be simplified and placed again within the context of the

three traditional pillars of Chinese society. In the choice of leadership that the Chinese had before them, there was Chiang Kaishek on the one hand, supported by foreign interests, a proven failure in the defense of the civilization and realm, and self-proclaimed ruler of a pyramid that had most of its essential lower masses looking elsewhere for leadership. On the other hand there were Mao Zedong's communists, comparative heroes for their guerrilla struggle against the Japanese, definitely not bankrolled nor bolstered by foreign governments (not even the Soviet Union at that stage), and, as a result of Maoist political policy and the grassroots nature of their guerrilla operations, intimately linked with the vast bulk of the peasant masses and workers without whose support the abiding structure of Chinese society could not be complete.

The outcome was inevitable: full civil war in which the communist forces drove the nationalist hierarchy further and further south, followed by the communist victory in which Chiang Kaishek and his die-hard followers fled to exile in Taiwan, followed in 1949 by the founding of the revolutionary People's Republic of China.

THE THREE MAOIST PILLARS

Much has been written about the tumultuous and yet largely misinterpreted 30 years of Maoist communism in China, and much of it has come from over-idealistic observers of the left or hysterical anticommunists of the right. Only an occasional incisive study and coldly objective pen has attempted to place the emotionally charged events and implications of the revolutionary era against the far broader background of Chinese history. Only then have the three pillars of that history been applied to the Maoist experience, and only then has it been considered not so much how Chairman Mao changed the society but what he restored to it.

Mao Zedong restored the traditional ruling principles of the dynastic past to the new Chinese society. These principles were essential if he was to successfully harness it to the painfully burdensome plow of recovery and reconstruction. He restored unity and national self-respect after many decades of chaos and humiliation. He restored the full vitality of protection and defense, and in ways that may have seemed bewildering to outsiders but were quite demonstrably satisfying to the Chinese in the very beginning.

Foreign presence and influence was removed entirely from Chinese soil. It was also swiftly countered whenever and wherever it threatened. (The Chinese response to the American-backed United Nations intervention in neighboring Korea in 1950, and India's military border incursion in 1962, are good examples of this protectionism.) Even in its close but short-lived 12-year cultural and technical pact with the Soviet Union, the Maoist government kept faith with the dynastic tradition. When Moscow's influence was seen as a threat (its insistence, for one thing, that revolutionary socialism should be achieved through the industrial proletariat, not Mao's peasant masses), the bond was severed, the Soviets charged with revisionism and their technicians and advisors sent packing. With that, the Chinese effectively shut the door once again on the outside world.

The basic character of Mao's society was a straight copy of that of imperial times. The pyramid was rearranged and restored, the various classes of Chinese society reaching upward once again from the vast, shifting peasant seas to the authoritative hand of the Great Helmsman. Mao's authority and popularity rivaled that of the emperors, not by unquestioned divine rule but by the constantly promoted "cult of the personality" that made him, nonetheless, a living god.

Mao's political base amongst the peasantry and his lifelong promotion of the peasant class came not just from his own modest rural beginnings but from an understanding of the lesson that all emperors before him had been forced to learn and heed. "The prince is the boat, the common people are the water," an old Chinese proverb had cautioned them. "The water can support the boat, or it can capsize it."

Mao's policy of industrial and agricultural self-sufficiency, manifested in the controversial Great Leap Forward, and its collapse in 1962, echoed the attitudes of the Ming, Yuan and latter Qing rulers toward foreign "manufactures." Mao even resurrected and harnessed the tradition of the mass campaign, only now the huge work brigades dug mammoth canals and constructed hydroelectric dams and power stations instead of imperial palaces, Great Walls and elaborate tombs.

THE RED GUARDS

Mao's most fateful mass campaign, the violent Cultural Revolution beginning in 1966, was launched against the growing power of moderates within the hierarchy whose ideas deviated in one crucial respect from the Maoist dream — they believed, and prob-

Mao Zedong, now regarded as "70% right and 30% wrong."

ably quite rightly so, that China could not modernize and develop behind closed doors, by its own sweat alone. It is tempting, as unlikely as it may seem, to recall the waning days of the Qing dynasty in the subsequent rampage by Mao's Red Guards and the events that took place next — the crackdown on "bourgeois revisionist" elements who were apparently willing to risk the sovereignty and integrity of China once again with "foreign" modernization and reform.

So fierce was the struggle between the Maoist and "revisionist" factions that the Cultural Revolution almost became an outright cultural civil war, and eventually the

Red Guards had to be forcibly reined and disbanded to prevent the conflict tearing the society completely apart. But for more than a decade the struggle continued, with moderate leaders such as Zhou Enlai and Deng Xiaoping attempting to promote Western-style modernization and Mao's opposing revolutionary line taken to the point of harsh and unacceptable social experiment by the so-called Gang of Four led by Mao's radical wife, the former actress Jiang Qing.

It was during this long struggle that the clock of progress virtually stopped in China, and society at large, weary of all the infighting, suddenly faced the cold and disturbing reality of its position in the global society with the twenty-first century rapidly bearing down upon it: It was technically, scientifically and militarily backward, even with its nuclear and aerospace programs, at a time when the other great powers of the world, the United States, Japan and especially the Soviet Union, were stepping into an age that was getting far beyond China's reach.

THE FOUR MODERNIZATIONS

When Mao Zedong died in September 1976, the moderates, now renamed "pragmatists," moved swiftly to prosecute and imprison the Gang of Four. In their place came the Four Modernizations, aimed at repairing and developing the country's infrastructure and sciences and boosting agriculture, industry, national defense and technology to the "front ranks of the world" by the year 2000. Deng Xiaoping emerged as the new Chinese leader, heading the campaign to steer China away from revolutionary socialism and into the economic fast lane of controlled free enterprise, expanded international trade and joint investment with foreign interests. In a moment that delighted the Western world, whatever it may have done to the die-hard socialists back home, Deng even appeared at a rodeo on a tour of the United States wearing a Texan 10-gallon hat.

TIANANMEN SQUARE MASSACRE

On the night of June 3, 1989, the Chinese leadership stunned the world by sending armed PLA troops into Tiananmen Square to brutally crush a huge carnival-like demonstration by students and young workers which was perceived as a major threat to Communist Party rule.

It's still not known exactly how many demonstrators and bystanders were killed in the square and adjacent streets that night: The government has since insisted that only a handful of "enemies of the state" perished in the night-long terror of gunfire and tanks, but foreign doctors who were on duty in Beijing that night reported the toll to be between 2,500 and 3,000. In any case, the bodies were spirited away and secretly disposed of, and in the aftermath the party chiefs launched a full-scale purge with much-publicized show trials, of "dissident" elements in Beijing, Shanghai and other major cities.

The Tiananmen Square Massacre, as it's since been known, caused worldwide revulsion, transforming China overnight from the great business and travel opportunity of Asia to an international pariah. American and European tourism slumped, Western and Japanese investment and economic aid took a similar nosedive; and in Hong Kong, upwards of a million people flooded into the streets in mass demonstrations against the killings and in support of the student pro-democracy movement — a show of popular and political feeling never before seen in this British colony. What came next was hardly surprising — a clamor by Hong Kong Chinese, suddenly fearful for their future in China's takeover of Hong Kong in 1997, to emigrate and obtain foreign citizenship.

The ruthlessness and violence of the crackdown reflected China's age-old imperatives: the perceived need for powerful central rule and national cohesion, and an ingrained fear at the highest levels of government of anything that could trigger disintegration. On top of that, the Communist Party, having opened the economic door to the world with a beaming promise of friendship and cooperation, made it patently clear that economic liberalization would not be matched with political reform. The jailing of dissidents, continued widespread execution of "criminal elements" — many of them convicted of crimes that would rate a minor jail term in the West — violent suppression of dissent in Tibet and hardline opposition to pre-1997 democratic development in Hong Kong only emphasized the Communist Party's determination to stay in power, apparently whatever the cost.

TOWARDS THE YEAR 2000

As the year 2000 approaches, "whither China?" remains a popular question for the pundits and China watchers. After all, so much has happened to feed speculation: the Tiananmen massacre, the dramatic collapse of Soviet and East European communism in recent history. Hong Kong's investment in manufacturing and processing in the Pearl River Delta — centered on the rapidly developing Shenzhen Special Economic Zone — has virtually doubled the size of the colony's economy. Tiny, Portuguese Macau, acting as a trade and investment gateway at Zhuhai, has broken out of its traditional Mediterranean slumber to transform its skyline with a rash of new hotels, casinos and commercial towers and to start work on major land reclamation and an international airport of its own.

1991, the mounting tensions over the "renegade province" of Taiwan, the death of patriarch Deng and the Hong Kong handover in 1997. If one thing is certain, it's that China-watching hasn't gotten any simpler.

The other certainty is that political chaos in China would benefit no one. With more than 1.2 billion people divided by regional, ethnic and even religious differences and ambitions, China is never going to be an easy place to hold together, as history has shown. It's no surprise then that both Hong Kong and Taiwan have channeled far more energy into business investment rather than political engagement.

Indeed, cross-border investment overshadows nearly everything else in China's

Taiwan, though still officially restricting its trade and investment with China to intermediaries in Hong Kong, has carved a powerful niche in Xiamen in Fujian province, dominating another flourishing coastal economy. The Japanese, though still moving cautiously as investors, have replaced the Americans as business leaders in Shanghai and are also very active in the northeastern zones of Tianjin and Dalian. The South Koreans have chosen Shandong province as their main site for cross-border manufacturing, largely because of its close proximity, just across the Yellow Sea.

Businessmen meet in the eighth floor café of a commercial tower in Shenzhen's rapidly developing Special Economic Zone.

Annual economic growth has been running at an astonishing 11%. The power built up through the Shenzhen and Xiamen Special Economic Zones, and the rich trading and financial benefits that they bestowed on Hong Kong and Taiwan, is now seen as just the initial stage of the development of a Chinese economic triangle, or trading and investment bloc, comprising China, Hong Kong, Taiwan and possibly even Singapore.

The reality of modern China is that it is the world's fastest growing economy held together by a single political party that still calls itself communist. A quarter of the world's population live there. It has a longer continuous history than anywhere else in the world. Question marks hang over its leadership, territory, world role. Contradictions and mysteries.

A journey to China is a pilgrimage through all of this and more.

THE CULTURAL LEGACY

PERFECT OBSOLESCENCE

The craft and artistry of Chinese culture owes much of its inspiration to animist beliefs and Daoist nature worship that originated in the nation's distant past; and it can thank the divine power and patronage of the various imperial dynasties for the creative heights that it aspired to and achieved over the centuries.

As for the extent to which it has survived, virtually unchanged for almost 5,000 years, that can be marked down to a fairly rigid discipline that has ruled most artistic and technological creation in China from the mists of prehistory. It's a simple discipline, but one that both preserved and, ironically, led to the eventual downfall of the Chinese cultural tradition. In a nutshell, the principle was this: if an art or craft has been brought to perfection, leave it alone. Don't fiddle with it. This explains many mysteries about Chinese art and technology—why ancient architectural styles, especially those of temples and pavilions, have basically survived to this day; why most of the Chinese painting, embroidery, ceramics, sculpture, cloisonnée, lacquerware and other artistic products offered in today's souvenir shops are almost

exact modern-day copies of those of the past. It explains why the key principle of traditional painting and calligraphy, for example, is an established and strict discipline of brushwork, hand-motion, color, light and shade, composition and even mental control, the rule being to achieve excellence or even brilliance within a perfection dictated by the masters of the past—this discipline certainly discouraging experimentation for its own sake.

Perhaps the best illustration of this discipline, and its consequences, is the traditional Chinese sailing craft, the junk. Evolving first from bamboo and inflated-skin river rafts, the development of the junk raced centuries ahead of all nautical technology in the West. It incorporated the principles of the watertight compartment, battened and easily maneuverable sails and the stern-post rudder and then undertook far-ranging expeditions and trading voyages throughout Southeast Asia while Western man was still paddling about in shallow waters in goat-skin coracles.

As oceangoing craft, huge four-masted junks struck out across the vast Indian Ocean on several great expeditions under the flag of the Ming dynasty nautical hero, Admiral Zheng He, reaching the coast of East Africa and, as some historians have claimed perhaps even rounding the Cape of Good Hope. At that time, Western vessels had barely reached the stage where they could confidently venture beyond the sight of land.

Yet while the junk was developed in myriad forms to suit various tasks and conditions on China's lakes, rivers and coastal waters, its basic principles, once considered perfected, were deemed to be just that — perfect. No further improvement or experimentation was really attempted. By the nineteenth century, when Western nautical technology had now far outstripped that of the Chinese, the "perfect" junk—rendered even more obsolete by the conservatism of the latter stage of the Manchu Qing dynasty — sailed bravely into the guns and Congreve rockets of the British ironclad, steam-pow-

The onlookers are as colorful as the performers at the Butter Festival OPPOSITE, which takes place at Ta'Er Monastery a short distance south of Xining.

ered warship, the *Nemesis*, and was literally blown out of the water.

What's left of the junk, the tattered sailing barges and fishing boats occasionally sighted on China's major lakes, on some of the rivers and in the fishing grounds off the coast, is a virtual replica, even today, of the craft that ruled the waves a thousand or more years ago. It is also a testament to the fundamental gulf between Chinese and Western cultures — discipline and tradition on the one hand, a constant drive for improvement and its inherent "planned obsolescence" on the other; and it is a cultural difference that must be considered in any study of Chinese arts and ingenuity.

THE ARTISTIC EXPLOSION

Chinese arts, both "art for art's sake" and the applied variety, are said to date back as distantly as around 4500 BC, during the reign of Huangdi, the Yellow Emperor, one of the three mythical fathers of Chinese civilization. It's said that sericulture, or silk-making, originated during his reign, his empress teaching others how to spin it from the silkworm cocoons and weave it into the elegant, diaphanous, fiercely strong material that has ruled fashion tastes all over the globe ever since.

Silk not only fostered a vast and innovative range of fashion and intricate embroidery over the ensuing centuries, it also formed the backdrop to the distinctive and variously acclaimed tradition of Chinese painting. Most early painting was done on silk and, as with many Chinese creative pursuits, what began as a technical expedient was later elevated into the realm of pure art.

During the time of that distant "Camelot" of Chinese history, the first written script was developed, with agricultural records, herbal medicine remedies and spiritual prophesies inscribed on tortoise shell, bones and bamboo strips. A quantum leap took place around AD 106 with the invention of paper, and from that point on the Chinese visual arts branched into the celebrated tradition of calligraphy — a combination of literature and art. Brushes of pig-bristle and inks of soot and glue were developed. A

discipline evolved that ruled the hand, the eye and, indeed, the state of mind that existed, or should exist, for each stroke of the brush. Different calligraphic styles were perfected, some of them branching again into carved stone tablets, or steles, others joining the illustrative arts in the ensuing crucial development of engraving and wood-block printing.

Pottery and decorative firing techniques appeared in Chinese art and crafts as early as the Neolithic period, but during the Shang dynasty (1600–1100 BC) bronze was discovered and yet another crucial artistic leap forward occurred. Stylized cast bronze tings, or cooking cauldrons, were among the first applications of this new art form, excellent examples of which can be seen in museums all over China.

In architecture, squat mud-brick huts of the Neolithic period gave way to increasingly palatial columned, glazed-roof buildings and pavilions as the dynastic tradition set in with the reign of the Shang rulers. Almost all early Chinese construction was of wood, and the constant risk and ravages of fire have naturally wiped out almost all trace of ancient architectural styles. However, because of the abiding philosophy of the "perfect obsolescence" — the preservation of a design once it has been perfected — fire-ruined homes, temples and palace buildings were often rebuilt on their original sites and quite close to their original design; so that while most of the present-day architectural monuments in China date back no further than the Ming dynasty, they remain fairly faithful to the styles of the more distant centuries.

Early roofs were thatched, but later clad with ceramic tiles which, in themselves, became an increasingly elaborate form of art. As the weight of all this tiling increased with each new architectural ambition, more and more complicated engineering techniques had to be developed to support it, and a study of any existing palace building or old temple will show the almost incredible system of brackets, columns, beams and levers designed to hold everything up. The distinctive curved or winged roofs are believed to have been adapted from Indian Buddhist architecture, and became universally popular and increasingly flamboyant from the time of the Song dynasty (960–1279). The Ming and Qing dynasties saw the same flamboyance extended to the ridge ornaments — sculptured animals, people, plants and other motifs — mounted at each end of the roof to repel evil influences.

The arrival of Buddhism in the first century gave Chinese art and crafts considerable new inspiration and impetus, especially in the fields of sculpture and rock carving, wall painting and bas-relief, silk painting and calligraphy and printing. Other than that, the irresistible demands and patronage of the various great dynasties added new artistic drive as they paraded, one after the other, down the annals of Chinese history.

THE DYNASTIC LEGACY

The Han dynasty (206 BC–220 AD) is noted as a major artistic period in which advanced silk weaving was developed, glaze was used on pottery, relief sculpture appeared and the early traditions of Chinese painting and portraiture were laid down. In the later "golden age" of the Tang rulers (618–906), sculpture and rock carving reached their "perfection," painting achieved almost unparalleled sophistication and porcelain made its debut on the vast artistic stage.

The Song period is regarded as possibly the most accomplished and elegant era of Chinese art, when poets — among them the acclaimed Su Dongpo — were established as literary heroes, when the field of landscape painting flourished with new color and composition. Boosted by the establishment of an Academy of Art, painters developed new perspectives in their work in which depth and elevation were illustrated with various subtle levels and shades of light and color. It was during the Song reign that the full discipline of brush strokes was established. Elsewhere, the Song era became famous for the introduction of the almost translucent celadon ware, and for the simple elegance of all arts ranging from ceramics to carved ivory and lacquerware.

But it was the Ming reign (1368–1644) that gave China much of the artistic tradition that is still widely evident today. It was a time of hot patriotism — the reins of power

returned to Han Chinese control after the short but bloody subjugation under the Mongols — and this was reflected in huge civil engineering feats like the reconstruction of the defensive Great Wall and in the boldness, brilliant color and general exuberance of painting. This burst of color was reflected in other arts — ceramics, sculpture and embroidery — and it also found its way into a new technique of multicolored wood-block printing. Porcelain became even finer and more elegant in design, and the distinctive blue and white porcelain that we see today originated in the Ming kilns. Cloisonnée — strikingly colored enamels fired onto intricate metal designs — developed in Beijing.

If there is a point in the history of Chinese arts where the principle of "perfect obsolescence" is turned upside down, it is in the ensuing Manchu Qing reign. Ironically, and unfortunately, the elegance and taste that had been achieved up to and during the Ming dynasty in almost all art and crafts deteriorated into a largely gaudy flamboyance and extravagance from then on — and in any study of existing Chinese traditional art and architecture today, the eyes and instincts search for that almost elusive simplicity of the past in a broad canvas of what can often be described as comparative kitsch.

Hong Kong, Guangzhou and the South

HONG KONG

ON JULY 1, 1997, 156 YEARS OF COLONIAL RULE came to an end, and the tiny enclave of diehard capitalism known as Hong Kong rejoined the communist "motherland." It rained through much of the leadup to the handover, and, despite celebrity concerts, processions, parades and an extravagant fireworks show over Victoria Harbour, when the clock struck midnight the crowds seemed puzzled about what to do next. Only one thing was certain, an era had come to an end.

BACKGROUND

The Chinese—who have a slogan for everything—say that Hong Kong and China equal "one country, two systems." The former colony is now the Hong Kong Special Administrative Region (HKSAR), and has been promised a high degree of autonomy and the freedom to continue its capitalist lifestyle for 50 years after 1997.

It's easy to forget that historically Hong Kong was part of China. After all, when the British annexed it in 1841, it was famously nothing but a "barren rock." And since then the colonial status of the island has reduced it in the popular Western imagination to a kind of Chinatown writ large. If China is the Great Wall, the Forbidden City, Mao and his adoring hordes armed with little red books, then Hong Kong is altogether more homey: junks in the harbor, joss smoldering in backstreet temples, tiffin on the peak. If for British "expats" Hong Kong was a home away from home, China was that place "over the border."

Nevertheless, Hong Kong *is* Chinese. The British got it as spoils of the first Opium War with China, an insult that has never been forgotten. From the beginning Chinese flooded in. They came first from Guangzhou (Canton) and the southern provinces fleeing famine and the harsh rule of the Manchu Qing dynasty, most of them with nothing to lose and thus, with thrift and hard toil, everything

The new Hong Kong Special Administrative Region bauhinia-flower flag and the national flag of China replace the Union Jack and Hong Kong colonial flags over the Legislative Building in Central Hong Kong.

to gain. The colony's second major attribute, its nineteenth century British and European venture capitalists, were always a small minority. But what a combination those armies of opportunity-grabbing Chinese and dour, ledger-worshipping inheritors of an empire made. Hong Kong couldn't help but make money.

It has never stopped making money. It probably does it better than anywhere else in the world. When the communist revolutionaries marched into Shanghai, the textile barons took their money and even their

economy back in order. In 1982, British Prime Minister Margaret Thatcher visited Hong Kong for the first talks on the handover of the New Territories, whose lease was due to expire in 1997. In the event, Britain agreed to hand the whole lot back. The merchants of gloom have had a field day ever since.

Although it's still early days, one thing is obvious: The much-feared Anglo-Chinese agreement didn't sink the territory at all. If anything, Hong Kong gets more prosperous by the day. It is the jewel in the crown of the Pearl River Delta — which includes Macau

manufacturing equipment to Hong Kong, and the colony retooled, fattened and diversified. By 1966, Hong Kong was not only the main Southeast Asian trans-shipment point for Vietnam war materials — its harbor packed with freighters — but it was also one of the most popular R&R (rest and recreation) venues for the American troops.

By the mid-1970s Hong Kong was moving from trade, textiles and toys to trade, international banking and finance and electronics, and vastly improving its housing and public transport infrastructure. By the early 1980s it was obvious that a new China was emerging, a more pragmatic China that was prepared to leave ideology simmering on the back burner while it got its moribund

and southern Guangdong — one of the frontrunners of the new wave of Asian economic "tigers". It welcomes more than 11 million visitors a year, including over two million business travelers and package tourists from mainland China. The "barren rock" of 150 years ago is now one the world's great cities.

GENERAL INFORMATION

Most countries have a consular office in Hong Kong. The main ones are:
Australia ((852) 2827-8881 FAX (852) 2827-6583; **Belgium** ((852) 2524-3111 FAX (852) 2868-5997; **Canada** ((852) 2810-4321 FAX (852) 2810-6736; **Denmark** ((852) 2827-8101 FAX (852) 2827-4555; **Finland** ((852) 2525-5385

FAX (852) 2810-1232; **France** ((852) 2529-4351 FAX (852) 2866-9693; **Germany** ((852) 2529-8855 FAX (852) 2865-2033; **Greece** ((852) 2774-1682 FAX (852) 2334-2738; **Italy** ((852) 2522-0033 FAX (852) 2845-9678; **Luxembourg** ((852) 2877-1018 FAX (852) 2869-6623; **Netherlands** ((852) 2522-5127 FAX (852) 2868-5388; **New Zealand** ((852) 2877-4488 FAX (852) 2845-2915; **Portugal** ((852) 2802-2587 FAX (852) 845-7944; **Singapore** ((852) 2527-2212 FAX (852) 2861-3595; **Spain** ((852) 2525-3041 FAX (852) 2877-2407; **Sweden** ((852) 2521-1212 FAX (852) 2596-0308; **Switzerland** ((852) 2522-7147 FAX (852) 2845-2619; **United Kingdom** ((852) 2901-3111 FAX (852) 2901-3066; **United States** ((852) 2523-9011 FAX (852) 2845-1598.

The **Hong Kong Tourist Association (HKTA)** (MONDAY TO SATURDAY (852) 2807-6390 and (SUNDAY (852) 2807 6177 provides advice and books on shopping, sightseeing, culture, dining and entertainment. Offices are at: Star Ferry Concourse, Tsimshatsui (open 8 AM to 6 PM, Monday to Friday; 9 AM to 5 PM weekends and public holidays); Hong Kong International Airport (arrivals terminal; open 8 AM to 10:30 PM daily); Shop 8, Basement, Jardine House, 1 Connaught Place, Central, Hong Kong (open 9 AM to 6 PM, Monday to Friday; 9 AM to 1 PM Saturday; closed Sunday and public holidays). For tourist information ((852) 2807 6177 (multilingual).

All Hong Kong clinics and hospitals have English-speaking staff. In an **emergency** dial (999.

The local **telephone system** is excellent, and local calls are free if they're made from a private phone; public phones cost HK$1 a call. Most hotels have International Direct Dialing (IDD). Cardphones for both local and IDD calls are located at some 500 sites and operate on stored-value phonecards available at most Telecom CSL shops, Hong Kong Telecom Service Centres and HKTA. For directory inquiries (1081.

Try to avoid **changing money** at Hong Kong's bureaux de change, particularly at the airport, where rates are nothing short of extortionary. Change large amounts at the banks: the Hong Kong Bank has good rates (it charges HK$50 per transaction); the Bank of America is the best place to exchange United States dollars.

Hong Kong, Guangzhou and the South

ORIENTATION

Hong Kong can be slightly confusing to the newcomer, simply because the region's namesake is a small island, amounting to just seven percent of the total area — the majority of "Hong Kong" is actually elsewhere.

Hong Kong divides into Hong Kong Island, Kowloon, the New Territories and the Outlying Islands. Hong Kong and Kowloon are where most of the action is, and these areas are easily accessible by MTR. The MTR runs under the harbor, but for visitors the Star Ferry is an obligatory rite of passage. The New Territories are serviced by the KCR, while the Outlying Islands have fleets of ferries connecting them to terminals in Central.

GETTING AROUND

The **Mass Transit Railway** (MTR) operates three lines that connect Hong Kong with Kowloon and even parts of the New Territories. Fares are inexpensive and the system is easy to use. MTR trains run from 6 AM to 1 AM, every two minutes during rush hour. An additional line, the Airport Railway, will open in mid-1998, linking Hong Kong's new airport at Chek Lap Kok with Kowloon and Hong Kong Island.

The **Kowloon-Canton Railway** (KCR) runs through Kowloon and the New Territories to Lowu at the Chinese border. But unless you have a China visa, Sheung Shui is the last stop as Lowu is a restricted area. The **Light Rail Transit** (LRT) operates in the western New Territories between Tuen Mun ferry pier and Yuen Long. The LRT has a number of lines, which can be a bit confusing, so be sure to study the route map before getting on any train.

Taxis are plentiful and reasonably cheap on both sides of the harbor, with urban taxis operating on a HK$14.50 flagfall for the first two kilometers (a bit more than a mile) and HK$1.30 for each 200 m (220 yds) thereafter and rural taxis on a HK$12.50 flagfall and HK$1.20 for each 200 m thereafter. If you cross the harbor you must pay an extra HK$20 for the Cross Harbor Tunnel fee — it's actu-

Pedder Street and old clock tower in late 1860s.

CENTRAL DISTRICT

Sheung Wan

Central
District

Mid Levels

The Peak

ally HK$10 each way; the driver gets to keep the extra HK$10 for his return toll. The toll for the new Lantau Link is expected to be about HK$100.

The HKTA provides **bus** timetables and information on routes. The main bus terminals are just west of Exchange Square on the island and the Star Ferry in Tsimshatsui. Fares are cheap, but you must have exact change.

For nostalgia on a budget, it's hard to beat the near-century-old tram service that runs from Kennedy Town in Western District right through the heart of Central, Wanchai and Causeway Bay and then into the North Point, Quarry Bay and Shaukeiwan. The fare is a flat HK$1.60, but at that price don't expect to get anywhere in a hurry.

The Star Ferry shuttles back and forth between Central District and Tsimshatsui for HK$2 first class from 6:30 AM to 11:30 PM. The Hong Kong Ferry Company ((852) 2542-3081 operates ferries from piers in Central district, just west of the General Post Office.

WHAT TO SEE AND DO

Central District and the Peak
Central is the Manhattan of Hong Kong. The best way to approach it is via the Star Ferry from Tsimshatsui — a first-class trip still costs only HK$2, making it probably the cheapest

Junk passes Exchange Square providing a contrast to Central District's stark architectural wonders.

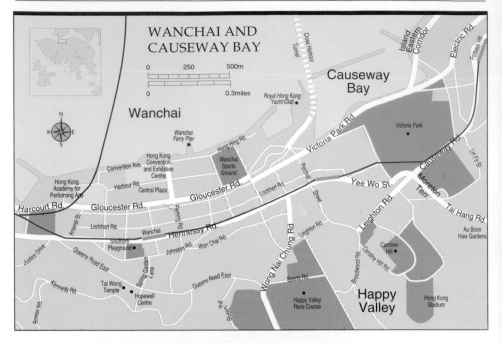

Map: WANCHAI AND CAUSEWAY BAY

scenic cruise in the world (see also ACROSS THE WATER TO THE PEAK in TOP SPOTS, page 30).

Attractions in the immediate vicinity of the Central Star Ferry terminal are mostly of the neck-craning variety. Stroll directly ahead to Statue Square for a striking contrast of tradition and the twenty-first century — the **Legislative Council Building** and the **Hong Kong Bank** respectively. British architect Norman Foster designed the latter, the most expensive building in the world on completion in 1985. The vast atrium has a soaring escalator ride that basks in natural light beamed in by a computer-controlled bank of 480 mirrors. The massive building next door is the **Bank of China Tower**, designed by Chinese-American, I.M. Pei. Behind the bank is **Hong Kong Park**, where you'll find **Flagstaff House**, home to some unassuming Chinese teaware.

Li Yuen Street East and **Li Yuen Street West** are back alley survivors, narrow streets closed to traffic, hedged in between the department stores and office blocks of Central, and crowded with stalls selling everything from newspapers to keyrings.

The **Hillside Escalator Link** is the world's longest outdoor escalator (800 m or 880 yds), running above street level up Cochrane Street, across Hollywood Road, up Shelley Street to Robinson Road in the Mid-Levels, then making its final ascent to Conduit Road. It only runs one-way, going down until around 10 AM, then up until 1 PM. Travel time is around 20 minutes.

Man Mo Temple, with its ornate green tiled roof, bell tower, smoke tower and main hall of prayer, is dedicated to the God of Civil Servants, Man Cheong, and a famous second century warrior, Kwan Kung, or Mo, since deified as the God of War, and guardian deity of pawnshops and curio dealers for good measure. The temple dates back to the 1840s and is at the corner of Hollywood Road and Ladder Street. After visiting Man Mo Temple, a stroll around this area is recommended for its hole-in-the-wall shops and temples.

The cable-operated **Peak Tram** is, like the Star Ferry, an obligatory Hong Kong experience. (Free, open-roofed, double-decker buses are also available from the Star Ferry.) Climbing smoothly up a disturbingly sheer series of hillsides, so sheer in some places that you have to stand at a 45-degree angle to move from your seat, it'll take you 397 m (1,223 ft) up the 552-m (1,817 ft) **Victoria Peak**, which dominates Hong Kong Island.

In the colonial past there was a direct corollary between your residential altitude and the heights to which you'd climbed in

Hong Kong's snooty social circles. Times have changed very little. The mansions up here command dizzying prices. Ogle them along with the view—one of the most breathtaking anywhere in the world.

Wanchai and Causeway Bay

Wanchai and Causeway are best seen from one of Hong Kong's rattling double-decker trams (fares are a flat HK$1.60).

Apart from the tram journey itself, however, Wanchai and Causeway Bay don't have a lot to offer the visitor. The world of Suzie Wong, much celebrated, long gone, is Wanchai's main claim to fame, but most of the bars are tired and overpriced these days. On the harborfront, the dramatic new Extension of the Hong Kong Convention Centre out into the harbor is worth a look. Inspired by the image of a seabird soaring into the sky, it was finished just in time to host the Change of Sovereignty Ceremony on June 30, 1997. The 155,000-sq-m (1.67-million-sq-ft) extension is purpose-built for meetings, conventions and special events and has a grand foyer whose 30-m (100-ft)-high glass wall gives spectacular 180° panoramic views of the harbor.

The main reason for going to Causeway Bay is, of course, to shop, both day and night, in the boutiques and giant Japanese department stores. But, there are a few other attractions — on the waterfront in a small garden opposite the Excelsior Hotel and World Trade Centre, you can actually watch the firing of the famous Noon Day Gun, whose origin to this day is still being disputed. Nearby, the Causeway Bay Typhoon Shelter houses junks and sampans alongside the luxury craft of the Royal Hong Kong Yacht Club.

The nearby Happy Valley Racecourse is, like its bigger and more modern sister track over in Shatin, the site of some of the world's most frenzied gambling.

On Tai Hang Road you'll see a large white pagoda standing in the shadow of monolithic housing estates. This is the famed Tiger Balm Gardens, now renovated and renamed Aw Boon Haw Gardens in memory of its 1935 founder, a flamboyant Chinese multimillionaire who came up with the recipe for the renowned balm that cures everything from a headache to a rattlesnake bite. Grotesque

but fascinating is the best description of this cornucopia of grottoes, pagodas and statuary of figures from Chinese mythology.

The Island Trail

From Central District, the main tourist route leads over or through the island's central mountain spine to Aberdeen, Repulse Bay and Stanley. Take the N° 6 bus from the Central Terminal at Exchange Square to Repulse Bay and Stanley, or the more scenic route on the air-conditioned express bus, also from Exchange Square, via the Aberdeen Tunnel

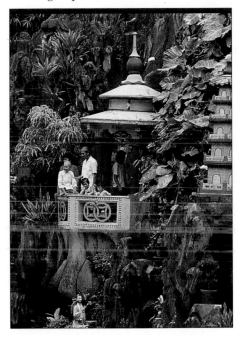

and Deep Water Bay. For Aberdeen itself, N° 7 and N° 70.

Thousands of fisherfolk still live on a small clutter of junks and their successors, new-style bullet-nosed trawlers, in **Aberdeen**. A sampan tour through the junks and to the floating restaurants should cost around HK$50 per person (for about half an hour's ride), depending on your bargaining skills.

Just south of Aberdeen **Ocean Park, Middle Kingdom** ((852) 2552-0291 and **Water World** ((852) 2555-6055, a huge playground and marine entertainment complex. All three are easily reached from Central by

Garish pavilions, sculptures and other attractions at Aw Boon Haw (formerly Tiger Balm) Gardens in Causeway Bay.

a special Citybus from Admiralty MTR station, but unless you have children with you they are of minimal interest.

Kowloon

A short hop across the harbor and you're in another world; not that this will be apparent immediately. Next to the Star Ferry terminal is **Harbor City**, a vast mall complex, and this — combined with the boulevard feel of Salisbury Road, the venerable Peninsula Hotel on one side and the modern **Hong Kong Cultural Centre** on the other — makes first

Built in 1928, the **Peninsula Hotel** was the glittering crown of Hong Kong high society through to the late 1970s, and even had the dubious distinction of being the headquarters of the Japanese military administration during the occupation in World War II. It's seen some of the most distinguished and most flamboyant names of the twentieth century come and go, and even today it's a place where you can play "Place the Face" in its ornate and renowned lobby.

Enter Nathan Road from here, and you're on the **Golden Mile**. By night this area prob-

impressions deceiving. Duck north into the tourist strip of Tsimshatsui's Nathan Road, and you'll soon discover that Kowloon is far more boisterously Cantonese than cosmopolitan Hong Kong island.

Next to Star Ferry is the old Kowloon-Canton Railway Station's **Clock Tower**, and beside it the Hong Kong Cultural Centre. Within the complex there's the world-class **Hong Kong Museum of Art** ((852) 2734-2167, which has a superb collection of oil paintings, lithographs of old Hong Kong along with other exhibitions of Chinese fine art and historical pictures. Next door is the domed **Space Museum** ((852) 2734-2722. Ring ahead to check times for shows in English.

ably packs in more neon per square meter than anywhere else in the world. If any spot gives itself over unrepentantly to that most beloved of Hong Kong pastimes — pursuit of a quick buck — it's this strip of Nathan Road. You'll also find the **Museum of History** ((852) 2367-1124, where relics of Hong Kong are on display, and the **Kowloon Mosque** ((852) 2724-0095. Guided tours can be arranged for the latter, but by appointment only.

The **Hong Kong Science Museum** ((852) 2732-3232, is in Tsimshatsui East. It has around 500 exhibits, more than half of them "hands-on."

OPPOSITE: Aberdeen and its famous floating restaurant looking out across the marine club. Scenic gondolas ABOVE glide past ornamental pagoda at Ocean Park.

In Yaumatei, **Temple Street** is a tourist fixture not only for bargain shopping but to watch the street theater of Chinese opera, fortunetellers and street dentists. Close by, on the corner of **Nathan Road** and **Public Square Street**, but best visited during the day, you'll find **Tin Hau Temple**, a complex of four temples originally built in the late 1870s but refurbished in 1972 after a fire destroyed the roof and rafters. Two blocks west, **Jade Market** sprawls its precious wares right across the sidewalks everyday from 1 AM until around 3:30 PM — expensive purchases should be left to discerning jade shoppers.

The New Territories

The New Territories, serviced by the KCR, sprawl over a large area, defying brief summary. But a good place to start your explorations is Shatin, where you'll find the **New Town Plaza**, a multilevel mall development of vast proportions. More worthy is the remarkable **10,000 Buddhas Monastery** behind Shatin Railway Station. The climb up 431 steps is enough to wind even the fittest of sightseers, but it's worth the effort. In the main hall you'll find not 10,000 but 12,800 Buddha images lining the walls.

In Tsuen Wan, the northernmost stop on the MTR, is the **Chuk Lam Shim Yuen Monastery**, also known as the "Bamboo Forest Monastery". Now an ornate, sprawling temple with a sweeping, curved and tiled roof, it houses three of Hong Kong's largest Buddha images. Also of interest is the **Sam Tung Uk Museum** ((852) 2411-2001, on Kwu Uk Kane, which re-creates a traditional Hakka village.

From Tsuen Wan, take a N⁰60M or N⁰68M bus to Tuen Mun, from whence it's a short Light Rail Transit (LRT) ride to **Ching Chung Koon Temple**, a Taoist temple, also known as the "Temple of Green Pines," and packed with garish images and altar guardians that were carved in Beijing 300 years ago. Nearby, at Castle Peak, is **Miu Fat Monastery**, a huge, multistory temple, packed on most days with worshippers and visitors and virtually lined throughout with thousands of small Buddha images and niches paid for by the faithful.

Another area of interest is **Sai Kung**, where a cluster of old villages around the

shallow bay are being transformed into marine resorts. If you feel like taking a rest from the shopping plazas and packed streets of the urban tourist districts, or feel the need to put your feet up after your New Territories tour, you'll find relative tranquillity, windsurfing and other water sports, blazing sunsets, interesting fishing communities and wonderful hiking in the country parks. To get to Sai Kung, take the MTR to Choi Hung and then take a bus N⁰92 or minibus N⁰1.

The HKTA and some private tour operators offer a number of New Territories tours. The HKTA Land Between Tour, for example, takes in such attractions as the Bamboo Forest Monastery, Tai Mo Shan mountain, the fish and duck farms of Shek Kong, the golf club at Fanling, Luen Wo market, the bird sanctuary at Luk Keng, Plover Cove Reservoir, a fishing village in Tolo Harbour, Tai Po, the Chinese University and Shatin. All this for HK$365 for adults and HK$315 for children.

The Outlying Islands

With so many things to see in Hong Kong and Kowloon, few short-term visitors get to see Hong Kong's outlying islands. Those who do are usually surprised at just how relaxed the pace of life is in these islands, which actually are not that far from Hong Kong at all.

Ferries and hoverferries to Lantau, Peng Chau, Lamma and Cheung Chau leave from Pier 6 and 7 in Central, west of Star Ferry.

LANTAU

Nearly twice the size of Hong Kong Island, Lantau is the site of the new Chek Lap Kok International Airport (slated hopefully, but unrealistically, to open in April 1998). For all that, the island remains surprisingly undeveloped. Hiking, camping, fishing and other recreational pursuits are popular. It also features a colossal Buddha statue, monasteries, temples, a fort and even has a small tea plantation.

The prime reason for visiting Lantau is **Po Lin (Precious Lotus) Buddhist Monastery**, which lies on the high Ngong Ping Pla-

You can still enjoy fresh air and open spaces on Hong Kong's outlying islands — this one is Lamma — before such peaceful spots catch the eye of developers.

teau close to Lantau Peak. To get there you take a bus from Silvermine Bay, where the ferries dock. First established in 1905, the present temple complex dates back to 1927. The main temple features three magnificent bronze Buddha images — including Sakyamuni, the Healing Buddha and the Lord of the Western Paradise; and an even more spectacular one, the "world's largest" outdoor bronze Buddha statue (34 m or 111 ft high and weighing 250 tons). It's the latter which attracts the crowds. Don't be mistaken, there are bigger Buddhas around, but this is the biggest "outdoor bronze Buddha." It's an impressive sight.

The village of **Tai O**, which can also be reached from Silvermine Bay by bus, is famous for its seafood restaurants, which cluster along the waterfront, and several restored temples, including the eighteenth century **Kwan Tai Temple**.

OTHER ISLANDS
Lamma Island is the closest of Hong Kong's other islands and, apart from an ugly electric power station, is otherwise a rustic retreat from city life. Ferries go to two destinations, **Yung Shue Wan**, (which has a large expatriate community) in the north near the power plant, and **Sok Kwu Wan** which lies in the island's narrow central spine.

Lamma features several good beaches, many countryside walks, including a strenuous climb up its main peak, Mount Stenhouse, interesting village life and two Tin Hau temples, one in each major town. But it's famous above all for its seafood restaurants which line the waterfront in both Yung Shue Wan and Sok Kwu Wan.

There's another crowded and popular huddle of seafood restaurants on the main waterfront, or Praya, of **Cheung Chau**, an island which lies close to Lantau. A huge fishing and trading fleet, including many junks, sits off the promenade. At the boat-building yard you'll see as you enter the harbor, traditional fishing junks, elegant teak and yakal pleasure junks were once constructed, in a confusion of crowded slipways. Nowadays, the yard mostly does repairs and the occasional building of a new fishing trawler.

Cheung Chau was once a thriving port, watering place and market town for junks

plying the South China Coast to and from Macau, and had a busy, well-developed society long before Hong Kong itself was settled. Much of that society remains — clans and trade guilds still dominate the island's industrious but carefully paced fishing and business life. The island comes to life in the week-long **Bun Festival**, in April or early May, held to appease the spirits of victims of a plague which swept Cheung Chau in the later 1880s. The island has several interesting temples, notably **Pak Tai Temple**, built in 1783, and enshrining images of the Spirit of the North, also known as the Supreme Emperor of the Dark Heaven and Protector of all Seafarers, along with the attendant gods Thousand Mile Eye and Favorable Wind Ear.

WHERE TO STAY

Living space in Hong Kong is highly sought after, and this is reflected in local room rates. Bargains are almost unheard of in this crowded city. Travelers trying to keep expenses down will find themselves being herded into shoebox-style digs. Those with money to throw around, on the other hand, can choose from some of the best hotels in Asia.

Luxury
Luxury hotels in Hong Kong charge rates that start at between HK$2700 and HK$3000. Typically there's a service charge of 10% and a government tax of five percent.

The Peninsula ((852) 2366-6251 FAX (852) 2722-4170, Salisbury Road, Tsimshatsui, is Hong Kong's most venerable hotel. The doors swung open in 1928 and the rich and famous have been arriving ever since. High standards are affirmed in countless tiny details, the classic look of the rooms, complete with marble bathrooms, fax machines and CD players. The hotel's restaurants are among the best in Hong Kong, notably Gaddi's and Felix, designed by avant-garde French designer Philippe Starck.

The Mandarin Oriental ((852) 2522-0111 FAX (852) 2810-6190, 5 Connaught Road,

Twice the size of Hong Kong Island and only marginally settled and developed, Lantau Island remains one of the territory's main areas of open-air recreation.

Central, Hong Kong, is the Peninsula's rival over the water. It has all the facilities you'd expect of a five-star hotel, including babysitting, health center, sauna, hotel doctor, indoor swimming pool, nonsmoking rooms. Of course it has arguably the best hotel location in all Hong Kong.

Back on Kowloon side, **The Regent (** (852) 2721-1211 FAX (852) 2739-4546, 18 Salisbury Road, Tsimshatsui, Kowloon, is less devoted to leisure and, consequently, more oriented to the needs of the business traveler, but it commands a loyal following all the same.

Mid-Range

Finding a room in Hong Kong for under US$100 is no easy feat. If you fly in, check with the Hotel Reservations desk at the airport — discounts are frequently available.

Garden View International House (HKYWCA) **(** (852) 2877-3737 FAX (852) 2845-6263, 1 MacDonnell Road Central, Hong Kong, is that most miraculous of things: an affordable hotel a brief stroll from the peak tram terminus. It overlooks the zoological gardens, and has business and health centers, babysitting services, an outdoor swimming pool, and even provides classes on Chinese arts.

Harbor View International House ((852) 2802-0111 FAX (852) 2802-9063, 4 Harbor Road, Wanchai, is similar to the Garden View. Wanchai is perhaps not such a fabulous setting, but a harbor view is hard to beat, and the hotel has all the facilities you would expect of a good mid-range hotel.

The **Guangdong Hotel (** (852) 2739-3311 FAX (852) 2721-1137, 18 Prat Avenue, Tsimshatsui, Kowloon, has an excellent location in the heart of bustling Tsimshatsui. The **Kowloon Hotel (** (852) 2369-8698 FAX (852) 2739-9811, 19-21 Nathan Road, Tsimshatsui, is behind the Peninsula Hotel, and for a third of the price of staying at the Peninsula itself you can stay here and use the Peninsula's swimming pool and other facilities.

The **Salisbury YMCA (** (852) 2369-2211 FAX (852) 2739-9315, 41 Salisbury Road, Tsimshatsui, has long been a favorite of repeat visitors to Hong Kong. The health club is widely celebrated, the rooms are spacious and service standards are very high. It's wise to book well in advance.

Inexpensive

The most infamous blot on Hong Kong's accommodation landscape is Chungking Mansions in Tsimshatsui. This 17-story complex of five blocks at 30 Nathan Road has the cheapest accommodation in town — around HK$200 for a single room or HK$300 to $400 for a double (usually with private bath). Most of the guesthouses are on the upper floors of Block A and B. Recommended places on A Block are the popular **Travelers' Hostel (** (852) 2368-7710, 16th floor and **Peking Guesthouse (** (852) 2723-8320. The only place recommended by the HKTA is **Chungking House (** (852) 2366-5362 FAX 2721-3570, Block A, 4/F. A superior guesthouse, Chungking House has a coffeeshop, laundry service, a dining area,

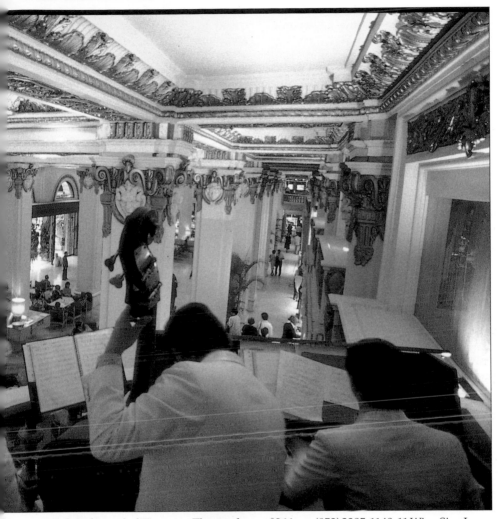

tour desk and a total of 75 rooms. The nearby **Golden Crown Guesthouse** ((852) 2369-1782, 66–70 Nathan Road, and the **Victoria Hostel** ((852) 2376-0621, 33 Hankow Road, are similarly priced alternatives to Chungking Mansions.

Hong Kong has seven **youth hostels**, though none is conveniently situated. Only one, Ma Wui Hall ((852) 2817-5717, on Hong Kong Island's Mount Davis, has anything approaching a central location. If you've got heavy luggage, you'd be best advised to take a taxi: Bus Nº 5B or Nº 47 from Central pass close by, but you're still faced with a stiff half-hour walk.

Moving up several notches in the price and comfort bracket, you could try the Salvation Army-run **Booth Lodge** ((852) 2771-9266 FAX (852) 2385-1140, 11 Wing Sing Lane, Yaumatei. Two other reasonable places in Yaumatei are the **Caritas Bianchi Lodge** ((852) 2388-1111 FAX (852) 2770-6669, 4 Cliff Road, where singles are around HK$750, doubles HK$850; and **King's Hotel** ((852) 2780-1281 FAX (852) 2782-1833, 473 Nathan Road, which has singles for around HK$570 and doubles for HK$700.

WHERE TO EAT

With around 19,000 restaurants, noodle shops, snack and fast food outlets throughout the territory, it is impossible to do justice

Old World grace and charm at afternoon tea in the lobby of the renowned Peninsula.

to Hong Kong dining in a brief section such as this. The best advice is to be adventurous and explore.

Central District

The imperial courts of Chinese cuisine in Central are the **Yung Kee Restaurant** ((852) 2522-1624, a multistory gaudily decorated Cantonese eating place in Wellington Street, and the famous **Luk Yu Tea House** ((852) 2523-5464, in nearby Stanley Street, which is such a popular *dim sum* establishment and restaurant that you virtually need to camp outside overnight to get a table.

For an absolutely superb *dim sum* experience, you can do no better than the **Diamond Restaurant** ((852) 2544-4708, 267 Des Vœux Road Central — but again, you need to be quick off the mark and determined to beat the hordes of office workers that pour into it at lunchtime.

For Indian, an establishment that has earned a reputation for good food and friendliness over the years is **Ashoka** ((852) 2524-9623, 57 Wyndham Street. You won't be disappointed. **Tandoor** ((852) 2845-2299, 3/F On Hing Building, On Hing Terrace, is another popular Indian restaurant in the area.

For superb Vietnamese cuisine, in a setting oozing with French colonial nostalgia, try the very upmarket **Indochine** ((852) 2869-7399, 2/F California Tower, 30–32 Lan Kwai Fong.

Western cuisine is also represented in mind-boggling abundance. You'll find all the major fast food chains if your tastes or budget run in that direction, but for fast food with a gourmet twist look out for **Delifrance** in Queensway Plaza and World-Wide Plaza. **Oliver's Super Sandwiches** are another excellent chain, and branches abound not only in Central but throughout Hong Kong.

The best areas to seek out Western food is Lan Kwai Fong and the up-and-coming SoHo (South of Hollywood Road) area — an old-fashioned residential neighborhood that is quickly becoming a funky alternative to Lan Kwai Fong. In both areas you'll find an extraordinary range of restaurants and cuisines.

In SoHo **Casa Lisboa** ((852) 2869-9631, 21 Elgin Street, was a pioneer, a romantic little haunt serving huge portions of Portuguese

dishes. **Le Fauchon** ((852) 2526-2136, 6 Staunton Street, sports minimalist decor and haute cuisine — with prices to match of course. In Lan Kwai Fong, **La Dolce Vita 97** ((852) 2810-9333, 8–11 Lan Kwai Fong, is a sleek, open-to-the-street Italian restaurant. For more good Italian food, try **Ristorante Il Mercato** ((852) 2868-3068, Basement, 34–36 D'Aguilar Street, and **Va Bene "stile veneziano"** ((852) 2845 5577, 8–62 D'Aguilar Street.

At the Mandarin Oriental Hotel ((852) 2522-0111, **The Pierrot** offers superb French cuisine, and for perhaps the most sumptuous and meticulously prepared Western food in Hong Kong the **Mandarin Grill** is in a class of its own.

Wanchai and Causeway Bay

The three most outstanding restaurants in this Wanchai and Causeway Bay are undoubtedly **Tao Yuan** ((852) 2827-8080, **Forum** ((852) 2892-0248, in Wanchai and the Grand Hyatt's **One Harbour Road** Cantonese restaurant in the Grand Hyatt. The Tao Yuan, 3/F Great Eagle Centre, near the Hong Kong Exhibition and Convention Centre, is an upmarket Cantonese establishment with harbor views. As is almost always the case with upmarket Cantonese, seafood is the specialty. At **Forum** one dish reigns supreme — braised abalone. The rubbery ear-shaped mollusk is braised for a full 15 hours in a stock of ham, chicken and beef, and the result (and the price) is truly sensational.

In Causeway Bay, the value-for-money **Farm House Restaurant** ((852) 2881-1881, 1/F AIA Plaza, 18 Hysan Avenue, has healthy dishes free of flavor "enhancers" like MSG (monosodium glutamate), such as scallops and shrimp hotpot, and braised pigeon with garlic. There are also a couple of good Sichuan restaurants in Causeway Bay: The family-run **Red Pepper** ((852) 2577-3811, 7 Lan Fong Road, for "strange taste" spiced shredded chicken and sizzling prawns; and **Sze Chuen Lau** ((852) 2891-9027, 466 Lockhart Road, where house favorites include spiced perfumed chicken, kumquat beef and chili and camphor-flavored tea-smoked duck.

Because of the big multistory Japanese department stores in Causeway Bay, the area abounds with Japanese restaurants. At the top of the range you'll find expensive places such as **Kanetanaka** ((852) 2833-6018, 22/F East Point Centre, 545–563 Hennessy Road. But for something a little different, and certainly more exciting, try the department stores themselves. The giant **Sogo**, for example, has a vast basement food stall which is divided into various Japanese and Cantonese kitchens and informal eating areas where you can enjoy full à la carte meals or just pick snacks from various stalls and counters.

Tsimshatsui

Ah Yee Leng Tong ((852) 2317-6082, Shop A, 1/F Hanley House, 68–80 Canton Road is a popular chain with four other branches in Kowloon and more on Hong Kong Island. Try the health-enhancing casseroles, and "male" and "female" soups. **Tai Woo Seafood Restaurant** ((852) 2369-9773, 14–16 Hillwood Road, offers reasonably priced seafood dishes such as hotpots, steamed garoupa, sautéed scallops and garlic prawns.

For those not watching their budgets, two excellent restaurants for shark's fin soup,

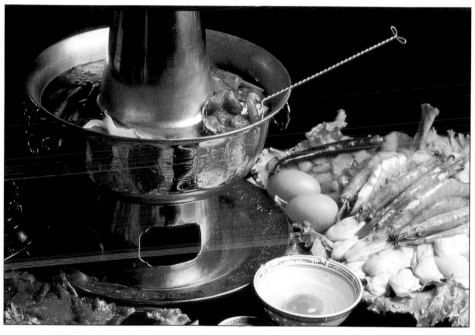

The Wanchai branch of the Indian restaurant **Ashoka** ((852) 2891-8981, in the Connaught Building, 185 Wanchai Road, makes a nice change, as does the **Chili Club** ((852) 2527-2872, 1/F 88 Lockhart Road, which has been doing a roaring business serving Thai fare for as long as most residents can remember.

For Mexican specialties, American steaks and seafood, margaritas and nightly entertainment, **Casa Mexicana** ((852) 2566-5560, G/F Victoria Centre, 15 Watson Road, North Point is a lively venue — not the place for quiet night out.

Homesick Brits should head over to **Harry Ramsden's** ((852) 2832-9626, 213 Queen's Road East, next to the Hopewell Centre, where they'll find authentic English fish and chips.

other seafood and game dishes are **Sun Tung Lok Shark's Fin Restaurant** ((852) 2730-0288, G/F Harbor City, 17–19 Canton Road, and **Fook Lam Moon** ((852) 2366-0286, 1/F 53–59 Kimberley Road.

Tsimshatsui is a good place to sample Chinese vegetarian cuisine: **Bodhi** ((852) 2366-8283, 1/F 32–34 Lock Road, has a wonderful selection of bean-curd, fungi and bamboo shoot dishes.

The Island Shangri-La's **Summer Palace** is one of the best Chinese restaurants that Hong Kong has to offer.

The infamous Chungking Mansions is swarming with Indian restaurants, but only

The traditional Chinese hotpot served in cold weather.

one is fully licensed, **Swagat** ((852) 2722-5350, 103 Chungking Mansions. At the famed **Gaylord Indian Restaurant** ((852) 2376-1001, 1/F Ashley Centre, 23–25 Ashley Road, tandoori is the specialty, and you can watch breads and kebabs being prepared for clay-oven baking.

Ah-So ((852) 2730-3392, 159 Craigie Court, World Finance Centre, South Tower, Harbor City, Canton Road, calls itself "Hong Kong's Only Floating Sushi Bar" — the food being served from floating "boats."

For years **Au Trou Normand** ((852) 2366-8754, 6 Carnarvon Road, has been rated the finest French restaurant in town, and its classic recipes, its variety of wines and decor are still five-star. Its main competition is at the Peninsula Hotel ((852) 2366-6251, which has excellent European restaurants in **Gaddi's**, the Swiss-style **Chesa**, the **Verandah Grill** and the extraordinary new East-meets-West **Felix**.

The Kowloon branch of **Grappa's** ((852) 2317-0288, Shop 105, 1/F Ocean Centre in Harbor City offers home-style Italian pastas, sausages, breads and desserts at reasonable prices. Other recommended Italian restaurants are the hip and trendy **Tutto Bene** ((852) 2316-2116, Knutsford Terrace and **Wild Poppies** ((852) 2368-8642.

Planet Hollywood ((852) 2377-7888, 3 Canton Road, is dining for the starstruck — Californian cuisine and trendy Hollywood decor; the **Hard Rock Café Kowloon** ((852) 2377-8118, 100 Canton Road, is a repeat performance around the theme of rock and roll.

NIGHTLIFE

As in all great cities, Hong Kong's nightlife scene caters for all tastes and is constantly evolving. In Tsimshatsui East, for example, three huge hostess clubs, the most well known of which is **Club Bboss** ((852) 2369-2883, LG/F New Mandarin Plaza, 14 Science Museum Road, are testimony to Hong Kong's towering status as a business center. Where else would you find a club measuring 6,510 sq m (70,000 sq ft) and with 1,000 hostesses on its books, up to 400 of whom will be on duty any night of the week?

But it is in areas like **Lan Kwai Fong** in Central that Hong Kong is at its most vibrant. If you find yourself in town on a Friday or a Saturday night, it is worth wandering through this area simply to soak up its ambiance — of course, you might stop off for a drink while you're at it.

Club 64 ((852) 2523-2801, Wing Wah Lane, has long been a favorite first stop, and the crowd often spills out onto the lane; the alfresco seating here is provided by the restaurants. Going upmarket — Club 64 is famously low-life, which in Hong Kong means drinkers loosen their ties — **Nineteen 97** ((852) 2810-9333, 8–11 Lan Kwai Fong, has drinks upstairs at **Post 97**, dinner downstairs in **La Dolce Vita 97** and dancing in **Club 1997**. Across the road, the **Jazz Club** ((852) 2845-

8477, 2/F California Entertainment Building, frequently features top international performers, along with their regular, first-rate house band.

Wanchai may have once been the **Suzy Wong** bar, brothel and nightclub district of Hong Kong, but it has now become a respectable business and restaurant area. For live rock and roll, Suzy Wong and old Hong Kong memorabilia, try **The Wanch** ((852) 2861-1621, 54 Jaffe Road. **Joe Bananas** ((852) 2529-1811, 23 Luard Road, is a Hong Kong institution and is known universally — there's no point pulling punches — as a "meat market." It gets packed on weekends. The nearby **Delaney's** ((852) 2804-2880, 2/F One Capital Place, 18 Luard Road is the place for real Irish ale (including, of course, Guinness

on tap). It gets packed on weekends. On the edge of Wanchai, one of the hottest nightspots in town is **JJ's** ((852) 2588-1234 in the Grand Hyatt Hotel, which features live rhythm and blues, disco dancing, videos and excellent bar food.

In Tsimshatsui, the **Bar City** nightlife complex ((852) 2369-8571, Basement 2, New World Centre, offers hi-tech disco in the **Zodiac**, live Latin music in the **Latino Bar** and a country and western theme in the **Crazy Horse Saloon**. The long-standing **Rick's Café** ((852) 2367-2939, 4 Hart Avenue, is still a popular spot for early drinks and late-night dancing. In Tsimshatsui's miniature version

The laser-lashed dance floor of Club Bboss, one of the biggest and most astonishing entertainment centers in the world.

of Lan Kwai Fong — Knutsford Terrace — you'll find **Bahama Mama's Coconut Bar** ((852) 2368-2121, one of Hong Kong's few reggae bars. Tsimshatsui also has a branch of **Delaney's** ((852) 2301-3980, 3 Pratt Avenue. **Mad Dogs** ((852) 2301-2222, 32 Nathan Road (there's a branch too in Central) is a popular English-style pub with counter lunches.

SHOPPING

Hong Kong has become the great Oriental emporium that the early China traders dreamed of. Local television advertisements parade Swiss watches, French perfumes, high-class jewelry and upmarket Japanese electronic consumer products. Huge self-contained, climate-controlled, luxury-packed shopping malls litter the landscape, making Hong Kong the ultimate shopper's theme park.

Before you leap into the fray, grab a copy of the HKTA's *Official Shopping Guide* (see SHOP TIL YOU DROP in YOUR CHOICE, page 52). Remember, especially in prime tourist territory (like Nathan Road, Tsimshatsui), there are some unscrupulous operators : Ascertain that you're getting the standard warranty and accessories on electrical goods; find out whether paying by credit card will make the purchase more expensive; bargain by all means but not too heatedly; and lastly, don't allow yourself to be lured into shops by touts.

Hong Kong's reputation as an electronics bargain basement needs some qualification nowadays. Always come armed with prices from back home, for comparison's sake, and shop around. The electronics shops of Tsimshatsui, for example, are generally at least 10% more expensive than their rivals just a mile up Nathan Road in Yaumatei and Mongkok — where, incidentally, prices are always labeled and not subject to the whim of an aggressive sales clerk.

Computer equipment can be reasonably priced (see SHOP TIL YOU DROP in YOUR CHOICE, page 53), and you'll find everything from mainstream dealers to hole-in-the-wall outlets selling everything from cables to Windows 2001.

For Chinese items and antiques there's really only one place to go: the area in Central starting from the upper end of Wyndham Street, continuing all the way along Hollywood Road until you reach "Cat Street," just by the Man Mo Temple (see SHOP TIL YOU DROP in YOUR CHOICE, page 52).

Temple Street is Hong Kong's most popular night market and can be reached by MTR, alighting at Jordan station. From the Jordan Road entrance you make your way through block after block of stalls and shops selling fake Rolex, and Cartier watches and designer clothes, more cheap watches, sunglasses, silk ties, trousers, shirts, sweaters, jackets, suits, men's underpants at HK$20 for three pairs and T-shirts for HK$15 to $20. You can pick up electronic keyrings that beep, solar calculators the size of credit cards (which also double as FM radios), or FM radios the size of cigarette lighters, or cigarette lighters that double as FM radios. You'll find Nepalese hawkers sitting on the sidewalk selling Nepalese jewelry, masks and colorful bags. You'll see street dentists, Chinese opera, and for HK$50 to $80 you can have some of your fortune told — the full story will cost more.

HOW TO GET THERE

Until the new Chek Lap Kok International Airport opens in mid-1998 you'll arrive at Kai Tak Airport in Kowloon. The **Airbus** coach service takes arrivals inexpensively to Taikoo Shing, Tsimshatsui, Causeway Bay and Central District, calling at most major hotels along the way. There is also a taxi stand outside the airport terminal.

From Hong Kong flights fan out into all corners of the world. Flights are also available to most major destinations in China. (For information on getting to Shenzhen and Guangzhou from Hong Kong, see under SHENZHEN and GUANGZHOU, below.)

SHENZHEN

BACKGROUND

Old China hands remember Shenzhen, in the days before the Open Door policy was launched in 1979, as nothing but ricefields, a hamlet and a border river — a popular

Like an apparition from the movie *Ghost Busters*, the 78-story monolithic Central Plaza streaks upward out of the harborfront business district of Wanchai.

place for tourists who were bussed to the Hong Kong side of the border for their first glimpse of the forbidden PRC. Today, Shenzhen is China's capitalist showplace, a city that sprang up overnight, taking mighty Hong Kong by surprise. It's easily China's most successful, most freewheeling Special Economic Zone (SEZ). You don't go there today to catch a glimpse of China, you go to take a look at the future — the combination of high-tech joint-venture manufacturing and processing and rapid urban development that is being repeated, at a somewhat slower pace, in cities right across the country. Many of these Chinese have the same idea in mind, and Shenzhen has become the target of so many domestic "migrants" — people from poorer areas seeking work, especially the higher-than-average wages it offers — that the city has had to throw an electric fence around its export processing zone to keep unauthorized people out. As for Hong Kong, Shenzhen has become both a major business opportunity and something of a pain in the neck. While it's the center of massive cross-border investment and trade, with many Hong Kong Chinese middle-management now moving there to live closer to their factories, it's also a den of corruption and a haven for large-scale smuggling of everything from black market cigarettes to stolen luxury cars — Mercedes Benzes, and others — from Hong Kong.

Shenzhen is also set to take some of the infrastructural strain off Hong Kong. The city has its own international airport, which lies around 40 minutes by taxi from the Hong Kong border — flights from here to other China destinations can be as little as half the price of flights bought ovrseas. It's also developing a major new deep-water port and container terminal at Yantai, aimed at providing a new southern conduit for China's trade.

GETTING AROUND

Shenzhen has arguably the best public transport system in China. The bus network is cheap and less crowded than elsewhere. The minibuses are privately operated and cheap but the signs are only in Chinese so you may

need help. Taxis are ubiquitous and are required to use their meters, though for long distances you will need to bargain a fare.

WHAT TO SEE AND DO

There's very little to do in central Shenzhen but stroll around and gawk at the high-rise hotels and prosperous shopping complexes. The western part of the Special Economic Zone is Shekou port, where you can get a hoverferry to Hong Kong, and where you will find Shenzhen's mind-boggling vacation resorts and Shenzhen University.

Splendid China and Window of the World

Two sprawling attractions at the western end of the Special Economic Zone, near Shenzhen Bay, Splendid China and Window of the World, are extremely popular with Chinese tourists but will seem tacky to most Westerners. Splendid China reproduces the historical sights of China in miniature; Window of the World does the same on a global scale. Minibuses run frequently from the Hong Kong border, or you might take a taxi. CTS and CITS book one day tours here from Hong Kong which also call at a traditional Hakka village (see TAKING A TOUR in YOUR CHOICE, page 66).

Chinese Ethnic Culture Demonstration Villages

Close by and similar in concept, you can see 20 re-creations of the villages of China's minorities, this time in original size, complete with dancing and daily enactments of minority festivals. Tacky in the extreme.

WHERE TO STAY

Shenzhen has a good range of accommodation, though whether the city is worth an overnight stay is debatable.

Luxury
There are a number of luxury hotels in Shenzhen nowadays. **The Landmark Hotel**

Nothing but ricefields, a hamlet and a border river in 1979, Shenzhen today is a burgeoning city, the center of the nation's most successful, most freewheeling Special Economic Zone.

((755) 217-2288 FAX (755) 229-0473, the **Century Plaza Hotel** ((755) 232-0888 FAX (755) 233-4060, the **Hotel Oriental Regent** ((755) 224-7000 FAX (755) 224-7290, and the **Shangri-La** ((755) 233-0888 FAX (755) 233-9878, all jostle for similar turf and offer high service standards.

Mid-Range

If you are looking for bargains, try Hong Kong travel agents (including CTS), which often have special package deals that would otherwise be difficult to find.

Good, centrally located, mid-range hotels with rates of HK$250 and up for a double include the **Petrel Hotel** ((755) 223-2828 FAX (755) 222-1398, the **Shentie Hotel** ((755) 558-4246 FAX (755) 556-1049 and the **Nanyang Hotel** ((755) 222-8110 FAX (755) 223-8927.

WHERE TO EAT

Dim sum breakfast and lunch is widely available and tends to be situated on the second and third floors rather than the lobby. Prices are slightly lower than in Hong Kong; you'll probably have to pay in Hong Kong dollars. **The Banxi Restaurant** ((755) 223-8076, on Jianshe Lu, has long been rated as one of Shenzhen's top places for a seafood meal.

Food Street is a small lane off Renmin Nanlu specializing in seafood and freshwater fish. Make sure you find out the price before you order even though prices are generally low. China's first **McDonald's** was set up here, and it is still a very popular place to eat.

NIGHTLIFE

The **Century Plaza** has a good, though expensive, disco on the top floor. The most popular late-night club in town is **Wall Street**.

HOW TO GET THERE

Shenzhen airport is around 40 minutes by taxi or an hour by minibus from the Hong Kong border. Direct hoverferry services run to the airport from the China Ferry Terminal (China Hong Kong City Building) ((852) 2736-1387, Canton Road, Tsimshatsui, Hong Kong, four times daily. The trip takes around one hour. Citybus ((852) 2736-3888, runs to Dongguan, leaving from the basement of the China Ferry Terminal, and stopping at Shenzhen airport.

The Kowloon–Canton Railway (KCR) has the fastest and most convenient transport to Shenzhen from Hong Kong. Take a train to Kowloon Tong station and change there for

Lo Wu. It's possible to get a one-day visa at the border, providing you stay in the Shenzhen SEZ. Citybus (see above) have eight departures daily to Shenzhen.

There are four hoverferries running daily from the China Ferry Terminal in Tsimshatsui (see above), and Shekou, a port on the west side of Shenzhen. The journey takes around 50 minutes.

GUANGZHOU (CANTON)

The capital of Guangdong province, Guangzhou is also the nation's preeminent southern gateway and a radial tour center from which you can strike out for major cities and cultural destinations in Guangdong, Fujian, Guizhou, Yunnan provinces, Guangxi Zhuangzu autonomous region and Hainan Island. Its air and rail links cover virtually all of China. The Pearl (Zhujiang) River, a major waterway, brings ocean shipping into the city's waterfront from the South China Sea and provides access right across the hinterland as far as Guangxi Zhuangzu autonomous region and Yunnan provinces.

BACKGROUND

Along with Shanghai and Beijing, Guangzhou is China's most modern and progressive city. For one, its Cantonese-speaking population of around 6.7 million live on the doorstep of one of the world's most prosperous cities — Hong Kong is just 111 km (69 miles) away. For two, as locals like to point out, Guangzhou has some 1,500 years history of foreign contact, starting with Arab merchant seafarers and then later with Portuguese Jesuits in Macau during the Ming dynasty, and the guns of the British "merchant princes" opening up Guangzhou itself as a trading port in the seventeenth century.

In the early nineteenth century Guangzhou was the main arena of the fierce test of strength between the British traders and the Qing throne over the alarming rate at which British opium exports were pouring into the society. In the two Opium Wars that followed, British warships and troops broke the back of the obsolete Qing defenses, grabbed Hong Kong as a colonial trading haven and triggered an international carve-up of Chinese territory and sovereignty that eventually caused the complete collapse of the 4,500-year-old dynastic order. As that collapse approached at the turn of this century, it was the sons and daughters of Chinese merchants and reformists in Guangzhou and the south — some who had been educated overseas, some of them influenced by local foreign missionaries, all of them hungry for modernization and reform — who led the first major rebellions against the Manchu rule. Sun

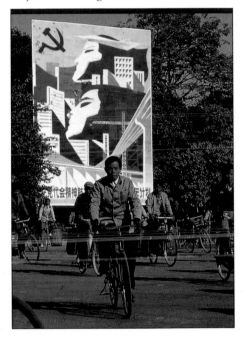

Yatsen, the exiled "spiritual" leader of the reformist movement and the first republican president, was born in **Huaxian** to the northwest of Guangzhou. In 1923, Guangzhou was where he gave the nationalist Guomindang Party its final form, the movement that later formed the military backbone of Chiang Kaishek's brutal campaign to exterminate the Chinese communists.

Guangzhou's climate, along with that of most of the southern region, is subtropical, hot and humid in summer (July and August

OPPOSITE: A Shenzhen seafood restaurant, where large selection of live fish and crustaceans are displayed in front of the restaurant for customers to choose from. ABOVE: Guangzhou street scene and mural, circa 1986.

average 29°C or 84°F), and from July to September the area is prey to heavy monsoon rains and fierce typhoons that boil up out of the Pacific south of the Philippines and dash themselves, virtually one after the other, on the China coast. The most comfortable time to visit is between October and March, though you should be prepared for cold weather in the height of winter.

GENERAL INFORMATION

American Express ((20) 8331-1771 is on the ground floor of the central lobby of the Guangdong International Hotel (see WHERE TO STAY, below).

Airlines represented in Guangzhou include **Air China (** (20) 8668-1319, **China Eastern Airlines (** (20) 8668-1688, **China Northwest (** (20) 8330-8058, **China Southern (** (20) 8612-3428, **Malaysia Airlines (** (20) 8335-8828 and **Singapore Airlines (** (20) 8335-8886.

Consular offices include **Australia (** (20) 8335-0909, and the **United States (** (20) 8188-8911.

ORIENTATION

Guangzhou is a flat, sprawling city, crossed from east to west by a main artery **Zhongshan Lu** that is all of 15 km (nine miles) in length, and from north to south by two main roads, **Renmin Lu** and **Jiefang Lu**. Circling the central city area is **Huanshi Lu**; the northeast section, Huanshi Donglu, is where many of the best hotels can be found.

If Guangzhou seems at first to be too vast and populous to make sense of, these three major thoroughfares help simplify it by linking up the three principal districts that are of interest to tourists — the **waterfront and Shamian Island**, site of the International Settlement in the Treaty Port days; the **northern commercial and tourist district** which includes the Railway Station, Dongfang and China Hotels, Trade Centre and Yuexiu Park; and the **cultural district**, running to the east along Zhongshan Lu, featuring the main temples and mosques and monuments to Guangzhou's more recent revolutionary history.

GETTING AROUND

The easiest way to get around Guangzhou is by taxi — the streets are teeming with them and fares are very reasonable — reckon on around ¥20 for trips around town, ¥30 to the airport. The only problem is communication: Few drivers speak much English; some of them, mutter locals, don't even speak Cantonese.

Bicycles are available for rent on the street close to the rear entrance of the White Swan

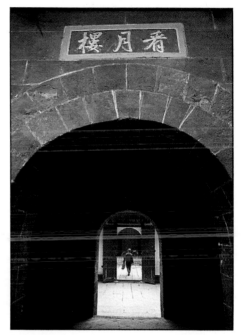

(see WHERE TO STAY, below). There's also a good trolley-bus service running between the three districts, but like public buses all over China they're overcrowded, slow-moving and distinctly uncomfortable in the Guangzhou humidity and heat. There's a good English-language tourist map in circulation that can be found at the desks of any of the top hotels.

WHAT TO SEE AND DO

Guangzhou and most of the entire south of China were isolated for many centuries from the imperial seats of power, and therefore are not exactly overloaded with great cul-

Main entrance to Huaisheng Mosque, Guangzhou.

tural attractions. However, Guangzhou does have the **Guangxiao Temple**, dating back to the third century BC, and to this it has added the relics of its foreign trading contacts, its monuments to latter-day rebellion and its special present-day social character to offer itself as a city well worth strolling about and touring.

Being as big and spread out as it is, covering about 60 sq km (36 sq miles), it's also difficult to get around in the space of a few days unless you approach it from the point of view of its three distinct tourist districts — **Shamian Island and environs**, **northern commercial** and **tourist district** including Yuexiu Park and the complex of temples, and monuments spreading to the east off **Zhongshan Lu**.

Shamian Island and Environs

Flat and partly reclaimed, Shamian Island is linked by two bridges to the Pearl River waterfront and is where the "foreign devil" British and French traders and taipans built their warehouses, homes, banks and business headquarters after the British victory in the Opium Wars. The buildings are still there, providing a timewarp of sedate or slightly pompous Victorian architecture. Efforts have been made to renovate some of the old buildings, and some boutiques and cafés have arrived, giving the area something of a facelift. Gentrification is proceeding at a snail's pace, though, and for the moment Shamian remains a charming mix of new and old, cafés and bars rubbing shoulders with busy *dim sum* restaurants.

With the entirety of Guangzhou bustling so prosperously it's difficult to believe now how "revolutionary" this area was back when market reforms were tentatively introduced at the tail end of the 1970s. Back then tourists were advised that **Qingping Market**, on Qingping Lu just to the north of Shamian Island, heralded a new era as they gawked at the caged animals and piles of vegetable produce. Nowadays it's just another market, though a particularly busy one. To the east, across the bridge and along the waterfront, **Renmin Nanlu** was another pioneering commercial district. It has retained that emphasis and is a fascinating district to explore on foot.

Qingping Market in particular is a raucous, friendly, crowded bazaar in which every step and turn of the head is living proof of the Cantonese taste for all things bright and beautiful, all creatures great and small: sugarcane, vegetables and fruit (look for succulent lychee fruits in June and pineapples in October); live catfish and carp; eels, snakes and tortoises in netted bowls and big fish tanks sprayed continuously from hoses to keep the water aerated; baskets full of chickens and pigeons; caged monkeys, dogs and raccoons; racks hanging with roast dog and a confusing array of butchered furry flesh and offal, all of it bound for the cooking wok. Of course, some animals end up here that shouldn't, and locals can sometimes get irate with shutter happy tourists. The Guangdong government is stepping up its efforts to stop locals eating endangered species but is finding it very difficult to enforce. Monkeys are seen less often in Qingping Market, but all this means is that prospective customers now have to ask for "behind the counter" service.

From the market area you can wander north along Haizhu Zhonglu which runs parallel to Renmin Lu, turn right on Huifu Xilu and find the Daoist **Wuxian (Five Immortals) Temple**. It's said to be the spot where five rams appeared more than 2,000 years ago, carrying ears of rice in their mouths and ridden by five gods. The gods vanished, but the rams stayed and turned to stone, whereupon the local people began planting rice. Since then Guangzhou has also been known as the City of Rams and City of Rice Ears.

The Wuxian Temple has a large rock in its courtyard bearing a hollow that is said to be the footprint of one of the gods. It also sports a huge Ming dynasty bell, three meters (10 ft) high and weighing five tons (which has no clapper and is believed would warn of impending disaster for the city should it ever make a sound).

North of Wuxian Temple on Guangta Lu, the **Huaisheng Mosque** represents the centuries of Islamic culture brought to Guangzhou by Arab traders. Like most Islamic places of worship it's quite severely free of ornamentation and idolatry, but its arched gateways and main hall of prayer are an interesting contrast of Moslem and Chinese architecture. It has a minaret that looms over the sweeping, tiled Chinese-style roofs and looks as though it's been rendered with concrete; but it's said to take its name, Guangta (Smooth Minaret) from this apparently unique surfacing. The mosque dates back to the year 627 in the Tang dynasty and commemorates the Arab missionary Saud Ibn Abu Waggas who was the first to bring the Koran to China.

Further north on the other side of the main east-west artery Zhongshan Lu, stand the two most interesting temples in Guangzhou, the **Guangxiao Temple** and the **Liurong (Six**

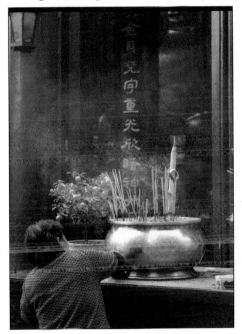

Banyan Trees) Temple with its towering nine-story **Hua Ta (Flower Pagoda)**. You can't miss the pagoda, and can reach it by walking north along either Haizhu Beilu or Liurong Lu from Zhongshan Lu.

The Liurong Temple was given its name by the renowned poet Su Dongpo who visited it some seven centuries ago and was captivated by the banyan trees (since gone) in its grounds. Both Liurong and the nearby Guangxiao Temple were built in honor of Hui Neng, the sixth patriarch of Chan (Zen) Buddhism, and in the grounds of the Guangxiao complex there's an open pavilion featuring frescoes of Hui Neng preaching to the monks and of the Indian monk, Bodhidharma, who is said to have visited Liurong at one stage.

Both temples attract large crowds of Cantonese sightseers and worshipers. Religion is coming back in Guangzhou, and none are happier about it than the old grannies who can be seen teaching their grandchildren how to light the joss stick, place it in the incense altars and kowtow to the images.

Part of the Guangxiao Temple is now the **Guangdong Antique Store**, with an interesting exhibition of Tang horses, camels and human figures. It has a "Sixth Patriarch's Hair-burying Pagoda," a Hall of the Sleeping Buddha and an ancient bodhi tree with

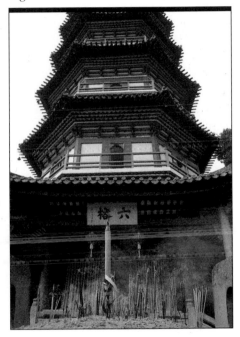

a sign below it declaring: "The age-old Buddha's Tree" (the Sixth Patriarch was given tonsure right underneath it). These two temples are about as far as you can comfortably go in one day's walking, and mark the boundary of Shamian Island and environs exploration.

At night, there's another treat in the Shamian Island district which definitely should not be missed — the Cultural Park. This large playground off Liu'ersan Lu and Renmin Nanlu just north of Shamian Island is where the Cantonese go at night to have

ABOVE: Religion re-emerges in the post-revolutionary age — joss and towering pagoda RIGHT and worshiper LEFT at Liurong (Six Banyan Trees) Temple, Guangzhou.

fun. It's just as much fun watching them enjoying themselves.

In the eerie, ill-lit tropical darkness you come across a fairground and ferris wheel, a roller-skating rink packed with teenagers, an early Buck Rogers rocketship space simulator, a shooting gallery with pneumatic "bazookas" that fire tennis balls, a pool hall and the very latest in modernized leisure in Guangzhou, a video arcade. But the most interesting attraction, and one that draws a couple of thousand spectators in the semi-darkness each night, is an open-air Chinese

you within close strolling proximity of a number of scenic and cultural attractions. To the north, heading toward the railway station, there's **Orchid Garden** where, in a landscaped setting, you can view more than 10,000 orchids from 100 species, and visit the seventh century **Mohammedan Tomb**, claimed to be the burial place of the same Moslem missionary Waggas to whom the Huaisheng Mosque is dedicated.

The **Youyi (Friendship) Theater** to the west of the tomb, off Renmin Beilu, is one of several in Guangzhou that present nightly

chess tournament in which the competitors play on a floodlit stage and when a move is made it's immediately marked up, to a chorus of gasps or groans, on giant boards on each side of the table and announced over the public address system.

Meanwhile, at an auditorium near the stage, the high-pitched singsong shriek and clash of gongs announces another act in the continuing story of Cantonese Opera, with its regal and lavishly-costumed princesses, kings and mandarins gliding and flapping about the stage.

Pet Birds and Pagodas
The Dongfang to China Hotels district between Renmin Beilu and Jiefang Beilu places

performances of Beijing and Cantonese opera, music, drama, dance and acrobatics.

Liuhua Park, to the west of the Dongfang Hotel, is a pleasant garden set among artificial lakes, but the much larger **Yuexiu Park** on the eastern side of Jiefang Beilu features at least two places of keen cultural and social interest. The remarkable **Zhenhai Tower**, a five-story red wooden and rectangular pagoda, is all that's left of the old city wall of Guangzhou, and from its wide balconies, decorated with fat red traditional lanterns, you can see out over the city.

Recently renovated for the second time in a decade, it houses the **Guangzhou City Museum** and its scrolls, porcelain, ceramic sculptures and other artifacts and relics covering the city's past from the Neolithic age to the 1911 republican revolution and World War II. Close to Zhenhai Tower there's a monument to Guangzhou's favorite son, Sun Yatsen, but it's a drab concrete monstrosity and could well be given a miss — except on Sundays, when it's a venue for hundreds of bird lovers showing off their caged warblers.

The **Sun Yatsen Memorial Hall** to the south of the park is also historically significant but relatively uninteresting. A much more fascinating spot to take a look at is the

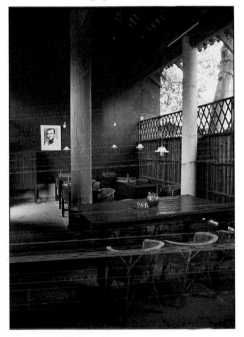

huge **Sculpture of the Five Rams**, west of Zhenhai Tower, a garish stone tableau of the legendary founders of Guangzhou that is nonetheless interesting because of the hordes of families that gather there each day to take photographs of each other against it.

You'll not only see amazing body–contortions as harried photography enthusiasts try to fit their impatient subjects into their upside-down viewfinders, but if you're smart about it you can also catch a good picture or two while all the posing and twisting and laughing and bickering are going on. For more candid photography in which you run little risk of offending anyone's sensibilities, the **Children's Park** to the southeast of the Sun Yatsen Memorial Hall is a good place to

go. You get there by going directly south from the memorial on Jixiang Lu and turning left on Zhongshan Lu.

The Revolutionary Tour

The third main tourist venue of Guangzhou begins roughly at the Children's Park and continues east along Zhongshan Lu. There you'll find the city's contemporary monuments, the **Original Site of the Peasant Movement Institute**, where in 1926 Mao Zedong trained the cadres, including Zhou Enlai, who were to spearhead his communist revolution. Nearby is the **Memorial Mausoleum to the Martyrs of the Guangzhou Uprising**, where, a year later, these same cadres headed a communist takeover of most of Guangzhou, only to be crushed by the ruling Guomindang forces.

Further to the northeast along Xi'anlie Nanlu, you can view the **Huanghuagang Mausoleum** of the 72 Martyrs, the monument to a similar, earlier uprising — and similar reprisal — in April 1911 in the last days of the Manchu Qing rule. Beyond that there's only one major attraction left, **Guangzhou Zoo**, which like most Chinese zoos is best passed up unless you're keen on watching pandas and other wildlife in old-fashioned, dank and quite dispirited captivity.

WHERE TO STAY

Guangzhou has a good range of accommodation. However, watch out for the Guangzhou Trade Fair, which is held for a week twice annually, in mid-April and in mid-October. During these periods rooms are scarce, and it's not unusual for rates to double.

Luxury

By Chinese standards, Guangzhou has a large number of luxury hotels, and you get better value here than in Hong Kong. Expect to pay from US$140 upwards in the luxury bracket.

The **White Swan Hotel (** (20) 8188-6968 FAX (20) 8186-1188, 843 rooms, was one of China's earliest luxury hotels, and it still remains top-class by any standards. Its tastefully decorated riverside coffee lounge and

Shrine-like setting LEFT at Peasant Movement Institute ABOVE where Mao Zedong's communist lieutenants were first trained.

vast atrium, features a traditionally styled pavilion and waterfall and a viewing deck on to which visiting Chinese groups are allowed each day to take photos of each other. But the White Swan's main selling point is its location on Shamian Island, the peaceful former foreign concession.

Most of Guangzhou's other luxury hotels are in the northeast of town, on the bustling commercial strip of Huanshi Donglu. The **Guangdong International Hotel (** (20) 8331-1888 FAX (20) 8331-1666, 339 Huanshi Donglu, though somewhat bland in appearance, is a good option for business travelers. Also in this area is the first-class **Garden Hotel (** (20) 8333-8989 FAX (20) 8335-0467, with its elaborate chandeliered lobby, bowling alley, swimming pool, roof restaurants, disco, coffee lounge, sun decks, bars, boutiques and beauty salons. Some travelers claim it is the best in Guangzhou.

The **China Hotel (** (20) 8666-6888 FAX (20) 8667-7014, Liuhua Lu, has an outdoor swimming pool, tennis court, bowling alley, an impressive health center on the fourth floor, and a Hong Kong-style basement Food Street. Most impressive of all, it is home to a branch of the Hard Rock Café.

Mid-Range

One of Guangzhou's outstanding mid-range options is the renovated **Guangdong Victory Hotel (** (20) 8186-2622 FAX (20) 8186-2413, 53 Shamian Beijie. The location, on charming Shamian Island, is a great plus, but the tastefully appointed rooms with rates from around HK$380 are also hard to beat. There's an excellent Cantonese-style restaurant with *dim sum* breakfasts on the ground floor.

The **Aiqun Hotel (** (20) 8186-6668 FAX (20) 8188-3519, 113 Yanjiang Xilu, (the name means "love the masses") is a massive, recently refurbished structure that overlooks the Pearl River. Foreign guests are rarely seen here, and beyond the front desk English is rarely spoken, but rooms are reasonably priced and a discount of around 20% is generally available upon request. Not far from here, the **Guangzhou Hotel (** (20) 8333-8168 FAX (20) 8333-0791, Haizhu Square, is a more upmarket option, where English is spoken and the hotel amenities include shopping, hairdressers, restaurants and so on.

Inexpensive

For as long as anyone can remember the **Guangzhou Youth Hostel (** (20) 8887-4298, on Shamian Island, has had a monopoly on Guangzhou's foreign budget travelers. In the past it was a grim place, where the staff were known to steal from the guests. It has cleaned up its act, renovated, and now has rooms (complete with satellite television) from around US$12 to US$25.

If you don't mind spending slightly more, a superb choice is the **Guangdong Shamian Hotel (** (20) 8191-2288 FAX (20) 8191-1628, 52 Shamian Nanjie, just around the corner. It may have little in the way of the amenities available in better hotels, but the rooms are clean and the staff are friendly.

WHERE TO EAT

For the Chinese, a visit to Guangzhou is a culinary pilgrimage. Some of the famous "old houses" have been serving customers for over 100 years. As was the case elsewhere in China, the fortunes of many of Guangzhou's best restaurants took a turn for a worse during the dark days of the Cultural Revolution, but nowadays Guangzhou's reputation as one of the best cities in China to eat out in is back on track.

Starting with the best, *dim sum* aficionados should head over to the **Taotaoju Restaurant (** (20) 8181-6111, 20 Dishipu Lu, an atmospheric place that was an academy of learning in the seventeenth century.

The **North Garden Restaurant (** (20) 8333-0087, 202 Xiaobei Road, is a series of rooms laid out around a Chinese garden where fish swim in a miniature lake crossed by a miniature bridge. Prices are close to those of Hong Kong. It gets packed early in the evening and has an extensive menu. The new annex next door is something of an eyesore, but business is business, and few Chinese guests are likely to complain.

West of the city, the **Panxi Restaurant (** (20) 8181-5718, 151 Longjing Xilu, is Guangzhou's busiest restaurant, and its dining rooms and pavilions are scattered through a romantic landscape of gardens, pools and ornamental bridges. Like the North Garden its menu is upmarket and gourmet — stewed turtle in pottery; swallow's nest and crabmeat soup;

white fungus (from stone) and bamboo pith with chicken slices in consommé; fried sea slug with chicken, perch, kidney, shrimp and vegetable. But it also offers fried prawns, fried frog and chicken slices, chicken with spicy sauce, fried noodles, and chicken slices in soup, with beer, at quite a reasonable price for a one-night blowout in a restaurant that, more than any other in contemporary China, recalls the splendor of the dynastic past.

It's worth sampling some Chinese vegetarian dishes, which are Buddhist in origin and use products like tofu to ingeniously duplicate the tastes and textures of various meats. The **Tsai Ken Hsiang Restaurant** ((20) 8334-4363, 167 Zhongshan 6-Lu, is a famous vegetarian restaurant.

With so many top-notch hotels around town, as you might expect there are also countless hotel restaurants to choose from. A couple of favorites are **Le Grill** ((20) 8331-1888, at the Guangdong International Hotel and **The Pizzeria** ((20) 8333-8989, at the Garden Hotel. In the China Hotel is the **Hard Rock Café** ((20) 8666-6888, where you can find that internationally tried and tested formula of loud rock music and overpriced treats such as hamburgers and french fries — don't forget to get the T-shirt.

For inexpensive dining there are any number of choices around town. Guangzhou has the full complement of fast food barns these days — **KFC**, **McDonald's** and **Pizza Hut** are just a few of the big names who have set up shop here. Popular Hong Kong chains like **Café de Coral** have also had considerable success.

HOW TO GET THERE

From Guangzhou, you can get to just about anywhere in China, and you can do it by air, rail, bus or river craft. There are daily express trains to Beijing and Shanghai, with both journeys taking about 33 hours, and there is also direct train service to Kunming.

AROUND GUANGZHOU: FOSHAN AND SHUNDE

Getting to the sights around Guangzhou under your own steam can be tiresome, especially in the hot summer months. A

good alternative is to take a tour. The tour offices in the major hotels run coach tours to cultural locations around the city, and their itineraries include visits to carving and other crafts factories. They also operate tours of Foshan, the famous ceramics and crafts city 28 km (17 miles) southwest of Guangzhou, where you have the opportunity to watch artists at the **Foshan Folk Art Research Society** making traditional lanterns, paper-cuttings and brick carvings, weavers producing silk in the city's mills and ceramic miniatures being painted in

their thousands at the **Shiwan Artistic Pottery and Porcelain Factory**.

Tours of Foshan also include a visit to the 900-year-old Song dynasty **Ancestral Temple**, whose remarkable architecture features dozens of ceramic figures and animals lining the crests of its roofs. It's possible to go on your own from the Guangzhou–Foshan (Guangfo) Bus Terminal, which you will find just off Daxin Zhonglu to the east of Shamian Island. It's a one-hour bus ride to Foshan, and once there, you can find reasonably-priced accommodation at the **Foshan Hotel** ((0757) 335-3338 FAX (757) 335-2347, or the **Overseas Chinese Hotel** ((757) 222-8328 FAX (757) 222-7702, if you want to stay overnight. You'll find the local CITS office at 75 Fenjiang Nanlu ((757) 335-3338.

Shunde is a small town—approximately 45 km (27 miles) away — famous among gourmets as the home of Cantonese cuisine. There are several hotels in town, of which

Historic Zhenhai Tower now houses a cultural museum.

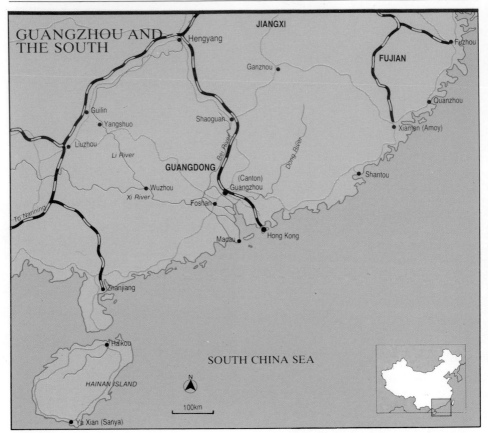

GUANGZHOU AND THE SOUTH

the **Century Hotel (** (765) 229-3333 is one. Access is not easy unless you are able to purchase a ticket from the railway station.

SOUTHERN CHINA: THE RADIAL ROUTE

North of Guangdong province there are two key junctions that open up the east-west rail routes — at **Hengyang** in Hunan province you change to the daily Shanghai–Kunming express trains for the dog-leg run west to Guilin and Kunming, and at **Zhengzhou** in Henan province you can connect with expresses from Beijing, Qingdao and Shanghai which will take you west to Chengdu, Lanzhou and Xi'an.

Buses leave the Long Distance Bus Terminal on the south side of Huanshi Xilu a short distance to the west of the Guangzhou railway station for up-country destinations in Guangdong province and beyond. Travel times are constantly being reduced by im-

provements to the roads. The new expressway between Shenzhen and Shantou means that a journey that once took 12 hours or more can now be covered in around four hours. You might stay overnight in Shantou on the east coast (perhaps making a sidetrip to the historically more interesting Chaozhou, just an hour away by bus), and carry on the next day to Xiamen (Amoy) in Fujian province. There's also a daily 10-hour bus service to Zhanjiang, the southern coastal jumping off point for Haikou on Hainan Island. For Guilin direct bus services are available (around 20 hours), but the better option (if you're not flying) is to take a high-speed ferry to Wuzhou (around four hours) and then take a second bus straight to Guilin, or go first to the beautiful Li River township of Yangshuo and carry on to Guilin by river ferry.

Ferries and hovercraft to Hong Kong, Macau and Haikou on Hainan Island leave from the Zhoutouzui Wharf on the south side of the Pearl River. To get to it you go across the Renmin Bridge and west along the extension of Tongfu Xilu to the waterfront. For boats to Wuzhou you go to the Dashatou Pier on Yanjiang Donglu.

Before you attempt to organize bookings yourself (always a headache in China), ask at the front desk of your hotel. In most cases your hotel reception can handle bookings, or at least refer you to a reliable nearby agent.

XIAMEN (AMOY) AND FUJIAN PROVINCE

The southeastern coastal city of Xiamen and the whole province with its capital Fuzhou are famous for their long-standing trade contacts with the rest of the world. Great Chinese fleets sailed from here in the Yuan and Ming dynasties to explore and establish trade throughout Southeast Asia, and waves of emigrants left these shores for all parts of the world in the last century. Yet for all this, Fujian languishes off the beaten tourist track and has yet to be fully explored by foreign visitors.

Compared with western areas of the southern region, Fujian's value as a mainstream tourist destination is debatable. But for the individual traveler looking for a relatively untrodden trail to follow, it offers some physical and cultural rewards.

A rugged mountainous province, Fujian is bounded on the west by the **Wuyi Mountains**, a 250-km (155-mile) range that's been a popular Buddhist retreat since Fujian was taken under the wing of imperial rule in the Tang dynasty. More than 100 monasteries were built among the heavily wooded slopes, and a wealth of surviving architecture and relics awaits the modern-day visitor. The mountains are also renowned for their Dahongpao tea, just one of the many Fujian brands that have made the province one of China's leading producers of the "lusty leaf."

The easiest access to the Wuyi range would be from Yingtan in Jiangxi province, the railway junction that links the Guangzhou–Shanghai line with Xiamen. There are hotels in **Yingtan** and a long-distance bus station where you should be able to get transport to either **Huanggang Shan**, one of the major Wuyi peaks, or to **Jianning** or **Nanping**, stopping off in the mountains along the way.

XIAMEN

Xiamen, which is actually an island linked to the mainland by a long causeway of road and railway, is, like Shenzhen, a Special Economic Zone. But while Shenzhen was piggybacked by booming Hong Kong, Xiamen is flush with Taiwanese investment. The local dialect, known as *minnanyu*, is nearly identical to the dialect spoken in Taiwan, and the nearest Taiwanese-controlled islands — Matsu and Quemoy (Kinmen) — are just a

couple of kilometers (a mile, or so) off shore from Xiamen.

Background

Historically, Xiamen was established as a major seaport in the Ming reign and returned the compliment by becoming a notorious pirate lair and the launching base for an ill-fated campaign in the seventeenth century to stem the southward influence of the Manchu Qing dynasty and restore the Ming rule. The campaign was led by one of the pirate chiefs Zheng Chenggong, better known as Koxinga. He didn't get far in his bid to drive the Manchus from China, but

Hengyang infant in bright New Year's costume.

turned around and kicked the Dutch out of what is now the island of Taiwan instead.

Xiamen was also an unofficial trading depot, doing a thriving under-the-counter business in silks with the Portuguese, Spanish and Dutch, until a British naval force stormed ashore after their victory in the first Opium War in 1841 and opened it up as a full Treaty Port. There is evidence today of its role as an international settlement in the surviving colonial architecture of parts of its skyline.

General Information
American Express ((592) 212-0268 is in Room 212 of the Holiday Inn Crowne Plaza Harbor View Hotel (see below).

Airlines represented in Xiamen include **Air China** ((592) 508-4381, **China Eastern Airlines** ((592) 202-8936, **Dragonair** ((592) 202-5433, **SilkAir** ((592) 205-3275, and **Xiamen Airlines** ((592) 602-2961.

What to See and Do
Although Nanputuo Temple is officially Xiamen's main attraction, most foreigners agree that Xiamen's charm reposes mostly in the small island of **Gulangyu**, which lies just off the city's waterfront and is linked to it by ferries that run with Star-Ferry-like efficiency through the day and into the night.

Foreigners started settling on Gulangyu in the 1840s, and in 1903 the island was declared a Foreign Settlement. The villas, churches and civic buildings you see today on streets blissfully free of motorized traffic are all that remains of the settlement. It's reminiscent of Shamian Island in Guangzhou, except on a grander and better preserved scale.

Apart from strolling around the island, admiring the architecture and work of cottage craftspeople (Gulangyu is one of the few places in the world where you can still buy masterfully executed oil portraits of Stalin, though who buys them is a mystery), Gulangyu also has two average beaches, the **Zheng Chenggong (Koxinga) Memorial Hall**, commemorating the pirate patriot of the Ming reign, and a viewing platform on top of **Sunlight Rock**. Below the rock is **Shuzhuang Garden**, which features a maze and one of the finest landscaped rockeries in southern China.

South of Xiamen is Xiamen University, which has an interesting **Museum of Anthropology**. Next door to the university is the remarkable Tang dynasty **Nanputuo Temple**. Although built in the Tang reign it was renovated in the Manchu Qing and features exquisite architecture and an impressive array of Buddhist statuary, including images of the Maitreya, or Future Buddha (also depicted as the rotund Laughing Buddha), several guardian deities, three images of Sakyamuni Buddha, four Bodhisattvas and other guardian figures.

Where to Stay
Xiamen has a good selection of hotels to suit all budgets.

LUXURY
Holiday Inn Crowne Plaza Harbourview ((592) 202-3333 FAX (592) 203-6666, 12–8 Zhenhai Lu, is one of Xiamen's top hotels. It has international restaurants and facilities, but its winning feature is its location in the heart of old Xiamen (other luxury hotels are out in the suburbs), near the harbor. For travelers looking for some luxury, it is easily the best choice.

The **Marco Polo Xiamen** ((592) 509-1888 FAX (592) 509-2888, 8 Jianye Road, Hubin Bei, is giving the Holiday Inn a run for it's money these days, though it doesn't have Holiday Inn's prize location. The **Xiamen Mandarin Hotel** ((592) 602-3333 FAX (592) 602-1431, 101 Mandarin Street, Huli, is a slightly less luxurious option; it's aimed mostly at business travelers.

MID-RANGE
Few foreign travelers stay there, but it's hard to beat the **Lujiang Hotel** ((592) 202-2922 FAX (592) 202-4644, 54 Lujiang Dao, for both it's location and general ambiance — it's in a restored old colonial structure right next to the Gulangyu ferry pier, in the heart of old Xiamen. The hotel is popular with Taiwanese tourists and business people.

Less conveniently located but cheaper and affording splendid views over Zhongshan Park, is the **Singapore Hotel** ((592) 202-6668 FAX (592) 202-5950, 113–121 Xi'an Road. It's a typical mid-range Chinese hotel, with a restaurant and basic amenities.

For very reasonably priced accommodation with some character, try the **Xin Qiao Hotel** ((592) 203-8883 FAX (592) 203-8765, 444 Zhongshan Lu, a rambling, restored structure that once served as a guesthouse for cadres.

INEXPENSIVE

You can save money and relax in beautiful surroundings at the **Gulangyu Guesthouse** ((592) 206-3856 FAX (592) 206-6060, 25 Huangyan Road, Gulangyu, on Gulangyu Island. This is a rare opportunity to retreat from the honk of traffic in coastal China.

The **Hubin Hotel** ((592) 202-5202 FAX 202-9964, Hubin Zhonglu, has some uninspiring bargain-priced rooms if you're prepared to beg for them. It's in a dull part of town.

Where to Eat

If you're prepared to be adventurous Zhongshan Lu, which runs through the old part of town down to the Gulangyu Ferry Pier, has many Chinese restaurants, though you'll be lucky to find an English menu anywhere. If you're not adventurous, there are fast food outlets about town, including a **Pizza Hut** down by the ferry pier.

The **Xiamen East Ocean Hotel** ((592) 202-1111, 1 Zhongshan Lu, has a highly rated seafood restaurant, while at the Holiday Inn, **Lao Sichuan** ((592) 202-3333 does upmarket Sichuanese cuisine — something of rarity in this neck of the woods.

Nanputuo Temple in Xiamen features an impressive array of Buddhist statuary and relics.

Gulangyu Island is celebrated for its seafood. You'll see seafood restaurants as you stroll around the island. Check prices as you order to avoid being presented with a horrifying bill when you finish.

How to Get There

Xiamen has an international airport, with direct access from Singapore and Hong Kong. Flights to local Chinese destinations are plentiful. There's access by train from either Guangzhou or Shanghai by changing at Yingtan and traveling south on the Xiamen branch line, but land travel out of Xiamen is mostly by bus.

QUANZHOU

Quanzhou, three hours up the coast by bus from Xiamen, is believed to have flourished long before Xiamen came into its own as a trading center, the site of ancient Zaiton, the "great resort of ships and merchandise" that Marco Polo wrote about after his epic travels in Kublai Khan's reign. An astonishing relic of that grand mercantile era can be seen in the grounds of the **Kaiyuan Monastery**.

Originally called the Lotus Monastery, Quanzhou was built in 686 in the Tang reign and renovated during the Ming dynasty, and not only features another impressive collection of Buddha images but also 72 panels of bas-relief carved with figures of lions with human heads that are reminiscent of Egyptian pharaonic art. But that's just the monastery. Behind it you'll find the **Museum of Overseas Communications History** which, despite its uninspiring name, deserves a close look; you'll find a magnificent relic of the power and glory of ancient Zaiton — the excavated hull of a huge ocean-going junk, dating back to the Song dynasty, and maps of the great oceanic expeditions that the eunuch admiral Zheng He commanded in the Ming reign to the distant shores of East Africa and Madagascar.

Where To Stay

Nearby Xiamen is a much more pleasant place to be based than Quanzhou. If you need to stay in Quanzhou, the **Quanzhou Hotel** ((595) 228-9958 FAX 218-2128, 22 Zhuangfu

Xi'ang, not far from the Kaiyuan Temple, is a good mid-range choice.

HAINAN ISLAND

If you were a mandarin, or government official, in the days of dynastic rule in China and you were transferred to the island of Hainan, you would have dragged yourself down there feeling quite thankful that you still had a head on your shoulders. Hainan was, and still is, the far southern limit of the Chinese civilization, a place of exile for any

bureaucrat or court official who had incurred the emperor's displeasure. There's a beach with two big boulders on the island's extreme southern tip that's called **Tianya Haijiao**, or literally "Edge of the Heavens, Corner of the Seas," and if you stand there in the sands and gaze out across the seas you can imagine the ghosts of the past standing there with you, still wondering how it all went wrong for them.

Hainan is a large tropical island, covering an area of 32,000 sq km (12,355 sq miles), much of it clothed in lush forests, ricefields and fruit growing plantations, low-lying in the north and mountainous in the central region and south. Its tallest hills, the Wuzhi Shan (Five-Fingered) Mountains, rise to nearly 1,900 m (6,234 ft) and can clearly be seen from the mainland 18 km (11 miles) away. Aside from forested slopes and balmy beaches, there are fertile valleys where a mixed population of Li and Miao minorities and Han Chinese settlers cultivate rice, rubber, sugarcane, tropical fruits, coffee, tobacco, pepper and cocoa.

The island has attracted overseas Chinese investment as one of the Special Economic Zones. It is also strategically important — much of its west coast is a burgeoning naval, air and military base facing Vietnam. The

From Hong Kong, Dragonair has flights to Haikou — tied in with vacation packages to Haikou–Sanya–Haikou — daily. You can also fly to Haikou and Sanya from Guangzhou. From Zhanjiang you can take a daily direct flight to Haikou.

Boats leave daily from Guangzhou and Zhanjiang to Haikou and Sanya.

If you want to do some sightseeing en-route, take a train from Guangzhou to Guilin, then travel by rail again to Zhanjiang, continue by bus and ferry across to Haikou and then travel right down the island by bus to Sanya.

west also happens to have the main concentration of Li minority villages, and while you can get to them quite freely nowadays you must keep in mind that this is a sensitive military zone. On the island's east coast you can find the Danjia boat people, who operate a fishing and pearling industry.

How to Get There

From the tourist's point of view, Hainan has three immediate destinations: the capital Haikou on the north coast, just across the Qiongzhou Strait from mainland Hai'an; the port and beach resort of Sanya (Ya Xian) on the south coast; and the mountains and colorful mountain folk in between.

CITS (see TAKING A TOUR in YOUR CHOICE, page 66) in Hong Kong handles all bookings.

Haikou

Haikou has its charm — the old part of town south of the Haidian River is reminiscent of Macau or Malacca — but for most travelers it's a whistle-stop on the road to better places.

General Information
The main branch of the **Bank of China** is at 33 Datong Lu, with its own ground floor

OPPOSITE: A lone monk descends the stairs at Xiamen's Nanputuo Temple, one of China's most important Buddhist centers. ABOVE: In spring the rape fields of northern Guangxi wash the landscape with yellow hues.

entrance in the huge Haikou International Commercial Centre. On the second floor of the same building, you can find **Dragonair** (677-3088. **CAAC** ((898) 677-2031 has an office at 9 Haixiu Lu, though most hotels around town sell domestic air tickets.

What to See and Do
In the center of Haikou is **Haikou Park**, a calm retreat from the traffic and a busy venue for teams of t'ai chi exponents in the early hours of the day. Just north of here **Donghu** and **Xihu** lakes mark the southern extent of the **Old Quarter**, a busy commercial district that teems with interesting architecture and fascinating street scenes. The Haidian River waterfront is being spruced up, but at the time of writing had little to recommend it.

Where to Stay
Given that luxury buses whizz through to Sanya in just three hours these days, there's probably no need to stay in Haikou. All the same, the city does have a good range of accommodation.

The newly completed **Mandarin Hotel** ((898) 845-8888 FAX (898) 851-1228, on Bihai Avenue, Haikou, is the best accommodation in town followed by the Hong Kong-managed **Huandao Tide Hotel** ((898) 626-8888 FAX (898) 626-5588, Heping Dadao, Haidian Island. Indeed, with tennis courts, a swimming pool, shops, restaurants, a food court, and a grand atrium lobby, this place is a self-contained city.

For quality mid-range accommodation, the **Overseas Hotel** ((898) 536-5999 FAX (898) 536-5333, is in the central business district and tries hard to please. **The Seaview International Hotel** ((898) 677-3381 FAX (898) 677-3101, 6 Haixiu Lu, is an older establishment where the rooms look slightly the worse for wear, but sizeable discounts are available on request, making this a reasonably priced, central hotel.

How to Get There
Making travel arrangements in Haikou is easy. Luxury buses go to Sanya and Wenchang every half hour or so from the corner of Daying Houlu and Jichang Lu (next to the Haikou Hotel).

The airport is in the middle of town, just five minutes from most hotels. Taxis are inexpensive.

SANYA (YA XIAN)

Sanya has the best beaches in all China, along with good seafood and comfortable beach-style accommodation.

What to See and Do
Dadonghai, the best of the beaches, is lined with resort-style hotels these days, but those fearing the worst are in for a surprise. The foreshore has been landscaped, with lawns and shady palms and firs, and the beach is free of litter.

Chinese tourists head up to **Luhuitou** to see a statue that immortalizes a local folk tale about a hunter who, after pursuing a deer to the top of this steep peninsula, was surprised to see the deer turn its head back to look at him and turn into a beautiful maiden (the two promptly settled into domestic bliss and lived happily ever after). The statue is a non-event, but the views of Sanya and the surrounding coast are a treat.

Tianya Haijiao is the southernmost tip of Hainan, and the site of famous rocks carved with the legend: "End of the World." This area is something of a tourist trap nowadays, with restaurants, an aquarium, ethnic traders selling pearls, and professional photographers. It's still worth making the 24-km (15-mile) trip out there.

Where to Stay
Dadonghai is the best place to stay. It has a good range of hotels, countless restaurants, and good swimming. Bear in mind that guests here are almost all Chinese, and even at the top hotels standards are still far from international.

The **South China Hotel** ((899) 821-3888 FAX (899) 821-3888 and the **Pearl River Garden Hotel** ((899) 821-1888 FAX (899) 821-1999 are the best of the Dadonghai hotels. The **Oriental Garden Hotel** ((899) 821-2188 FAX (899) 821-3049 is slightly cheaper, and in need of some maintenance.

If you don't mind taking a step down in the comfort stakes, the **Seaside Holiday Inn Resort** ((899) 821-3898 is an economical option, with well maintained doubles and cottages in delightful landscaped grounds.

The **Gloria Resort Sanya** ((899) 856-8855 FAX (899) 856-8533 is a luxury hotel at nearby Yalong Bay, and is where tour groups settle.

GUANGXI–ZHUANGZU AUTONOMOUS REGION

THE KARST HILLS

Chinese culture abounds with literary superlatives, paintings, embroidery, murals, sculp-

In fact and in legend, these hill rocks have been littered over the centuries with the wine-flasks of inebriated poets, one of whom, Han Yu, got as far as describing the Li River (Lijiang) as "a turquoise gauze belt, the mountains like a jade clasp." Another managed to start a poem but couldn't finish it and promptly turned to stone. Yet another gave up trying to express himself altogether and simply drank himself to death.

What they were struggling to capture in prose was a geological phenomenon called karst—the erosive action of rivers and drain-

ture and other artwork that all attempt to express the beauty of Guilin and its Li River scenery. Even the very meticulous and businesslike *Official Guide to China* produced by the Imperial Japanese Government Railways in 1915 had to cast about for a little poetic inspiration. "The neighborhood (of Guilin) is rich in picturesque scenery," it observed. "The mountains are singular in that the peaks all rise immediately from the plains, each by itself, so that they have been fitly compared by the poet Fan Shih-hu to young bamboos sprouting out of the ground, apparently without any connection with each other. On the river banks there are innumerable grotesque and singular rocks which form objects of interest and attraction to poets."

age over many millions of years on a belt of limestone that extends right across the southern provinces, carving away the softer rock to produce abrupt and fanciful hills and extensive underground caves.

GUILIN

This sprawling city of 680,000 attracts so many visitors for its famous Li River scenery and surrounding necklace of karst hills that its tempting to dismiss the place as a tourist trap these days. Guilin is certainly highly industrious in its pursuit of the tourist dollar, and there is much industrial ugliness to bemoan

Tourist ferry glides through fairyland setting of karst pinnacles and hills along Li River from Guilin.

around town, but it remains one of the most fascinating travel destinations in China. When the rat race in downtown Guilin becomes too much for you, remember that rural Yangshuo is just an hour or so downstream.

General Information

The main **Bank of China** ((773) 282-4810 is at 5 Shanhu Beilu, but you can change money at most of the major hotels too.

Dragonair ((773) 282-5588 has an office on the 2nd Floor of the Sheraton Guilin Hotel (see WHERE TO STAY, below).

shops on Zhongshan Lu. Check the brakes and the tires before deciding on a bike. Some bikes are in poor condition.

But once you're out there, bicycling is safe (reasonably), a lot of fun, easier than trudging by foot, and you tend to merge into the masses rather than being the center of attention. Don't try to race — you'll get frustrated in the crush, have a collision and lose a lot of face (perhaps literally). You'll also wear yourself out. Save the energy for the uphill sections and don't be too proud to get off and walk the bike up — the Chinese

CITS ((773) 282-3518 is at 14 Ronghu Beilu. CTS ((773) 282-6235, is at 29 Xinyi Lu.

Getting Around

When you fet off the train at Guilin's main railway station at the southern end of the city's north-south artery Zhongshan Lu, you will likely be swamped by a clamoring mêlée of taxi drivers and minibus touts. If your destination is the airport or a hotel in Guilin, take a taxi (make sure the meter gets turned on); if you're going to Yangshuo or the airport, take a minibus.

Once you have somewhere to stay, the best way to get around Guilin is by bicycle. Bikes are available for hire for around $2 to $3 (with a deposit of around $30) a day from the hire

certainly do. Learn to coast and rest on the downhill runs, and on the flats take it at a sedate pace and rhythm and let the weight of the feet rather than muscle power glide you along. You're in no real hurry, and neither is anyone else.

What to See and Do

Guilin's main attractions are all in town. With your hired bike, you can combine a lot of social activity with the main tourist attractions by picking a scenic or cultural spot to ride to and nosing around the streets on the way.

OPPOSITE: Thousand Buddha Cave in Guilin vies with the Wind Cave for rock sculptures dating back to Buddhism's grand age in China. ABOVE: Rounded karst hills beyond Guilin.

For example, a ride to the Qixing Gongyuan (Seven Star Park) on the eastern side of the Li River will take you along the waterfront east of the Lijiang Hotel to the Liberation Bridge over Li River, passing open markets, an open-air wooden bed bazaar, crowded gambling spots, sampan life and a cluster of old floating restaurants along the way.

The park itself is a well landscaped strolling spot with gardens and traditional humpbacked stone bridges over streams and pools, a precipitous climb that takes you up through viewing pavilions and restaurants to the top of its craggy karst hill, an interesting Ming dynasty bridge called Hua Qiao (Flower Bridge) and six caves with rock formations that have been given evocative names by the Chinese — Monkey Picking Peaches, for instance — but you'll require a great deal of imagination to transform these stalactites and stalagmites into such fanciful images.

The same richly descriptive names have been given to all the karst landmarks in and around Guilin — Duxiu Feng (Solitary Beauty Hill) north of the Lijiang Hotel and the Liberation Bridge over Li River, Diecai Shan (Piled Silk Hill) on the city's northern outskirts, Xi'angbi Shan (Elephant Trunk Hill) to the south, Laoren Shan (Old Man Hill) to the northwest. While they look interesting from a distance they offer little more than a grueling climb and various views of the city when you reach them. But again, there's a great deal of interesting street-life to be seen on the way.

Choose the formations that have more than city views to offer. For example, at Fubo Hill on the river bank east of Duxiu Feng you'll find the Qianfo Dong (Thousand Buddha Cave) with many Tang and Song dynasty Buddha images carved into its rock faces. Further north at Diecai Shan you'll find more Buddha carvings in its Wind Cave. But the most fascinating cave by far is in Ludi Yan (Reed Flute Cave) which lies about 15 km (nine miles) to the northwest of the city and can be reached by bicycle if you head out west along Jiefang Lu, cross the railway line and ask directions from there. Another way to get there is by bus Nº 13 from Seven Star Park.

Reed Flute Cave is a tour of the underworld as seen through a Disney cartoonist's fantasies — it's an extensive network of beautiful and bizarre natural grottoes, galleries and vast caverns such as the Dragon King's Crystal Palace, which was a local secret for several centuries and used as a place of refuge in times of civil war. Visitors are taken through in groups and the whole attraction is well presented, with imaginative lighting effects adding a touch of magic at each turn of the narrow, winding stone stairways. As you pass through each area the lighting dies to pitch blackness behind you, so be careful to keep up with the group.

Where to Stay

As one of China's premiere tourist attractions, it's small surprise that Guilin has hotels to meet almost every budget. But if it's solitude and backpacker prices you want, head down to Yangshuo, just over an hour away by minibus.

LUXURY

The **Sheraton Guilin Hotel** ((773) 282-5588 FAX (773) 282-5598, Binjiang Nanlu, is the best of Guilin's many hotels that aspire to international luxury standards. Ask for a room with a view of the Li River when you book.

Another reliable luxury hotel is the **Holiday Inn Guilin** ((773) 282-3750 FAX (773) 282-2101, 8 Xihuan Yi Lu, in a central but quiet location overlooking the small Banyan Lake. The **Guilin Royal Garden Hotel** ((773) 581-2411 FAX (773) 581-2744, Yanjiang Lu, is in the north of town, on the far side of the Li River looking out across the Wave Subduing Hill. This is a pleasant part of town to base yourself, if you don't mind being slightly isolated.

MID-RANGE

Once Guilin's top hotel, the **Lijiang Hotel** ((773) 282-2881 FAX (773) 282-2891, 1 Shanhu Beilu, still puts on a good show, with the full complement of services and rooms with

INEXPENSIVE

For years the **Overseas Chinese Hotel** ((773) 383-5373, Zhongshan Lu, just a short stroll south of the main railway station, has been a favorite with budget travelers. It's gone slightly up market in recent years, but it still offers very reasonable rates — for around $20 you will get a clean, simple double.

The **Yugui Hotel** ((773) 282-5499, Nanhuan Lu, is slightly more expensive but in a quieter and more picturesque part of town; some of the rooms look out over the Li River.

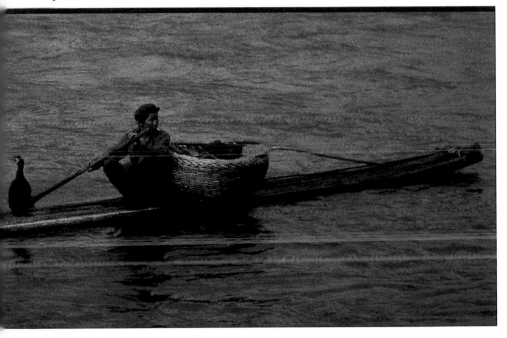

views that rival those of the four and five-star monsters like the Sheraton and the Holiday Inn. It's right in the center of town, overlooking Fir Lake.

The **Guilin Osmanthus Hotel** ((773) 383-4300 FAX (773) 383-5316, 451 Zhongshan Nanlu, is not in the same league as the Lijiang, but if it's mid-range value for money you're looking for, the Osmanthus is probably the best bet in town.

Not far from the Holiday Inn, and also overlooking the small Banyan Lake, is the **Ronghu Hotel** ((773) 282-3811 FAX 282-5456, 17 Ronghu Beilu, another long-runner and one that does a good business with budget tour groups. It's a reliable mid-range hotel, with rates slightly higher than the Osmanthus.

Where to Eat

The north-south Zhongshan Lu is packed with eating places, enough to fill an entire chapter. You'll find that they offer mainly Cantonese cuisine with local specialties and local variations. They appear to have mushroomed in such numbers to cash in on the seasonal droves of visiting Hong Kong Chinese. There are a couple that also offer exotic game dishes — monkey, civet cat, raccoon and the like — which are also aimed at the Hong Kong Chinese palate.

All the major hotels have restaurants, the best of them being in the **Sheraton** and the **Holiday Inn**. For good Chinese fare at very

Trained cormorants are a fisherman's best friend in Guilin, Guangxi Province.

affordable prices, the **Hong Kong Hotel** ((773) 383-3889, 8 Xihuan Yi Lu, has a revolving restaurant on its nineteenth floor.

At night **Zhongshan Lu** transforms into a long strip of alfresco food stalls offering a better range of cuisine than even the hotels. The section near the Guilin Hotel, is the best. It's one big tumultuous open-air food market, lit by hissing gas lamps and doing a roaring trade in fresh meat and vegetable hotpots, noodles and soups. Elsewhere you can find little sidewalk snack stalls — knee-high tables and tiny bamboo stools — which do a delicious and very cheap sweet bean soup with eggs. Overcharging has long been a problem here: It's best to clarify prices when you order.

How to Get There

To get to Guilin you can fly directly from Hong Kong on Dragonair and CAAC, or by CAAC from Guangzhou. There are also daily flights from Kunming. The Shanghai–Kunming railway pauses in Guilin, which means that you can jump on a train to either of those destinations — subject to ticket availability, and there can often be long waits on this busy line.

The popular route from Guangzhou for budget travelers is to take a ferry to Wuzhou and change there to a direct bus to either Guilin or Yangshuo. Slow ferries take around 24 hours, but the express services from both Hong Kong and Guangzhou power upriver to Wuzhou in around six hours. The bus from Wuzhou to Guilin takes around six hours.

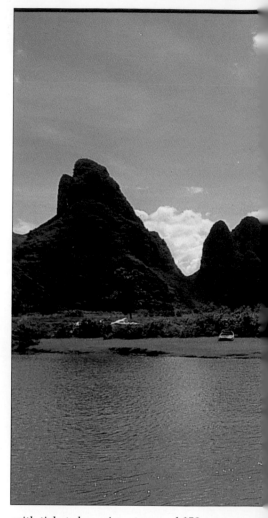

YANGSHUO

"The rivers and hills of Guilin are the most beautiful in China," says one of the many historic tributes to this karst region, "and those of Yangshuo's surpass Guilin." In fact, the prime reason for visiting Guilin is to take the six-hour, 80-km (50-mile) boat cruise to this small river village, winding down through a fairyland of mounds, towers, cones and craggy pinnacles soaring sharply out of a silken swathe of flat rice land. In the evenings, fleets of lantern-lit bamboo fishing rafts spread down the placid waters, the fishermen using tame cormorants to dive for the fish.

In times past, most travelers approached Yangshuo by cruise boat from Guilin, but with tickets hovering at around $50, many travelers opt for a minibus ride to Yangshuo, where inexpensive riverboat trips can be organized. If money is no object, CITS in Guilin will be only too happy to put you on one of their cruise boats to Yangshuo.

Getting Around

Yangshuo is small enough to stroll around, but for longer trips, bicycle is the only way to go. Bicycles (even mountain bikes nowadays) can be rented, and there are plenty of viewpoints outside the town where you can sit for hours with a picnic lunch and beer or wine and do what the poets of old did — contemplate the karst skyscrapers thrusting up out of the rice paddies and try to put it all into words.

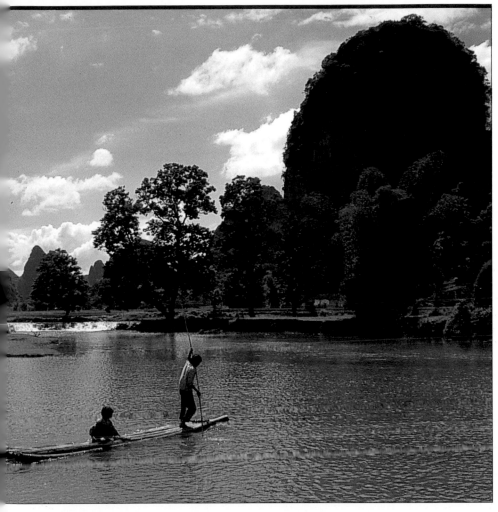

What to See and Do

Yangshuo has enough to see and do to keep you busy for three or four days at least. Many travelers become so bewitched by the place that they linger for a week or more. Yangshuo's pulling power derives not in small part from its small village atmosphere. How many places in China give you the opportunity to stay in a small community, hire a bicycle and explore the surrounding countryside, with its patchwork paddy fields and stunning karst peaks?

Yangshuo village itself has little to see, though the harbor area on the Li River is charming, and it's easy to while away an afternoon shopping for crafts. **Yangshuo Park** is a pleasant spot for a stroll if you don't mind paying the overpriced gate charge.

High on every visitor's agenda is **Moon Hill**, a one-hour bicycle trip out of Yangshuo. It's a steep walk up the hill, which earns its name from the massive moon-shaped hole near the summit, but the views are ample reward for the effort of the climb. Not far away, enterprising locals will take you on tours of cave systems with names like **Black Buddha Caves** and **Dragon Cave**.

The village of **Xingping** is another popular bike excursion. The village is on the bank of the Li River three hours downstream with even more impressive mountain scenery than Yangshuo. Xingping's **market** is the same day as Yangshuo's, but it's larger and worth a special trip to see (see CORMORANTS, CAVES AND LIMESTONE PEAKS in TOP SPOTS, PAGE 20).

A punter navigates the river Li at Yangshuo.

Where to Stay and Eat

Yangshuo is one of the few places in China where backpackers get some choice. In fact, Yangshuo is teeming with hotels charging as little as $2 to $3 for a bed in a dorm, and around $5 for a double with attached bathroom.

It's difficult to make recommendations in such a competitive and volatile market, but the long-runners are the **Zhuyang Hotel**, the **Sihai Hotel**, the **Yangshuo Youth Hostel**, the **Good Companion Holiday Inn** and the **Xilang Hotel**. There's little that differenti-

Mei You Café is another restaurant that packs in the diners: The name will make sense to anyone who's been in China more than a week or two. Be adventurous, duck into restaurants for afternoon tea and mid-morning snacks (everything is very inexpensive) and plan your evening meals accordingly.

How to Get There

Direct buses run from the Wuzhou ferry terminal (which has connections to Guangzhou and Hong Kong) to Yangshuo and take around five to six hours. From Guilin mini-

ates them, though the Zhuyang Hotel has always been slightly ahead of the competition in a shabby, try-as-try-can way.

The **Yangshuo Guesthouse** has been refurbished and is the only place in town offering comforts such as air-conditioning.

On the food front, Yangshuo is brimming with cafés that are not afraid to attempt anything. Don't be surprised to find *chow mein* rubbing shoulders with pizza on the menu. Ever-popular standbys such as banana pancakes and muesli feature on everyone's breakfast menus. As with the hotels, making recommendations is difficult. **Lisa's** deserves a mention for the fact that it's been running longer than virtually anywhere else and still manages to pull in the crowds. The

buses run all day (every 15 to 20 minutes) and take one and half hours.

NANNING

Once a poor nondescript port on the Yong River, Nanning has grown and flourished over the years to become the cultural and administrative capital of Guangxi-Zhuangzu autonomous region. There's very little to see or do in town, and most travelers who turn up here are on route to Pingxiang, the Vietnam border town. The Zhuang and Dong minorities inhabit Nanning in great numbers, but you're not likely to recognize them on the streets—they dress and look almost identical to their Han Chinese counterparts.

Background

Nanning has also revived one of the most exciting of all the cultural events in southern China, the **Dragonboat Festival**, staged on the fifth day of the fifth lunar month (usually June), which commemorates a statesman named Qu Yuan who drowned himself in a river in 295 BC as a protest against government corruption. He was so admired and respected for his virtue and fidelity, the story goes, that the villagers rowed out to where he'd disappeared and beat gongs and drums and dropped rice cakes to keep the fish away from his corpse.

Nowadays, slim shallow-draft "dragonboats," 40 m (130 ft) long and manned by up to 60 rowers, race up and down the rivers on Dragonboat Day with gongs and tom-toms beating the rhythm, spectators screaming encouragement and water exploding and cascading everywhere.

General Information

The head branch of the **Bank of China** is at 15 Gucheng Lu. **CITS** ((771) 280-4960 is at 40 Xinmin Lu. Go to CITS if you want to visit Vietnam but don't have a Vietnam visa.

What to See and Do

Nanning is a good walking and bicycling city with a lot of activity in its streets, especially in the cool of the evenings when the farmers and open-air market vendors move into the side-streets with their stalls. The main cultural attraction is the **Guangxi Museum**, east of the Yongjiang Hotel (see below), which features, among other relics and artifacts, more than 300 ancient bronze drums, the largest collection of its type in China. **Bailong Park** is an unassuming spot, but worth a short visit if you are in Nanning for a day.

Twenty kilometers (12.5 miles) northwest of the city are the **Yiling Caves**, a karst formation as interesting as Guilin's Reed Flute Cave with splendid stalactites and stalagmites. It winds for about one kilometer (around half a mile) under ground.

Where to Stay

LUXURY

The closest Nanning gets to luxury is the **Mingyuan Xindu Hotel** ((771) 283-0808 FAX (771) 283-0811, 38 Xinmin Lu, which is rated with four stars and lists its room rates in Hong Kong dollars. There is nothing particularly distinguished about this hotel, and unless you are the fastidious type, you will be better off going down market and saving yourself some money.

MID-RANGE

The **Yongjiang Hotel** ((771) 280-8123 FAX (771) 280-0535, 48 Jiangbin Lu, is in the south of town, near the Yongjiang Bridge, and is a serviceable mid-range hotel with air-conditioned doubles with attached bathroom costing from around $25 and up.

The **Yongzhou Hotel** ((771) 280-2338 FAX (771) 281-0951, 59 Xinmin Lu, is in a pleasant part of town, not far from Bailong Park. Room rates are similar to those at the Yongjiang.

INEXPENSIVE

As is often the case in China, the railway station area is the place for accommodation bargains. Some of the station hotels, such as the **Yingbin Hotel**, even have inexpensive dorm beds. The **Airways Hotel**, a five-minute walk up Chaoyang Lu away from the station, has functional singles and doubles for around $10.

How to Get There

There are direct air services between Nanning and Guangzhou, Kunming and Beijing and you can get there by train from Guilin. There are also special express train links with Beijing, and trains south to Zhanjiang, the mainland access point for Hainan Island.

ONWARD TO VIETNAM

From Nanning you can get to the Chinese border town of Pingxiang either by train or by bus. You will need to get a taxi or hitchhike to the Friendship Gate, which is not far from the Vietnamese town of Lang Son. Providing you set out early from Nanning there's no reason why you shouldn't be in Hanoi enjoying a cheap bottle of east European plonk and a fairly decent *coq-au-vin* by evening.

Smiles light the faces of a group of young Dong minority women in northern Guangxi.

Kunming and the West

KUNMING AND YUNNAN PROVINCE can be regarded as another radial tour center interlocking with the southern tour route from Guangzhou and, at the same time, opening up the western tour trail that runs north to Chongqing and Chengdu in Sichuan province, and the capital of Tibet, Lhasa.

YUNNAN PROVINCE

Yunnan, which translates into "South of the Clouds," is a mountainous subtropical province and a kind of Chinese Golden Triangle, bordering Myanmar (Burma), Laos and Vietnam. It shares four main rivers with these neighboring states, including the mighty Mekong, and has a certain cultural intercourse too through its minority hill tribes. The most prominent of these, the Dai, have their own tribal homeland, the Xishuangbanna autonomous district to the south of the province, which was opened up in 1986 to foreign travel without special permits. There are also Lisu, Lahu and Yao clans whose tribal domains spread as far as the northern border region of Thailand.

Originally part of a southern kingdom called Nanzhou, Yunnan was conquered by the Yuan Mongols in the thirteenth century and brought under imperial rule. It was the scene of a violent Moslem rebellion and an equally bloody government reprisal in the nineteenth century and then became a foothold for French incursions into China from their colonial bases in Laos and Vietnam. A legacy of the French presence is a narrow-gauge railway linking Kunming with Hanoi, which is now back in operation and is a popular overland route with backpackers.

In World War II Kunming became one of the bases of Chiang Kaishek's beleaguered nationalist government and swelled with refugees from the east, who were fleeing Japanese forces. The British and Americans kept the city alive with vast shipments of supplies from Burma, bringing them in along the famous Burma Road and by airlift from India.

KUNMING

Kunming easily rates as one of China's most charming provincial capitals. The year-round

Kunming and the West

balmy weather helps, no doubt. But it's more than just weather. As soon as you fly into Kunming (if that is how you arrive) you will notice the difference: Things happen slower here; there's space and light and, despite the arrival of modern architecture, oodles of character in the back streets. It's worth allotting a few days for Kunming and its surrounding attractions.

On a less positive note, many of the narrow older streets lined with traditional prewar "bamboo"-tiled and lattice-windowed homes and shops are under threat from de-

velopers. If you hire a bicycle or set off on a long walk, however, you can still enjoy the city's busy street life, its grand parks, open markets and nighttime food stalls. Kunming also has several interesting temples, and there are more in the Western Hills overlooking the vast, freshwater Lake Dian. It is also the access point for bus tours of the Stone Forest and air and bus transport to Dali and the tribal minorities of the Xishuangbanna region.

General Information

The **Bank of China** is at 444 Beijing Lu. The **International Post Office** is around a kilometer (about half a mile) south of here, also on Beijing Lu, and is the place to collect poste restante mail and send parcels.

Kunming has some overseas air connections, and foreign airlines represented in town include **Dragonair (** (871) 313-8592,

Winged roof OPPOSITE hangs over Kunming watchtower and canal bridge. ABOVE: Separated from bicycle traffic, buses and cars take the fast lane on Kunming Boulevard.

KUNMING

- Lianhua (Lotus) Pond
- Kunming North Station
- Huancheng Beilu
- Huancheng Beilu
- Chuanjin Lu
- Yuantong Zoo
- Yuantong Temple
- West Bus Station
- Cuihu (Green Lake) Park
- Panlong River
- Yuantong Jie
- Kunshi Lu
- Cuihu Nanlu
- CITS
- Renmin Xilu
- Wucheng Lu
- Qingnian Lu
- Beijing Lu
- Renmin Donglu
- Changchun Lu
- Huancheng
- Daguan Jie
- Dongfeng Xilu
- Zhengyi Lu
- Nantaiqiao
- Dongfeng Donglu
- Baita Lu
- Daguan Lu
- Daguan River
- Yunnan Provincial Museum
- Huancheng
- Beijing Restaurant
- Lu
- Donglu Lu
- Xilu
- West Temple Pagoda
- Jinbi Lu
- Tuodong Lu
- Jinbi Xilu
- East Temple Pagoda
- East Bus Station
- Dongsi Jie
- Beijing Lu
- Minhang Lu
- Haigeng Lu
- Huancheng Nanlu
- (Panlong River)
- Jinzhi River
- Chengdu – Kunming Railway
- Guiyang – Kunming Railway
- Kunming Railway Station
- N
- 500m

Golden Dragon Hotel, 575 Beijing Lu, **SilkAir** ((871) 316-6450, Holiday Inn Hotel, 25 Dongfeng Lu, and **Thai Airways** ((871) 313-3315, King World Hotel, 28 Beijing Lu. For domestic flights contact **CAAC** ((871) 313-7465, 146 Dongfeng Donglu.

CITS ((871) 313-2895 has its office at 220 Huancheng Lu, but unless you are in Kunming on a tour, they probably won't have much to offer you.

Getting Around

Bicycle is the best vehicle for sightseeing in Kunming. Both the Kunming and Camellia hotels (see WHERE TO STAY, below) rent them.

What to See and Do

Green Lake Park (Cuihu Park) is a landscaped cultural park and leisure area with attractive gardens and traditional halls and pavilions set around ornamental pools. It's a good place to meet locals and watch them rowing on the lake, rollerskating and photographing each other. There are often art and crafts exhibitions in the grounds and outside, and at weekends the adjacent street is full of market stalls, ice cream vendors, "sugar sculptors" who fashion elaborate filigrees of dragons, butterflies and other subjects out of thin strands of hot toffee, shooting galleries, paper silhouette artists and even old fairground "Test Your Strength" machines.

Southwest of the park at the main traffic circus at **Dongfeng Xilu**, **Daguan Jie** and **Renmin Xilu**, you can watch minority tribespeople arriving in town to sell their produce; and at night, alongside the Yunnan Arts and Crafts Store, the street turns into one of the most colorful and clamorous open-air eating places to be encountered anywhere in China.

East of the Green Lake Hotel, on Yuantong Jie, you'll find the **Yuantong Monastery**, constructed in the Yuan dynasty between 1301 and 1320 and featuring a huge, ornately sculptured gateway, an elegant triple-arched stone bridge, an eight-sided pavilion and spectacular Buddha images in the main hall. It's another excellent place to study the religious liberalization that's occurring now in China — the brisk back-to-business reverence with which the older matrons plant their

joss sticks and kowtow to the images and altars. Another easily accessible cultural attraction is the **Golden Temple**, which lies about seven kilometers (four miles) northeast of Kunming and can be reached by bicycle or a № 10 bus. It was built in the Ming dynasty and became the summer residence of a Manchu military turncoat, General Wu Sangui, who was sent south in 1659 to put down a rebellion and set himself up as a rebel warlord instead.

THE BAMBOO TEMPLE

The most fascinating temple you'll find is by far the **Qiongzhu Si (Bamboo Monastery)** about 12 km (7.5 miles) northwest of

Kunming and the West

Kunming. It's recognized as the first Chan (or Zen) monastery to be built in Yunnan province, but the original Tang dynasty buildings burned down and were replaced in the fifteenth century. During another facelift between 1883 and 1889 the Sichuan sculptor Li Guangxiu was commissioned to decorate one of the halls with images of the 500 *arhats*, or immortal beings commanded to remain on earth and protect the laws of Buddhism.

Li and five assistants produced a lifelike but bizarre and even Boschian human tableau, filling the walls of the hall, that was later condemned as a sick caricature of some of the important personalities of the time. Thankfully, no one doubted the artistry enough to have it destroyed, and today it ranks amongst China's most impressive cultural relics.

To get to the Bamboo Monastery you take a bus from outside the Yunnan Hotel on Dongfeng Lu. The journey takes around 30 minutes.

LAKE DIAN

For a rewarding full day's excursion from Kunming, and one that combines physical exercise, fresh air and cultural interest, take a № 6 bus from the Xiaoximen bus depot near the traffic circus just down from the Green Lake Hotel (see WHERE TO STAY, below) and head out to the **Western Hills** and **Lake Dian**. You can also take bus № 4 from the **Yuantong Temple** to **Daguan Park** at the lake's northernmost point and from there take a boat cruise, departing at 8 AM, to Haikou, passing under the sharply rising hillsides which are called Sleeping Beauty because their contours are said to resemble a maiden at rest.

From the № 6 bus terminal the road winds upward through forested slopes to provide panoramic views of Lake Dian — the second largest freshwater lake in China — with its spreading thickets of fish traps and elegant square-sailed cargo junks that flutter lazily like white moths down its main channel. The road winds higher and higher, and there are several interesting temples and grottoes along the way — the eleventh century **Hua-**

Abbot of Bamboo Monastery, Kunming.

ting Temple, the biggest around Kunming, the Ming dynasty **Taihua Temple** with its magnificently grotesque door gods, and the **Sanqingge Temple**, a temple pavilion and former country villa built in the Yuan dynasty and later turned into a Daoist place of worship.

At the top of the climb you'll find the **Longmen (Dragon Gate)** complex of grottoes and pavilions set high in a cliff face and commanding another panoramic view of the lake. Dragon Gate was built some two centuries ago in the reign of the Qing emperor Qianlong. The paths and caves took 72 years to hack out of the rock, and then a sculptor named Zhu Jiage spent another eight years fashioning the various images that adorn the main cave, including a large statue of the god

of literature. One day, so the story goes Zhu was shaping a pen-brush in the statue's hand when it snapped off. He was so mortified that he hurled himself from the precipice to his death.

You can finish off your tour of the Western Hills by climbing down to the lake itself. Below Dragon Gate there's a steep pathway that zigzags down to a sleepy fishing village right at the water's edge. From there you can stroll out along a causeway to a narrow channel and rest a while watching the sailing junks pass through. There's a sampan ferry there that is usually packed with day trippers and their bicycles being poled across the narrow neck of water. On the other side you can walk about a kilometer (just over half a mile) to Haigeng Beach and climb on board a Nº 44 bus for your trip back to Kunming.

THE STONE FOREST

Everyone who goes to Kunming goes to the Stone Forest (Shilin), a bizarre mushroom patch of fungus-shaped gray rocks that are believed to have been formed and sculpted by two natural forces — the earth's crust pushing upward and the wind and rain eroding the bared limestone outcrops. They are quite a remarkable spectacle, and what is also remarkable about a visit there is the tenacity with which hordes of colorfully-costumed souvenir hawkers, mostly women and girls of the Sanyi, a clan of the Yi minority tribe, will try to sell you ornately embroidered "hill tribe" bags, purses and other items.

Kunming and the West

Although the Stone Forest is interesting, there's a truly fascinating attraction around the small lake at the forest's entrance — the **Five Tree Village** with rustic old mud-brick homes featuring "horned" roofs and traditional doorways, wandering pigs, goats, donkeys and other livestock and, in the autumn and winter, huge bunches of corn hanging high in the trees above the homes to dry.

There are various ways to get to the Stone Forest, but the easiest and least expensive way is to book a ticket at the long-distance bus station. The journey will take around three hours, which means you should catch the first bus of the day; it leaves at 7:30 AM. Most Kunming hotels run tours out to the Stone Forest, but these involve time-consuming pit stops at souvenir shops and minor attractions.

The old French narrow-gauge line, which runs all the way to Hanoi, provides access to the Stone Forest via Yiliang. Buses from Yiliang to the Stone Forest take just 45 minutes but are infrequent, making this combination of train and bus an inconvenient travel option.

Where to Stay

LUXURY

Kunming's premiere luxury hotel is the **Holiday Inn Kunming ℂ** (871) 316-5888 FAX (871) 313-5189, 25 Dongfeng Donglu. It has all the amenities you'd expect — restaurants, travel services, health center, a popular disco and so on — and also has a central location.

At other luxury hotels around town expect standards to be slightly patchy. The **Green Lake Hotel ℂ** (871) 515-5788 FAX (871) 515-3286, 6 Cuihu Nanlu, has a superb location overlooking Green Lake Park. Having started out its days as a government guesthouse, it now offers four-star accommodation in a new extension. The Chinese restaurants here are excellent.

Borderline mid-range to luxury accommodation, with starting rates of around $80, is available at the **King World Hotel ℂ** (871) 313-8888 FAX (871) 313-1910, 28 Beijing Lu,

Lanterns and pavilions at eventide in Green Lake Park.

and at the **Golden Dragon Hotel** ((871) 313-3015 FAX (871) 313-3781, 575 Beijing Lu.

MID-RANGE

The **Green Lake Hotel** (see above) has excellent mid-range rooms in its original guesthouse section, now refurbished. Staying here gives you access to the hotel's first class amenities, excellent restaurants and of course you are just a hop, skip and a jump from one of Kunming's tourist highlights, the Green Lake Park.

The **Kunming Hotel** ((871) 316-2063 FAX (871) 318-8220, 145 Dongfeng Donglu, is a sprawling place with a wide variety of rooms to choose from. The north wing sports luxury prices, but rooms in the South Wing are very good value at around $50. This is one of those hotels that guests rarely have to leave, with shops, amusement arcades, travel agents and restaurants.

The **Camellia Hotel** ((871) 316-8000, Dongfeng Donglu, has some reasonably priced mid-range rooms, with air-conditioning and attached bathroom.

INEXPENSIVE

The **Camellia Hotel** (see above) is where you'll find most backpacking travelers. The dormitories here have been a fixture on the China circuit for as long as anyone can remember. The other popular budget option is the **Kunhu Hotel** ((871) 316-1704, 44 Beijing Lu, where staff — whose surliness is celebrated the length and breadth of China — will sometimes admit to the existence of dormitory beds.

Where to Eat

Most of the good hotels have excellent Chinese restaurants, and prices that are surprisingly cheap. Elsewhere, there's a wide range of restaurants and cuisine to choose from. The **Yingjiangdou Moslem Restaurant**, 360 Changchun Lu, serves excellent Hui minority cuisine — mainly mutton and beef dishes — and there's even an English menu. It's in a teeming old-style district in which you can stroll at night and gaze upon lanterns glowing softly through the distinctive latticework of the tenement buildings.

The busy commercial district around Dongfeng Xilu is a good hunting ground for restaurants. Look for Xi'angyun Jie, where the long-running **Beijing Restaurant**, at № 77, does fabulous northern style cuisine at reasonable prices. The Sichuan-style **Chuanwei** is on the same street, as are a host of other snack vendors and small restaurants. Not much English is spoken here, but if you're willing to be adventurous, you'll undoubtedly come up with some delicious rewards.

Not far from here, on Nantong Jie, is the **Yunnan Across the Bridge Noodle Restaurant**. "Across the bridge noodles" (*guoqiaomian*) is Kunming's most famous local dish and you'll find it served with much pomp and ceremony at all the major hotels in town. But for the real thing, in down-to-earth plebeian surroundings (and at rock-bottom prices), this restaurant is the place to go. The noodle dish itself is a winter dish in which a thin film of oil over a bowl of broth keeps the heat in and allows condiments to cook — you will hear the story of how it came into being countless times if you visit Kunming.

How to Get There

Kunming is connected with frequent flights from all the major Chinese cities. Dragonair flies from Hong Kong, SilkAir from Singapore, and Thai from Bangkok. Daily trains run there from Chongqing and Guilin via the junction of Guiyang. Getting a sleeper on the Shanghai–Kunming Express will normally require at least three-days advance booking.

Onward to Vietnam

With the proper paperwork — you will need a Vietnam visa with Lao Cai indicated as the port of entry — it is possible to travel by train from Kunming to Hanoi. Trains running on this narrow-gauge, French-constructed railway take around 18 hours either way.

DALI

The old walled city of Dali lies around seven to eight hours by bus to the west of Kunming, and has become one of the most popular destinations in all of Yunnan. There's no denying the beauty of the place. Nestled between the turquoise Erhai Lake and snow-capped Cangshan mountain range, Dali is one of the most picturesque corners of China.

Dali was originally the capital of a kingdom ruled by the Bai minority tribe until it was conquered by the Yuan Mongols in the thirteenth century and absorbed into their empire. In many respects, the this town still rests somewhere in the Middle Ages, trapped in timewarp of traditional winged-roof and neatly whitewashed homes, an encompassing wall and old town gates that are still the main access for a daily parade of farmers from the surrounding countryside with their horses and carts. Bird cages hang in the narrow streets and alleys, householders can

What to See and Do

It's easy to while away a day wandering the back streets of Dali, shopping for souvenirs and ducking into the travelers cafés that line Huguo Lu, the street locals refer to as "Foreigner's Street."

Most of the attractions are out of town. If you rent a bicycle (as always, recommended), you can ride down to the **Erhai Lake** in about 10 minutes, where you will find the small village of Caicun. From here ferries go to the villages of Wase and Haidong (check with locals for times in Dali before setting out).

actually be seen scrubbing the outsides of their homes. Things are changing fast here, however. New hotels are springing up, and the construction of an airport has turned this formerly sleepy town into a major tourist destination.

When to Go

The best time to go to Dali is in April, when Bai tribespeople from all over the region flock to the **Third Moon Fair**. Next best is June, when the town stages a spectacular **Dragonboat Festival**. At other times the Bai pour into Dali every Saturday for the open-air markets, and another market is held every Monday at **Shaping**, two kilometers (one and a quarter miles) away.

Dali is the sort of place that if you sit around in a café for a short while you will meet people who are doing interesting things, such as heading off on hikes or extended trips into the country. A popular hike is up to **Zhonghe Temple**, to the west of Dali. It's not an easy walk, but when you get up there you are rewarded with stunning views.

Where to Stay and Eat

There are actually two Dalis, a point which causes some confusion. Old Dali is the place to stay, not New Dali, which is a sprawling uninteresting town, also known as Xiaguan.

Remarkable Stone Forest (Shilin) was formed by massive upheaval and erosion of limestone.

The top hotel in Old Dali is the **Jinhua Hotel** ((872) 267-3343, which is right on the corner of Huguo Lu and Fuxing Lu, in the center of town. The **Red Camellia Hotel**, 32 Huguo Lu, also known as Nº 2 Guest House, is just up the road, close to all the restaurants and has a wide range of rooms, from dormitories to basic singles and doubles. It is often full. The **Old Dali Inn** ((872) 267-0382, Bo'ai Lu, is a relative newcomer, but is fast becoming a favorite with everyone from backpackers to mid-range travelers. The Bai-style rooms and flower gardens are a hit.

As in Yangshuo, that other backpackers' haven, it's difficult to make recommendations for restaurants in Dali. Follow the crowds initially and then do some exploring. Huguo Lu is the place to start your search. The **Yunnan Café**, once known as the Coca Cola Café, has been pulling in the crowds for its pizzas and burritos for years and is still popular. The café has rooftop dining and a modest book exchange. **Marley's Café** is legendary, as is **Café de Jack**, which once went by the less ostentatious name, Jack's Café. There are many more worth trying.

How to Get There

Dali has its own air port, and flights turn up four times a week from Kunming. Bus transport fans out from Dali to Baoshan and Dehong, a minority region on the Myanmar border, and to Lijiang. To get to Xishuangbanna, you will need to go to Baoshan first.

LIJIANG

If you've visited Dali it may be hard to believe, but Lijiang is equally, if not more, beautiful. The new town is just what the name suggests, but the old quarter is a fascinating maze of canals and old buildings. On February 2, 1996 an earthquake measuring around seven on the Richter scale struck Lijiang, killing approximately 300 people. The town has bounced back from the disaster, and most of the buildings damaged have been faithfully restored. The surrounding valley is a treat to explore, with many Tibetan monasteries, some beautiful frescoes, and, presiding over it all, **Jade Dragon Snow Mountain**.

Lijiang is famous above all as the home of the Naxi minority. Much has been made of the fact that the Naxi were (perhaps in some remote areas still are) a matriarchal society. You will see very little evidence of this in Lijiang and its surrounding villages, but for those willing to go farther afield the Naxi are still a matriarchal tribe by all accounts. In the Naxi world, women own all property and they choose their mates. Their written language is, like Chinese, pictographic.

Good books on the area include *The Ancient Nakhi Kingdom of Southwest China* by Joseph Rock, a pioneering anthropologist, who lived in the area from the early 1920s until 1949, and who is still remembered by some locals. Easier reading, and giving an insight into the man himself and the Naxi is *In China's Border Provinces: The Turbulent Career of Joseph Rock, Botanist-Explorer* by J.B. Sutton — essential reading for anyone who has an interest in the region.

What to See and Do

Travelers use Lijiang as a base from which to do treks and make day trips into the surrounding countryside. The immediate attractions are Lijiang's monasteries, which belong to the *kagyupa* (red hat) sect of Tibetan Buddhism. You won't see many monks nowadays, but the monasteries are often scenically located and command stunning views. **Yufeng Monastery**, at the foot of **Mount Yulongxue** (Jade Dragon Snow), about 20 km (12.4 miles) north of Lijiang, is particularly worth a visit and can be combined with a trip to **Baisha**.

Baisha is just a small village. It's hard to believe that it was once capital of the Naxi kingdom, before Kublai Khan made it part of his Yuan empire in the fourteenth century. Baisha's main attractions are its frescoes executed in Tibetan style with Tibetan Buddhist, Muslim, Taoist and Dongba elements. They illustrate well the mixed lines along which Naxi religion developed as a result of its situation as a crossroads for Mongols from the north, Tibetans from the west, Turko-Mongols from the northwest and Chinese from the south and east. The frescoes can be seen at the **Dabaoji Palace**, **Dading Pavilion**

A ferryman on Erhai Lake, Dali.

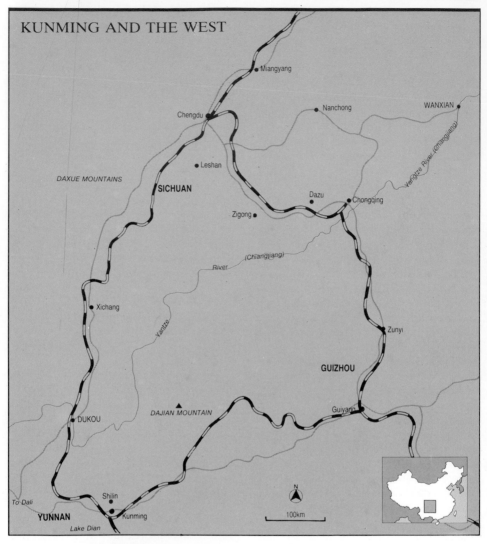

KUNMING AND THE WEST

and **Liuli Temple**. Baisha's other attraction is Dr. Ho, a local herbal doctor who has been made famous by visiting travel writers such as Bruce Chatwin. He will no doubt hail you on the street and sell you some of his miraculous herbal tea.

Tiger Leaping Gorge is one of the world's deepest, and the two-day trek through it has passed into backpacker legend. Overnight accommodation — extremely basic — is available midway at a small village that somehow has ended up with the name Walnut Grove. Check in the cafés of Lijiang on the latest details about doing the trek. Don't do the trek alone — a number of individual trekkers have gone missing over the years.

Unfortunately a road has been cut through the gorge recently.

Back in Lijiang itself, evenings are enlivened by performances of the local **Naxi orchestra**, conducted by Mr. Xuan Ke. His explanations tend to ramble, but the performances themselves are captivating.

Where to Stay and Eat

As the name suggests, the **Lijiang Grand Hotel** ((8891) 212-8888, a Chinese–Thai joint venture, is Lijiang's top hotel. The **Guluwan Hotel** in the north of town has inexpensive doubles with attached bathroom, while the nearby **N⁰ 2 Guesthouse** is the favored haunt of backpackers. Another popular budget

174

hotel is the **Red Sun Hotel** ((8891) 212-1018, which is nearly opposite the Guluwan.

The so-called Mao Square, with its impressive Mao statue, was once home to a lively café scene, but the action has moved to the square in the old quarter. Check to see whether **Mama Fu's**, a long-running and very popular café on the Mao Square, has reopened.

Yinjiu has a 500-year history and has a lychee-based wine tasting like a medium sweet sherry. Try it.

How to Get There

Lijiang has its own airport these days, and flights connect it with Kunming four times a week. Flights are frequently full, so book early.

Buses run daily between Lijiang and Dali and take around five hours. Minibuses do the trip slightly quicker. Buses to Kunming can take up to 15 hours, a marathon trip. For onward travel to Sichuan, buses run between Lijiang and Jinjiang, a town on the Kunming–Chengdu rail route. It can take up to nine hours to get to Jinjiang, an uninspiring town just over the Sichuan border, by bus.

XISHUANGBANNA

This special autonomous prefecture, in the south of Yunnan province bordering Burma (Myanmar) and Laos, is the heartland of the Dai minority. They are Buddhists and are famous for their elaborate Burmese-style temples and their homes, which are built on stilts, leaving room underneath for boats and livestock, and their traditional dress — the women wearing an exotic combination of colorful turbans, silver bracelets and necklaces and long slim ankle-length sarongs.

The Dai are also renowned for their spectacular rites and festivals, and there's hardly a tourism documentary on Chinese television that doesn't promote their tribal dances, with their blaze of strange animist costumes and headdresses — particularly their ceremonial Peacock Dance. The best time to see this ritual performed is in April, at the time of the **Dai New Year**, when it's presented along with Dragonboat races and the Water Festival. In this day-long Mardi Gras — also a feature of the festive calendar in Thailand —

the revelers drench each other with water in a very enjoyable "wringing in" of the New Year.

Xishuangbanna is not only popular with Western travelers, it has also become a mini-Thailand for Chinese tourists, who find the combination of tropical heat, colorful minorities and spicy food every bit as exciting as Westerners do.

JINGHONG

Jinghong lies on the Lancang Jiang, or Mekong River, about 29 km (18 miles) from the Burmese border, and acts as the gateway to the rest of Xishuangbanna. There's little to do around town, except enjoy long lazy meals and watch some local Dai dancing in the evenings.

Those with time should make a side-trip to **Menghan** (also known as Ganlanba), a village just two hours by bicycle from Jinghong with some splendid nearby *wats* (temples). Menghan has some basic Dai-style accommodation.

Where to Stay and Eat

There are plenty of hotels around Jinghong, but none has the pedigree or the character of the **Banna Hotel** ((691) 212-3679, 37 Jialian Lu. Renovations and additions have stripped it of some its charm, but for around $20 to $30 you can get a comfortable air-conditioned double with views of the Mekong. The **Tai Garden Hotel** ((691) 212-3888 FAX (691) 212-6060, 8 Nongxin Nanlu, is Jinghong's luxury option. The **Banna Mansion Hotel** ((691) 212-5100, corner of Jinghong Nanlu and Jinghong Xilu, right in the center of town, is another mid-range to luxury hotel.

Budget travelers all head to Manting Lu, in the south of Jinghong, where a string of very basic Dai-run hostels provide beds for around $2 per night and offer home-cooked meals that many remember for years afterwards as among the most delicious on their entire China trip.

BEYOND JINGHONG

Trips to other destinations such as **Menghai, Menghun, Jingzhen, Nannuoshan, Damenglong** and **Menyang** can be arranged through CITS (in the Banna Hotel) or the Tai Garden Hotel or you can strike out on your own by local bus. Distances are not great in Xishuangbanna, which means that most towns and villages can be reached in two or three hours of traveling. Most villages have basic accommodation.

SICHUAN PROVINCE

CHONGQING

Chongqing is a grimy, hilly industrial city at the confluence of the Jialing and Yangtze rivers that is smog-bound for more than a hundred days of the year and in the summer is so fiercely hot that it is known as one of the Three Furnaces of the Yangtze. Having said that, there are three good reasons why it should be included in any western travel itinerary.

First, it has one of the most architecturally stunning hotels in China, the **Renmin Hotel**, with its magnificent triple-eaved "Temple of Heaven" domed auditorium and huge columns along its two residential wings. Secondly, the city is the western starting point for the Yangtze River ferry services that cut right across the heart of China. Thirdly, you go to Chongqing to get to Dazu (see below), one of the four most famous centers of Buddhist cave sculpture in China.

Although it has a long past, Chongqing's contemporary history is much more relevant to its current appeal. It was the headquarters of Chiang Kaishek and his Guomindang forces during Japan's relentless drive to occupy all of China in the 1930s and suffered devastating Japanese bombing as a result. A legacy of that violent period is a network of tunnels and shelters cut into its many hillsides, some of which have since been turned into small factories. At one point the city was a command post for both nationalist and communist forces in their brief military pact against the Japanese. The communists based their command at Red Crag Village on the Jialing River 10 km (six miles) from the city center, and Zhou Enlai and his wife lived in house Nº 13 and also at 50 Zengjiayan in the city itself.

General Information
Dragonair ((811) 280-3380 is in the Holiday Inn Yangtze Chongqing hotel (see below). **CAAC** ((811) 386-2970 is on the corner of Zhongshan Lu and Renmin Lu.

The main branch of the **Bank of China** ((811) 383-4344 is on Minzu Lu in the city center.

CITS ((811) 385-0188 is at 175 Renmin Lu. They can help with Yangtse cruise bookings.

What to See and Do
Being hilly, Chongqing isn't the sort of city you want to bicycle around. The buses are also particularly crowded. Thankfully, most of the city's attractions lay within the narrow peninsula that make up central Chongqing and are easily reached on foot. A stroll along the southern bank of the **Jialing River**, past the main bridge, will take you over clusters of European-style rooftops and homes that date back to Chongqing's days as a Treaty Port. If you head down Minzu Lu toward Chaotianmen Dock at the eastern end of the peninsula, you'll find the **Liberation Monument**, which is a huge clock tower, and, close to there, the interesting and very ancient (over 1,000 years, it is said) **Luohan Temple**, which has an impressive collection of 500 terracotta *arhats* and an imposing seated golden Buddha. The temple also has an inexpensive vegetarian restaurant of a very high standard. The Liberation Monument is also the center of the city's main commercial and tourist district, and around it you'll find department stores, crafts shops, several restaurants and the Xinhua Bookstore, where you can buy a good English-language city map.

Taking Zourong Lu southwest toward the Yangtze River, you climb steps toward one of the city's urban ridges and, on the other side, you'll find a small recreational area where the city's old-timers gather to gamble in the afternoons and show off their caged birds. Below the park there's a big roller-skating rink where you can watch the youngsters enjoying themselves. Another interesting strolling spot is a bustling open-air market that tumbles down a steep "ladder street" toward the railway station, and which you can reach by going south on Zhongshan Lu from the Renmin Hotel and crossing over to it from the giant Shancheng Cinema. On the way down Zhongshan Lu you might call into **Pipashan Park**, where you will find the **Chonqing Museum** and a pagoda at the summit with good views over the city.

Where to Stay
LUXURY

The remarkable **Chongqing People's Hotel** ((811) 385-1421 FAX (811) 385-2076, 173 Renmin Lu, is by no means a luxury hotel, but it's the only place in China where you

can stay in a palace. If that sounds like a contradiction, let's just say that the rooms don't live up to the promise of the hotel's imposing exterior. Room rates start at around $50.

For true luxury standards the **Holiday Inn Yangtze Chongqing** ((811) 280-3380 FAX (881) 280-0884, 15 Nanping Beilu, is the best bet, though it's location on the southern bank of the Yangtze River leaves you rather a long way from the hustle and bustle of downtown Chongqing.

MID-RANGE

The **Chung King Hotel** ((811) 343-9301 FAX (811) 384-3085, 41–43 Xinhua Lu, is a joint-venture operation near Chaotianmen Dock.

The facilities include post and telecommunications, clinic, taxis, foreign exchange and a small gift shop. There is also a shuttle service. The **Chongqing Guesthouse** ((811) 384-5888 FAX (811) 383-0643 235 Minsheng Lu, is another good mid-range choice. It has a wide-range of rooms and prices and also has a couple of very good Chinese restaurants.

INEXPENSIVE

Huixianlou Hotel ((811) 384-5101, close to the Liberation Monument, has long been popular with budget travelers for its seven-bed dormitory rooms, which have panoramic views.

How to Get There
Being a junction city, Chongqing is accessible directly by air from virtually every airport in China. There are direct trains to Beijing and Chengdu, and if you're approaching on the clockwise route from the south you travel directly on a dog-leg route via Guiyang.

YANGTZE RIVER FERRIES

The most popular Yangtze trip is to go downriver from Chongqing to Wuhan. The three-day deluxe cruises offered by CITS and CTS (see TAKING A TOUR in YOUR CHOICE, page 66) take in the three gorges—Qutang, Wuxia and Xiling — with several scenic and historical stops along the way. However, once you get beyond the gorges to the town of Yichang (Hubei province), the Yangtze becomes a wide dun-colored sweep of river with an occasional passing cargo boat or string of barges and relative nondescript river cities.

Steamers go as far as Shanghai and tickets can be obtained in Chongqing and Wuhan through CITS or directly from the booking office on the dock (see also WUHAN, page 270).

DAZU

From the tourist's point of view, Dazu is Chongqing's *raison d'être*. Along with remote Dunhuang, this small town has China's most impressive collection of Buddhist cave sculptures.

Mechanical dragon breathes "fire" at Chongqing New Year fair.

Dazu Buddhist Caves

To get to the **Dazu Grottoes** you continue up from the main street and continue on out of the town, climbing toward **Bei Shan (North Hill)** which has a pagoda set dramatically on top of it. If you climb directly on up to the pagoda you'll find something of immediate interest — three beautiful Song dynasty Buddha images sitting side-by-side in the courtyard of a farmhouse. The cave sculptures themselves — among some 50,000 of them dating back to the Tang and Song reigns and found at 45 sites scattered

throughout this region — are back down the hill from the pagoda; but while they're interesting, and while Bei Shan offers stunning aerial views of the surrounding ricelands, this is really not what you've come to Dazu to see.

Baoding Shan (Treasure Peak Mountain) is what you've come here for. It lies 15 km (nine miles) northeast of Dazu and you can get a bus there from the town's main square. Baoding is a huge horseshoe-shaped grotto, something like an amphitheater, lined with more than 15,000 statues, engravings and bas-relief images. They were started during the Southern Song reign and took from 1179 to 1249 to complete. Most of the sculptures refer to epic Buddhist stories, and many depict animals and rural life and the stages of childhood, but they are dominated by two magnificent examples of Buddhist art — the ornate **Thousand-Hands-Thousand-Eyes Bodhisattva**, which you'll find in one of the pavilions, and a huge 31-m (102-ft) recumbent **Sakyamuni Buddha (The Sleeping Buddha)**, which fills one

entire wall of the grotto. This one dramatic and inspiring sculpture explains why Baoding is rated with Dunhuang, Luoyang and Datong in the immense legacy of Buddhist art.

Where to Stay

Dazu has a couple of hotels. The **Dazu Guesthouse** is a plush mid-range place that has been renovated to meet the needs of affluent tour group travelers. The **Beishan Hotel** is cheaper, though a night here is unlikely to rate high on your list of memorable China experiences afterwards.

How to Get There

Dazu lies 160 km (100 miles) northwest of Chongqing. Buses run approximately every half hour from the Chongqing long-distance bus station (next door to the railway station), and take around three hours.

CHENGDU

Chengdu, the Sichuan provincial capital, has had many names in the past. During the Han dynasty it was called the City of Brocade for the beautiful silks that it produced. In the tenth century it was the City of Hibiscus for the flowers planted along its main wall. Nowadays its name translates into Perfect Metropolis and it is an important industrial city that has somehow managed to retain an atmosphere of clean, well-ordered and expansive leisure, with wide boulevards, interesting monuments and temples and fine parks.

Chengdu is also another vital access city for tourists, it is the most convenient departure point for the exciting new frontier of travel in China, Lhasa and Tibet, and the gateway to one of the nation's most extraordinary Buddhist relics, the Grand Buddha at Leshan.

The city itself features another remarkable but more contemporary relic, a towering, centrally located statue of the Great Helmsman of the Chinese Revolution, Mao Zedong. Chengdu also has a somewhat important link with the post-Maoist society as well: Its province was the birthplace of Deng Xiaoping, who steered China to its current prosperity after the death of Mao.

General Information
Dragonair ((28) 675-5555 is in the lobby of the Sichuan Hotel (see below). **China Southwest Airlines** ((28) 666-5911 is opposite the Jinjiang Hotel on Renmin Nanlu.

The main branch of the **Bank of China** is in the center of town at 60 Shuwa Bei Sanjie, but money can be changed at most hotels. There is a **Consulate General of the United States** ((28) 558-9642 at 4 Lingshiguan Lu, which is on the fourth sector of Renmin Nanlu.

Getting Around
Chengdu is flat, spaciously laid out and thus another good bicycling town, and you can rent bicycles at a number of places close to the Traffic Hotel (see below). Taxis are easy to flag down, though not much English is spoken by drivers.

What to See and Do
The first stop on any sightseeing tour around Chengdu is the five-story **Exhibition Hall**, a giant department store, and the towering **statue of Mao Zedong** that looms over the city's busiest traffic circus at the junction of Renmin Nanlu and Renmin Xilu/Remin Donglu north of the Jinjiang Hotel. From there you can bicycle over to the **Wuhou Temple**, which is in the southern suburb of Nanjiao across the Jinjiang River (or Nanhe as this part of the river is also called) to the southwest of the Jinjian hotel. Built in honor of Zhuge Liang, a brilliant military strategist and advisor to Emperor Liu Bei of the Three Kingdoms Period (220–265), the temple features the tombs of both men, several shrine halls built in the much more recent Qing dynasty and a nearby lake and parkland with pavilions and a pleasant tea house.

Another pleasant temple park is **Wanjiang Lou (River Viewing Pavilion)**, which is dedicated to the Tang dynasty poetess Xue Tao and lies to the southeast near Sichuan University. Five kilometers (three miles) to the west of the city center, following the road from Xinximen, you can reach the famed **Thatched Cottage of Du Fu**, where one of the most illustrious poets of the Tang reign retired after serving in various official posts and wrote some 240 melancholic works that

summed up his most vivid impression of all those years of official duties — the suffering of the people.

If you venture beyond Chengdu's western gate, heading north to the Ximen Bus Station, cross a creek and then turn left into the back streets, you'll find the **Temple of Wang Jian**, a Tang dynasty general who proclaimed himself emperor of Shu in the tenth century. The central coffin chamber has interesting wall carvings of female musicians, dancers and musical instruments of that era, along with jade tablets, imperial seals and a carved stone portrait of Wang Jian himself.

Another popular spot is the **Wenshu (God of Wisdom) Monastery** which was built in the Tang reign and reconstructed in the seventeenth century and features a striking Tibetan Buddha image. Wenshu is worth a visit not only for its architecture and relics but also for a busy tea house within the grounds and the religious street life that goes on around its gates, with stalls loaded with devotional joss sticks, candles and fireworks.

If you have time to make a day of it, you could also bicycle about 18 km (11 miles) to the northeast of the city, out along Jiefang Beilu to the **Baoguang Si (Temple of Divine Light)**. It's a big monastery, founded in the ninth century and featuring a Qing dynasty Arhat Hall housing 500 clay sculptures of Buddhist immortals, including the Qing emperors Kangxi and Qianlong. Among the other treasures and relics there you'll find a Burmese white jade Buddha, paintings and calligraphy from the Ming and Qing reigns and a stone tablet engraved with hundreds of Buddha images.

Most of these cultural attractions — and others such as the ancient **Dujiangyan Irrigation System** (from the third century BC), 50 km (31 miles) northwest of Chengdu — are included in one-and two-day organized tours offered by CITS at the Jinjiang Hotel. Their tours also cover three popular destinations outside Chengdu: the **Su Dongpo Mansion** in Meishan, the mountain **Emeishan**, and one of China's most remarkable sights — the monolithic **Grand Buddha** at Leshan.

The huge sleeping Buddha dominates the cave sculptures at Baoding, near Dazu.

Where to Stay

LUXURY

Chengdu is well provided for in the luxury stakes. The **Jinjiang Hotel** ((28) 558-2222 FAX (28) 558-1849, 36 Second Section, Renmin Nanlu, is the granddaddy of Chengdu's tourist hotels, having hosted foreign guests since the pioneering days of China's open-door policy. Nowadays it is a vast, modern complex with Chinese, Western, and Korean restaurants, a business center, nightclub, and swimming pool.

The **Holiday Inn Crowne Plaza** ((28) 678-6666 FAX (28) 678-9789, 31 Zongfu Jie, is the most expensive hotel in town, and has all the amenities you will have come to appreciate if you've stayed in other Chinese Holiday Inns. The **Yinhe Dynasty Hotel** ((28) 661-8888 FAX (28) 662-4313, 99 Xiaxi Shuncheng Jie, is a luxury joint-venture with a good central location. It has the usual features — close to four hundred well appointed rooms and suites, a business center, swimming pool, recreational facilities, and restaurants offering Chinese and Western cuisine.

MID-RANGE

The **Sichuan Hotel** ((28) 666-1115 FAX (28) 666-5263, 31 Zongfu Road, is a good mid-range hotel, though definitely at the upper end of the category, with room rates starting at around $60. If you are looking for something less expensive, the **Jing Rong Hotel** ((28) 333-7878, Erhuan Beilu, up near the railway station, manages to provide reasonably comfortable doubles from around $30.

INEXPENSIVE

Like the nearby Jinjiang Hotel, in the luxury bracket, the **Traffic Hotel** ((28) 555-1017 FAX (28) 558-2777, 77 Linjiang Road, is a budget institution. Standards have improved over the years and rates have gone up accordingly, but it's still a popular option — the doubles with attached bathrooms and satellite television are a bargain at less than $20.

Where to Eat

Like Guangzhou, Chengdu is celebrated China-wide for its restaurants. Indeed, it is the best place in China — and thus the world — to sample Sichuan's justly celebrated cuisine.

Sichuan food is known mostly as the spicy arm of Chinese cuisine, but this is only part of the story. It is in fact a diverse cuisine, and has a whole armory of delicious (and occasionally mouth-numbing) sauces with which it converts the edible into the delectable. One special treat is Sichuan duck, which in many ways is more sophisticated than its Beijing counterpart. Sichuanese chefs have developed dozens of ways of preparing duck without the fat and grease of the Beijing variety, a famous recipe being Zhangcha duck, the masterpiece of a Qing dynasty chef, in which tea, camphor leaves and cypress twigs are used to flavor the skin and flesh. Another popular recipe is roast duck with a jelly made from the root of a taro. Yet another is savory and crisp duck in which the bird is first soaked in salt water, then smoked, steamed and fried and seasoned with prickly ash.

One of Chengdu's great attractions is the fact that the streets teem with snack shops and hole-in-the-wall restaurants that serve up the best of Sichuan cuisine at budget prices. Not much — if any — English is spoken in such places, however, and if you are only just finding your way into Chinese cuisine, it's probably a good idea to stick with the hotel restaurants initially. All the top hotels in town have outstanding Chinese restaurants, but the place to go is the **Rooftop Chinese Restaurant** at the Jinjiang Hotel.

Chengdu's most famous restaurant is the **Chengdu Restaurant** at 134 Shandong Dajie. In the comfortable dining area upstairs, you'll find an English menu that guides you

through most of the Sichuan repertoire. Some favorites you might consider trying include *gongbao jiding* (chicken, chilies and peanuts), *guoba roupian* ("crispy rice" and pork), *mapo doufu* (bean curd, pork and chilies — the quintessential Sichuan dish, say some), *yuxiang qiezi* (fish-flavored eggplant) and of course the aforementioned duck.

Sichuan is also renowned for its snacks — though this reputation is eclipsed in the West by Cantonese *dim sum*. **Long Chao Shou Special Restaurant**, on Xia Dong Dajie, has sampler courses which allow you to graze at random through the Elysian fields of Sichuan budget snack heaven.

At Leshan, visitors flock to the feet of the astounding 71-meter (230-ft)-high Grand Buddha which towers over the Min River.

Lastly, no trip to Chengdu is complete without a visit to a Sichuan tea house, as much an institution here as the pub is in Britain. Known as *chadian*, you will see them all over Chengdu, but mostly in parks. Just look for the tatty bamboo furniture and the clusters of animatedly gesticulating oldies. The **Renmin Teahouse** in the middle of Renmin Park is the biggest in town and a treat. Tea comes in bottomless pots and costs next to nothing.

Nightlife

There are several pubs directly across from the Jinjiang Hotel. They're worth mentioning as there is little non-karaoke entertainment in this part of the world, and they offer a good opportunity to fall into conversation with locals over a few drinks.

The **Jinjiang Theatre** on Huaxingzheng Jie provides visitors with a fabulous opportunity to see Sichuan opera, or *chuanju*. Some hotel tours will even arrange a backstage visit, an opportunity not to be passed up on any account.

How to Get There

You can reach Chengdu from all directions by air, with direct flights from Beijing, Guangzhou, Chongqing, Kunming, Guilin, Nanjing, Shanghai, Wuhan, Xi'an and Lhasa and Hong Kong. You can get there directly by train from Xi'an, Lanzhou and Beijing, and from Chongqing. (See LIJIANG, page 173, for information on the overland route between Sichuan and Yunnan provinces.)

LESHAN

Once a sleepy little town, Leshan has joined China's go-go race to economic reform and is busily transforming itself into an affluent small city. Who can blame it? After all, Leshan has one of the world's most impressive man-made sights, and with all those visitors — domestic and foreign alike — flocking in, one likes to look one's best.

Leshan dates back to the Tang reign and is set alongside sweeping river flats at the confluence of the Min, Qingyi and Dadu rivers about 165 km (102 miles) south of Chengdu. In the eighth century it was decided that something had to be done to control the dangerous torrents at this river meeting place and a monk named Haitong suggested that only a monumental spiritual force could possibly tame the waters. The result is the awesome 71-m (233-ft) sitting Buddha carved into the face of Mount Lingyun, right across the waters from Leshan.

The Grand Buddha

The Dafo (Grand Buddha) is so immense that 100 people can congregate on his head. You could fit a couple of football teams on his toes. When first built he was painted and gilded with gold leaf and a 13-story pavilion, or "Buddha House," protected him from the elements. That shelter was destroyed in the Ming reign, and since then the monolith has been totally exposed — but saved from serious erosion by an ingenious internal drainage system. You can climb all over the statue, view it from the Grand Buddha Temple alongside its head, or take a ferry trip from the Leshan Pier which will give you astonishing perspectives of its size from the river.

Unfortunately Dafo is in danger of collapsing due to soil erosion. An accumulation of water on his left side has also caused him to "bloat." He was entered into the UNESCO heritage listing in 1996, and Chinese and foreign experts are looking at ways to ensure that he doesn't bloat any more (or worse still, take a tumble into the river at his feet). This may mean that Dafo views are marred by scaffolding and drainage works when you visit. Ask for the latest news before making the trip.

Two-day package tours are widely available in Chengdu. These allow you an hour and a half at the Grand Buddha before rushing you on to the Su Mansion at Meishan followed a lot of hiking an overnight stop and at Mount Emei. You'd be better off doing the trip on your own and overnighting at Leshan. With more time on your hands you can study one of the world's greatest religious monuments from all angles, in your own good time.

Where to Stay

In town, top of the range is the **Jiazhou Hotel** ((833) 239-888. The **Nanlou Guesthouse** is above the Grand Buddha, next door to the

Grand Buddha Temple, a very agreeable place to be based. The **Leshan Education Hotel** ((833) 234-257 is the most popular spot with budget travelers.

How to Get There
Buses do the trip from Chengdu to Leshan in as little as three hours. Buses leave from Chengdu's Xinnanmen bus station, near the Jinjiang Hotel. Trains take around four hours. Buses to Chongqing take around 10 hours — you would probably be better off to go back to Chengdu and travel to Chongqing from there.

EMEISHAN

Emeishan is one of China's four Buddhist sacred mountains, and has been a pilgrimage destination for well over a millennium. For those with the endurance for a couple of days of steep climbing, this is an exciting opportunity to join thousands of Chinese in a celebration of old myths about the sacredness of mountains and the aesthetic of the views they offer. Some thirty (reduced from an original of 150) temples and monasteries provide simple accommodation along the way.

Come prepared with warm clothes and sturdy boots if you're planning to climb Emei, particularly between October and April, when temperatures can plummet. Even in summer, it can be very cold on the summit, which is close to 3,000 m (9,850 ft).

Access is via **Emei Town**, and true pilgrims begin their ascent from the nearby **Baoguo Temple**. Given that this route involves a demanding three-day round trip, most foreign visitors start with a minibus to **Qingyin Pavilion**, from where you are looking at 10 hours of climbing to get to the **10,000 Buddha Summit**, via **Wannian Temple**, **Xixiang Pond**, **Jieyin Hall** and the **Golden Summit**. At Jieyin Hall you can cheat by taking a short cable car ride up to the summit, saving yourself two hours of hard slog. This is what you may have to do if you want to get up to the summit in one day. Dedicated cheaters can take a minibus all the way to Jieyin Hall, jump into the cable car and arrive at the summit refreshed and ready for the descent.

The popular descent route is identical to the ascent as far as Xixiang Pond, making the cable car option a sensible one for at least one leg. After the pond, the descent veers west to **Xi'anfeng Temple**, from where it's around four hours to Qingyin Pavilion. At Jieyin Hall, you have the option of taking a minibus back down to Emei Town if you have run out of puff.

How to Get There
Emei Town is just 30 km (19 miles) from Leshan, and minibuses between the two are

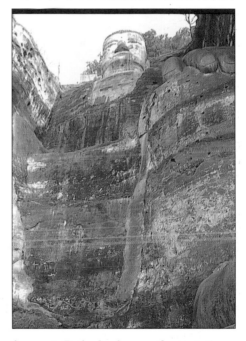

frequent. Both also have railway stations, which means that it is possible to catch a train to one, bus on to the other and catch another train back to Chengdu. Note, though, that buses run between Chengdu and Leshan in just three hours.

The Grand Buddha at Leshan — "so immense that 100 people can congregate on his head."

Lhasa
and
Tibet

TO PAY A VISIT TO TIBET is to step through a portal from the materialism of the modern age to a society which is still, to a large extent, ruled by deep medieval spiritual impulses. Tibet is transcendental — even the main route to Lhasa by air from Chengdu is a journey toward the heavens, soaring upward over the vast and awesome snow-tipped ranges of the Tibet–Qinghai Plateau to touch down in a dusty valley two miles above sea level.

Tibet is also vividly hued compared with the far more mundane revolutionary char-

THE LAND AND THE PEOPLE

There is a striking incongruity about Tibet — that it's people are so warm and welcoming and yet its geography so inhospitable. It covers an area of close to 750,000 sq km (290,000 sq miles) bordered by China, India, Nepal, Burma, Sikkim and Bhutan, and it is mostly mountainous, very sparsely inhabited, has few serviceable roads and no railway. And it has a climate in which the temperature can fall to freezing point on

acter of the Chinese "lowlands" — a sudden blaze of tribal costume, coral and turquoise beadwork, gilded temple roofs, garish gods and demons, fluttering prayer-flags, spinning prayer-drums, silver and brass and rich golden yak butter, priests in flowing crimson robes, lamas in deep maroon, saffron and yellow — and through the seemingly incessant whirl of color, the mournful squeal and rumbling bellow of temple pipes and horns.

For centuries, Tibet was isolated, almost inaccessible, a forbidden citadel hidden in the eaves of the very roof of the world. Today it is the most coveted of all the tourist destinations in China, the place where just about every China traveler wants to go.

mountainsides even at the height of summer and plunge to minus 40°C (minus 40°F) in winter, bringing heavy snowfalls that block the mountain passes and make many areas more isolated than ever.

Its main travel artery is the bumpy highway that runs west from Lhasa to Shigatse and then cuts south to the border with Nepal. Another key mountain road carries on from Shigatse and skirts the Himalayas, following the western border, skirting the holy mountain of Kailash, before pausing in Ali and heading north to Yecheng and Kashgar

Three faces of Tibetan culture: Animism of Bon and refinement of Buddhism OPPOSITE in Potala Palace wall painting; Beaded market woman ABOVE LEFT; tribeswoman RIGHT prays at Lhasa temple.

in the Xinjiang Uygur autonomous region. Lhasa is also linked with the "lowland" by a road that runs to Golmud in Qinghai province.

The Tibetan people are believed to be of mixed Mongoloid-Turkic lineage. Before the arrival of Buddhism, Tibetan armies rampaged through Turkestan, Pakistan, Nepal and even China, at one time overrunning the Tang dynasty capital of Chang'an (contemporary Xi'an). But when Buddhism arrived it took hold with a vengeance, so that by the tenth century the Tibetans had gone from

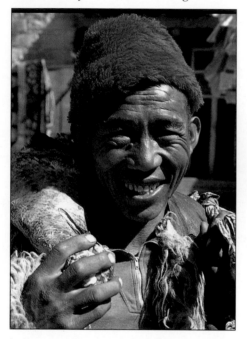

being a warlike, much-feared race to being a nation of monasteries, a people ruled by monks.

The evolution of the various Buddhist sects that contend (mostly peacefully) in Tibet is very complex. It's enough to say that by the seventeenth century the Dalai Lamas of the Gelugpa order had become the most revered incarnate lamas in all Tibet. Today's Dalai Lama is the fourteenth, and he is adored by his people as a God King. He fled Tibet in 1959, during an unsuccessful uprising by the Tibetan people in protest at the Chinese occupation of their country. The Chinese had marched into Tibet and "liberated" it in October 1950, shortly after the Communist Party finally came to power.

Under Chinese military rule most of the country's 4,000 monasteries were shut down and the monkhood disbanded. Nowadays, monasteries are reopening the length and breadth of the land. The Beijing government would even like to see the Dalai Lama return, and have in fact renovated his private apartments in the Potala Palace in Lhasa, but there appears to be little chance of this former religious monarch regaining any real measure of power.

BUDDHISM AND BON

Tibetan Buddhism, or Lamaism, was bonded onto a form of animism called Bon, which ruled Tibetan spiritual life in ancient times. Some of its imagery and ritual have been absorbed quite comfortably into the Buddhist practices — spirit and demon worship, prayer-flags and offerings to the guardian spirits of mountain passes, for instance — adding the color, reverence and mystique that distinguish its ceremony and monastic life, and death rites, from all other Buddhist schools of thought.

For more than two decades after the Chinese takeover, Tibetan religion was virtually driven underground. But in the current liberalization it is beginning to flourish again, and starting from early 1986 the regular "summonses" of the various sects and temple festivals have been restored in Lhasa and throughout the mountain domain. There is still a running rivalry between the occupying Chinese and Tibetan independence groups, though, as the riots in 1988 violently proved, and travelers are warned that this tension could close the region to visitors at various times.

HOW TO GET THERE

There have never been any easy answers when it comes to travel around Tibet. In theory, of course, the Chinese government is much in favor of tourism up on the high plateau, but on the other hand, they take a dim view of individual travelers spending long periods of time in Tibet, particularly when there's the risk that they'll make disaffected Tibetan friends and come away sympathizing with the Tibetan plight, which is just the opposite of what the Chinese government wants tourists to do. The idea, essentially, is to cash in on Tibet's ethnic appeal and show tourists Tibetans who look happy about life in the New Tibet. Obviously, when protests occur on the streets of Lhasa, Tibet-bound tours can end up stranded in Chengdu or Lhasa.

As for tours versus individual travel, the official position is "no individual travelers." For all that, individual travelers have been going to Tibet for over 10 years, and will probably continue to do so. In Golmud, CITS

HEALTH

Attractive and challenging as Tibet is, any plan to visit the country must take health into account. Because of the high altitude it is definitely no place for anyone with a heart condition, anemia or any other form of chronic ill-health. Elderly people, particularly, should think twice about risking it. Even young, healthy visitors are affected by the 4,000-m (13,100-ft) altitude, the most immediate symptoms being a slight shortness of breath,

sell bus tickets at tour-group prices that actually include a three-day tour of Lhasa. Once you step off the bus, you can do what you like. Flights are another matter. Usually it's a lost cause trying to buy a ticket to Lhasa in Chengdu, but if you plan ahead it can often be possible to buy one elsewhere — in Hong Kong for example.

Again in Kathmandu, boarding a flight to Lhasa is near impossible. The main problem is that the Chinese embassy in Kathmandu will not issue visas to individual travelers. The simple way around this problem is to organize your visa before you go. Armed with a Chinese visa you can march up to the border at Kodari and walk over into Tibet.

an initial sense of lightheadedness and a gradually consuming lethargy. On a long bicycle ride or a trudge up the endless stone stairways leading into the Potala, all these symptoms come together in panting exhaustion and headaches if frequent rest stops are not made along the way.

Some people, young or old, suffer a more severe form of altitude sickness, with chronic nausea and headaches caused by an insufficient supply of oxygen to the brain. Altitude sickness strikes at random, and whether you come down with it or not will depend on

OPPOSITE: Tribesman carries dried mutton for sale in Lhasa bazaar while three Tibetan pilgrim women ABOVE sport spring hats and ornately silvered costumes.

your own metabolism. It can often be eased with aspirin and a period of complete rest, but if it persists and is extremely debilitating there's only one cure — get a plane back down to the "lowlands."

Otherwise, the simplest way to cope with it is to always take things easy, attempt only one major excursion or errand a day, drink plenty of tea, and if you wake up gasping for breath in the middle of the night don't panic — it's just your brain changing your pattern of breathing to suit the high-level conditions. Just go back to sleep and await the sun's nine o'clock alarm call.

LHASA

A visit to the Sacred Tibetan city of Lhasa is a highlight of any China tour. Lhasa is so utterly different from anything you will have experienced before that its sights and smells will stay with you for the rest of your life. It is very easy to spend a week, acclimatizing to the altitude and slowly taking in Lhasa's many sights.

GENERAL INFORMATION

The **Bank of China** is at 13 Linkuo Lu. Air tickets for foreigners are sold at the Tibet Hotel (see WHERE TO STAY, below), where there is a ticket outlet for **CAAC (** (891) 633-6784. For overland travel bookings, few people bother with **CITS**, which has an office opposite the Holiday Inn. The small, privately run travel agents, which are legion in the old quarter of Lhasa, are the best places to make bookings.

GETTING AROUND

You'll find that the street map of Lhasa is dominated by two main arteries. **Xingfu Lu** runs east-west right through the heart of the new and old sections of the city, linking the Potala with the newer tourist hotels and, five kilometers (three miles) to the west of the city, the famed Drepung Monastery. To the east it links the post office with the main bazaar and pilgrim's path, the Barkhor, the holiest of all Tibet's temples, the Jokhang, and, beyond them, the most popular low-priced Tibetan guesthouses and restaurants.

LHASA AND TIBET

TIBET

TANGGULA MOU

Tingri   Sakya   Xigaze   GAN
                              Gyanze

Gamba

HIMALÁYAS

To the north, starting from the rear of the bus station, **Jiefang Beilu** runs into dusty wastelands beyond the Sports Complex toward another huge religious center, the Sera Monastery. South of the city, the Lhasa River trickles and bubbles east to west over wide, flat pebbled beds and sand banks. Beyond the river, further south, the city is guarded by a high, sharply sculptured mountain range which acts as a kind of natural clock, or regulator of the rhythm of tourist life. In winter, for example, when the night air is absolutely frigid, only the brave or most brazen visitor stirs and moves from the bed covers before the dot of 9 AM, when the sun blasts over the range and begins softening the bitter chill.

Unless you're staying in one of the high-priced tourist hotels east of the Potala, there's only one readily available form of transport in Lhasa — a bicycle. The city is flat and its social atmosphere so dreamy and laid-back that any other means of perambulation would be tantamount to reckless haste.

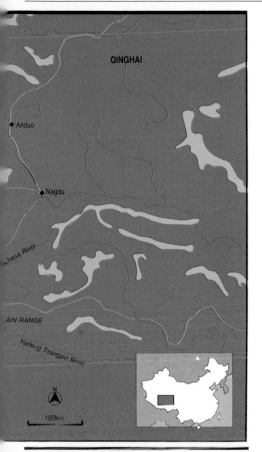

QINGHAI

• Anduo

• Nagqu

Lhasa River

AIN RANGE

Yarlong Tsangpo River

N

100km

WHAT TO SEE AND DO

Lhasa's main cultural attractions are involved with its religious life, so agenda planning oftens begins with finding out about "events" at the local temples and monasteries. Because of the long suppression of religious activity, the full religious calendar is only now being slowly restored, and "events" can often be announced only days before they are about to happen. But if a temple is opening up for a day of worship by pilgrims, or if new lamas are being chosen or inducted, or if a new *thangka*, or sacred tapestry, is being unveiled, word quickly buzzes around the tourist community (see ALL ROADS LEAD TO LHASA in TOP SPOTS, page 27).

First, though, any new arrival needs an immediate immersion course in the Tibetan social and cultural character, and the place to get this is in the **Barkhor**, where you find the main bazaar and a bustling and picturesque rabbit warren of streets that form a sacred pilgrim's path around the Jokhang Temple. The **bazaar** is a crowded, kaleidoscopic whirl of friendly faces, the stunned expressions of out-of-towners, "Honest Joe" bead and artifact traders and colorful costumed tribespeople from all over the country — their mahogany faces so hauntingly reminiscent of another time and another culture that the entire pageant looks like a massive gathering of the North American Indian nations.

The Jokhang

As for the Jokhang Temple, it is the sacred spot around which everything else revolves. Built in the seventh century by King Songsten Gampo, a fierce military campaigner and the founding father of Buddhism in Tibet, it is the nation's holiest shrine and contains its most revered religious relic, a gilded and bejeweled image of Sakyamuni Buddha. The Jokhang is beautiful and fascinating, its roof laden with gilded bells, birds, beasts, dragons and two deer holding the Buddhist Wheel of Dharma. Its forecourt is usually packed with worshipers either prostrating before the doors or lighting fragrant juniper in a tall hearth to please the gods. Inside, among its shrine halls and relics, a vast gallery of brass prayer-drums spin in unison as the lines of faithful file through.

The area in front of the Jokhang was once part of the walled precincts of the Old City. Now it's been cleared and turned into a wide pedestrian square, flanked by crafts and provisions stores, and is the city's main social hub. Several cafés with rooftop seating have set up shop on the square, and there can be few more pleasurable ways to while away a late afternoon than sitting in one of these places, sipping tea and gazing out across the square at the Jokhang.

The Potala

The Potala Palace dominates all cultural sightseeing in Lhasa. It's such a magnificent structure that you could spend days studying it from all angles and in all weather and lighting before actually going inside. In the morning it blazes with gold in the first rays of the sun, and then, as the sun climbs higher, it settles back into white and ocher. If there's an early morning mist or dust storm about, it seems to float on a bed of clouds.

The Potala was built by the Great Fifth Dalai Lama, a military and religious strongman who ruled from 1617 to 1682. He brought the Tibetans together as one sovereign people, established the ruling supremacy of the Yellow Hats — one of the three main Buddhist sects in Tibet — and provided the Potala as the seat of Tibetan government and both palace and tomb of the Dalai Lamas for centuries to come. The section that the Great Fifth built is known as the **White Palace**, the administrative and residential section, entered from the soaring eastern stairways and huge doors above the village of **Sho** at the foot of the temple-fort.

The western half of the Potala is the **Red Palace**, the religious center, and it is packed with chapels and shrines, golden stupas, the tombs of eight Dalai Lamas and vast libraries full of Buddhist scriptures. The entrance to this section is a massive ornate gateway at the western end of the Potala with heavy medieval wooden doors decorated with knotted yak hair left as devotional offerings by pilgrims.

The Potala is subject to irregular opening hours. Check locally on the latest hours before heading out to explore it. It would be a pity to make the long climb to the entrance in vain.

Behind the Potala you'll find **Chingdrol Chilling Park** with a pavilion called the Lukhang set in the middle of it. This was a trysting spot built by one of the black sheep of the dynasty, the Sixth Dalai Lama (1683–1706) who became so debauched that he was kidnapped and murdered by his subjects.

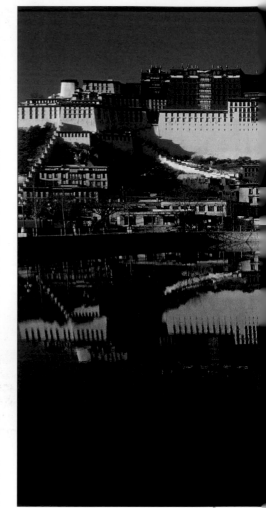

The Summer Palace

Three kilometers (two miles) to the west of the Potala, near the Holiday Inn Hotel, you'll find **Norbulingka (Jewel Park)** the Summer Palace. It was laid out by the Seventh Dalai Lama (1708–1757) who ascended to the throne with the backing of China's Qing dynasty and whose reign brought Tibet under Chinese control.

The park features woods and gardens, pavilions, a small zoo and palace buildings erected by several rulers, including a new palace constructed by the present Dalai Lama before he fled Tibet. The whole complex is worth a full day's visit, and is less exhausting than the Potala. One interesting section that should not be missed is the **Kasang Temple**, where you can study some 70 magnificent hanging *thangkas* depicting Buddhist stories and mandalas. Some of these fantastic weavings, some of them so big that they're draped right down the central façade of the Potala Palace during special religious events, are so treasured and revered that they're often unveiled only once every 20, 30 or even 50 years.

Drepung Monastery

Drepung (Rice Heap) Monastery, about five kilometers (three miles) west of Lhasa city, or an hour's sedate travel by bicycle, was where the powerful Great Fifth Dalai Lama

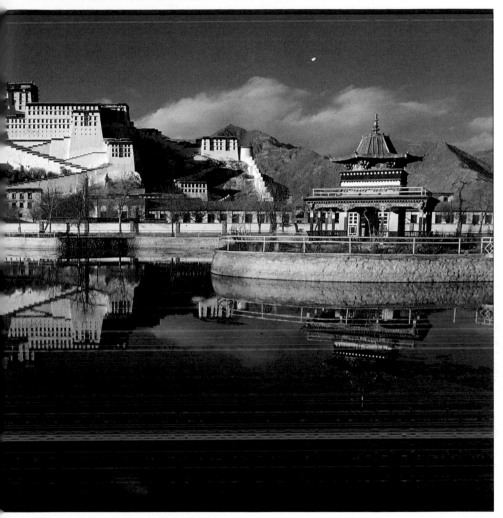

resided and ruled while the Potala Palace was being built. It's a huge monastery — in its heyday it had rich estates, held sway over about 700 subsidiary monasteries and was staffed by no fewer than 10,000 monks. Most of its high lamas fled to India with the Dalai Lama in the Chinese military crackdown.

Nowadays only a few hundred monks and novices are left there, and part of the northwestern section, the Gwoma, is in ruins. A striking aspect of any visit is the vehemence with which some of the lamas will sometimes speak of the Chinese — the monastery fared badly in the Cultural Revolution. Wandering through Drepung is like stepping through a medieval town, with narrow stone alleyways rising and winding between the monastery's main temples, col-

leges and chanting halls. It is rich in relics, religious and historical, and as you move from one building to another you can find huge *thangkas* and murals, gold stupas, the tombs of three Dalai Lamas, yak butter sculptures, ancient weapons and armor, garish oracle dolls and the monastery's holiest treasure, a huge gilded Buddha.

In the hills to the west of the monastery you may stumble across young lamas practicing the temple pipes and long bronze trumpets that are sounded in religious rites. One of the hills, **Mount Gyengbuwudze**, is a sacred spot where on certain occasions in the summer pilgrims flock to spend the night chanting and dancing. Again, you need to

The magnificent Potala Palace.

keep an ear to the ground to learn when these devotional sing-alongs are to take place.

Sera Monastery

North of Lhasa, Sera (Merciful Hail) Monastery is a easier distance to ride. It takes about half an hour to get there along Jiefang Beilu, turning off to the right before you reach the Regional Military Hospital. Founded in the fifteenth century, Sera has a reputation for rebellious behavior, and in 1947 its high lamas actually plotted to overthrow the Dalai Lama and put their own man in the Potala.

The monastery features three interesting chanting halls and a wealth of religious artwork including an image of Ayaguriba, a horse-headed demon that typifies the blending of animist Bon and Buddhist beliefs, a huge image of the Maitreya Buddha, rock paintings, a magnificent array of murals in its Drezame chanting hall and its holiest relic, an image of the many-handed, many-eyed Bodhisattva Chenrezi — Tibet's version of the Avalokitesvara of India and China's goddess of mercy, Guanyin.

In the hills to the west of Sera the maps pinpoint a spot called the **Sky Burial Site**, a place upon which fierce debate is centered among the traveling community in Lhasa. It's where the traditional Tibetan funerals take place, the bodies broken up and cast among vultures and other scavengers to be picked clean. This practice, gruesome as it may seem to outsiders, is necessary because the frozen ground won't allow normal burial and fuel is too scarce for elaborate cremations. It has taken on a spiritual significance over the centuries, representing a fundamen-

tal principle of the Tibetan death ceremonies — that the spirit is sacrosanct and the earthly body means nothing.

The debate is whether it should be regarded as a tourist attraction or not. If the answer is not immediately obvious, the domdens, or body breakers, settle the matter quite effectively: Unwanted visitors are chased off in no time.

Street Sights

Aside from the color and splendor of its monasteries, Lhasa offers a few cultural sideshows that should not be missed — the **Moslem Mosque** in the heart of the Islamic Old Quarter south of the Banak Shol, for instance, and the **Lhasa Carpet Factory**, the biggest rug weaving center in Tibet, to the southeast of the city near the University of Tibet.

If you're interested in medicine, go along to the **Tibetan Traditional Hospital**, on Renmin Lu just west of the Jokhang Temple, which practices the complex folk-science of Tibetan medicine based on herbal treatments, astrology, acupuncture, moxibustion and even the Buddhist sutras. One interesting fact is that it forbids surgery: It was banned "forever" in the ninth century when the mother of the ruler of that time died during what must have been a primitive and agonizing operation.

WHERE TO STAY

Luxury

There is only one hotel that comes close to qualifying as luxury lodging in the whole of Tibet: the **Holiday Inn Lhasa** ((891) 633-2221 FAX (891) 633-5796, 1 Minzu Lu. The management here do a remarkable job with very limited resources. The hotel has over 480 rooms and suites, all of them fitted with satellite television, air-conditioning, International Dial Direct phones and, of course, essentials such as 24-hour hot water.

The only other hotel in Lhasa where you can stay with some degree of luxury is the

ABOVE: Sacred wheel and deer sculptures
OPPOSITE TOP and BOTTOM: Rooftop apartments of the Potala Palace, the former stronghold of the Dalai Lamas, now a vast museum of palace treasures, chapels and shrines, libraries and tombs of eight supreme rulers.

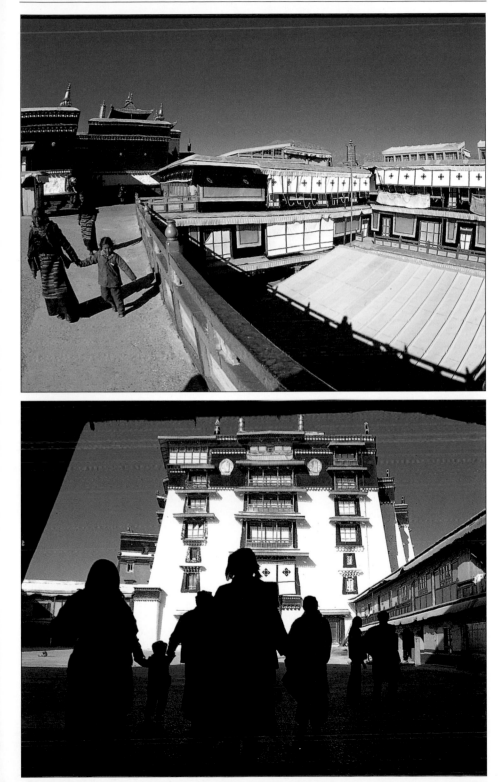

Tibet Hotel ((891) 633-6787, 221 Beijing Xilu, which is close by. It can't compare with the Holiday Inn, however, and some tour groups who get put up here complain of faltering service standards and other problems. Room rates, however, start at about half of those of the Holiday Inn.

Mid-Range

Lhasa scarcely has any mid-range hotels. The only places in town that qualify are soulless, drafty places, and most travelers who aren't in the Holiday Inn or the Tibet Hotel opt to

inexpensive dorms to "luxury" rooms with attached bathrooms (the supply of water here is erratic, particularly once winter arrives). The main attraction is not so much the rooms — decorated with Tibetan motifs — than the big courtyards lined with sofas, where young travelers sun themselves by day and chat and strum guitars during the evenings.

The **Banak Shol** ((891) 632-3829, on Beijing Donglu just down the road from the Yak, has been catering to Westerners' Tibetan fantasies nearly as long as individual travelers

go down market and stay in one of the more hospitable and atmospheric Tibetan-run hotels.

The **Himalaya Hotel** ((891) 632-3775 FAX (891) 633-2675, is not exactly a shining exception to this rule, but it does have a little more character than most places. Its location, to the southeast of Barkhor Square is less than ideal.

Inexpensive

If you're young at heart, the only place to be is in one of budget hotels in the old Tibetan quarter of Lhasa.

For many years now, the most popular hotel in Lhasa has been the **Yak Hotel** ((891) 632-3496. It has a wide range of rooms, from

have been making their way to Tibet — old-timers reminisce about it and sigh that it isn't what it once was, but the Banak Shol is still an atmospheric warren of courtyards and corridors, wobbly flights of stairs and precarious ladders. It even has some mid-range rooms with attached bathroom these days.

The **Snowlands** ((891) 632-3687, has been surviving on the same formula for more than a decade — cheap rooms, dingy shared toilets, not always reliable water supply, but always beaming smiles from the staff. Anyways, it works at this place. Some repeat visitors to Lhasa would stay nowhere else. The views of the Jokhang from the upper floors of the hotel are delightful.

WHERE TO EAT

Traditional Tibetan cuisine is very bland: salted tea mixed with yak butter and *tsampa*, a barley flour, dried yak meat and mutton, cheese and yogurt were the staples of these hardy mountain people. Tourism and the arrival of large numbers of Han Chinese have changed all that, and Lhasa nowadays has plenty of good food.

The best restaurants in town are all at the **Holiday Inn Lhasa**. The evening buffet fea-

its views than its meals. At the very least have a drink here at some point.

HOW TO GET THERE

There are just a handful of points from which you can fly to Lhasa. Regular flights are available from Chengdu, Chongqing and Kathmandu, while there is less frequent service from Xi'an. The rumor mill has had flights starting up from all over China for over a decade, but the fact is that most travelers enter from Chengdu.

turing Indian and Tibetan cuisine at the **Himalaya Restaurant** is not to be missed. The decor is sumptuous, and the musical show is a rare opportunity to hear Tibetan performers. Full marks are reserved too for the **Hard Yak Café**, where yak burgers and French fries are featured on a menu that does commendable job of satisfying Western cravings with the resources at hand.

In the Tibetan quarter, **Tashi's**, on the Barkhor Square has long been popular with travelers. The menu is simple — most people order the chepati-like *bobi*, which comes either with meat or vegetables. Tashi's cheesecakes are the stuff of legends. Also on the Barkhor Square is the **Barkhor Café**, a rooftop terrace that is better recommended for

After arriving by air from Chengdu there's a two-hour bus ride between the Gonggar airstrip and Lhasa. Nothing about getting to Tibet is easy, and if you've made it this far the bumpy two-hour bus journey will seem a fitting final hurdle.

The only viable overland routes to Lhasa are by bus from Golmud or Kathmandu.

THE TIBETAN TRAIL

Beyond Lhasa, one of the world's most forbidding and yet exciting landscapes awaits the intrepid visitor to Tibet. The hinterland offers rugged adventure, breathtaking

ABOVE: Sky Burial Site. OPPOSITE: Jokhang Temple prayer wheels.

views of the Himalayas and Mount Everest and a gem-string of relatively undisturbed Buddhist wonders. Travel is arduous, accommodation and living conditions are primitive, but the rewards are well worth the struggle.

The standard overland trail from Lhasa is the Lhasa–Nepal overland route via **Shigatse, Gyantse, Sakya, Tinggri, Everest Base Camp** (an exciting optional extra) and **Zhangmu (Kasa)** on the Nepalese border.

CITS, which has an office opposite the Holiday Inn, offers tours to destinations around Tibet, but few travelers bother with their services. Clustered around the Yak and Banak Shol hotels in the Tibetan quarter of Lhasa are a number of private operators who can offer reasonably priced tours. The notice boards at both of these hotels are always bristling with requests for travel companions to help share the costs on trips to dozens of destinations.

GYANTSE

Since the construction of the Lhasa–Shigatse Highway, Gyantse has begun to miss out on much tourist traffic. Be sure to include it on your agenda. The old Shigatse highway, which goes via Gyantse, might be slow and potholed but it follows the edge of Yamdrok Lake, surely one of the world's most stunning sheets of turquoise water.

Gyantse itself is the closest thing you'll see to a true Tibetan town, short of traveling the arduous road out west towards Mount Kailash. It also has one of Tibet's premiere attractions in the magnificent stupa temple, the **Kumbum**. Equally impressive is **Palkhor Monastery**, which has an interesting array of Buddha images. Presiding over the town is the **Gyantse Fort**, a crumbling structure on a hill top that was the site of fierce fighting between the British and Tibetans during the Younghusband Expedition of 1903.

Gyantse has several places to stay and they all seem to be called the **Gyantse Hotel**. None of them is recommended for anything other than an overnight stay and it would be foolhardy to expect anything in the way of creature comforts; consider yourself lucky if you get some hot water. The best restaurants are in the newer Chinese quarter.

SHIGATSE

Shigatse is Tibet's second largest city and the junction for the route south to the Nepal border. It's also the traditional seat of power of the Panchen Lamas, the divine "prime ministers" of the Tibetan Buddhist hierarchy, appointed from within the city's huge **Tashilhunpo Monastery**.

One of the four greatest Buddhist monasteries in Tibet, Tashilhunpo was founded in the fifteenth century, sacked and looted

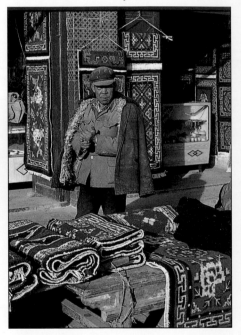

by an invading army of Nepalese Gurkhas in 1791, stormed and closed down by the People's Liberation Army in 1960, yet survives today as one of the most splendid of all Tibet's religious centers. It is famed for its immense nine-story *thangka* wall from which huge Buddhist tapestries are displayed during festivals, its 26-m (85-ft)-high Maitreya Buddha, and the Panchen Lama's Palace, the main treasure of which is a priceless gold and silver stupa studded with precious gems. It also has its own exhibition of grotesque demons to recall the psychic horrors of Bon animism.

There are two other interesting Buddhist monasteries close to Shigatse, both built in the Mongolian style. **Shalu Monastery**,

22 km (13.6 miles) south of the city, was a center for psychic training in which lamas are said to have developed incredible paranormal powers, and some of the feats that they allegedly performed are depicted in a series of murals. **Narthang (Ladang) Monastery**, 15 km (9.3 miles) west of Shigatse, built in the twelfth century, was a leading theological center and printing house. It was almost completely destroyed by the Red Guards in the 1960s.

One other interesting center of culture is still flourishing in Shigatse, the **Silver Crafts Factory** where visitors can watch craftsmen and their young apprentices fashion traditional cups, bowls and yak butter lamps from gold, silver and copper, working over charcoal furnaces and yak-skin bellows.

The top hotel in town is the **Shigatse Hotel**, which gives the appearance of striving hard for a star rating of some kind. The resulting effect is somewhat bizarre, but it does at least manage to provide some comforts for travel-weary guests.

Elsewhere in Shigatse there is nowhere that is really worth recommending. The **Tenzin Hotel**, across from the market, does has superb rooftop views of the Shigatse Fort, but a stay here is only for the more adventurous.

HIMALAYAN GRANDEUR

The 530-km (320-mile) stretch to the border town of Zhangmu crosses three high mountain passes, the third of which, Lalung Leh (at 5,214 m or 17,106 ft), beyond the town of **New Tinggri**, offers the grand physical and spiritual spectacle that draws almost every foreign pilgrim to Tibet—a panoramic view of the majestic snow-capped peaks of the Himalayas. On the way there are other fantastic sights, the monolithic **Sakya Monastery**, a Mongolian temple-fortress 26 km (16 miles) off the main highway from the Sakya River Bridge, which is 128 km (79 miles) from Shigatse. **Rongbuk Monastery**, near New Tinggri, at 5,000 m (16,404 ft) is probably the highest in the world and offers a clear view of Mount Everest; it is just six kilometers (almost four miles) below the Everest Base Camp. As for New

Tinggri itself, there is a reasonably comfortable guesthouse with three-to-a-room beds and a restaurant.

Beyond New Tinggri the road climbs up through the high Lalung Leh pass and breaks through the Himalayan barrier — and from there it plunges 3,000 m (9,842 ft) over a mere 90 km (56 miles) down to the Zhangmu border crossing and the warm, lush "lowlands" of Nepal. It's a fabulous journey. If you start out early enough in the morning from New Tinggri, you will be enjoying your evening dinner in Kathmandu

with memories of one of the world's most awe-inspiring journeys swimming around your head.

OPPOSITE: Rug seller. ABOVE: Sidewalk stall offers watch repair.

Xi'an
and the
Northwest

XI'AN

Xi'an is one of China's oldest and most illustrious cities — the capital of Shaanxi province, cultural hub of north-central China and the principal gateway to the remarkable oasis towns and cities, Islamic minorities and Buddhist treasures of the arid northwest. It is the north-central crossroads of China, providing access by train between east and west and linking the northern and southern provinces.

The city has played a strategic role in Chinese history for more than 3,000 years. Known as Chang'an, it served as the capital of 11 dynasties covering a period of 1,100 years up to the reign of the Tang (618–907). It was also the eastern terminus of the Silk Road and, lying in the path of the main Central Asian conduit into the heart of China, was a heavily fortified frontier post for several centuries.

In 1374, engineers of the Ming rule, already strengthening the Great Wall, bolstered Xi'an's defenses by tearing down and reconstructing the wall that had encircled the city since ancient times. The massive structure, 12 m (39 ft) high and 14 to 18 m (46 to 59 ft) thick and running for about 12 km (7.4 miles) around the city, still stands today and is the first vivid impression of Xi'an's historic importance that visitors get as they arrive by train.

Its historic prominence has endowed modern Xi'an with one of the greatest treasure troves of ancient culture to be found anywhere in China, and it's given the city a new strategic role as the nation's number one tourist mecca. In the high summer season it is packed with tour groups and, unfortunately, it is also a clamoring beehive of frantically persistent souvenir hawkers, especially at the most renowned and astonishing of all its cultural attractions — the life-size terracotta "army" of the iron man of Chinese history, Qinshi Huangdi.

GENERAL INFORMATION

Northwest Airlines ((29) 870-2299 is the local arm of CAAC. **Dragonair** ((29) 426-2988, has an office in the lobby of the Sheraton Xi'an Hotel (see WHERE TO STAY, below).

There is a branch of the **Bank of China** at 318 Dong Dajie, but most hotels can change money.

The head office of **CITS** ((29) 526-2066 is at 32 Chang'an Beilu.

GETTING AROUND

Xi'an, flat and fairly compact (at least the section within the walls), is another city ideally suited to the bicycle. They can be hired at Mum's and Dad's restaurants, opposite the Flats of Renmin Hotel on Fenghe Lu (see below).

Taxis are easy to flag down, they use meters and are inexpensive. The bus system is chronically overcrowded and best avoided if you have much luggage.

Xi'an's Xiguan airport is a long, 40-km (25-mile) drive from central Xi'an. It's best to take a CAAC bus. The taxi drivers out at the airport are a rapacious crew.

WHAT TO SEE AND DO

Xi'an is of interest in itself and for the cultural attractions that lie around its ancient walls, such as the Qinshi Huangdi Mausoleum. In Xi'an, the **City Wall** is worth more than a casual inspection, especially at its four main gates to the north, south, east and west, over which the Ming engineers built small multistory forts with firing points from which teams of archers and sappers could shower hostile forces with arrows, gunpowder bombs and blazing oil and naptha.

As for the **Bell Tower**, transplanted to the hub of the city from an earlier fourteenth century site during the Qing dynasty, it's such a central landmark and so festooned with trolley-bus cables that you can't help but notice it every day. Before the 1949 revolution it was used as a garrison and prison by the Guomindang nationalists. There's a smaller and more interesting **Drum Tower** just slightly to the west of it, and beyond that the fascinating **Qingzhen Si (Grand Mosque)**, one of the biggest Islamic places of worship in China. Once you've visited the mosque don't neglect to take some time out

Verdant river bed contrasts with the sunbaked slopes of Turpan's Huoyan Shan (Flaming Mountains).

XI'AN

Provincial Exhibition Hall

Gongnong Lu
Xinghuo Lu
Ziqiang Xilu
Qianwei Jie
Beiguan Zhengjie
Caotan Lu
Ziqiang Donglu
Taihua Lu
Huaqing Lu
Changying Lu
Beimen Gate (North Gate)
Xi'an Railway Station
Geming (Revolutionary) Park
Huancheng Xilu Beiduan
Lianhu Lu
Damaishi Jie
Lianhu (Lotus Lake) Park
Bei Dajie
Xi 5 – Lu
Dong 5 – Lu
Changle Xilu
Huancheng Donglu
Sichuan Cuisine Restaurant
Beiduan
Xingqing Lu
Children's Park
Bell Tower
Xixin Jie
Dongxin Jie
Jiefang Lu
Renmin Lu
Huancheng Xilu Nanduan
Ximen Gate (West Gate)
Hongguang Jie
Xi Dajie
Drum Tower
Dong Dajie
Heping Lu
Huan Cheng Donglu
Dongguan Zhengjie
Xingqinggong Park
Xi'an Restaurant
Duanlumen
Taibai Lu
Huancheng Nanlu Xiduan
Nanmen Gate (South Gate)
Nanguan Zhengjie
Huancheng Nanlu Dongduan
Wenyi Lu
Nanduan
Xianning Lu
Youyi xilu
Youyi Donglu
Xiaoyan (Small Wild Goose) Pagoda
Lingyuan Lu
CITS / CTS
Chang'an Lu
Cuihua Lu
Yanta Lu
Flood Control Canal
Big Xingshan Temple
N
500m
Xiaozhai Xilu
Xiaozhai Donglu
Dayan (Big Wild Goose) Pagoda

and explore the neighboring Muslim Quarter, where you'll see storeholders roasting kebabs and flatbreads, and where sheep heads jostle with sweetmeats for your attention.

The **Shaanxi Provincial Museum**, lying close to the old city's South Gate, is part of an old Confucian temple with exhibition halls rebuilt in the 1960s to the Ming and Qing architectural styles. Its three main halls are packed with relics covering the period from prehistory to the Tang dynasty, and they include terracotta horses from the Qin reign, gilded Sui dynasty Buddha images, carvings from the Warring States period and Tang pottery, figures, horses and camels.

The museum's most prized exhibit is the extraordinary Forest of Steles — 2,300 large stone tablets engraved with imperial edicts, commentaries on the classics, celebrated styles of calligraphy and other records of the ages back to Han times. One stele dated 781 records the appearance of the Syrian Christian school of thought, Nestorianism, which found its way to ancient Chang'an via the Silk Road.

South of the city wall there are two Tang dynasty pagodas, **Dayan (Big Wild Goose)** and **Xiaoyan (Small Wild Goose)**, the larger one built to honor the Buddhist monk Xuan Zang, who first brought the Buddhist scriptures from India to China, and to house the 1,335 volumes of translations that he spent virtually the rest of his life producing.

Farther south again is Xi'an's other important museum, the **Shaanxi History Museum**, which opened its doors in 1992. The ground floor traces the evolution of Chinese civilization from its Shang dynasty beginnings through the upstairs collections from the Zhou and Han to the side room collections from the Tang, which being the most recent are the best preserved and most interesting to the nonspecialist.

Geming (Revolutionary) Park and the nearby (**Memorial Museum of the Eighth Route Army**, in the north of the city near the railway station, commemorate the communist revolutionary drive against the nationalists and the Japanese in the 1930s. It's a place of special interest to Canadians, because Norman Bethune, the Montreal medic who joined Mao's forces and became one of the most beloved foreign heroes of the communist cause, lived and worked here with Zhou Enlai and Deng Xiaoping at one stage of the campaign.

The Terracotta Warriors

The plains surrounding Xi'an are dotted with tombs, pagodas and temples, but there's really only one great attraction to make every effort to see — the **Qinshi Huangdi Mausoleum** and its terracotta army. There's also **Banpo Museum**, where you can view an interesting reconstruction of a Neolithic mudhut hamlet and relics of that distant age — including clay jars in which children were buried — and the **Huaqing Hot Springs Resort**, a complex of baths, temples and halls in which the Qin, Han and Tang rulers languished and bathed.

The **Tomb of Qinshi Huangdi** is nothing short of awe-inspiring — the packed ranks of some 1,000 life-size fully armed and armored warriors, each of them bearing the distinctive features of the men they were modeled on, standing with their horses under the sweeping roof of a protective exhibition hall. Of all the historic landmarks of the great China pilgrimage, this is perhaps the place of deepest sanctity (see an ARMY IN STONE in TOP SPOTS, page 26).

SHOPPING

Xi'an is the perfect place for souvenir shopping. The vast hordes of tourists passing through ensures variety and a good turnover. Some of the tourist sights (the **Small Goose Pagoda**, for example) have selections of high quality souvenirs. The **Grand Mosque** is a good place to shop for bargains, though you must be prepared to haggle. Just east of the South Gate is an area called **Shuyuanmen**, where the shops have been given a facelift to make them resemble a scene from a Hong Kong drama set in Qing dynasty China. The **Friendship Store**, on the corner of Nanxin Jie and Dong Dajie, is a good place to survey Xi'an's souvenir plenitude.

WHERE TO STAY

Luxury

Xi'an is an important tourist destination where you will have no problem finding luxury accommodation.

The **Hyatt Regency Xi'an (** (29) 723-1234 FAX (29) 721-6799, 158 Dadong Jie, is one of the city's best, a gleaming citadel a world apart from the rest of Xi'an.

The **Sheraton Xi'an Hotel (** (29) 426-1888 FAX (29) 426-2188, 12 Feng Hao Lu, has 438 rooms and 16 suites. Apartments with kitchenettes are also available. Along with restaurants it has a cocktail lounge and disco, and there's an indoor heated pool and a gym.

The **Shangri-La Golden Flower Hotel (** (29) 323-2981 FAX (29) 323-5477, 8 Changle Xilu, is recommended for its spacious rooms. Doubles come with two queen-size beds, while deluxe doubles have the same, with the addition of a sofa and large writing desk.

The Holiday-Inn-managed **Bell Tower Hotel Xi'an (** (29) 727-9200 FAX (29) 721-8767, on the southwest corner of the Bell Tower, may not be up to the standards set by the typical Holiday Inn hotels, but it has the best location of any luxury hotel in town.

Mid-Range

If you're staying in a mid-range or budget hotel, make it one that's inside or at least not too far outside the city walls — though you may find this advice difficult to adhere to as choices are limited. Three options are worth considering.

The **Xi'an People's Hotel** (also referred to by its Chinese name, the **Renmin**) ((29) 721-5111 FAX (29) 721-8152, 319 Dongxin Jie,

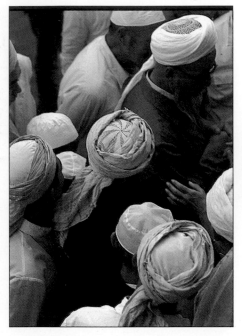

is one of those sprawling Soviet-inspired guesthouses, which like most others around China these days has been blandly renovated. Rooms here are good value, however, from around $40.

The **Jiefang Hotel** ((29) 727-8946 FAX (29) 721-2617, only just creeps in as an "inside the walls" hotel, being part of the walls. Don't expect it to be a medieval keep; it's another big Chinese hotel, but the price is right and the location directly opposite the railway station is a godsend for those early morning starts.

The **Wuyi (May Fifth) Hotel** ((29) 721-3824, may not be the best hotel in town, but the location is second only to that of the Bell Tower Hotel (above), the staff are friendly,

and there's a good restaurant downstairs. It's a bargain.

Inexpensive

There are just two popular budget hotels: the **Flats of Renmin Hotel** ((29) 625-2352, 9 Fenghe Lu, which is in an isolated but not unpleasant area just west of the city walls; and the long-running **Victory Hotel** ((29) 789-3040, on the corner of Huancheng Nanlu and Yanta Lu, just south of the city walls.

The Victory has the advantage of being closer to the sights than the Renmin. On the other hand, the Renmin is is directly across the road from two popular restaurants, which provide bicycle hire and travel advice, decent breakfasts and a constant stream of companionship.

WHERE TO EAT

Obviously, with all those four- and five-star hotels around, there's no shortage of excellent hotel restaurants. But after you've eaten your fill at the Hyatt or the Sheraton, don't forget there are some very good and reasonably priced restaurants out on the streets too.

Laosunjia, 384 Dong Dajie, can't be recommended too highly. For those who are not spending much time in the west of China, it represents a rare opportunity to try Chinese Moslem cuisine at its best. The house specialty is the *yangrou paomo*, in which a couple of cakes of bread are laboriously "crumbed" (by you, with your fingers) into a big soup bowl, to which a broth with noodles, lamb and sauces is added, producing a delicious meal.

The huge **Xi'an Restaurant**, 298 Dong Dajie, a short walk east of the Bell Tower, offers cuisine ranging from Beijing duck to steak and fries in its 14 dining rooms containing 300 tables and capable of seating a total 1,800 diners. Unless you're in the market for a splash out meal, it's best to stick to the downstairs area, where they throw together tasty Chinese meals in plebeian surroundings.

The **Wuyi Restaurant**, 351 Dong Dajie, is part of the hotel of the same name. Again the downstairs section is best, but for a sit-down meal the upstairs area, specializing in the cuisine of Jiangsu, is not a bad choice.

The **Dongya (East Asia) Restaurant**, 46 Luoma Shi, just south of the Bell Tower, is something of an institution, having been founded in 1916 in Shanghai, and brought to Xi'an in the 1950s.

An excellent choice for a meal is the **Sichuan Restaurant**, 151 Jiefang Lu, east of the Renmin Hotel. It doesn't look promising, but if you have an interest in China's spiciest cuisine, you will enjoy a meal here.

The local's favorite eating places can be found in the two Muslim food quarters in the Drum Tower district. Food stalls in the **Damaishi Jie** and **Majia Shazi** open until midnight. They offer snacks like fried persimmon cakes, soup dumplings and barbecued lamb and beef.

Backpackers gather at **Mum's Home Cooking** and **Dad's Home Cooking**. Both of them are on Fenghe Lu, opposite the Flats of Renmin Hotel, next door to each other. Dad's was the pioneer, Mum's followed shortly after: Both offer tasty, inexpensive Chinese and Western food, cheap beers and useful travel information.

HOW TO GET THERE

Xi'an can be reached by air from almost any airport in China. There are also direct trains from Beijing, Shanghai, Chengdu, Qingdao and Wuhan and direct rail services in turn to Xining and Urumqi, opening up the "wild west" of Qinghai and Xinjiang, and the route of the old Silk Road. Dragonair flies from Hong Kong. You can sometimes fly direct between Xi'an and Lhasa, Tibet on China Southwest Airlines, but as flights are not regular, it is best to check with a reputable China tour operator prior to departure.

MAIJISHAN GROTTOES

If you are traveling between Xi'an and Lanzhou by train, an extremely worthwhile diversion is the Maijishan Grottoes. The grottoes are around 35 km (22 miles) south of Tianshui, which in turn is around half way between Xi'an and Lanzhou.

Tianshui itself is an uninspiring urban sprawl that divides into the two centers: Beidao (which is where the train stops) and Qincheng (which is where buses arrive). If

you time things right, there should be no need to stay overnight in either district, but there is accommodation if you need it.

Maijishan (Wheat Stack Mountain) is China's fourth largest Buddhist cave complex, built from 384–417 AD. The others are at Dunhuang, Luoyang and Datong. One of the main attractions is a 16-m (52-ft)-tall Buddha, which announces itself from quite a distance before you reach the spectacular site.

The central section of the cliffs was damaged by an earthquake in 734 AD, but the east and west sections (particularly the latter)

contain some fine sculptures and murals. Since many of the caves are locked up, in order to get the most out of your tour you need a guide with keys. To organize an English-speaking guide, contact CITS ((938) 213-621, at the Xibing Hotel in the Qincheng district of Tianshui.

You'll find a better selection of hotels in the Qincheng district than in the Beidao railway station area. The best hotel is the **Tianshui Hotel** ((938) 214-542, on Yingbin Lu, which has comfortable doubles from around $40. Budget travelers head for the **Government Hostel** (Zhengfu Zhaodaisuo), next door to the railway station in Beidao.

LANZHOU

If Xi'an is the crossroads of central China, Lanzhou, the capital of Gansu province, is its radial right arm. From this former Han

OPPOSITE: Muslims gather for prayer at Xi'an's Grand Mosque. ABOVE: Boisterous, colorful souvenirs and hawkers at tomb of the terracotta soldiers.

dynasty garrison and frontier post there is access by rail to the heart of Qinghai province, and from there by road to Tibet. Another rail route runs directly to the old Silk Road oasis towns of the northwest, and yet another sweeps across the northern reaches of China, across the vast grasslands of Inner Mongolia, toward Beijing.

A key industrial city, Lanzhou is modern, well laid out with wide streets and boulevards, and has good hotels and department stores. It also sports a huge Beijing-style central city square (Dongfanghong, or East is Red, Square), about 10-minutes' walk west of the Lanzhou Hotel. Thousands of people meet here every day to fly kites and balloons and climb a strange and novel sightseeing tower which looks like a Moslem minaret with a children's slide winding around it.

The city's Moslem community is quite large, and it is really the first major center heading into the northwest where you can recognize the distinctive, surprisingly Middle Eastern features of the region's Turkic lineage. It also has a number of historic and cultural attractions, including an interesting set of Buddhist cave sculptures dating from the Tang dynasty.

WHAT TO SEE AND DO

Lanzhou lies on the south bank of the Yellow River. On the north bank is **Baita Shan (White Pagoda Hill)**, a hilly park with Ming and Qing dynasty pavilions and a Buddhist pagoda. A cable car swings over there (across the river) from just west of the Zhongshan bridge.

The **Gansu Provincial Museum**, opposite the Friendship Hotel, has the skeleton of a prehistoric mammoth dug up in 1973 and an interesting array of Neolithic and Han era pottery, murals, clay and bronze figures and the revered "Flying horses" that gave the Han and Tang cavalries the speed, mobility and endurance they needed to fight the nomadic Huns and the Turkic tribes. This is one provincial museum that is worth visiting, and it even has some English labeling.

The city's prime attraction is the **Bingling Si Caves**, near the hamlet of **Yongjing** on the Yellow River in Dasi Valley, a beautiful area of mountains, sheer cliffs and deep ravines.

From Lanzhou the journey by bus and boat takes about six hours, but during the summer months access may not be possible because of flooding.

First dug about 1,500 years ago, one of the grottoes has an inscription that is recognized as the oldest example of cave writing in China.

In the year 420, Buddhist monks extended the grottoes and began work on an impressive parade of carved Buddhas and other devotional art. More were added over the centuries until there were 183 caves crammed with art and relics by the time of the thirteenth century Mongol rule. They contain nearly 700 Buddha images, including a 27-m (88.5–ft)-high Maitreya sculpture, more than 80 clay figures and a big display of Qin and Tang dynasty murals.

WHERE TO STAY

The **Lanzhou Legend Hotel** ((931) 888-2876 FAX (931) 888-7876, 599 Tianshui Lu, is right on the Xiguan traffic circle and the best of Lanzhou's hotels. The **Ningwozhuang Hotel** ((931) 882-4180 FAX (931) 841-7649, 365 Tianshui Lu, is that rambling institutional style of guesthouse much beloved by tea-sipping cadres back in the 1950s. The grounds are very pleasant, but some of the rooms could do with refurbishing.

Just across from the Lanzhou Legend, and also on the Xiguan traffic circle is the **Lanzhou Hotel** ((931) 841-6321 FAX (931) 841-8608, 434 Donggang Xilu, which is a good mid-range choice.

Most of the budget accommodation is beside the main railway station. **Lanzhou Mansions** ((931) 841-6321, the huge block on your left as you exit the station has some three-bed dorms with attached bathroom. North of the station on Tianshui Lu is the **Yingbin Hotel** ((931) 888-6552, which is cheaper still.

HOW TO GET THERE

There are direct air services to Lanzhou from Beijing, Guangzhou, Nanjing, Xi'an, and Shanghai, and, coming from the northwest,

Which came first? A trader in Lanzhou ponders an age-old question.

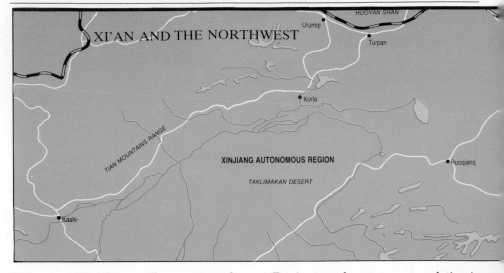

Urumqi and Dunhuang. There are two alternative train routes linking the city with Beijing, one sweeping over Inner Mongolia via Baotou, Hohhot and Datong, and the other cutting across the center of China via Xi'an and Zhengzhou. Direct trains to and from Shanghai also take the Xi'an-Zhengzhou route.

XIAHE

Nine hours south of Lanzhou is the enchanting town of Xiahe with its famous **Labrang Monastery**. "Little Tibet" might be a good name for this area, and for those who don't have time to get up to the high plateau a visit to Xiahe is a perfect second-best. Like Tibet, be prepared for some acclimatization problems: Xiahe is 2,920 m (9,580) above sea level, which is more than enough to leave you short of breath and slightly insomniac for few days.

Labrang, one of the great Gelugpa, or Yellow Hat, monasteries is very active, even by Tibetan standards. Although the erstwhile monk population of 4,000 has been reduced by half, the monastery still has more monks than any monastery in Tibet has. They come from all over the Tibetan regions of western China — Gansu, Qinghai, Sichuan and Tibet itself. There are daily debates, and you will frequently see performances of traditional Tibetan music (which, incidentally, is unmelodic to the Western ears, consisting mostly of chants and tortured blasts from enormous horns).

Don't expect luxury accommodation in Xiahe, which is quite an off-the-beaten track destination. The **Labrang Hotel ⟮** (9412) 21849, several kilometers to the west of town, past a small Tibetan village, is furnished in Tibetan style and has a wide range of rooms, from dormitories to delightful doubles with attached bath.

THE RADIAL ROUTE

From Lanzhou you can travel by train and bus all the way to Lhasa, crossing one of the most rugged, least explored tourist areas of China, Qinghai province.

There are daily trains to Xining, the capital of Qinghai, and the trip is short enough to take a first-class soft-seat or even venture into the hard-seat section. You'll roll along through green-swathed terraced loess landscape in summer — the ancient sculpture of the Yellow River — or, in midwinter, witness bleak scenes of dun-colored terraced mounds and hills, looming over frozen rivers and streams, mud-bricked walled compounds and villages huddle in the loess fields, the only sign of life an occasional donkey kicking its heels in the morning sun and dust, following its master out into the neat flat farming plots.

XINING

Xining, the capital of Qinghai province, started its days as a military garrison and

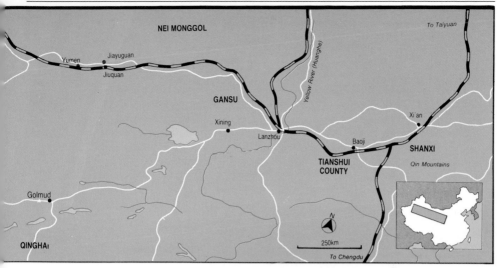

trading center in the sixteenth century. Like the rest of Qinghai it has long been a place of exile, and even today some sources calculate that one in 10 residents of the province are either prisoners or released prisoners who cannot return to their home provinces.

Despite such grim statistics, Xining today is a fairly modern industrial city populated by an interesting mix of Han Chinese, Moslem Huis and Tibetans. Its eastern inner-city district is where you'll find the **Moslem Quarter**, a crowded market enclave around the picturesque fourteenth century **Grand Mosque**.

The city is remarkable for its huge well-stocked department stores, probably a reflection of its continuing frontier role as a supply and provisions depot for the vast and largely inhospitable Tibet–Qinghai Plateau which sweeps away to the west and south right to the foothills of the Himalayas.

WHAT TO SEE AND DO

Xining is not brimming with sights, but for those who have travelled here across China, the unique character of the place will be apparent immediately. There's more space here, the light is harder, the air crisper, and if you feel yourself slightly out of breath as you stroll around town, it's because you're at an altitude of 2,200 m (7,000 ft).

The chief attraction in town is the **Moslem Quarter**, with its impressive **Grand Mosque**. If you're feeling particularly ener-

getic, you might consider climbing for about an hour up into the hills north of the Huangshui River to visit **Beishan Temple**. At around 1400 years of age, this is an ancient place of worship, and the views of Xining from up here are fabulous. From the railway station, a Nº 11 bus will take you to the foot of the hills.

Huangzhong, about 25 km (15.5 miles) to the southwest of Xining, is where you'll find the magnificent Tibetan-style **Ta'Er Monastery**, one of the six greatest lamaserais of the Gelugpa, or Yellow Hat Sect (Labrang at Xiahe, above, is another). This is a good taste of what is to come in Tibet, if that is where you are headed. Note the beautiful Hall of Meditation, with its silk *thangkas*. Ta'Er was built in 1560 in memory of the founder of the sect, Tsongkapa, and is famous for its ornate yak butter sculptures of human figures, animals and landscapes.

If you can, pay a visit to the monastery early in the day. There's plenty here to keep you busy for a full day, wandering through the many halls of the monastery, hiking up around the surrounding hills for a stupendous panoramic view, and finally enjoying a hearty bowl of inexpensive noodles at one of the stalls that surround Ta'Er. Buses leave from the long distance bus station across from the railway station, while minibuses leave throughout the day from the Ximen bus station in town next to the gymnasium (as for the *tiyuguan*). The trip takes around an hour.

WHERE TO STAY AND EAT

Xining's finest is the **Qinghai Hotel** ((971) 614-4888. It's aimed mostly at tour groups and business people, and inconveniently located 10 km (six miles) from the railway station.

For a basic but clean and friendly stop-over, the most popular hotel with foreigners is the **Yongfu Hotel** ((971) 814-0236, directly opposite the railway station.

Some of Xining's best dining takes place

on the streets (not that you'd want to do this in the winter months, when temperatures plummet). Look out for sizzling kebabs and simmering pots of noodle broth. Around the Yongfu Hotel are several Moslem restaurants.

TO LHASA

There are two trains a day from Xining to **Golmud** in the center of Qinghai province, where you face the bus journey from hell: anywhere from 25 to 35 hours nonstop and much of it along precipitous mountain roads. Buses also run from Golmud to Dunhuang in Gansu province, home of the Mogao Buddhist Grottoes, the most famous surviving treasures of the old Silk Road.

THE NEW SILK ROAD

From Lanzhou, a northwest rail route opens the door to the great garrisons, oasis towns, cities and Buddhist relics that were among the wonders of the Silk Road and have survived the ravages of time since its death. **Jiayuguan** is the first convenient radial point on the Lanzhou–Urumqi railway, providing access by bus to **Jiuquan**, a similar outpost that was prominent in the Han dynasty's expeditions against the Xiongnu, and to **Dunhuang** and its fabulous **Mogao Caves**.

Jiayuguan was also an important Han military outpost, but it was not until the Ming dynasty that its strategic position, guarding the Jiayuguan Pass, was considered critical to the defense of the northwest frontier. The Ming emperor Hongwu bolstered the garrison by building the **Tianxia Xiongguan**, a huge stronghold which, from that point on, served as the western extremity of the Great Wall. The Ming engineers were so meticulous, and their specifications so exact, that when this "Impregnable Defile Under the Heavens" was completed, only a single brick was left over. It is now proudly displayed in one of the fort's halls.

The fort is one of northwest China's most impressive sights. Be sure, too, to visit the **Overhanging Great Wall**, a reconstructed stretch of the wall. It provides wonderful views of Jianyuguan, the fort and the snow-capped mountains in the distance.

Jiayuguan's top hotel is the **Changcheng Hotel** ((9477) 225-277 FAX (9477) 226-016. It has a variety of rooms, but you can get some comfort here for around $30 and up. The **Jiayuguan Guesthouse** ((9477) 226-983 FAX (9477) 227-174 has both inexpensive dorms and tourist-class rooms, and has a good central location with a post office and bank right across the street and buses outside that leave four times a day for the 15-minute hop to the fort.

DUNHUANG

The reason to visit this hot and dusty oasis town is its nearby **Mogao Buddhist Grottoes**, 25 km (15.5 miles) to the southeast. In these caves, all 492 of them, you can see

China's best preserved cave art (over 45,000 murals) and some of the most impressive Buddhist statuary (over 2,000 items) in the whole country.

More than 1,000 caves were originally excavated here and filled with carvings, murals, clay sculptures and other artwork. The work began in the fourth century AD and continued for several centuries. The surviving grottoes are crammed with treasures: murals covering a total of 4.5 hectares (11 acres), 3,400 bas-relief and three-dimensional wall sculptures, several thousand pil-

lars with the lotus motif and floral floor tiles, and five ornate Tang era wooden shrines. At the turn of the twentieth century a Daoist priest broke through to a sealed grotto and came upon another 50,000 relics dating from the Jin to Song period.

This massive endeavor was started by the Turkic-speaking Toba rulers of the Northern Wei dynasty (386–594 AD) and added to in the ensuing Sui, Tang, Five Dynasties and Song reigns—each dynasty stamping its own artistic style on this amazing exhibition. The aesthetic high point was reached in the Tang reign, and the sculptures, and murals of that time reflect the dynasty's three thumb-rules to acceptable art—richness, exuberance and opulence. The Buddha images are made of

clay and painted, and range in height from a few centimeters to a towering 33 m (108 ft). Among them is a huge sculpture of the Maitreya Buddha executed by Ma Sizhong between the years 713 and 741 AD.

The Chinese are very sensitive about the Mogao Grottoes, and photography is strictly forbidden. Over a period of years from the late 1800s to the 1930s, several Western scholar-adventurers, notably the Swede Sven Hedin, the German Albert von Le Coq, the Frenchman Paul Pelliot and Great Britain's Aurel Stein, infiltrated the paths of the Silk Road from the west and virtually ransacked its "lost" and barely surviving oasis centers, including Dunhuang, of some of the most splendid Buddhist artwork, manuscripts and relics — an act for which the Chinese have never really forgiven the West. Read *Foreign Devils on the Silk Road* by Peter Hopkirk to gain an appreciation of the part of the world you are in.

Where to Stay

Though small, Dunhuang has a good selection of places to stay. There are a couple of luxury options, such as the **Jinshan Hotel** ((9473) 882-1077, but the best choice is the mid-range **Dunhuang Hotel** ((9473) 882-2512, 14 Yangguang Donglu. Don't confuse the latter with the other, very grotty, Dunhuang Hotel on Xinjiang Lu: the first is a *bīnguǎn*, the second a *fàndiàn*.

How to Get There

Daily flights are available all through the summer season from Xi'an and Lanzhou, and on a less frequent basis the rest of the year.

To get back on to the main Lanzhou–Urumqi railway line, there are buses from Dunhuang to the station at Liuyuan, about three and a half hours away. From there, the path is open to the second great frontier of modern travel in China — the barren, but fascinating "wild west" of Xinjiang Uygur.

XINJIANG–UYGUR AUTONOMOUS REGION

This is classic "great game" country, with politics, espionage, disguise, murder, mys-

OPPOSITE: Tibetan worshiper at Ta'Er Monastery near Xining. ABOVE: Crowd watches at Ta'Er Butter Festival, one of the main spiritual observances of Lamaism.

tery and intrigue. Read another of Peter Hopkirk's books, *The Great Game*, which tells with immense readability and historic detail the importance of these desolate but strategic locations.

The Uygurs are the most numerous and most prominent of some 13 Moslem Turkic-speaking or Mongol minorities that inhabit this harsh, sun-baked region. The others include ethnic Russians, Tartars, Uzbeks, Tajiks, Xibes, Dours, Khalkhas, Kazakhs, Kalmucks (Kalmyks) and Hui in this huge melting pot of previously fierce nomadic tribal groups of Central Asia. The region itself has had a variety of names over the centuries, including High Tartary, Chinese Turkestan, Kashgaria and Serinder (the Silk Route).

Divided by the Tian Mountains into two vast desert basins, Xinjiang is one of the most geographically hostile places on earth. In the south lies the dreaded Taklamakan — an 800,000-sq-km (308,880-sq-mile) inferno with 100-m (67-ft)-high shifting dunes and fierce sandstorms — which in the Turkic tongue is known as the place where travelers "go in (and) don't come out." To the north lies the Gobi, which stretches up into Mongolia and, to the southwest, is another waterless sea of dunes known as the Land of Death. In the central region the desert sinks more than 150 m (492 ft) below sea-level to form the pitilessly hot Turpan Depression.

TURPAN

At the heart of the furnace, Turpan is the first major tourist destination on the northwest trail. This oasis town was an important link in the Silk Road, and a jewel in the Buddhist crown, until the eighth century when Islam spread from the West, its forces destroying much of the region's Buddhist statuary as they went. The town now presents an interesting contrast of the two religious influences, a key center of the Moslem Uygur culture and an access point for some of the surviving Silk Road Buddhist relics.

CITS is at the Oasis Hotel.

Getting Around

Turpan, though flat, is one place where few feel inclined to leap onto a bicycle; the heat is soporific. For short jaunts around town, a

donkey and cart is a perfect way to jolt to your destination. For longer trips, get together with a group of other travelers (there are always plenty in town) and hire a minibus for a day of sightseeing. Figure on spending around $50 to $60 for a minibus.

What to See and Do

The eighteenth-century Afghan-style **Emin Minaret** is a couple of kilometers (a mile and a quarter) southeast of town and is easily Turpan's most impressive sight.

Most of Turpan's other attractions lay quite a distance out of town. Notable are two ruined cities that once played prominent roles on the old Silk Road. **Gaochang**, about 46 km (28 miles) to the east of Turpan, was the capital of the Uygur state established by the Uygurs when they migrated into Xinjiang from Mongolia in the ninth century. While **Jiaohe**, 20 km (12.4 miles) west, was a Tang dynasty garrison in the wars against the Turkic tribes.

Both towns are derelict but give a clear impression of the mud-brick and rammed earth architecture of that age, and the thoroughfares and lanes, official halls, monasteries and pagodas, homes and courtyards, corridors and underground passages and thick earthen walls of what were, in fact, relatively sophisticated settlements. Underground chambers were dug below each dwelling to give shelter from the fierce daytime heat. At Gaochang you'll find the remains of a monastery with some parts of it still reasonably intact. To the northwest of Gaochang there's an ancient burial complex, the **Hastana Tombs**, with murals of some of the dead.

North of Turpan, right in the central pan of the Turpan Depression, the **Huoyan Shan (Flaming Mountains)** offer a vivid experience of the intense heat of the region. The daytime temperature on the slopes often reaches 70°C (158°F). The rock and red soil flare into shimmering "fire" when the sun strikes, hence the name. One Ming dynasty novel describes how a famous monk and his disciples were caught in the raging "fires" on the range and were saved by the Monkey

---

Classic lines of Islamic architecture TOP and ornate Islamic decoration on new Turpan mosque BOTTOM.

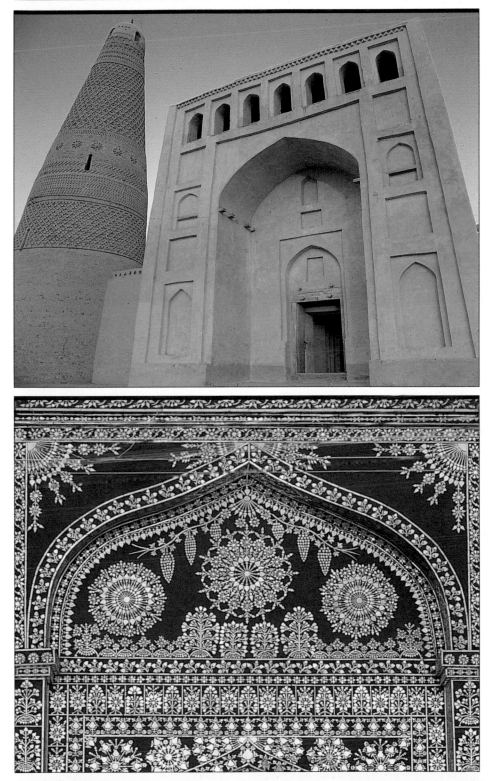

King, Sun Wukong, who put out the flames with a fan so that they could continue on their way.

BEZEKLIK GROTTOES

The Turpan region's most famous attraction, the Bezeklik Grottoes about 50 km (31 miles) northwest of town are, for almost everyone who visits, a disappointment. They were cut into the western slope of Huoyan Shan in the Northern Wei period just before the rise of the Tang dynasty—64 grottoes excavated or built of mud-brick, featuring Buddhist shrines and chambers. Nowadays they look worn, and besides, most of the finest artwork was swiped by the German Silk Road explorer, Albert von Le Coq. The murals were shipped to the Berlin Museum, where they were destroyed by Allied bombing in World War II.

Where to Stay and Eat

The **Turpan Guesthouse** ((995) 522-301 has been the choice abode of foreigners in Turpan for as long as anyone can remember. Backpackers crowd into the dorms, while the well-heeled cool off in the air-conditioned rooms, which start at around $25. **John's Information & Café**, an essential stop on the Turpan dining circuit and a mine of useful information on the area, is just across the road. Best of all are the vine-covered verandahs where you can sit in the cool of the evening, dining, nibbling on Turpan's justly famous grapes, and wondering if you'll ever feel the chill of winter again. In the evenings, all through the summer months, Uygur song and dance performances are held in the hotel grounds.

The other popular lodging in Turpan is the **Oasis Hotel** ((995) 522-478, with spacious grounds and a host of useful amenities. Like the Turpan Guesthouse it has both dorms and more upmarket tourist rooms.

URUMQI

This, the Xinjiang capital and the next stop along the northwest railway line, is a disappointingly drab city at first glance. Certainly it lacks the small town oasis atmosphere of Turpan. But as you explore the place, stumble across a Uygur bazaar, visit a museum or two, and chance upon the mosques of Jiegang Nanlu, you begin to realize that below the familiar Han exterior of this city run some fascinating Middle Eastern undercurrents.

General Information

The **CAAC** booking office ((991) 484-3762 is at 62 Youhao Nanlu, in the northwest of town.

The **Bank of China** has its main branch at 343 Jiefang Nanlu. **CITS** ((991) 282-1427 is at 51 Xinhua Beilu.

Getting Around

Until some enterprising local starts renting out bicycles (ask at John's Café), you're stuck with either the overcrowded bus system or the just-plain-crowded minibuses. One look at the former should be enough to put off most sensible travelers. Take a minibus, or better still, take a taxi; they cost just $2 to most destinations.

What to See and Do

Among Urumqi's parks, **Renmin Park** and **Hongshan Park** are worth visiting. The Renmin Park lies near the center of town, and is superb early in the morning when locals come out in force to do their daily calisthenics. Hongshan Park is a hilly area in the north of town. At the summit is a pagoda, and from here you get stunning views of Urumqi, the desert and the faraway mountains.

The **Xinjiang Regional Museum**, as the name suggests, is the best in the region. The museum could be better organized, more English labeling is needed, but overall it's

an interesting insight into Xinjiang and the old Silk Road that once crossed it. In particular look for the four 3000-year-old bodies, which were mummified in the scorching desert sands and are now on public display. One of the females is reckoned quite a beauty.

For a closer look at the minorities and their lifestyles there's a pastureland called **Baiyanggou (White Poplar Gully)**, about 60 km (37 miles) south of Urumqi and accessible by bus or taxi. It's a traditional gathering place for the Kazakh herders. Visitors can watch them tending their sheep, horses and cattle and, for a fee, can spend the night in their yurts feasting on mutton and rice and being entertained with Kazakh song and dance.

Weathered ruins of ancient Jiaohe.

But the area's most splendid attraction lies 115 km (72 miles) east of Urumqi—**Tian Chi (Heaven Lake)**, 2000 m (6400) up, on the slopes of Mount Bogda, the 5,445-m (17,860-ft)-high principal peak of the Tian Mountains. This towering range rises in central Xinjiang and marches 2,500 km (1,550 miles) into the heart of Central Asia, presenting a stunning contrast of soaring snow-capped peaks set amidst the fiery flat desert wastes. The marauding Xiongnü regarded the Tian range as heaven. It has an astounding number of glaciers—6,896 of them—forming an enormous reservoir of ice which, as it melts, feeds six great rivers in Xinjiang, as well as the region's vital subterranean cisterns.

Heaven Lake is alpine in its beauty, unspeakably refreshing after the desert lowlands. Heavily wooded slopes roll down to the edge of the turquoise water. In the warmer summer months (it gets bitterly cold through the winter, and may even be inaccessible at this time), it's possible to hire horses for less than $10 a day and trek up into other valleys, where you can stay in yurts with the local Kazakh herders.

Buses to Heaven Lake leave at around 9 AM from the north end of Renmin Park in Urumqi. It's a good idea to buy your ticket the day before departure from the Hongshan Hotel (see below).

Where to Stay
Top of the range is the **Holiday Inn Urumqi** ((991) 281-8788 FAX (991) 281-7422, 168 Xinhua Beilu, which given its remoteness does a remarkable job of catering to the luxury needs of its guests. You'll find a good health club, a disco, excellent restaurants and a top-floor lounge. The nearby **Laiyuan Hotel** ((991) 282-8368 is another luxury setup, but if you're going to pay the rates they want for their (albeit very comfy) doubles, you may as well go that little extra and check into the Holiday Inn.

The **Kunlun Guesthouse** ((991) 484-0411 FAX (991) 484-0213, 38 Youhao Beilu, is an expensive mid-range hotel, but still a considerable step down in price from the Holiday Inn, and reasonably good value. Its one drawback is that it is somewhat remote. The **Peafowl Hotel** ((991) 484-2988, is closer to town (opposite CAAC), and its air-conditioned doubles are quite a bargain.

The most popular budget hotel in town is the **Hongshan Hotel** ((991) 282-4973. It has a fine central location close to the shops, restaurants and buses for Heaven Lake. The hotel has both dorms and inexpensive doubles.

Where to Eat
Save breakfasts (and lunch too if you like) for the **Holiday Inn** buffet, which is an unimaginable treat after pulling into town from the rigors of the northwestern trail. If breakfast and lunch leave you hungry for more, the Holiday Inn has a good selection of restaurants, including **Kashgaris**, which does *haute cuisine* Moslem-style.

Opposite the Hongshan Hotel, John has set up another **John's Information & Café**. If it's information and decent affordable meals you want, John's is the best place in town to get them.

Elsewhere, be adventurous and try some local Uyghur street food. The area around and in **Erdaoqiao Market** is a good place to sample kebabs and flat breads. Pop into a noodle shop, too, and try the local noodle soup — just ask for *lamian*.

How to Get There
Urumqi is well connected with the rest of China by air these days. Daily rail services run to Lanzhou, Xi'an, Zhengzhou, Nanjing and on to other parts of China. For travel farther west, however, you have just two choices: bus or air.

On to Central Asia
An adventurous route out of China is from Urumqi into Kazakhstan. It is now possible to walk into the Urumqi railway station and buy a train ticket for less than $100 to Almaty. If you're game to fly Kazakh Airlines ((991) 383-6400, you can fly to Almaty for around $120; CAAC will fly you there too, but at nearly double the price. Buses are the cheapest way to get to Almaty, but few travelers relish the thought of a 24-hour bus journey into the unknown. You *will* need a visa; they are available from the Kazakh Airlines office in Urumqi.

Aptly named Heavenly Lake TOP, near Urumqi; Mongolian yurts BOTTOM on the shores of Sky Lake.

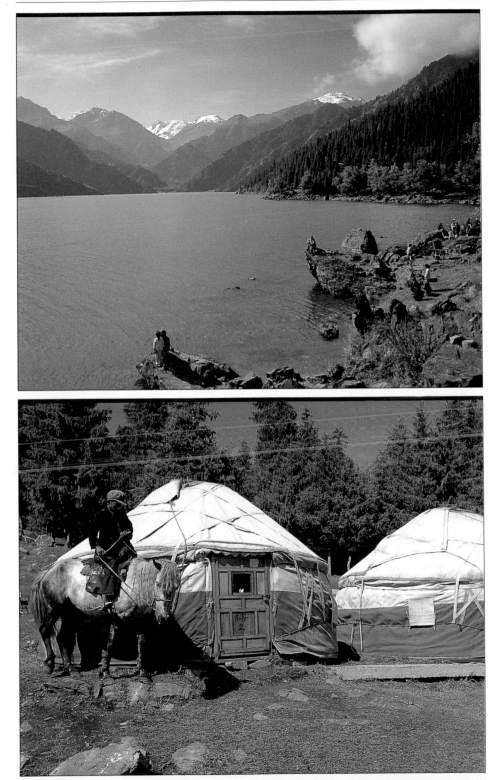

KASHGAR

If anywhere is the heart of old Chinese Turkestan, it is this faraway place called Kashgar (in Chinese, Kashi). The name has a ring to it. It speaks of caravan routes snaking through desert, of the long-dreamed-of shade of palms, the splash of water, of pomegranates and dates. Of course, Kashgar nowadays evokes little of such romance, but it still provides a fascinating glimpse into the rhythms of Uyghur urban life as it must have been a century or more ago.

Kashgar is in a sense the only true surviving Silk Road watering hole. Merchant camel caravans, Buddhist pilgrims and the occasional explorer like Marco Polo — they all passed through here. They passed through a lot of other places too; but, most of these have fallen into neglect. Only Kashgar continues to prosper.

Back in the nineteenth century it was a great bazaar in which Indian, Afghan and Russian traders rubbed elbows with Moslem and Mongolian tribesmen, Chinese settlers and exiles, bandits, brigands, corsairs, tomb and temple robbers and some of the scurviest, most dangerous human flotsam of Central Asia. It had its spies too — agents of a Russian intrigue centered on Afghanistan that the British took so seriously that they established a consulate and dispatched the redoubtable George and Lady Macartney there for 28 years to keep an eye on things. From their official residence, a fine colonial mansion called Chini-bagh, they kept tabs on the Russian consul and offered hospitality to archaeologists like Hedin and Stein as they trekked through to ransack the crumbling ruins of the Silk Road. Both Chini-bagh and the Russian consulate are now hotels.

Kashgar today continues to function as a watering hole. Since May 1986, the border for travel to and from Pakistan via the Friendship Highway, which runs to the southwest and crosses the Karakoram Mountains, has been open. It's not unusual to see Pakistani and Indian traders in town.

Getting Around

Donkey carts are not allowed into central Kashgar — they do tend to bestow a certain air of bucolic poverty, after all — so you will have to get around by bicycle. These are available from John's Information & Café or from outside the Chinibagh Hotel.

What to See and Do

Kashgar is an ethnic microcosm of the northwest, with a population that mixes Kazakhs, Mongols and Uygurs. Its **central bazaar** (the best in China) and nearby **Id Kah Mosque** and main square are where all the daily trading and pageantry take place. The mosque is designed in the typical Moslem, rather

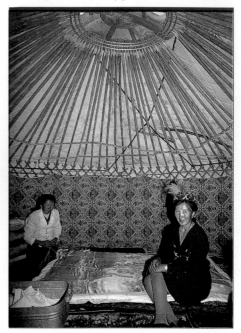

than Chinese style, with a huge arched main entrance and doors, elegantly tiled minarets and a domed prayer hall, and there are others in the backstreets around it including a large one that has fallen into quite colorful ruin.

Travelers lucky enough to be in Kashgar on a Sunday can visit Xinjiang's most colorful and boisterous **Sunday market**. It's on the eastern edge of town. Just follow the crowds.

But the main attraction of Kashgar is the stunning Moslem architecture of the **Abakh Hoja Tomb** on the eastern outskirts of the town, a seventeenth century family mausoleum that grew in the ensuing centuries into a major burial spot for the Moslem aristocracy of the region. Today it presents a contrast of both the severe simplicity and ornate architecture of Islam — it is surrounded by cone-shaped graves the color of baked clay, and out of the center of them rises the principal grave chamber with its splendid domed roof, decorated with green and amber tiles. Minaret-style towers stand at its four corners.

This main tomb contains 72 burial places, most of them decorated with mosaic tiles and draped with colorfully patterned shrouds. It's said that the tomb became a popular spot for wealthy Moslems because they wanted to lie in rest beside the central sarcophagus which, as legend has it, contains the costumes of Xi'angfei (Fragrant Concubine), a renowned beauty of the region who was kidnaped by a Qing dynasty ruler and taken to the Forbidden City in Beijing.

Kashgar's other big attraction is its access via the **Friendship Highway** and forbidding Karakorum Mountains to Pakistan. CITS are the people to go to for information about exit visas and buses for the cross border journey.

Where to Stay and Eat

Kashgar's best hotel is the **Kashgar Guesthouse** ((998) 222-368. Don't expect a great deal of this rambling, slightly neglected tourist-class hotel. It has, as they say, seen better days. The location too, three or four kilometers (one or two miles) out on the western edge of the town, is not a major selling point.

Chinibagh Hotel ((998) 225-929, is the old Macartney residence and consulate, and has an excellent location near the central market. It has some good mid-range rooms.

The most popular hotel in town, however, both with budget and mid-range travelers is the **Seman Hotel** ((998) 222-129, which is housed in the former Russian consulate. The rooms range from noisy dorms to very comfortable mid-range rooms. Another reason for its popularity is the proximity of a number of small restaurants serving delicious food via that most important of media, the English menu. And in case you were wondering, **John's Information & Café** is across the road doling out that client-winning combination of food and facts.

How to Get There

For the brave and the impecunious Kashgar is a two- or three-day bus journey from Urumqi. Slow buses stop overnight in towns along the way. There are no more Holiday Inns out there on the northern edge of the Taklamakan Desert (think of those poor Silk Road merchants huddled up with their camels if the conditions get depressing). Daily flights between Kashgar and Urumqi are a civilized addition to Xinjiang's travel network. In Kashgar **CAAC** ((998) 222-113, is on Jiefang Nanlu.

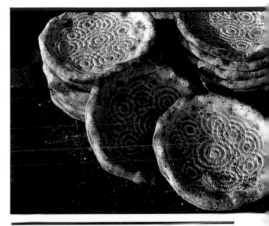

ONWARD TO PAKISTAN

The Karakorum Highway spans 1,300 km (800 miles), over the Khunjerab Pass to Rawalpindi in northern Pakistan, from whence you can travel on to Islamabad. You need at least four days to reach Islamabad, and you will also need a Pakistan visa — organize one in Beijing or in Hong Kong. From the beginning of May until the end of October, which is when the pass is open, there should be daily departures from Kashgar.

OPPOSITE: Yurt interior on the shores of Sky Lake. ABOVE: Unleavened bread on Urumqi market stall.

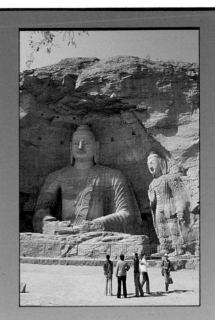

Across
the North

IF YOU ARE ENTERING CHINA along the Friendship Highway, Urumqi is the railhead for the swing right across the north of the country, through the boundless grasslands of Inner Mongolia to Beijing. If you've cut up into the northwest from Lanzhou there's no alternative, other than an expensive plane flight (Urumqi–Kashgar), to retracing your route by rail back to this key junction for access across the north.

There are, in fact, two rail routes to the north from Lanzhou, and care must be taken when booking tickets not to be stuck aboard the wrong one. One direct service heads to Beijing via Baotou and Hohhot in Inner Mongolia, then Datong, the third of the four greatest centers of Buddhist cave art in China. The other cuts back southeast to Xi'an, then across the heartland of China through Luoyang, the site of the Longmen Grottoes, and Zengzhou, the access point for the Shaolin Monastery, after which it heads north to Beijing through Shijiazhuang in Hebei province.

Luoyang and Zhengzhou can be approached just as easily from the east, from Beijing, Shanghai and Guangzhou, leaving the trip across the northern plateau the most exciting route from Lanzhou.

THE GRASSLANDS

The grasslands route takes you through the panoramic flat green seas of Gobi scrubland and lusher pastureland that stretch from horizon to horizon across Nei Menggu (Inner Mongolia), broken only by occasional settlements of yurts, the animal skin tents of the nomadic sheep and cattle herders. Until the railway line was pushed across the plains, the Dahingan Range, a thickly wooded stretch of hills running northeast to southwest across the plateau, effectively isolated the Mongolian tribes, or "banners," from the rest of the world, and for the most part kept the rest of the world out of Mongolia.

As for the Mongolians themselves, they were a warring, fragmented and greatly feared "barbarian" race ruled by khans, or tribal chiefs, until one man turned their solitary, idyllic existence upside down for them — Genghis Khan. In one of the most incredible, explosive events of history these sheep and cattle herders — brilliant horsemen and cavalry tacticians, to be sure — suddenly banded together under this savage warlord's command and thundered out of the wilderness to conquer China and carve an empire that stretched beyond the western borders of Russia and Persia. And, just as swiftly as they pillaged and subjugated much of the vast Eurasian landmass, so their terrible adventure ended: Within less than a century they had been crushed in China by the Mings, pushed back out of the territories to the west and were straggling and limping back into the grassy wilds far beyond the Great Wall.

From that time of retreat and withdrawal, the Mongolian "nation" was divided between the tribes of the north and the remnants of the China "expedition" in the south — a division that the Manchu Qing dynasty was happy to maintain for its own sake when it brought the entire region under Chinese control in the seventeenth century. By the turn of the twentieth century the Russians were competing for control of the region, and in 1924 the Soviet Red Army moved in and promoted the establishment of the autonomous People's Republic of (Outer) Mongolia in the north, leaving the southern Nei Monggol to Beijing. The region is now heavily settled with Han Chinese, who vastly outnumber the estimated two million Mongols, many of whom have returned to their greener but far less ambitious pastures with little to show for their historic glory but two spiritual legacies — Tibetan-style Buddhism and Islam.

BAOTOU

The first major stop on the journey to the east is Baotou, the autonomous region's largest city, and an ugly industrial center supported by iron and coal mining. It is, however, the site of one of the main centers of lamaist Buddhism in China, the magnificent **Wudang (Willow Tree) Monastery** which lies on a hillside 70 km (43 miles) northeast of the city.

Wudang is one of the finest surviving lamaseries in Inner Mongolia, and its size alone testifies to its importance — it contains more than 2,500 living units, classrooms, temples and prayer halls. Its origins are similarly illustrious. It was built in 1749 by the thenreigning Dalai Lama himself and has since been a temporary residence for at least seven Tibetan rulers. Its architecture is flat, white-washed and Tibetan on the outside with blazes of color inside in its temples and schools. Ornately woven pillar rugs, beautiful Tibetan carpeting and huge murals decorate the main hall, Suguqindu, where the lamas pray and chant the scriptures. Other halls are filled with images of Sakyamuni Buddha, including one bronze statue that's 10 m (33 ft) tall.

Baotou itself, however, is not a particularly pleasant place to find yourself in need of lodging. If you get stuck there, try to make sure you're stuck in East Baotou (Donghe), where you will find the **Beiyang Hotel (** (472) 417-5656.

HOHHOT

Hohhot (in Chinese Huhehaote), the capital of Inner Mongolia, is a far more attractive city than Baotou. It only became the capital in 1952, and prior to this time it was a center for Mongolian Buddhism.

WHAT TO SEE AND DO

Xilitu Temple is set into the old city walls. Built in the Ming dynasty, Xilitu has an architecture that is mainly Han Chinese with a main shrine hall and sutra hall in the Tibetan style and features an eight-sided pavilion inscribed with details in Chinese, Manchu, Mongolian and Tibetan of the Qing emperor Kangxi's victorious military expeditions against unruly tribes in the northwest.

The great sutra hall, or Dajingtang, has walls inlaid with peacock-blue tiles with silver decorations. The roof of the building is strictly Tibetan, mounted with an ornate gilded vase, prayer-wheel, flying dragon and a deer, all cast in copper.

Near the People's Park you'll find the **Jingangzuo Sheli Pagoda**, popularly called Wu Ta (Five Pagodas) a series of five square brick and stone towers faced with glazed tiles and richly carved with Buddhas, Bodhisattvas and bodhi trees, images of lions, elephants and birds, mandalas, and a total of 1,119 small

Buddha niches. These towers, mounted on a stone base, are all that survives of a much grander Cideng Monastery which was built there in the eighteenth century.

The **Wanbu Huayanjing Ta** (Pagoda of the 10,000 Volumes of Avatamasaka Sutra) is in the eastern section of Hohhot; you can call it the **Bai Ta** (White Pagoda), which most of the citizenry call it. It's a lofty 43-m (141-ft)-tall eight-sided tower of wood and brick, probably built between 983 and 1031 when Buddhism flourished again in the wake of the late-Tang dynasty crackdown, and it

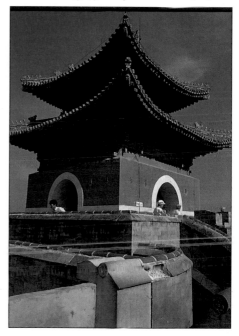

stands on the site of what was once a monastery called Daxuanjiao. It features an interesting display of ancient graffiti — inscriptions carved by visitors as far back as the twelfth century and written not only in Chinese but also Mongolian, Nuzhen (an old Chinese tribe), Kitan, ancient Syrian and Persian.

For one of the city's most prized Buddhist relics you have to visit the **Dazhao Monastery** in Hohhot's southern district. The Chinese call it Yinfo Si (Silver Buddha Monastery) in honor of its most treasured possession, an image of the Sakyamuni Buddha cast entirely in silver. Again, the monastery's

Sweeping double-eaved roof of Qing dynasty tomb.

design is half Chinese and half Tibetan, built in 1580 and extended during the reign of the Qing warrior emperor Kangxi.

Nine kilometers (six miles) south of Hohhot on the south bank of the Dahei (Great Black) River there's a tall loess mound, 33 m (108 ft) high, which isn't much of a sightseeing attraction — just a huge bump in the terrain — but is worth a picnic while you sit and ponder over the legend and superstition that goes with it. It's the **Tomb of Wang Zhaojun**, who is said to have been a concubine of the Han dynasty ruler Emperor Yuan.

When a prince named Huhanye of the dreaded Xiongnü came to the court and asked to marry Wang Zhaojun, the emperor naturally saw the union as a god-given opportunity for some peace and quiet on the northern border.

Despite the harsh conditions that she had to endure beyond the Great Wall and the fringe of the Han civilization, Wang Zhaojun is said to have been a dutiful consort and ambassadress, her stoicism and dignity keeping the barbarians under reasonable control. Since her death, her tomb has been endowed with the power to cure infertility in women, and childless visitors take a pinch of soil from the mound and pray there in the hope that it will help make them pregnant.

The **Museum of Inner Mongolia** features an interesting display of costumes, weapons, cavalry trappings and a traditional yurt — along with another huge skeleton of a mammoth that was excavated from a coal mine. The present-day yurts and their inhabitants are found in Mongolian communes north of the city, and group excursions, known as **Grassland Tours** and lasting two days or more, are organized by CITS and other agencies in town. Very few travelers who join these tours enjoy them. The reason is mostly to do with the way they are shepherded around sights that would obviously not exist if tourists didn't either.

WHERE TO STAY

Hohhot's top hotel is the **Zhaojun Hotel** ((471) 696-2211 FAX (471) 686-8825, 53 Xinhua Dajie, right in the center of town, opposite the Bank of China and just down the road from the Museum of Inner Mongolia. It's not the best hotel you'll ever stay in, but the joint Hong Kong management keeps things ship shape.

The two most popular hotels with foreigners are the **Xincheng Hotel** ((471) 696-3322 and the **Inner Mongolia Hotel** ((471) 696-4233, which is where CITS is housed. Both hotels are a couple of kilometers (a mile and a quarter) from the railway station, making it best to take a taxi. The Xincheng is the budget option, but it also has some mid-range rooms, and the grounds are extensive and well maintained. The Inner Mongolia is a good mid-range choice.

HOW TO GET THERE

Access from Hohhot is by bus to Datong or Baotou, or by train to Baotou and Lanzhou or Datong and Beijing. There are also direct flights to Beijing, Guangzhou, Shanghai and Xi'an, among other places.

Decorated wooden door ABOVE and colorful interior hangings OPPOSITE BOTTOM grace Kazakh herdsman's yurt near Urumqi. OPPOSITE TOP: Mother and child of the Mongolian grasslands.

Beijing and the Northeast

BEIGING

Great Bell Temple

isanhuan Xilu Beisanhuan Zhonglu Beisanhuan Donglu

Xihuang Temple

Xueyuan Xtucheng Nanlu Qingnianhu Park Hepingli Beijie Dongli

Xinjiekouwai Deshengmenwai Dajie Ande Lu Ditan (Temple of Earth) Park

Xishimen Station Deshengmen Xidajie Deshengmen Andingmen Xidajie Andingmen Dongdajie Dongzhimen

Beijing Zoo Dajie Xizhimennei Dajie Dongjie Gulou Xidajie Gulou Dongdajie Dongsi 10-Tiao Gongren Tiyuchang B

Chegongzhuang Dajie Fuchengmen Beidajie Ping'anli Xidagjie Di'anmen Xidajie Di'anmen Dongdajie Chaoyangmen Beidajie

Fuchengmenwai Dajie Fuchengmennei Dajie Beihai Lake (North Lake) Jingshan Park China Art Gallery Chaoyangmennei Dajie Chaoyangmenwai Dajie

Yuetan Beijie Beihai Park Jingshan Qianjie Wenjin Jie

Yuetan Nanjie Zhonghai Lake Gugong (Palace) Museum Heping (Peace) Hotel Ritan (Temple of the Sun) Park

Fuxingmenwai Dajie Fuxingmennei Dajie Zhongshan Park Tian an Men (Gate of Heavenly Peace) Beijing Hotel

Nanhai Lake Jianguomennei Dajie Jianguomenwai Dajie

uachi Donglu Xuanwumen Xidajie CITS Chairman Mao Memorial Hall Beijing Station

Tianning Temple Qianmen Xidajie Qianmen Dongdajie CITS Head Office Baiqiao

Guang'anmenwai Dajie Guang'anmennei Dajie Luomashi Dajie Beijing Roast Duck Restaurant (Quanjude) Huashi Dajie Guangqumen Dajie Xizhaosi Jie

Guang'anmen Station Changchun Jie Zhushikou Dajie Tiantan Lu Jingsong

Lianhua Baizhifang Jie Taoranting Lu Tiantan (Temple of Heaven) Park Tiyuguan Lu Fangzhuang

Sanluju Lu You'anmen Dajie Taoranting Park Yongdingmen Dongjie Longtan Lake

River Yongdingmen Nansanhuan

Nansanhuan Xilu Maliapu Nansanhuan Zhonglu Nansanhuan Do

N
1000m

BEIJING

China is many things, and here in the capital, at the heart of it all, you'll find something of all of them. Beijing is the Chinese world in miniature. You'll see grand palaces, pagoda studded gardens, crowded markets, acrobatic troops, five-star hotels, late-night discos, old-world *hutong*s (alleys); in short everything that China is famous for, and quite a lot more that it isn't. Give yourself plenty of time. This vast, busy and exciting city will, like any great city, soak up as much time as you have to give it.

BACKGROUND

The capital of China is a city of broad ceremonial thoroughfares and monumental architecture that is more awe-inspiring than liveable. It is a place of eminence and imperial might. Stand on the edge of the vast Tiananmen Square, in the sweeping courtyards of the Forbidden City, or before the majestic blue-tiled Ming roofs of the once-sacred Temple of Heaven and sense, even in this irrelegious age of clamoring traffic, bicycles and tourist crowds, the power and unquestioned authority of the 24 emperors who ruled from here; imagine the fear that struck at the heart from the traditional exhortation that ended each of their imperial edicts: "Tremble and obey!"

In another sense it is China's Washington DC, another grand architecture of the ego, a repository of pomp, sentiment and grandiose pride, the tomb of all the mortal fantasies and follies that history endows with immortal greatness and nobility. It is where the triumphant Jurchens of the Jin dynasty quaked and cowered and awaited horrific mass murder and destruction as Genghis Khan's cavalries smashed their way through the Great Wall to the north; where the boulevards and squares of the new capital that Kublai Khan built were designed so that the Mongol cavalrymen could get a good unhindered run along them on their horses; where the illustrious rulers of the Ming dynasty bathed and caroused in the treacherous care of their eunuch courts, unable to see or hear the rage swelling be-

yond the walls; where the long and harsh Qing reign of the Manchus committed virtual suicide, encircled by its own angry masses and the armed might of the Europeans; where, amid billowing revolutionary flags, the biggest mass rallies the world has ever seen chanted and waved little red books in homage to their new and perhaps last imperial figure, Chairman Mao Zedong. It is where, in April 1976, the same masses turned in rage on the same revolution — prevented by the Gang of Four from paying homage to the newly dead Premier Zhou

Enlai — and the course of Chinese history swerved dramatically once again.

Beijing began its life as an insignificant border outpost, pitted with the sweeping dust-storms that blow regularly from the Gobi Desert. The barbarians beyond the wall were the first to take its location seriously. The Khitan Tartars of the Liao dynasty made it their southern capital, calling it Yanjing or Swallow City, and in 1125 AD their triumphant rivals, the Jin, established it as Zhongdu, their capital. In both cases the city appealed to them because it was close to their tribal domains on the Mongolian Plateau to the north.

Woman and grandchild pose at Spring Festival in Beijing.

Genghis Khan ravished, depopulated and looted the place and burned it to the ground, and his grandson Kublai, the Great Khan, rebuilt it completely and established it as the Yuan capital Dadu, the most splendid of all the cities of the Mongol Empire. Marco Polo stood amidst its vast halls, palaces, temples, walls and squares as awed and open-mouthed as any visitor who contemplates the grandeur of the city today.

Much of Beijing's present historic character and architecture is the legacy of the Ming rulers, who, after crushing the Yuan and razing their magnificent Dadu to the ground, rebuilt it as their capital, Beiping, or "Northern Peace." It was the Ming emperors who gave it its real strategic value — for them it was a powerful garrison, listening post and command center from which they could maintain a vigil on the dangerous tribal lands beyond the Great Wall. When the Manchus grabbed the imperial throne in 1644, Beiping was a convenient center of power for them because of that same close proximity to their own homelands.

Most of Beijing's historical heritage dates from the Manchu Qing dynasty. Much has been lost. When the Communists took over Beijing in January 1949 they found a city that was backward, dirty and chaotic. To their minds, there was only one way to modernize: They began to clear away the old *hutong*s, widen the boulevards, and create a modern — Soviet-style — city of wide open spaces with Tiananmen Square at the center. It has been pointed out that in this the Communists were simply following historical precedent and inaugurating a new period of dynastic rule with the construction of a new capital. This process is still ongoing. To be sure, "old Peking" lingers in some historical monuments, in the occasional *hutong*, but what you are most likely to remember of Beijing is its thrusting confidence, its intimidating overpasses and busy roads. "Modernization" is the key word in the new China, and nowhere more so than in the capital.

ORIENTATION

Beijing's main boulevards and backstreets follow a neat and very convenient "chessboard" grid that was established in the Yuan

reign and maintained through the Ming and Qing periods. Not that grid-like necessarily means easy to use. The vastness of Beijing's boulevards, some of them seemingly stretching forever, changing names confusingly every couple of kilometers or so, can be daunting to the new arrival. Even after you've been in the city for some time, that feeling of looking out of a taxi window and not having a clue where you are will be familiar to most Beijing visitors and even residents.

The main thoroughfare is Chang'an Lu — in its east (*dong*) and west (*xi*) sections — which runs between the two focus points of the city: the **Forbidden City** and **Tiananmen Square**. The latter, along with Beijing's modern revolutionary monuments — the Great Hall of the People, Monument to the People's Heroes and the Chairman Mao Memorial Hall — lie to the south of Chang'an Avenue. To its east and west, radiating from the square, lie the main tourist centers — the central Beijing Hotel, Beijing railway station, the Friendship Store, International Club, Long Distance Telegraph Office and the major department stores, restaurants and bookshops.

The city center is surrounded by the Second Ring Road and the Circle Line of the Beijing Subway, whose 18 stations make most of the main cultural attractions readily accessible. The Third Ring Road (Sanhuan Lu) essentially encompasses the city proper — base yourself outside it and you'll probably have a longish commute in store before you can begin sightseeing.

New arrivals generally find the street names appallingly difficult. Some of them are mind-bogglingly long and full of "q"s and "x"s and "zh"s. The first step, if you haven't already done so, is to familiarize yourself with the official *pinyin* spelling system. The second step is to learn the following words: *dong* — east; *nan* — south; *xi* — west; *bei* — north; *nei* — inside; *wai* — outside; *men* — gate; *lu* — road; *jie* — street; *dajie* — boulevard. Thus Chongwenmenwai Dajie, is "Outside Chongmen Gate Boulevard." Simple… with a little practice.

Incidentally, the *nei* and *wai* (inside and outside) distinction refers to the now torn down city walls. The gates were usually gates in the walls.

GENERAL INFORMATION

Before you do anything else, get yourself a good fold-out map of the city, preferably one labeled with both English *and* Chinese — the latter is essential for letting taxi drivers (and anyone else) know where you want to go. You should be able to get one at your hotel.

Some of the major airlines represented in Beijing are:

Air France ((10) 6505-1818; **Alitalia** ((10) 6591-8468; **British Airways** ((10) 6512-4070

credit cards. The head office of the **Bank of China** is at 410 Fuchengmennei Dajie, and the Beijing branch at 8 Yabao Lu is another good place to do bank business.

Some foreign embassies in Beijing include: **Australia** ((10) 6532-2331, 15 Dongzhimenwai Dajie; **Austria** ((10) 6532-2061, 5 Xiushui Nanjie, Jianguomenwai; **Belgium** ((10) 6532-1736, 6 Sanlitun Lu; **Canada** ((10) 6532-3536, 10 San Li Tun Lu; **Denmark** ((10) 6532-2431, 1 Dongwujie, Sanlitun; **France** ((10) 6532-2631, 3 Dongsan Jie, Sanlitun; **Germany** ((10) 6532-2161, 5 Dongzhimen-

Canadian Airlines ((10) 6463-7901; **China Eastern** ((10) 6513-3671; **China Northwest** ((10) 6601-7589; **Dragonair** ((10) 6505-4343; **Japan Airlines** ((10) 6513-0888; **KLM Royal Dutch Airlines** ((10) 6505-3505; **Korean Air** ((10) 6505-4639; **Lufthansa** ((10) 6465-4488; **Malaysia Airlines** ((10) 6505-2681; **Qantas Airways** ((10) 6467-3337; **SAS** ((10) 6512-0575; **Singapore Airlines** ((10) 6505-2233; **Thai Airways International** ((10) 6460-8899; **United Airlines** ((10) 6463-1111.

American Express ((10) 6505-2888 has an office at Room L115D, in the Shopping Arcade of the China World Tower, 1 Jianguomenwai Dajie. The **Commercial Bank**, CITIC Building, 19 Jianguomenwai Dajie is a good place to change money and get advances on

wai Dajie; **India** ((10) 6532-1856, 1 Ritan Donglu; **Ireland** ((10) 6532-2691, 3 Ritan Donglu; **Israel** ((10) 6505-2288, 405 China World Trade Tower; **Italy** ((10) 6532-2131, 2 Donger Jie, Sanlitun; **Japan** ((10) 6532-2361, 7 Ritanlu, Jianguomenwai; **Mongolia** ((10) 6532-1203, 2 Xiushui Beijie, Jianguomenwai; **Netherlands** ((10) 6532-1131, 1-15-2 Ta Yuan Building; **New Zealand** ((10) 6532-2731, 1 Donger Jie, Sanlitun; **Russia** ((10) 6532-2051, 4 Dongzhimen Beizhongjie; **Spain** ((10) 6532-3629, 9 Sanlitun Lu; **Sweden** ((10) 6532-3331, 3 Dongzhimenwai Dajie; **Switzerland** ((10) 6532-2736, 3 Dongwu Jie, Sanlitun;

The Ancient Palaces, better known as Beijing's Forbidden City, are the largest surviving cluster of wooden buildings on such a scale in the world.

United Kingdom ((10) 6532-1961, 11 Guanghua Lu; **United States** ((10) 6532-3831, 3 Xiushuibeijie, Jianguomenwai.

For the latest on **cultural events** in Beijing, pick up a copy of the free listings magazine, *Beijing Scene*.

GETTING AROUND

Outside the central core around the Forbidden City, Beijing is so spread out that it'll wear you down and send your shoe repair bills soaring if you try to walk it. As with Guangzhou and the other major cities, the best way to get around is either by bicycle, choosing a particular cultural site or section of the city each day, or by taking a taxi to each area of interest and strolling about from there.

Beijing has taxis, huge fleets of them in fact, operating from all the main hotels, and they are surprisingly cheap and for the most part honest (it still pays to be alert to rip-offs). Most of them have meters, and most drivers use them.

The subway runs right around the core of the city and west along Chang'an Lu and Fuxing Lu, from 5 AM to 11 PM. Rides cost next to nothing. It does, however, get extremely crowded, especially at peak commuting times when the vast bureaucracy of Beijing pours in or out of its offices — but not as crowded as the buses get, some of which are the stuff of which Guinness records are made.

Bicycle hire is widely available, though prices vary remarkably from place to place — at the better hotels, you might easily spend ¥100 per day on a rented bike, while at cheaper digs ¥20 per day is the norm. Shop around.

WHAT TO SEE AND DO

Beijing is so huge, its attractions so various that a plan of action is essential. The place to start is the center of the city, and indeed the center of China — **Tiananmen Square**, with its **Tiananmen (Gate of Heavenly Peace)** and **Palace Museum (Forbidden City)**. These three sights alone will probably fill an entire day.

The square itself, expanded to its present vast dimensions after the communist revolution, is a central place of congregation for the people of Beijing and a particularly popular spot for spring and summer kite flying — the colored paper and silk butterflies and various other designs darting and swooping against a backdrop of huge red revolutionary flags billowing across the front of the **Monument to the People's Heroes**. The 36-m (118-ft) granite obelisk and graphic stone sculpture, almost an epithet of the Maoist era — soldiers, peasants, workers and women in a dramatic revolutionary tableau — breasting the tide of the future, commemorates the revolution. Inevitably this focal point of revolutionary idealism has become the focus of new "revolutions." In 1976 thousands gathered to publicly mourn Zhou Enlai, and were roughly dispersed. In 1989 hundreds of thousands gathered to protest official corruption and rampant inflation. The result: several thousands dead.

Beside the monument, the memory of the Great Helmsman remains revered in the **Mao Zedong Mausoleum**, open to the public as a museum, where the leader who is now accredited with having been 70% right and 30% wrong during his tumultuous reign lies in state in a crystal coffin. Two other sacred institutions flank Tiananmen Square. To the east stands the huge museum building which houses the **Museum of Chinese History** and the **Museum of the Chinese Revolution**, to the west the equally huge **Great Hall of the People**, which is where the Chinese parliament, the National People's Congress, meets and where you can take a look at the 5,000-seat Great Banqueting Hall.

The Forbidden City

Everything in Tiananmen Square focuses on one point — the **Gate of Heavenly Peace** and the mecca of all pilgrims to China, the renowned portrait of Chairman Mao. Rallies of a million or more people took place before this gate, from where the communist leader and his party lieutenants acknowledged the thunderous slogan-chanting adoration and acclaim — standing where the dynastic leaders before them, going back to the great Ming reconstruction of the fifteenth century, had occasionally emerged from their divine seclusion to exhort and review the mood of their common subjects. Now, tour-

234

ist parties are invited to stand where Mao and his lieutenants presided over the masses.

The Gate of Heavenly Peace opens the way into the huge Forbidden City, the largest complex of antique wooden buildings of such scale left in the world, and, all in all, a fascinating but daunting tourist challenge of 800 palaces, halls, shrines and pavilions and no fewer than 9,000 rooms. This vast museum, formerly the seat of power and isolated inner sanctum of the rulers of the Ming and Qing dynasties, is far too big to cover in fine detail unless you have a week or so in

which to do it. All that you can achieve in a half-day or so is to identify its main halls and relics and contemplate the ghosts of autocracy, pride, wrath, folly, intrigue, debauchery and murder moving restlessly about you.

Take a walkman with you when you go to the Forbidden Palace and you can be personally guided around by the dulcet tones of Roger Moore. Tape players are also available at the front gate for a refundable ¥100.

Beyond the Gate of Heavenly Peace lies a sweeping courtyard leading to the massive **Meridian Gate (Wumen)**, the exclusive gateway of the emperors and where, at the stroke of noon on certain days, they issued edicts, had miscreant mandarins publicly flogged and had common criminals executed.

Beyond the Meridian Gate, five marble bridges lead across the bow-shaped **Jin (Golden) Stream** to the **Supreme Harmony Gate**, which in turn opens on to the ceremonial quarter of the palace complex, a huge courtyard that could hold 100,000 people at imperial audiences and the three **great halls** of **Supreme Harmony**, **Complete Harmony** and **Preserving Harmony**, each of which played a particular role in the most important imperial rituals: coronations, New Year's observances, imperial birthdays, court banquets and the awarding of degrees to lucky would-be mandarins in the imperial examinations.

North of these halls you step through the Heavenly Purity Gate into the inner palaces or living quarters of the Forbidden City and reach **Qianqing Guan (Palace of Heavenly Purity)**, which is surrounded by more than 40 mansions, libraries, medical consulting rooms and quarters for servants, concubines and palace eunuchs. Qianqing is where the emperors chose their successors. Each ruler would write the name of his intended successor on two slips of paper, one to be kept in his personal possession and the other hidden behind a plaque inscribed with the words "Upright and Bright". Upon his death his advisers would compare the papers, and if the names tallied, the new ruler would be announced.

One tragic aspect of the Forbidden City is that while it's big on imperial architecture it's surprisingly light on imperial relics and treasures. For that the world can blame Chiang Kaishek and his nationalists, who ransacked the palace of its most precious ceremonial artwork and shipped them to Taiwan, where are now on display in the National Palace Museum in Taipei.

This, in any case, is the official story. In fact the treasures were removed in the thirties and transported on the backs of coolies to Chongqing to protect them from the advancing Japanese. (It is claimed that on that march of nearly 2,000 miles not one object was broken.) In the late forties they were transported by American military aircraft to Taipei when it was clear that "Shanghai Jack" had lost the mainland to Mao. Bearing in

Flower beds surround the Forbidden City, Beijing.

mind what was destroyed during the Cultural Revolution by the Great Helmsman's marauding Red Guards, Chinese posterity owes the Nationalists an unfashionable debt of gratitude for ensuring the survival of the greatest collection of Chinese art in existence.

What's left in the Forbidden City isn't much, and some of it has been brought there from other parts of the country, but it includes the fabulous Suit of Jade and a collection of terracotta warriors on display in the **Hall of Preserving Harmony**; Qing dynasty sedan chairs in the **Hall of Complete Harmony**; an old water clock and several mechanical clocks presented by Western rulers in the **Hall of Union**; a magnificent collection of traditional paintings in the **Palace of Peaceful Old Age**; a **Treasure Room** filled with costumes, jeweled ceremonial swords, gold Buddhas and stupas encrusted with precious gems, a five-ton block of carved jade, bronzes, flowers fashioned from semiprecious stones and crafts of both dynasties in the aptly named **Palace of Mental Cultivation**; murals from the celebrated Qing dynasty novel *A Dream of the Red Mansions* in the **Palace of Eternal Spring**; and other palace halls displaying silks, furniture, jewelry, gold and jade artifacts and the personal possessions of some of the supreme rulers and the many concubines and high officials of their courts.

You emerge, slightly dazed and footsore, by way of the Palace Museum's north gate, **Shenwumen (Gate of Divine Military Genius)** to face a climb up **Coal Hill Park**, directly opposite, where the last Ming ruler, Chongzhen, hanged himself after murdering his family as the Manchus hammered at the city gates. From there, the path leads to **Beihai Park** which was the site of Kublai Khan's grand palace and now features the distinctive **Bai Ta (White Pagoda)** and the **Yongan Si (Temple of Everlasting Peace)**, both built on an islet in Beihai Lake in 1651 in honor of the visiting Dalai Lama.

On the southern side of the lake, the **Chengguang Dian (Light Receiving Hall)** has a beautiful jade Buddha presented by the Burmese to the Empress Dowager Ci Xi, but shorn of one of its arms when British and "allied" troops stormed and occupied much of Beijing in 1900 to put down the anti-European Boxer Rebellion.

Temple of Heaven (Tiantan)

While the Ming and Qing emperors sat enthroned in the Forbidden Palace at the very center of the Chinese civilization, and that meant the entire universe to them, the firmament itself was represented by four temples beyond the palace walls, one at each of four points of the compass. To the north stood **Ditan (Temple of the Earth)**, to the west **Yuetan (Temple of the Moon)**, to the east **Ritan (Temple of the Sun)** and to the south, close to the canal on the edge of the inner city, the most architecturally inspiring and

spiritually significant of all these sacred places, **Tiantan (The Temple of Heaven)**.

It was here, close to each winter solstice and in the spring, that the emperor was borne in a spectacular procession accompanied by his imperial guards, advisers, priests and musicians to pray for good harvests and to offer sacrifices to heaven — performing his most crucial role as the nation's spiritual messenger to the gods and translator to the nation of the favor or wrath of the deities.

The emperor was taken first to the **Imperial Vault of Heaven**, the smaller of the two ornate halls, to pray amidst the tablets of the gods of the firmament and elements — sun, moon, stars, rain, wind, thunder and lightning. Around this hall, built in 1530, stands the remarkable **Whispering** or **Echo Wall**, a circular wall with the acoustic "magic" that you find in the oracle caves of the Mediterranean — where, if you speak to the smooth stonework you can telegraph your voice to someone some distance around it.

From this complex the emperor was taken south along the marble terrace, **Red Steps Bridge**, with its tall carved arches, to the **Circular Altar (Huanqiu Tan)**, a three-tiered white marble terrace decorated with blue tiles that are arranged concentrically in odd numbers, considered to be extremely propitious

in ancient times. Here, on the central dais, the forces of heaven and earth came together in the most crucial of the ceremonies as the emperor, surrounded by the sacred tablets, prayed from what was regarded as the very center of mortal existence and then presided over the sacrifice of a bull calf.

The magnificent **Hall of Prayer for Good Harvests**, with its renowned triple-tiered blue-tiled roof, is where the ruler spent the night resting and meditating between the two great rituals. Built on a three-decked marble terrace, it ranks with the Great Wall and Tiananmen Square as a visual symbol of Chinese history and culture, and features a sensational carved, gilded and decorated domed ceiling as complex as a mandala, with

a dragon set in the center of it. In fact, the temple is relatively "new." Built originally in 1420 it burned down in 1889 and was rebuilt in the following year in the Ming design and using the construction techniques of that age — supported by 28 cedar pillars with not one cross beam, nail or dab of cement anywhere in the structure.

The Lama Temple (Yonghe Gong)

This beautiful Tibetan Buddhist lamasery, the third most remarkable cultural attraction in Beijing, can be found to the northeast of the Forbidden City at the intersection of Andingmen Dongdajie and Yonghegong Dajie, and the best way to get to it is to bicycle north from the Beijing Hotel. A former palace of the Qing emperor Yongzheng, it was established as a Tibetan monastery in 1744, largely as a symbol of Chinese suzerainty over Tibet, and assumed a spiritual significance as important as that of the Jokhang Temple in Lhasa. It has several halls featuring some of the most splendid Tibetan Buddhist artwork and relics found anywhere in the Chinese "lowlands," including a 26-m (85-ft)-high Maitreya Buddha carved from a single block of sandalwood, a large bronze statue of the founder of the Gelugpa, Yellow Hat Sect, Tsongkapa, a host of other Buddha images representing the various stages of Buddhahood and a bronze mandala portraying the Buddhist "Western Paradise."

Buddhas and Pagodas

There are many other temples around the city, some of them in reasonably good shape and others derelict or destroyed all but for their pagodas. The most attractive are the **Binyin Si (Temple of Azure Clouds)** in Xi'angshan Park in the Western Hills, a Yuan dynasty temple extended in the Qing reign and noted for its striking white marble pagodas in the early Indian architectural style; the **Wofo Si (Sleeping Buddha Monastery)**, also close to Xi'angshan Park, with a giant bronze statue of Sakyamuni Buddha in the reclining position which is said to be the pose he took when discussing with his disciples his impending departure from all earthly matters; the **Dazhong Si (Big Bell Temple)**,

Tiantan (Temple of Heaven) and detail of the temple's decorative gilding and tilework.

two kilometers (one and a quarter miles) northwest of the city center near the Friendship Hotel, with an immense 46-ton Ming dynasty bell with Buddhist sutras inscribed on it; the **Guangji Si (Temple of Universal Rescue)**, just west of Beihai Park, with many good Buddha statues; and the **Mahakala Miao** at the southern end of the Forbidden City, which is one of the centers of Mongolian lamaism in Beijing.

Other Sights

As you go east on Chang'an Avenue, heading toward the huge Friendship Store, you'll find on the right the ancient **Guanxiang Tai (Observatory)**, built in the Ming dynasty and now notable for its collection of Chinese maritime maps and instruments and astronomical gadgets built by Jesuit priests. These scholars, headed by Father Matteo Ricci, were employed in the Ming court to work on a Chinese calendar, and in return were given the freedom to seek Chinese converts — not many of whom ever turned up.

CITS operate daily tours of **Underground Beijing**, a network of subterranean defenses and shelters throughout the capital, some of which have factories, shops, restaurants and even, it's said, some 100 "hotels." They're a legacy of the Cold War and Yellow Peril period when the Chinese feared nuclear attack by the United States or the former Soviet Union, or both.

The **Junshi Bowuguan (Military Museum)** on Fuxing Lu, the western extension of Chang'an Avenue, has exhibitions recounting the history of the People's Liberation Army, its role in the Korean War (and American jets that it shot down) and captured weapons and documents of its most recent military foray, the 1979 military "lesson" that it attempted to teach Vietnam. In the Military Museum you will see staged photos of the Tiananmen incident attempting to show how the students massacred innocent soldiers.

The **China Art Gallery**, just east of Beihai and Jingshan (on Coal Hill) parks, has changing exhibits, mostly modern. Check the *Beijing Scene* listings to see what's on.

The **Former Residence of Soong Ching Ling** on the northern bank of Shisha Lake, just north of Beihai Park, is worth a visit

for the symbol that it now represents of the chaotic republican era after the collapse of the Qing dynasty. Soong Ching Ling was one of three daughters of "Charlie" Soong, a wayward Hainanese Chinese who became a Methodist preacher in the United States and was sent back to China to convert the "heathen" nation with American-style holy rolling evangelism. Charlie decided to get rich instead, backing Sun Yatsen and his republican cause and becoming, in the process, the wealthiest magnate in China.

Of his three daughters, Ching Ling, the "thinking" one, married Sun Yatsen and this placed her in the annals of the revolutionary heroes, while Meiling, the "clever" one, became Madame Chiang Kaishek, thence to use her particular talents for power, guile and false piety to hoodwink the Americans into one of their biggest ever diplomatic blunders, their dogged, shortsighted support of Chiang's corrupt military regime. If you go to the Soong Ching Ling museum, take along a copy of the book that exposes it all — Sterling Seagrave's epic *The Soong Dynasty*. It makes illuminating reading.

Temple of Virtue OPPOSITE in Qing dynasty Summer Palace, and detail ABOVE of opulent architecture.

Yihe Yuan (Summer Palace)

This Qing dynasty summer retreat, about 12 km (seven miles) northwest of the city center, was built in the early years of the Manchu reign but has since become more popularly associated with its most famous, or infamous, resident, the Empress Dowager. She put a great deal of money into the place — most of it, as already mentioned, grabbed from funds established to modernize the antique Qing navy — and had a great deal of trouble keeping it in one piece.

It was torn apart by an Anglo-French force in 1860, damaged again by foreign troops in the Boxer Rebellion in 1900, and, each time, the Dragon Lady put it all back together again. Nowadays it's a public recreational spot, perhaps the most popular around Beijing, reclining along the shore of Lake Kunming and featuring splendid gardens, pavilions, mansions, temples and bridges — and the remarkable **Long Corridor**, a 7,000-m (7,655-yd) long, covered gallery full of frescoes with mythical themes. And in the lake itself there's the ultimate in imperial kitsch, the Empress's white marble paddlewheel steamboat. In winter time the lake is the place to go for one of Beijing's favorite seasonal recreations, ice skating.

The Great Wall

The greatest man-made barrier in the world, said to be the only concrete sign of human existence that can be seen from outer space, the world's longest cemetery, the abiding symbol of China, the scene of incredible bloodshed, the wall that ultimately faced the wrong way.... All this, and more, you can reflect upon atop the sweeping, crowded **Great Wall** at **Badaling**, 75 km (46 miles) northwest of Beijing, the main section of the 6,000 km (3,720 miles) wall that is open for tourism. It's the ultimate and, in many respects, the final destination of the China pilgrimage. See the Great Wall, and die. Not right away, though.

It is everything that you can imagine it to be — monolithic, magnificent, sweeping and snaking up and over steep hills as though a blind man's blundering had directed its path. In fact, when the great Qinshi Huangdi built the ancient first sections of it, the surveying technique followed by his engineers was to

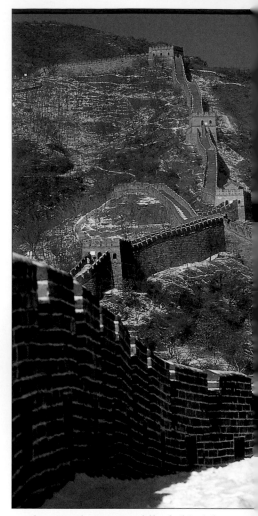

send ponies dragging saddles behind them over the hills and peg out the path they chose.

Along its full length, much of the wall has fallen into disrepair, its watchtowers left standing like tombstones in the desert wastes and on the loess hills of the west. You can see decrepit sections of it north of Lanzhou and follow a reasonably intact winding section on the railway ride between Beijing and Datong. The section at Badaling was repaired with a view to attracting tourists in 1957, and since then other renovations have been going on in the province. **Mutianyu**, 90 km (56 miles) northeast of Beijing is less overrun with tourists and their hangers-on, and makes a good alternative to Badaling. To get there take a morning minibus from the area just south of the Great Hall of the People.

Another good Great Wall viewing area is **Simatai**, which is 110 km (68 miles) from Beijing. This is the least developed section of the Great Wall, with just a scattering of souvenir stands and hawkers. Get bus tickets at the Jinghua Hotel (see below) in Beijing. Farther away again is the wall's dramatic eastern terminus called Old Dragon Head at **Shanhaiguan** on the Bo Hai (Sea). There's a beach here, a small village and a couple of hotels too. Close by is Beidaihe, a seaside resort popular with China's elite.

It seems that every hotel in Beijing offers a Badaling tour, which probably accounts for all the tourists out there. Most of these tours will drag you to a dozen "attractions" before you set sight on the wall itself, and charge you ludicrously inflated prices to do so.

You're better off catching a bus out there yourself from outside the Qianmen subway station, near KFC. Ask for Badaling. The buses start at around 6 AM and run approximately every 20 minutes through the day. Doing it by train is much more troublesome.

Unless you have oodles of time or have a keen archeological interest, it's best to avoid tours that include the **Ming Tombs**. They may be the resting places of 13 of the 16 Ming emperors, but nowadays they are virtually empty of relics and artwork and are little more than decorated concrete blockhouses surrounded by tourist restaurants, tea gardens and souvenir stalls.

The ultimate destination of every China pilgrimage: the Great Wall.

WHERE TO STAY

Luxury

The **Beijing Hotel** ((10) 6513-7766 FAX (10) 6513-7307, 33 Dong Chang'an Jie, was Beijing's first true luxury hotel, and in many eyes it is still Beijing's best. Built in 1900, right in the center of Beijing, the hotel comprises three wings, each fitted out in a different architectural style. The west wing is the place for views looking out over the Forbidden City. Essentially, this hotel has everything —

The Palace, run by the Peninsula Group, is obviously in close competition with the nearby Holiday Inn. Both offer very high standards of accommodation, and services such as 24-hour medical attention (only if you need it), gyms with training staff, swimming pools, and the full complement of international restaurants. The Palace even offers martial arts classes, but then so probably does the Holiday Inn by now. The Holiday Inn is better on the Western food front.

The **Grand Hotel** ((10) 6513-7788 FAX (10) 6513-0048, 35 Dong Chang'an Jie, next door

shopping arcade (from "traditional silks to Pierre Cardin fashions," the blurb goes), dancing, sauna, billiard room, gym, business center, conference facilities, and the list goes on. Restaurants in the hotel include the Sichuan-style Yiyuan Garden and the Japanese Gojin Hiakusho. Bear in mind that the Beijing is not universally lauded; it has its share of critics, who mostly find fault with the service.

For more central luxury accommodation, but at lower rates, two good choices are the **Palace Hotel** ((10) 6512-8899 FAX (10) 6512-9050, 8 Jinyu Hutong (Goldfish Lane), Wangfujing, and the **Holiday Inn Crowne Plaza** ((10) 6513-3388 FAX (10) 6513-2513, 48 Wangfujing Dajie.

to the Beijing Hotel, is a relative newcomer, and plays on the imperial Beijing theme — stylish fake antiquities in the rooms and so on. Some of the rooms do have excellent views over the Forbidden City, as does the rooftop terrace, but some may find the efforts this hotel has taken to achieve a grand style slightly pompous.

Another well located five-star hotel is the **New Otani** ((10) 6512-5555 FAX (10) 6513-9810, 26 Jianguomenwai Dajie, a link in the well known Japanese chain. It's probably one of Beijing's best luxury hotels, though some may find its style a trifle stuffy.

The **Shangri-La Hotel** ((10) 6841-2211 FAX (10) 6841-8006, 29 Zizhuyuan Lu, Haidianqu, is somewhat remote (around 30 minutes drive from downtown) but the landscaped gardens compensate for this. With 657 well appointed guestrooms, seven different restaurants and a 24-hour business center (among other services), the Shangri-La is rated very highly by those who stay there.

Mid-Range

One of the best centrally located mid-range hotels is the **Chongwenmen Hotel** ((10) 6512-2211 FAX (10) 6512-2212, 2 Chongwenmen Xi Dajie. Rooms start at between $50

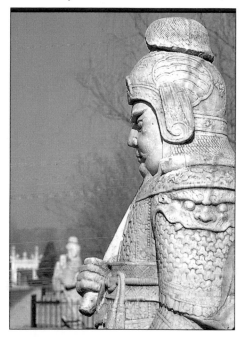

and $60, which for a hotel with such good access to Beijing's prime attractions is a bargain. Amenities are scarce — this is a hotel with few pretentions. Similarly priced is the **Taiwan Hotel** ((10) 6513-6688 FAX (10) 6513-6896, 5 Jinyu Hutong (Goldfish Lane), which is even better located just off Wangfujing. Again, this is simply a basic mid-range hotel, with nothing in the way of extras.

If you are interested in a bit more comfort but want to keep you accommodation budget under $100, the **Tiantan Sports Hotel** ((10) 6711-2277 FAX (10) 6711-6833, 10 Tiyuguan Lu, is not a bad choice. Incidentally, there's nothing particularly sporting about the place, except perhaps the sports shops in the neighborhood.

Beijing and the Northeast

Inexpensive

The most popular budget hotel in Beijing these days in the **Jinghua Hotel** ((10) 6722-2211, Nansanhuan Xilu. It may not be in an ideal location, on the southern section of the Third Ring Road, south of the Yongdingmen bus and railway station, but with inexpensive dorm beds and doubles with private bathroom from around $20, this place can't be beaten.

The **Sea Star Hotel** ((10) 6721-8855, 166 Yongdingmen Dajie, is another popular budget hotel, and under the same management as the Jinghua. The attraction is less the somewhat grotty dorms than the spacious doubles, which come in at less than $30.

WHERE TO EAT

Despite rival claims by Guangzhou and Chengdu, Beijing is the best place in all China to eat out. Simply put, the capital has the best of everything, and diners are spoiled for choice, whether it comes to local fare, a regional speciality, or even an ethnic surprise from beyond the Himalayas.

The local cuisine, classified as "Peking" style, comprises dishes served in the imperial court of the emperor. You can find restaurants serving imperial cuisine, particularly in the banquet departments of the five-star hotels, but it won't be cheap. The local street cuisine, on the other hand, is hearty and inexpensive. Unlike the south, where rice is the staple, in Beijing it's noodles, dumplings, and breads (baked, steamed or fried) that fill up the empty spaces between the tasty bits. A great treat in Beijing is to watch an experienced noodle chef turning a lump of dough into a skein of perfect noodles, or *lamian* (literally "pull noodles") as they're known.

But Beijing's most famous dish is, of course, Peking duck (or Beijing duck if you insist). Strictly speaking, this is a dish for a party of at least six people, but as a visiting foreigner you can eat alone or with just one friend providing you can pay the bill, which is rarely that expensive anyway. The crispy skin is the most prized portion — wrap them

Bicyclist and bystanders OPPOSITE at Ming dynasty guardian statue ABOVE on triumphal route to Ming tombs.

in thin pancakes with a little spring onion and a dollop of plum sauce. Nothing is wasted. What's left is fried up with bean sprouts; the bones are used to make soup.

Beijing's most famous dish has given birth to a chain that has itself become a Beijing institution. **Qianmen Quanjude Roast Duck** ((10) 6701-1739, 32 Qianmen Dajie, and **Quanjude Roast Duck** ((10) 6301-8833, 14 Qianmen Xi Dajie, are the two main branches, with the latter earning the moniker, Super Duck, for its expansive pack-'em-in dining hall. Expect to pay around $20 per head for your duck at either of these, touristy but fun, places. Look also for **Wangfujing Quanjude Roast Duck** ((10) 6553-3100, 13 Shuaifuyuan, Wangfujing. For a budget roast duck meal, the place to head to is **Bianyifang Roast Duck** ((10) 6711-2244, 2 Chongwenmenwai Dajie. There are two dining halls here. It's the one at the back you want. A whole duck — more than enough for two people — costs around $10. It's a popular place.

Beijing's famous Sichuan restaurant goes by the same name: **Sichuan** ((10) 6603-3291, 51 Rongxian Hutong. Housed in the former residence of the general who would be emperor, Yuan Shikai, this traditional-style structure, complete with a courtyard, is as much the attraction as the fiery Sichuan cuisine it serves.

Another regional specialty is Moslem, or Hui. The best restaurant for this delicious cuisine is **Hongbinlou** ((10) 6601-4832, 82 Xi Chang'an Jie. It's one of those shabbily genteel establishments that reflect the character of Beijing a decade ago — couldn't care less, sloppy and complacent — but the dishes, when they finally arrive, are the real thing. The plebes' dining hall — for budget meals — is upstairs on the right. Among other things, Hongbinlou is acclaimed for its *jiaozi* (dumplings), another dish for which Beijing is famous.

For Chinese vegetarian cuisine, which is actually Buddhist temple food, **Gongdelin** ((10) 6511-2542, 158 Qianmen Nan Dajie, not only serves up superb and fabulously inventive vegetarian dishes (many of them duplicating meaty dishes that Chinese Buddhists must forego), but does so at rock-bottom prices.

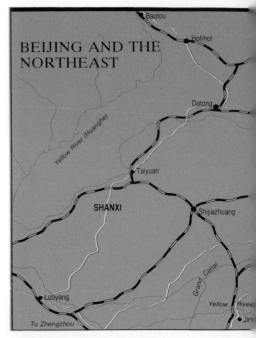

BEIJING AND THE NORTHEAST

There was a time when Western food was the preserve of the cavernous Moscow restaurant — which served jam and bread with its main courses. Amazingly the Moscow still survives as the **Peking Exhibition Hall Restaurant**, which will serve up an unremarkable but authentic enough borscht for you if that's what you require. But nowadays Beijing is teeming with Western restaurants: everything from **T.G.I. Friday**, on Dongsanhuan Lu, which is an upmarket American-style diner (part of a chain), to **McDonald's** and company (**KFC**, **Pizza Hut**, **Baskin Robbins**, and others) to the much appreciated croissant and coffee chain **Vie de France** (there's one next door to the Friendship Store) to upmarket establishments like **Maxim's de Paris** ((10) 6505-4853, and trendy bistros like **Mexican Wave** ((10) 6506-3961, on Dongdaqiao Lu. The latter is much celebrated by Beijing's large expatriate community, not least for its excellent set lunch deal.

Don't forget to explore Beijing's street markets for delicious snacks and even meals. One excellent place to sample not only local dishes but also regional specialties is the **Donganmen Night Market**, at the northern end of Wangfujing. The action takes place nightly from 6 to 9 PM. Another place to go is the **Dongdantoutiao Night Market**, on

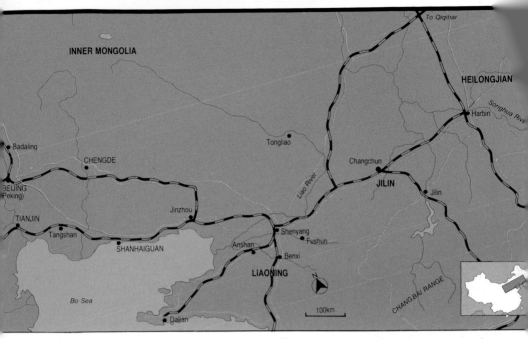

Chang'an street, and the **Chongwenmen Night Market**. The latter is very much a local affair, but there's nothing stopping you sitting down and slurping back a bowl of noodles with them.

NIGHTLIFE

The China Daily lists current events and exhibitions, but a better listings source is *Beijing Scene*, which should be available at most major hotels around town. For a relaxing drink after a day's sightseeing, try **Mexican Wave**, already mentioned above; it's close to the Jianguo Hotel. **Brauhaus**, in the basement of the World Trade Centre, on Jianguomen Dajie, is another popular spot for a quiet drink. One of the most popular bars in town is **Poachers Inn**, 7 Sanlitun Road. It's an English-style pub, and arguably the best all-round bar in China.

For Beijing Opera, again check the *The China Daily* or *Beijing Scene* for the latest performances. Bear in mind that a real opera performance will last up to four hours, and unless you have a reasonable grasp of the proceedings or are happy to sit and wonder at the spectacle of it all, sitting through the genuine article is no mean feat. With this in mind, the somewhat touristy (but still very entertaining) performances at the **Liyuan Theatre** ((10) 6301-6688, Qianmen Hotel, 175 Yong'an Lu, are the perfect teaser.

With a 2,000-year history, the acrobats have had plenty of time to perfect their act and put all other acrobats to shame. The best place to see a performance is at the **Chaoyang Theatre** ((10) 6507-2421, Dongsanhuan Beilu. Tickets are available through CITS.

Beijing is no slow coach when it comes to late night action, despite its reputation as a haven for fusty bureaucrats, staid diplomats and number-crunching correspondents. The biggie is **JJ's** ((10) 6607-9601, 74–76 Xinjiekou Bei Dajie, which is a warehouse-sized cavern of sci-fi effects and techno beat. DJs are sometimes even flown in from London — "spiritual pollution" of the worst kind and lots of fun too.

HOW TO GET THERE

Beijing has access by air and rail to all parts of China and to the Mongolian Plateau to the north and the former Manchurian territory of the northeast. For rail travelers, **Beijing Station**, with its cavernous halls, crowded concourse and unusually decorative clock towers, is one of the most convenient in the country. No booking struggles here — you simply make your way to its International Traveler's section, through the central hall and down along the left of the escalators, to find a CITS-style reservations room, just for foreign guests, with two big boards listing destinations all over China, train numbers, departure times and ticket prices.

Outside the reservations section this VIP inner sanctum has a large waiting room, with comfortable furnishings and a Friendship desk, where you can await your train far from the madding crowds and even be escorted to it by an attendant when it's time to go. By average rail travel standards in China it's so comfortable and efficient that it's almost decadent.

THE NORTHERN TRAIL

There are two main northern routes, the "over the top" Beijing–Lanzhou run to **Datong** and across Inner Mongolia, and the northeast Beijing–Harbin route with major intermediate tourist destinations at **Chengde**, **Shenyang**, **Changchun** and **Harbin**.

The region itself is one of the most physically dramatic in all of China, bounded to the north, east and southeast by four great rivers, the Heilong, Wusuli, Tumen and Yalu (where, in its eastern reaches, Chinese forces stormed into the Korean War), and featuring four principal mountain ranges. The most beautiful of these, the Changbai Range, includes Mount Baitou, the tallest peak in the northeast, capped with snow all the year round. On its upper slopes lies the pristine but moody Sky Lake (Tianchi), a huge volcanic crater lake surrounded by 16 lofty peaks, that can be beautifully placid and serene one day and a maelstrom of crashing wind-whipped waves the next.

The Changbai Range also produces the Songhua River, the major tributary of the Heilong Jiang, which flows through the region's two most interesting and attractive "river cities," Harbin, completely iced in and a popular resort in the winter months, and **Jilin** (in Jilin province, the capital of which is Changchun), famous for its frozen "tree hangings," a riverside filigree of ice formed by warmer moisture on banks of willow trees.

Culturally, Shenyang and Chengde have magnificent buildings and relics reflecting the region's former status as the cradle of the Manchu expansion that overran China in the seventeenth century and established the last of the nation's imperial dynasties. The founding emperor of the Qing reign established Shenyang, now the capital of Liaoning province, as the imperial capital before moving triumphantly to the Forbidden City in Beijing. That brief moment of glory has endowed the city with the Imperial Palace, the mausoleums of two Qing emperors and some 70 courts and administrative complexes that rank in architecture with Beijing's "Great Within."

Chengde features the Imperial Summer Villa, the traveling lodge of the early Qing court at Shenyang, northeast of which lie several interesting monasteries and the world's largest wooden Buddha statue. At the region's farthest edge, the town of Mohe on the bank of the Heilong Jiang, the northernmost inhabited point in China, is called the Arctic City for its bitterly cold winter climate as low as 50°C below freezing point (minus 58°F) and the City of the White Night for its spectacular summer displays of the Aurora Borealis.

DATONG

At first sight, Datong is an unspectacular industrial and coal mining center, situated in the north of Shaanxi province close to the Great Wall and the Inner Mongolia border and eight hours by train from Beijing. But it has a surprisingly interesting monastery and another major cultural attraction that makes it an important place of pilgrimage — it lies close to the **Yungang Grottoes**, one of the four greatest examples of Buddhist cave art in China, started by the Toba rulers of the Northern Wei when they made Datong their capital in 398 AD.

What to See and Do

In Datong itself, the main cultural center is the huge, brooding twelfth century **Huayan Monastery**, set on two levels right in the center of the city. Currently under renova-

French tourists dwarfed by huge Sakyamuni Buddha image at Yungang Grottoes, near Datong.

tion, the monastery looks a bit derelict and drab, but inside, the main hall is crammed with fantastic Buddhist artwork. Not only does it feature five huge Ming dynasty Buddha images, gilded and flamboyantly decorated and seated on lotus thrones, but these in turn are flanked by honor guards of 31 Liao dynasty statues of soldiers, officials and Bodhisattvas. Around them, the walls are decorated with murals and paintings of Sakyamuni Buddha, *arhats*, thousand-eye Bodhisattvas and other deities added by the artist Dong An in the late Qing reign.

To the south of Huayan, the **Shanhua Monastery** dating back to the Tang dynasty features another five splendid Buddha images and many murals. There's also a far more modern, yet still antique, attraction in Datong which should not be missed — the **Steam Locomotive Factory** where, on visits arranged by CITS on weekdays, you can watch the last of China's beautiful early industrial thoroughbreds being assembled.

YUNGANG GROTTOES

These dramatic Buddhist caves, carved into the northern slope of **Mount Wuzhou** more than 1,500 years ago, lie 16 km (10 miles) north of Datong in the heart of the region's coal mining communities. To get there you can either organize a minibus or taxi through CITS or take the public bus, or rather two buses — N° 2 from a terminal west of the city's main square, connecting with bus N° 3 on the western outskirts of the city for the direct journey to Yungang.

There are 53 caves covering about one kilometer (over a half mile) of the cliff face and containing about 50,000 Buddhist statues and bas-relief carvings. Along the western face, the complex is dominated by a marvelous sitting Sakyamuni Buddha, 13.7 m (44 ft) high, with a slightly amused expression that is typical of the Northern Wei style.

To the east, three ornately decorated wooden pavilions with double eaves and several galleries, built right into the cliff, form the entrance to caverns containing immense Sakyamuni and Maitreya statues and wall carvings and niches reaching right up to the ceilings. These depict the life of Buddha and also include flower motifs, altars, musicians and instruments; some were added as re-

cently as the Qing dynasty. Although three different periods of Buddhist art are represented at Yungang, each grotto contains a Buddha image at least 13 m (43 ft) high that is said to have been modeled on a Northern Wei ruler.

Where to Stay

Datong's ludicrous setup vis-a-vis tourists and hotel accommodation is in need of a drastic overhaul. Despite the fact that there are numerous perfectly adequate lodgings in Datong, foreigners are herded into either the **Datong Guesthouse** ((352) 203-2476, to the south of the city center and the **Yungang Hotel** ((352) 502-1601. The Yungang Hotel is probably the better choice. Take bus N° 15 to get there.

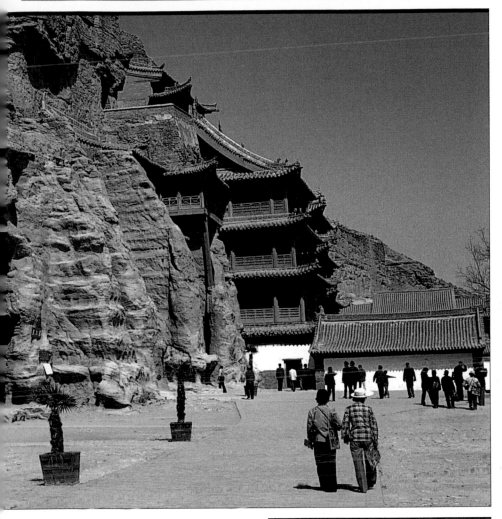

Where to Eat

There isn't much in the way of eating out in Datong, but the two hotels have good dining rooms and there are a couple of restaurants directly opposite the Yungang Hotel, notably the **Hongqi Restaurant**.

How to Get There

There's only one way to get to Datong: by train. And there are two ways of doing it — stopping off on the west-to-east Lanzhou–Beijing route, or taking the overnight express west from Beijing. Leaving Datong you can take a daytime train to Beijing, riding hard-seat, and enjoy remarkable views of the Great Wall snaking around and over the hills to the east, and old walled towns along the way.

Beijing and the Northeast

HARBIN

The capital of Heilongjiang province, 385 km (238 miles) northeast of Beijing, Harbin was a sleepy fishing village — its Manchurian name meaning "where the fishing nets are dried" — until the Russians obtained parts of Manchuria as a concession in 1898 to give themselves access to the east, and built the railway line through to Vladivostok. They then lost the entire region to the Japanese as a result of their humiliating naval defeat of 1905 but continued to make a cultural impression on the area after the 1917 Bolshevik

Yungang Grottoes near Datong date back to Northern Wei dynasty and feature about 50,000 Buddhist statues and bas-relief carvings covering three great dynasties.

revolution, when Harbin became a refuge for White Russian escapees. This is largely what Harbin is famous for today: its surviving Russian character, particularly the architecture of its old Orthodox churches. That, and the city's harsh winter climate, when the temperature plummets as low as minus 30°C (minus 25°F) and when the city becomes a winter recreation resort and the venue for a spectacular winter festival.

General Information
CAAC ((451) 263-2337 is at 87 Zhongshan Lu. **Shanghai Airlines** ((451) 263-7953 is at 224 Zhongshan Lu.

There's a **Bank of China** at 37 Zhaolin Jie and another (the head provincial branch) at 19 Hongjun Jie. **CITS** ((451) 262-1655 is on the ground floor of the Swan Hotel, 73 Zhongshan Lu.

What to See and Do
Harbin is more of a recreational spot than a cultural center. While it's a big summer resort, with boating, swimming, hunting, trekking and cruises on the Songhua River, its most exciting season is midwinter. The Songhua freezes over and becomes an ice skating rink and a winter playground for ice yachting, ice hockey, sledding and sleigh rides. A long runway of ice for sledding sweeps 150 m (159 yards) down the riverbank and on to the ice at Stalin Park. Elsewhere you can take rides around the town on donkey and horse sleighs, clad to the eyeballs in fur fashions bought at the **Fur Product Shop** and **Harbin Fur Factory** at 88 Zhongyang Dajie, catching a glimpse here and there of a surviving cupola or onion-shaped dome and quietly humming the theme from Doctor Zhivago in your partner's frozen ear.

But the big attraction is the **Ice Lantern Festival** from January 1, to the end of February, when Zhuolin Park and other areas are decorated with fantastic ice sculptures of animals, plants, temples and pavilions, tableaux from Chinese legends and anything that strike's the ice artist's fancy — all lit up from the inside at night. The festival is already attracting 16,000 visitors a year, and the city has plans to make it a major international attraction, with ski resorts to go with it.

Of Harbin's Russian architecture, the orthodox **Nigula Jiaotang (Nicholas Church)** is the only surviving structure in any reasonable repair. It was built in 1899 and was regarded as the finest of some 17 Orthodox churches that were eventually established throughout the short-lived Czarist concession.

Where to Stay
Being a summer and winter resort for the top echelons of the Chinese administration as well as foreign visitors, Harbin has no

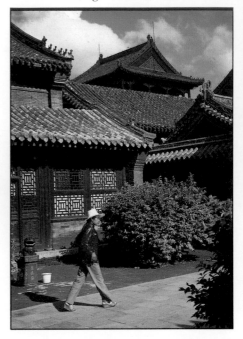

shortage of mainstream hotels and private *dasha*-style villa hotels for overworked party officials. But note that during the January and February Ice Lantern Festival prices go up at least 20%, and it's essential that you book ahead at this time.

The best luxury hotel is the **Holiday Inn City Centre Harbin** ((451) 422-6666 FAX (451) 422-1661, 90 Jingwei Street. As the name suggests, it has a convenient location and is about the only place offering true international standards. Mind you, the **Songhuajiang Gloria Inn** ((451) 463-8855 FAX (451) 463-8533 is out to give the Holiday Inn a run for its money. This Hong Kong managed hotel can also be booked in Hong Kong ((852) 2833-0298.

If you have an early morning flight (the airport is nearly 50 km or 30 miiles out of town), the **Swan Hotel (** (451) 230-0021 is a mid-range place within walking distance of CAAC and the airport bus. Mid-range travelers may be tempted to go a little upmarket and spend around $70 on a room at the **Modern Hotel (** (451) 461-5845 FAX (451) 461-4997. Contrary to the name, this hotel was built in 1906 and despite a complete interior overhaul it still oozes character.

Budget travelers should go to the **Tianzhu Hotel (** (451) 363-3725, next to the railway

Jiangbin Fandian (Riverside Restaurant) is good for Han Chinese cuisine and seafood.

Red lanterns hang outside the restaurants as a rating system, i.e. the more lanterns the better and more expensive the restaurant.

Har Har Le Restaurant is housed in the same building as the Overseas Chinese Hotel. It offers cheap cafeteria-style food, which you order by pointing at what you want.

How to Get There

There are direct air services to Harbin from Beijing, Guangzhou, Shanghai, Changchun

station, where they should be able to get a clean, comfortable room for under $20.

Where to Eat

Outside its many hotel restaurants and dining rooms, Harbin is noted for its Beijing duck, Mongolian hotpot, shish kebab, Korean dog soups and other less orthodox dishes, Russian bread the size of pillows and its glacé ice cream, all of which can be found in its eating houses and its streets.

For roast duck try the **Futailou (** (451) 461-5278, 19 Xi Shishan Dao. **Beilaishun** near Zhaolin Park features local mutton dishes and Mongolian hotpot in the winter; **Huamei Canting** at 142 Zhongyang Dajie has a Western menu with Russian borsch; and the

and Shenyang, and daily express trains from Beijing. If you are flying out of Harbin, give yourself at least an hour to get to the airport.

SHENYANG

This industrial hub of Liaoning province was a trading center for the nomads beyond the Great Wall 1,000 years ago. In the seventeenth century it became the capital of the Manchus, and after they fought and connived their way to the imperial throne in Beijing, it remained as the secondary seat of power, known by its Manchu name, Mukden.

Two views of the magnificent early Qing Imperial Palace in Shenyang — seat of the Manchu warlords.

The city has changed hands several times since then. The Russians controlled it as a center of their Manchurian enterprise until the Japanese booted them out in savage warfare in 1904 and 1905. The Russians took it back after the World War II defeat of Japan, and then Mao Zedong's communists marched in and established it as a key northern base from which they launched their nationwide campaign that led to the triumph of 1949.

Nowadays, Shenyang is a huge industrial and manufacturing city supported by the region's coal and steel, and would be a venue for the joint-venture businessman rather than the tourist, were it not for its magnificent footprint of the Manchu march to power, the Imperial Palace.

General Information
CAAC ((24) 386-3705 has its office in the center of town at 117 Zhonghua Lu. **China Northern Airlines** ((24) 829-4431 is at 3 Xiaoheyuan Lu.

The **Bank of China** is at 6 Shiwei Lu.

CITS ((24) 680-5858 extension 8680 is close to the Phoenix Hotel, at 113 Huanghe Nan Dajie.

Shenyang has a **United States Consulate** ((24) 322-1198, at 52 Shisiwei Lu.

What to See and Do
Of Shenyang's **Manchu tombs**, the **North Tomb** is easily the best. It is the burial place of Abahai, the son of Nurhaci, who founded the Qing dynasty in the early seventeenth century. The tomb is set in an expansive park and the approach is lined with statuary reminiscent of the Ming tombs near Beijing. Bus Nº 220 goes to the park from the railway station. The **East Tomb** is the burial place of Nurhaci himself and, though less impressive than the North Tomb, is worth visiting if you have time; get there by bus Nº 18.

The main reason for visiting Shenyang is of course the **Imperial Palace** in the eastern section of the city, which was the Manchu court and seat of power until the takeover of China was completed and the first Qing emperor, the warrior Shunzhi, moved the court to Beijing in 1644.

In scale and architecture this palace rivals the Forbidden City where the Qing emper-

ors continued their long and dramatic reign. It was built in three sections, beginning in 1625, and expanded by successive rulers until it comprised some 70 pavilions and halls dominated by the octagonal **Dazheng Hall**, where Emperor Shunzhi was crowned before being borne triumphantly south. It has a militaristic design — rows of five pavilions on each side, extending north to south, that give the effect of two lines of tents guarding the commander-in-chief.

The nearby **Pavilions** off to the south are a series of administrative centers where the Manchu ruler's ten most important lieutenants — two princes and eight ministers — got together and met each day to plot the combination of political intrigue and military strategy that was to win them the empire. These days it is a museum of Manchu armor, carriages, military costume, campaign banners and weapons — and a sword that was worn by the eighteenth century ruler, Emperor Qianlong, which today, more than two centuries after his reign, is still untarnished.

Back in town, close to the south railway station, look for Zhongshan Square, with its massive — for some the ultimate — **Mao statue**. He stands mightily over the busy traffic, his arm gesturing with a flourish, the sculpted proletariat brandishing little red books at his feet. It is a reminder of a China that is fast disappearing.

Where to Stay and Eat
The northeast of China is different from the rest of the country, and not least when it comes to foreigners' accommodation. The authorities in this part of China have decided to standardize all room prices, which in effect is just another form of price gouging.

The Gloria group have arrived in Shenyang in recent years and erected two luxury hotels, though like most upmarket hotels in this part of China their market is more business travelers than tourists. The best of the two is the **Gloria Plaza Hotel** ((24) 252-8855 FAX (24) 252-8533, 32 Yingbin Jie, close to the north railway station. The **Gloria Inn** ((24) 482-5225 FAX (24) 482-5875, 8 Wenhua Donglu, is around 15 minutes from the center and is even more of a business hotel than the Plaza.

In the old China, "friendship" was always a byword for bad service and institutional standards of comfort. In Shenyang, little has changed and at the mid-range **Friendship Hotel** ((24) 680-1222 FAX (24) 680-0132, 1 Huanghe Dajie, you can take a little trip down memory lane. This Soviet-style villa hotel is north of the Phoenix Hotel.

The **Liaoning Hotel** ((24) 782-9166, 2 Zhongshan Lu, is a better mid-range choice. Complete with views of the waving Mao statue, it was built by the Japanese and, with its art nouveau windows, is one of the most attractive buildings in town.

If you're looking to keep expenses down (not easy in Shenyang), the **Zhongxing Hotel** ((24) 383-8188, 86 Taiyuan Beijie, has a wide-range of rooms, encompassing Shenyang's version of budget (around $30) and more upmarket offerings. It's near the south station, and has a distinctive red-brick pyramid roof — you can't miss it.

Dining out is a chore in Shenyang. The hotels all have their restaurants, but with the exception of the two Gloria hotels and a couple of other luxury places, the meals are not great. Even street food is not particularly exciting, and many visiting foreigners end up resorting to **KFC**, which has a pioneering branch on Zhonghua Lu in front of the south railway station

How to Get There
Shenyang has direct air connections with most major Chinese cities. Korean Airlines has direct flights to Seoul. Shenyang is also the junction of six major railway lines in the northeast, and lies on the route of the Beijing–Harbin express trains. Note that Shenyang-bound trains stop at either the north *or* the south stations.

Overnight sleeper buses to Beijing leave from the north railway station area.

CHENGDE

The Hebei provincial city, 250 km (155 miles) northeast of Beijing, Chengde was an insignificant backwater called Jehol until 1703 when the Qing emperor Kangxi took a good look at its surrounding natural beauty and hot springs and transformed it into his **Imperial Summer Villa**. He called his palace

Bishu Shanzhuang (Fleeing the Heat Mountain Villa), and his successors expanded it until it reached such magnificent proportions that it covered an area the size of the Forbidden City and Summer Palace combined. It is still the biggest garden palace complex in China.

Emperor Qianlong later endowed the palace with three Tibetan-style temples, one of them, the Putuo Zongcheng, a smaller version of the Potala Palace, to bind his authority to the Tibetan Buddhist rule after bringing the mountain stronghold under imperial control. Today the palace's gardens and temples, surrounded by a 10-km (six-mile)-long red wall, are in varying states of neglect and disrepair, awaiting renovations that will obviously have to be carried out if it is to become a major tourist draw.

Getting Around
Chengde is a sprawling place, and seeing the attractions on your own is almost impossible unless you have infinite patience and almost as much time. The best bet is to take a tour. These can be arranged cheaply once you arrive in Chengde.

What to See and Do
Bishu Shanzhuang's main **Central Palace**, now a museum, is in reasonable shape; so too are its **Misty Rain Mansion, Pine and Crane Studio** and **East Palace**. Of the temples, only five of an original 11 remain standing, but they still present a striking reminder of the power and artistry of the dynastic age. The **Puning Temple**, featuring a beautiful five-story Tibetan style pavilion, houses an impressive 22-m (72-ft) wooden Bodhisatta image — a Thousand-Hands-Thousand-Eyes Guanyin — fashioned from five different timbers and one of the largest images of its type in the world.

The **Pule Temple** has a main building which is almost a carbon copy of the Hall of Prayer for Good Harvests in Beijing, and inside you'll find a three-dimensional mandala, at the center of which is set a bronze sculpture of the Maitreya Buddha. The Potala style **Putuo Zongcheng** features a huge statue of the Buddhist Heavenly Mother, mounted on a horse, while the Xumi Fushou

Temple, built in 1780 to accommodate the sixth Panchen Lama on a visit from Tibet, is a near-replica of the Tashilhunpo Monastery in Xigaze.

Where to Stay

Chengde is quite a distance from Beijing, so you may have to stay the night. An unusual and fairly luxurious option (though with mid-range rates) is the **Mongolian Yurts Holiday Inn** ((314) 202-2710 in which you get to do the yurt thing with all modern conveniences, inside the grounds of the Imperial Summer Villa. Closer to town, near Bifeng Gate, the Qing dynasty style **Qiwanglou** ((314) 202-2192 is slightly more expensive but not by much.

In town, the **Chengde Hotel** (*binguan*) ((314) 203-3157, 33 Nanyingzi Dajie has basic doubles that hover somewhere between budget and mid-range. It's perfectly adequate for an overnight stay in Chengde.

How to Get There

There are daily early morning trains from Beijing to Chengde. The journey takes around four hours.

SHANHAIGUAN

This dramatic coastal location, six and a half hours by train out of Beijing, is where the Great Wall terminates in the **Old Dragon Head**, the place where the wall ends (begins really) its journey by tumbling down from the hills to the remains of a walled garrison on the shore of the Bo Hai (Sea). It's an opportunity to view the wall without the tourist hassle of the conventional visit to Badaling, and even though the structure at Shanhaiguan is in relatively poor shape, it still has a great deal of physical and romantic appeal. Still, bear in mind that Shanhaiguan has become a popular destination for Chinese tourists. It's not quite the rustic, neglected by tourists attraction it was five years ago. Avoid weekends if possible.

Apart from the so-called Old Dragon Head, the main attraction is the **First Pass Under Heaven**, a massive gate that for many centuries was the northern route in and out of China. Climb up on the wall, and you will discover a small military museum.

Shanhaiguan also offers a temple commemorating one of the many romantic legends associated with the Great Wall, or rather its reputation as the "world's longest cemetery." The **Temple of Mengjiangnu**, six kilometers (four miles) from the town, deifies a lady of the same name who went in search of her husband who had been pressed into service along with thousands of other conscripts during its initial construction in the reign of the ruthless Qinshi Huangdi. "Suddenly there was a great rumble," so the story goes, "and a gaping hole appeared in the wall. The bones of not one but thousands of dead workers were exposed to the icy winds." Those of Meng's husband were among them. Life, tragically, was cheap in the struggle it took to build the defensive barrier. It's also said that a sorcerer told the Iron Emperor that the wall would not be completed until 10,000 men had been buried in it. Qinshi Huangdi immediately tracked down a worker whose name included the character meaning "ten thousand" and had him slain and buried in the foundations instead.

Where to Stay

Shanhaiguan's most popular lodging is the **Jingshan Hotel** ((335) 505-1130, on Dong Dajie near the First Pass Under Heaven. It's a wonderfully atmospheric hotel that gives you the illusion of resting up in a Qing guesthouse. Rates are very reasonable for doubles with attached bathroom and television. The **North Street Hotel**, on Mujia Hutong, is another surprising atmospheric accommodation; rates are slightly cheaper here than at the Jingshan.

Poplars line boulevard BOTTOM of Chengde, home of an imperial summer retreat that rivals the grand landscaping and architecture of Forbidden City's palace gardens TOP.

The
Road
South

THE TRAIL between Beijing and Shanghai is not littered with grand cultural attractions, but there are some worthy stopovers all the same. The city of Tianjin has a fascinating foreign concession district that rivals that of Shanghai (minus the river views), while in Shandong province, Qingdao, another Treaty Port, is home of China's most famous brew and some charming German villas. Elsewhere in the province, Qufu was the birthplace of Confucius, China's grand old man of letters, and nearby Taishan is one of the country's most famous Taoist peaks.

TIANJIN

Tianjin is worthy of note for two reasons. The first is its compact enclave of colonial buildings, a legacy of the Treaty of Tianjin, signed in 1856 and granting the right to the European powers to establish concessions. The second is its sheer size: With a population of close to 10 million, Tianjin is China's third largest city.

Although an important port since Ming times, nowadays the port has shifted 50 km (30 miles) east to Tanggu. Some travelers arrive in and leave China from Tanggu, which has shipping connections with South Korea and Japan.

GENERAL INFORMATION

Dragonair ((22) 330-1234 has an office in the Hyatt Tianjin Hotel. **Korean Air** ((22) 319-0088 is at Room 2415, Tianjin International Building, 75 Nanjing Lu. **CAAC** ((22) 730-5888 is at 242 Heping Lu.

The **Bank of China** is at 80 Jiefang Beilu. **CITS** ((22) 835-8499 is at 22 Youyi Lu.

GETTING AROUND

Tianjin is a vast urban conglomeration, and getting around it is not much fun unless you're prepared to travel by taxi. The city has one subway line, which runs from the West Railway Station to Nanjing Lu.

WHAT TO SEE AND DO

One of Tianjin's most worthwhile attractions is **Dabei Yuan Temple**, in the north of Tianjin,

on an alley off Zhongshan Lu. It was built in the early seventeenth century, and to this day it remains very active. Note the nearby shops selling Buddhist accessories.

Other attractions include a **Confucius Temple** on Dongmennei Dajie and just east of here the main drawing card for both local and foreign visitors: **Ancient Culture Street**. Essentially the idea is to time warp travelers into the China of centuries past and fleece them of their tourist dollars in the process. Still, it makes for an interesting couple of hours of browsing (virtually every imaginable Chinese souvenir is on sale here), and there's a small **Tianhou Temple** to take a look at as well.

In the city center, the European streetscapes are to be found south of the Hai River. A good place to start is the Zhongxin Park roundabout, which marks the heart of the old **French concession**, a delightful area to explore on foot. This central area is perfect for combining some architectural sightseeing with a little shopping. Go to Binjiang Dao, the length of which is virtually one long market, for clothes shopping, and go to Shenyang Dao for antique shopping. The **antique market** here is probably the biggest in China. South of Nanjing Lu, is an impressive **Catholic Church** — you can't miss it. Five-minutes' walk farther east along Nanjing Lu, opposite the Friendship Hotel is the **Earthquake Memorial**, which commemorates the quarter of a million who perished in the Great Tangshan Earthquake of 1976; Tangshan is just 70 km to the north, and the earthquake destroyed much of Tianjin too.

WHERE TO STAY

Tianjin has a couple of luxury accommodations, some very decent mid-range hotels, but virtually no budget hotels. Backpackers, indeed anyone who is counting their yuan, are better off visiting Tianjin as a day trip from Beijing, which is just two hours away by train.

Tianjin's two international class luxury hotels are the **Hyatt Tianjin Hotel** ((22) 331-8888 FAX (22) 331-1234, 219 Jiefang Beilu, in Central Tianjin, and the **Sheraton Tianjin Hotel** ((22) 334-3388 FAX (22) 335-8740

Shuishang (On the Water) Park is a pleasant retreat from urban Tianjin.

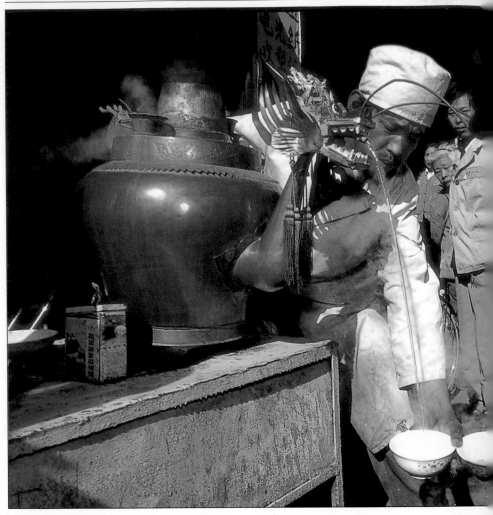

Zijinshan Lu, in the south of town overlooking Yanyuan Park.

At the top end of the mid-range scale is the **Friendship Hotel** ((22) 331-0372, 94 Nanjing Lu, an uninspiring but reliable option with a reasonably good location close to the concessions part of town. The **Tianjin Number One Hotel** ((22) 331-0707 FAX (22) 331-3341, 58 Jiefang Beilu, makes up for what the Friendship lacks in charm, and does so at cheaper rates.

WHERE TO EAT

The first stop on any culinary tour of Tianjin (and the offerings are surprisingly good) is **Food Street (Shipin Jie)** just east of Nanmenwai Dajie. With two stories of restaurants, 50 or so per floor, it's easy to spend an hour or so just deciding where to eat. Regional cuisines are well represented here.

Tianjin's other famous restaurant is **Goubuli**, 77 Shandong Lu, which some claim serves the best dumplings — *jiaozi* — in all China. Such claims are difficult to dispute. And if you didn't get your fill of duck in Beijing, Tianjin has a branch of the chain **Quanjude** ((22) 735-0046, at 53 Rongji Dajie.

HOW TO GET THERE

Direct flights from Hong Kong are available with Dragonair or with CAAC. Korean Air has flights from Seoul.

From Beijing, the easiest way to get to Tianjin is by bus. It saves queuing for train

German troops took Qingdao in 1897, after two German missionaries were killed there. A year later China ceded the town to the Germans for 99 years. Before the locals could start muttering, "What have the Germans ever done for us?" a railway line was built to connect the town with the provincial capital Ji'nan, electric lighting was installed and—importantly—a brewery was established. The brewery is still going strong, and makes China's only internationally known beer: Tsingtao. The Germans lost their foothold in China (and their brewery), when the Japanese marched on the city in 1914.

GENERAL INFORMATION

Dragonair ((532) 589-6809 has its office in the Grand Regency Hotel, 1 Taiwan Lu. **Korean Air** ((532) 387-0088 has its office in the Haitian Hotel, 39 Zhanshan Dalu. **CAAC** ((532) 287-6204 has its office in the Huanghai Hotel, 75 Yan'an 1 Lu.

The **Bank of China** is at 64 Zhongshan Lu, not far from the main railway station.

CITS ((532) 286-1513/4 is at 9 Nanhai Lu, behind the Huiquan Hotel.

GETTING AROUND

There is no bicycle hire in Qingdao. Fortunately, with the exception of Zhongshan Park, central Qingdao is small enough to explore on foot. Taxis are abundant and are metered.

tickets, and the journey takes less than three hours. Buses leave frequently from the west section of the car park in front of Beijing railway station.

QINGDAO

For those with the time to make a slight detour off the Beijing to Shanghai trail, Qingdao is a fascinating corner of Shandong to pay a visit to. Being a former German Treaty Port, people often refer to Qingdao as a tiny slice of Europe, a town miraculously transplanted from Bavaria. For many decades, before China opened up to the west, when a Chinese director needed a European street scene for a production, chances are it would be filmed here.

WHAT TO SEE AND DO

Qingdao's main attraction is its **German concession**, and the best area in which to see what's left of it is in the vicinity of the railway station. Take a stroll up Zhongshan Lu away from the station and look for a fine **Catholic church** on your right. The church itself is only open for services on Sunday mornings, but a wander around the area to the rear of the church will reward architectural buffs.

The **Tsingtao Brewery** is, of course, a popular destination. Unfortunately the only way to get inside is to go on a tour with CITS (see GENERAL INFORMATION above).

Souvenirs, and tea served in bowls are highlights of a visit to Tianjin's Ancient Culture Street.

For Chinese visitors — and in the summer months the city is swarming with them — Qingdao is a beach resort. To Western eyes, the beaches will probably seem unappealing, and if you settle on one of them for a spot of sunbathing it's very likely that representatives of the China-wide fraternity of English students will descend on you in no time. Still, it's worth taking a stroll along the very pleasant esplanade that overlooks **N° 1**, **N° 2**, **N° 3** and **N° 6 beaches**. N° 6 is usually the busiest.

Northwest of N° 1 Beach is Xinhao Park, which has a beautiful old German mansion on its grounds, now transformed into a hotel: the **Xinhao Hill Hotel**. Underneath the park is a bizarre underground shopping complex called the **Longshan Underground Market**. It's well worth visiting. **Zhongshan Park** is a huge garden made for strolling, and is famous for its cherry trees, which bloom between mid-April and early May.

WHERE TO STAY

There are no truly luxurious hotels around town, but some places try hard. The **Badaguan Hotel (** (532) 387-2168 FAX (532) 387-1383, 19 Shanhaiguan Lu, is not the top hotel in town, but it has a good location close to N° 2 Beach, has some character and can also organize accommodation in villas around town.

The **Qingdao Huiquan Dynasty Hotel (** (532) 287-3366 FAX (532) 287-1122, 9 Nanhai Lu, is also well located, and is more a standard luxury hotel, if a little bland. The Gloria Group has a new hotel in Qingdao: the **Huanhai Gloria Inn (** (532) 387-8855 FAX (532) 386-4640, 21 Donghai Lu.

For mid-range accommodation, the central **Qingdao Hotel (** (532) 289-1888 FAX (532) 286-2464, 53 Zhongshan Lu, may look expensive from the outside, but room rates are very reasonable — discounts are often available if you ask politely. For sheer convenience, the **Railway Hotel (** (532) 286-6693, next door to the railway station, is hard to beat. Room rates start at around $25.

HOW TO GET THERE

Qingdao has international air connections with Hong Kong and Seoul, and is well connected with domestic destinations. Ji'nan, the provincial capital is the nearest transport hub. The easiest way to get there is by bus, which take four to five hours and leave frequently from the bus stand next to the railway station. From Ji'nan, the provincial capital, there are buses to Tai'an (for Taishan and Qufu) and trains north to Tianjin and Beijing, and south to Shanghai.

TAI'AN

Tai'an is a small dusty town and there would be no reason to stop here were it not for its Dai Temple, and the nearby cultural attractions of Taishan and Qufu.

The **Dai Temple** came into being as a pit stop for pilgrims visiting nearby Taishan — some say as early as the Qin dynasty (221–206 BC). It has gone through countless reconstructions since then, most recently in the mid-1950s. Today it's remarkably well preserved, and even if there is a museum-like atmosphere to the place, a visit is still an essential prelude to climbing Taishan; if you're feeling particularly energetic, you can walk up to the mountain, starting at the temple.

Notable sights in this large temple include a magnificent Song dynasty mural housed in the Main Hall, which depicts the god of Taishan in the guise of Emperor Zhen Zong, who commissioned the painting. In the temple grounds is a large collection of steles, some of them very ancient.

WHERE TO STAY

Tai'an's top hotel is the **Overseas Chinese Hotel (** (538) 822-8112 FAX (538) 822-8171, Dongyue Dajie, which given its location does a very good job. It even has a swimming pool and a bowling alley, though after slogging up Taishan and back, bowling is unlikely to be foremost on your mind.

The popular place to stay, for backpackers and mid-range travelers alike, is the **Taishan Binguan (** (538) 822-4678, on Hongmen Lu, just north of the Dai Temple and en route to Taishan. The doubles with air-conditioning and attached bath are very reasonably priced, while budget travelers pile into the three-bed dorm rooms.

HOW TO GET THERE

If you're coming from Qingdao, change to a minibus in front of the Ji'nan main railway station. Tai'an is also connected by train to Ji'nan and to Beijing and Shanghai. The onward train journey to Shanghai takes around nine to 10 hours.

TAISHAN

Taishan is China's most sacred Daoist mountain. Its crags and peaks are littered with pagodas and temples and calligraphy, the legacy of inspiration-seeking artists, poets, and leaders. Imperial sacrifices were once held on its summit, emperors have toiled up its slopes, as did Confucius (who was born nearby) and more recently even Mao.

Taishan is the domain of the female Daoist deity Bixia, whose name is usually rendered in English as the Princess of the Azure (or pink, perhaps) Clouds. She has traditionally had a loyal following in Shandong, and among other things she is said to bestow long life on those who climb to the summit of her mountain — 100 years, specifically. But the most captivating thing about Taishan, after the views, is the tide of people. Don't be surprised if you see some gnarled old Daoist priest skip past you as you pant your way up the more than 6,000 stairs that climb ever upwards; move aside as the porters trip nimbly past carrying huge loads; watch for the honeymoon couples taking it easy on a two-man palanquin, a time-honored mode of conveyance on China's sacred mountains.

There are a number of different approaches to the summit. The combination of minibus and cable car is the easiest one, and given that the proper pilgrimage trail from Tai'an to the summit involves four to five hours of uphill trudging it's tempting. One possibility is to "half cheat" and take a minibus to **Zhongtianmen**, which is where the cablecar starts, and walk from there, which takes around two hours — don't worry you're legs will know that they've been busy when you get to the top. Once you're on the summit, you can decide whether you want to walk back down or take the cable car (it takes just eight minutes).

There is accommodation on the mountain at the **Zhongtianmen Guesthouse** ((538) 822-6740, and at the **Shenqi Guesthouse** ((538) 822-3866, which is at the summit. In both cases you should expect basic standards despite the high cost of the rooms (the Shenqi costs around $100 for a double).

QUFU

An interesting daytrip from Tai'an is the small hamlet of Qufu. Confucius, the Great Teacher, was born here in 551 BC and spent much of his life teaching with little in the way of recognition. His attempts to achieve influence foundered; his efforts, as he traveled around China, to reach the ears of the powerful were roundly ignored, and it was only after his students gathered together his ideas in a book known as *The Analects* that he achieved posthumous success.

Today it's easy to spend a day wandering around Qufu's **Confucius Temple** and the **Confucius Mansions**. Both of them are massive, testifying not only to the eminence that Confucius achieved after his death, but also to the extent to which his impecunious pursuit of his ideals enriched his ancestors. The Kong family (Confucius is spelled Kong Fuzi in Chinese) became the First Family Under Heaven, and they lived in their Qufu mansion for some 2,500 years, building on to it, enhancing its magnificence, until when the last family head of the Kongs, Kong Decheng, decamped (sensibly given his lifestyle) to Taiwan in 1948, the family residence, with its 466 rooms, resembled the Beijing's Forbidden City.

WHERE TO STAY

If you decide you need more time in Qufu, there are places to stay. The **Queli Hotel** ((537) 441-1300 is an upper mid-range hotel that is right next door to the mansions and temple complex. **Confucius Mansion** ((537) 441-1783 is the top budget hotel in town, and it also has comfortable mid-range rooms. It's in the south of town, next to the bus stop.

Buses run from Tai'an to Qufu through out the day, and there are also buses to the provincial capital, Ji'nan.

Shanghai
and the
River
Cities

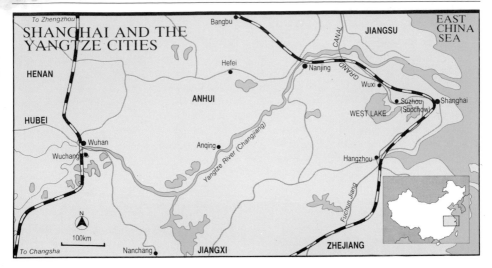

SHANGHAI AND THE YANGTZE CITIES

THIS DRAMATIC east-west stretch of the long China trail offers an exciting and quite refined gateway to the heart of the nation for travelers starting from Shanghai — and for those taking the clockwise grand tour, it offers relative comfort, good cuisine and sophistication for the end of a China adventure.

The Yangtze River route is the central axis on which all travel in China swings. On the rail route north from Guangzhou it provides access to Shanghai, Suzhou and Hangzhou in the east and Chongqing, Chengdu, Lhasa and Xi'an in the west. It offers the same east-west access coming, of course, south from Beijing. And from whichever direction you approach it, the two pivotal junctions are Zhengzhou and Wuhan.

ZHENGZHOU

A busy, prosperous industrial city, once a Shang dynasty imperial seat and now the capital of Henan province, Zhengzhou is one of the two most strategic railway junctions of central eastern China — the other being Hengyang on the east-west rail corridor to Yunnan and the west. It's also one of the most difficult cities in China for foreigners to tackle — very few locals speak English, and, unless you're staying in the Holiday Inn, tourist facilities remain primitive. The main cultural attraction is Shaolin Monastery, 80 km (50 miles) to the southwest, considered to be the birthplace of Chan (Zen) Buddhism and the martial art kung fu.

GENERAL INFORMATION

CAAC has outlets in most hotels. The **Bank of China** is at 40 Huayuan Lu. CITS ((371) 595-2072 is at 15 Jinshui Lu.

WHAT TO SEE AND DO

Zhengzhou only has one overwhelming attraction, and that's **Shaolin Monastery**. Built in the time of the Northern Wei dynasty, it was established in tribute to Bodhidharma, the Indian monk (also featured on a mural in the Guangxiao Temple in Guangzhou) who brought the message of Chan (Zen) to China and is said to have been the first champion of the martial arts — teaching his disciples boxing and unarmed combat for self-protection in those unstable and dangerous times. Legend has it that he was so transcendental that he was able to cross a river on a flimsy reed.

In the monastery's most glorious age, during the Sui and Tang dynasties, it sported 5,000 shrines, halls, pagodas and pavilions. Only four major buildings remain — the Bodhidharma Pavilion, Thousand Buddha Hall, White Robe Hall and Bodhisattva Ksitigarbha Hall — but they offer surviving artwork and relics that echo the monastery's martial role. In the White Robe hall, for example, there are stunning murals depicting scenes and techniques of kung fu, including

Daoist monk — Daoism flourishes alongside Buddhism.

the epic "Thirteen Monks Rescuing the King of Tang" — a celebrated punch-up that took place when the monks of Shaolin acted as imperial retainers in the Tang dynasty. In the Thousand Buddha Hall you can study rounded hollows in the tiled floor — worn there over the centuries by daily kung fu training.

To get to the monastery, either take a CITS tour or a daily bus that leaves from outside the Zhongyuan Mansions opposite the railway station. Buy your ticket the a small white booth on the edge of the station concourse.

Although there are a few would-be contenders Zhengzhou's other hotels are either blandly mid-range or horrifyingly bottom range, and if you doubt the last take a look at the Dickensian Zhongyuan Mansions opposite the railway station.

The **Asia Hotel** ((371) 696-8888, is probably the best mid-range choice. It has a good location next to the Erqi Pagoda traffic circle, not far from the railway station, and the joint-venture status of the hotel should ensure that standards will not slip much. Doubles start at around $60.

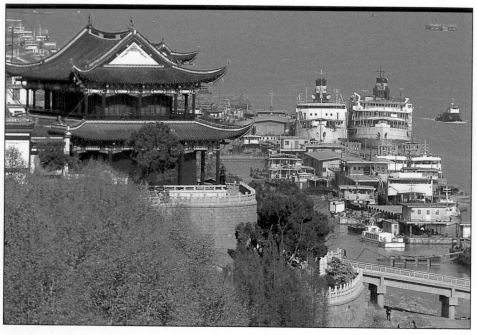

Note that if you take the daily bus, you should try to bring along a ticket request written in Chinese.

Aside from the monastery Zhengzhou provides easy access by train or bus to the cultural jewel of central China, Luoyang.

WHERE TO STAY

Zhengzhou's finest is the **Holiday Inn Crowne Plaza** ((371) 595-0055 FAX (371) 599-0770, a hotel with an interesting history. It has been converted from a "foreign expert's" guesthouse built in the 1950s, but from the moment you step into the massive, glitzy lobby area there can be no doubt that the conversion has been a thorough one.

For budget travelers the **Erqi Hotel** ((371) 696-8801, on the same traffic circle as the Asia Hotel, is a basic place to lay your head down for a night — nothing in the way of amenities, but the price is right.

HOW TO GET THERE

Zhengzhou is connected by air with most major Chinese cities. For access by train, it's on the main north-south Guangzhou–Beijing express route, the cross-country Beijing–Xi'an–Lanzhou service and the east-west route between Shanghai and Xi'an. There are comfortable express rail services to Xi'an which take around seven and half hours.

LUOYANG

Luoyang, west of Zhengzhou, is another city whose modern industrial façade obscures its long, illustrious history. Not only was it the founding center of Buddhism in China — the site of the Han dynasty **White Horse Temple**, built to celebrate the arrival of the first sutras from India — but it was the imperial capital of nine dynasties until it was destroyed by the armies of the northern Jin reign in the twelfth century.

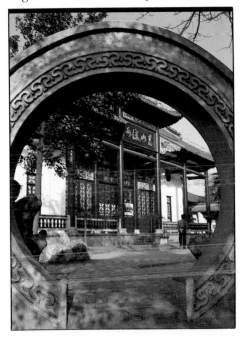

Its most magnificent legacy is, of course, the **Longmen Buddhist Grottoes**, first excavated and decorated in the time of the Toba Northern Wei dynasty when Luoyang was the imperial court, and also the site of more than 1,300 Buddhist temples.

WHAT TO SEE AND DO

Longmen Grottoes

Around 16 km (10 miles) south of Luoyang on the banks of the Yi River, the Longmen (Dragon Gate) Grottoes were dug and carved around the year 493 in the time of the Northern Wei dynasty and added to in the Tang dynasty. More than 2,000 of them are found along the cliff face overlooking the Yi River, packed

with some 100,000 sculptured images, 40 stone towers and 3,600 stone carvings and inscribed steles and plaques. The Buddha images are magnificent, with their full, benign Han Chinese features that reflect the cultural assimilation that occurred as the Toba dynasty extended its control south.

The two most impressive galleries are the **Binyang Caves** at the entrance to the complex, featuring 11 large Buddha images of the Toba period, and the **Fengxian Temple**, now without its protective roof and actually an open-air grotto, which was built in the Tang era and is dominated by 11 huge statues, the biggest of them a 51-m (59-ft)-high Vairocana Buddha. One of the statues supports a pagoda in the palm of its hand and is in the act of crushing a demon underfoot. Aside from the Buddhas and attendant statues, there are sculptures throughout the grottoes of emperors, princes and nobles of the 400-year period over which the immense tableau was completed.

WHERE TO STAY

Luoyang won't go out of its way to pamper you. The top hotel in town is the very Chinese **Luoyang Peony Hotel** ((379) 491-3699 FAX (379) 491-3668, 15 Zhongzhou Xilu. It does a good job considering its in faraway Luoyang, and the lobby restaurant is not bad.

The best mid-range hotel in town is the **Luoyang Friendship Hotel** ((379) 491-2780 FAX (379) 491-3808, 6 Xiyuan Lu, whose lobby sees constant streams of overseas Chinese tour groups. Its inconveniently located in the southwest of town.

Budget travelers mostly stay around the railway station, which has a few inexpensive hotels and has the added advantage of being close to the minibus departure points for the White Horse Temple and the Longmen Grottoes. Choose between the **Luoyang Hotel** and the **Tianxiang Hotel**, neither of which are particularly salubrious.

HOW TO GET THERE

Luoyang is not very well connected to the rest of China by air. Consider flying to Zheng-

Sensuously rounded gateway ABOVE to restored pavilion at Guiyuan Monastery OPPOSITE.

zhou and continuing from there to Luoyang by train or bus. The daily Zhengzhou-Xi'an express stops in Luoyang. Buses from Zhengzhou to Luoyang take around three hours. Minibuses to Longmen and to the White Horse Temple leave from in front of Luoyang station. Some of these buses are in fact Chinese tour buses, and their itineraries will include both sights. Tours are also available at the Friendship and the Peony hotels in Luoyang.

WUHAN

Hubei's provincial capital, one of the largest cities in the interior of China, Wuhan is actually made up of three cities clustered at the confluence of the Yangtze and Han rivers. **Hankou**, on the Yangtze's west bank, is the main attraction. A former fishing village that became a major Treaty Port in the days of British and European military and trading pressure, its architectural character is similar to that of Shanghai.

Hanyang, south of Hankou, over the Han River, is a largely industrial center. Although it doesn't have the narrow teeming streets and old Victorian commercial buildings of Hankou, it features the city's most historically interesting attraction, the Qing dynasty **Guiyuan Temple**.

Wuchang, on the Yangtze's eastern bank, is the oldest, dating back to 221, but is ironically now more representative of modern China — wide boulevards and high-rise administrative buildings — and includes the huge Wuhan University, the Hubei Provincial Museum and the popular recreational resort, East Lake (Dong Hu). Wuchang is linked to Hankou by the spectacular Yangtze River Bridge, built in 1957 and the first to span the great river, its eastern expressway sweeping under the beautiful multiwinged roofs of the city's most remarkable historic landmark, the renovated Ming dynasty Yellow Crane Mansion (Huanghe Lou).

Wuhan's place in contemporary history centers on an accidental bomb explosion on October 10, 1911 that triggered an anti-Manchu army rebellion and in turn became the long-awaited flashpoint of the republican campaign to sweep the Qing dynasty from power.

GENERAL INFORMATION

The Hankou branch of **CAAC(** (27) 284-4841 is at 102 Yanjiang Dadao. The **Bank of China** is at 1021 Zhongshan Dadao. **CITS(** (27) 282-1265 is at 48 Jianghan 1 Lu.

GETTING AROUND

Taxis are widely available, as are auto rickshaws. There are ferries and speedboats that run back and forth between Hankou,

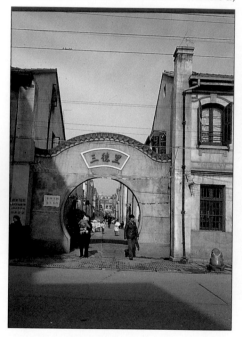

Hanyang and Wuchang, but they are often very crowded.

WHAT TO SEE AND DO

If Wuhan has a saving grace as a destination for travelers it's the street life in **Hankou**. There are no sights as such here, but take a stroll in the area between **Yanjiang Dadao** (beside the river) and **Jiefang Dadao**, and between the push and shove of the crowds and the delightful cultural clash of old Chinese and Treaty Port Victorian architecture, there's never a dull moment. Take a look

Classic architecture ABOVE in gateway to residential backstreet. OPPOSITE: The historic Ming dynasty Yellow Crane Mansion, Wuchang.

at the Victorian-style Bank of China building on the corner of Jiangshan Lu and Zhongshan Dadao.

For those on a strict sightseeing agenda, **Guiyuan Temple** should top the itinerary. It's close to the waterfront in **Hanyang** — a Qing dynasty monastery, on the grounds of a Ming dynasty park, now springing back to life after the repression of the Cultural Revolution. Billowing with joss-stick smoke, it features a gloomy but fascinating main hall full of Buddha images, sculptures of *arhats* and a looming, moon-faced guardian deity, all staring from dark and dusty glassed alcoves. Its most treasured relic is a Burmese jade Buddha presented to it in 1935.

As for the **Yangtze Bridge** (the old one, not the new one in the east of town), you can climb up its stone towers and right onto its top traffic deck and cross the 1,156-m (3,800-ft) span enjoying a bird's-eye view of the river traffic and the packed city ferries disgorging hundreds of commuters and their bicycles along the **Wuchang** waterfront — the crowds streaming like hordes of ants up the ferry ramps, the chrome of their bikes flashing in the sun. Ahead of you, on the Wuchang side, you can also marvel at the towering, golden, multi-eaved **Huanghe Lou (Yellow Crane Mansion)**. It's really a rebuilt pagoda — the original is said to have been built in the Three Kingdoms days (220–265) and rebuilt time after time. The last but one, a Ming dynasty structure burned down in 1884 — and although this one is completely new it's a popular recreation spot for Chinese and foreign visitors alike. The view from its upper balconies is a dramatic panorama of the bridge, its huge expressway, the Wuchang riverfront and the Hanyang foreshores.

East Lake (Dong Hu)

Out on the eastern fringe of Wuchang, East Lake (Dong Hu) is one of the largest freshwater lakes in China and a long-established recreational resort that has interesting pavilions, boating, good bicycling paths, a botanical garden and three lakeside restaurants, the **Renmin**, **Liyuan** and **Tingtao**. It's also the site of the small **Hubei Provincial Museum** with a remarkable exhibition of

bronze tripods, lacquered furniture and trunks, carvings, sculpture, jewelry and gold bowls and ornaments unearthed in 1978 from the tomb of the Marquis Yi of Zeng, one of the nobles of the Warring States period of 475–221 BC, just before the rise to power of the Iron Emperor Qinshi Huangdi.

The most splendid relic from the tomb is a huge ancient musical instrument, a bronze bell chime — 65 ornately decorated bells set on a heavy three-level frame which, as the museum's brochure explains, "were played

by five musicians… Ancient and modern music, both Chinese and foreign, has been played on it, and the sound is melodious and beautiful."

There's a another notice that strikes a chilling tone in this important tomb excavation, too. It calls attention to the "immolated remains" of concubines and attendants found in 21 plain wooden coffins around the duke's sarcophagus. " Skeletons found in the coffins are those of young females, the oldest being about 25 and the youngest 13 years old. Obviously they were immolated for the master of the tomb. This is an indictment against the feudal exploiting class for their cruel oppression of the laboring people."

Where to Stay

Luxury

The arrival of the **Holiday Inn Tian An Wuhan** ((27) 586-7888 FAX (27) 584-5353, 868 Jiefang Dadao, is a sure sign of Wuhan's increasing importance as a destination for business travelers. It's currently the best hotel in town.

For those less in need of modern international standards and more in search of local ambiance, the **Jianghan Hotel** ((27) 281-1599

FAX (27) 281-4342, 245 Shengli Jie, is an excellent choice. It was built by the French in 1914, and although it has subsequently been completely refurbished, it still retains much of its charm.

The **Wuhan Asia Hotel** ((27) 380-7777 FAX (27) 380-8080, 616 Jiefang Dadao, was Wuhan's top hotel until the arrival of the Holiday Inn.

Mid-Range and Inexpensive

Mid-range hotels are not thick on the ground in Hankou. Recommended is the central **Yinfeng Hotel** ((27) 589-2700, 400 Zhongshan Dadao, where spacious, very clean doubles with attached bathroom cost from around $25, which is about as cheap as

rooms come in Wuhan. The **Victory Hotel** ((27) 283-2604 FAX (27) 283-2604, 11 Siwei Lu, is another good mid-range hotel, though the location, north of the central Hankou district, could be better. Its rates start at around $50.

Where to Eat

There is some good hotel food in Wuhan, notably in the Holiday Inn and at the **Ramada Hotel** ((27) 578-7968, 9 Taibei 1 Lu, which until the Holiday Inn came along held up the fort alone on the Western food front with its lobby coffeeshop.

Elsewhere around town, you might like to drop into one of Wuhan's longest running and most famous restaurants, **Lao Huibin**, on the corner of Minquan and Qianjin Lu. It's a good place to try Hubei dishes such as brown-sauce fish. The basic but wildly popular **Laotongchang**, 1 Dazhi Lu, is a cheap and friendly eating establishment offering very tasty and nourishing chicken soup in clay pots and a famous stuffed bean curd snack known as *doupi*.

How to Get There

Wuhan is China's central rail and Yangtze River access. It lies on the main Guangzhou–Beijing express route and the east-west routes from Shanghai to Kunming and Xi'an. The Yangtze River ferries ply east to Nanjing and Shanghai and west to Chongqing. Both the main railway station and river ferry terminal are in Hankou. There are also direct air links with almost every airport in China.

Yangtse River Ferries

Tickets for the Yangtse River ferries are readily booked in Wuhan at any of the tourist hotels, or if you feel up to it at the Yangtse Ferry Terminal in Hankou.

If you want to enjoy the trip (and why else would you do it?) take a second-class passage. Second class is two-a-cabin, and is fairly comfortable: the third- and fourth-class berths are not only packed with people but

OPPOSITE: "Liberal era" young people sport latest fashions and suburban woman ABOVE heads off to market.

dozens more crowd aboard at each stop along the river and bed down along the decks and corridors until there's hardly room to move. Because of the vessel's constant hot water supply, the passengers all wash their clothes the moment they step aboard, and the decks become festooned with flapping shirts, dresses, underwear and long johns. But it's a restful run, with an occasional stop to pick up cargo and passengers along the way, and, now and then, the sight of a passing moth-winged sailing junk thrown in for excitement.

Treaty Ports to free trade. In the Taiping Rebellion of 1853 the city was again besieged, conquered and established as the rebel headquarters. In 1911 it became the republican capital for a brief period and was where Sun Yatsen was declared president of the provisional government. In 1937 it was the headquarters of Chiang Kaishek's government until the Japanese advance drove it up the Yangtze to Wuhan and then to Chongqing. In April 1949, Mao Zedong's communist forces poured across the Yangtze and raised the red flag over its rooftops.

NANJING

Nanjing, (Nanking) the old southern capital of the dynastic age, now the capital of Jiangsu province, is a prosperous, attractive city with a fascinating history, dating back to 473 BC, in the Warring States period; it was later to become the Song dynasty capital. It was also the temporary capital during the early Ming period, and has always been regarded as an alternative to Beijing as a seat of power. Indeed Nanjing means "southern capital"; Beijing means "northern capital."

In 1842, British troops and gunboats laid siege to Nanjing in the first Opium War, forcing the Qing dynasty to sign the historic Treaty of Nanking which opened up the five

The city is now a leading center of culture and higher education, and a powerhouse for joint-venture business projects in Jiangsu. It is, in fact, a business city, but its strategic position on the Yangtze River ferry route and its cultural attractions make it well worth a stopover.

GENERAL INFORMATION

Dragonair ((25) 331-9500 is in the Grand Hotel, 208 Guangzhou Lu. **CAAC** ((25) 449-9378 is at 52 Ruijin Lu. **China Eastern Airlines** ((25) 664-0739 is at 350 Taiping Nanlu.

The **Bank of China** is at 3 Zhongshan Donglu.

CITS ((25) 334-6444 is at 202 Zhongshan Beilu, and does very little except sell airline tickets.

WHAT TO SEE AND DO

The commercial heart of Nanjing is the **Xinjiekou** traffic circle, where you will find the upmarket Jinling Hotel, and where Zhongshan Lu intersects with Zhongshan Nanlu. North of here, at the intersection of Zhongyang Lu and Beijing Lu, you'll find the **Drum Tower** (Gulou) traffic circle,

Farther east is **Zijin Shan** (Purp Mountain), with a number of famous tions. Of most interest are the buil around **Linggu Temple**, a small but active Buddhist place of worship. The la **Beamless Hall** dates back to 1381, and is named because its large frame is supporte by columns without the aid of a beam. From here you can take a shuttle bus up to the **Sun Yatsen Mausoleum**. Although for many Chinese visitors — particularly from overseas — a visit the tomb of the man who the Nationalists refer to as the *guofu*, literally the

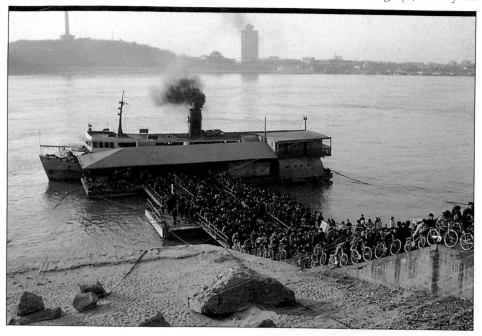

another center and a useful landmark. The other area you need to know about is **Fuzi Miao**, a Confucian temple in the south of town, surrounded by many shops and restaurants.

East of Xinjiekou, on Zhongshan Donglu, the **Nanjing Museum** is wide ranging and always interesting. West of Fuzimiao, the **Memorial to the Nanjing Massacre** is a chilling account in pictures and displays of the darkest moment in the Japanese attempt to annex China to its colonial ambitions in the Second World War.

Xuanwu Lake Park, in the northeast of town is a landscaped park that provides a chance to watch the Chinese at play, but otherwise is nothing to write home about.

"national father," is something of a pilgrimage, for most Western visitors the views over Nanjing and the surrounding hills are likely to be more of a draw. Carved over the mausoleum entrance are the Three Principles, as expounded by Sun Yatsen (in Chinese, Sun Zhongshan), and still upheld by the Nationalist government in Taiwan: Nationalism, Democracy and People's Livelihood.

The **Zheng He Memorial Hall** and park and the **Qixia Monastery** are 20 km (12 miles) northeast of the city. The former commemorates the Ming dynasty eunuch admiral who

Two views of Yangtze riverfront. OPPOSITE: A bridge spans the mighty river at Nanjing, Jiangsu Province. ABOVE: Evening ferry disgorges rush hour commuters, in Wuhan.

Shanghai and the River Cities

seven great oceanic voyages to the an coast between 1405 and 1433, almost ntury before Columbus discovered the w World. The hall and surrounding pavilns are packed with relics and exhibits of life n the Ming reign, graphs, maps and models depicting the Moslem seafarer's expeditions and the 1,456 sailing junks that were under his command, and a brass bell that was cast to announce his safe return from the last of these "Silk Road of the Sea" odysseys.

WHERE TO STAY

Luxury

The magnificent 37-story **Jinling Hotel** ((25) 445-5888 FAX (25) 470-3396, Xinjiekou Square, with its revolving restaurant on the 36th floor, is the city's most luxurious accommodation, and superbly located right in the center of town. Just north of here, is the **Nanjing Central Hotel** ((25) 440-0666 FAX (25) 441-4194, 75 Zhongshan Beilu, which is smaller and more intimate but lacks the facilities that the nearby Jinling has.

If you want to be based in the lively Fuzi Miao district in the south of town (the best area for dining and nightlife), the **Nanjing Mandarin Garden Hotel** ((25) 220-2555 FAX (25) 220-1876, 9 Zhuangyuanjing, is an excellent choice.

Mid-Range

The great attraction of the **Shuangmenlou Hotel** ((25) 800-5961 FAX (25) 880-1421, 185 Huju Beilu, is the fact that in typical guesthouse style it's located in rambling gardens in a series of wings. Most of the rooms have been renovated tastefully and come in at around $40 to $50. Some less expensive rooms may also be available.

The **Hongqiao Hotel** ((25) 330-1466 FAX (25) 342-0756, 202 Zhongshan Beilu, is a comfortable tourist-class hotel in the northwest of town next door to CITS. It's a comfortable place to be based and the staff at reception can help with transport queries and bookings.

The **Nanjing Hotel** ((25) 330-2302 is opposite the Hongqiao, giving you two midrange choices within easy walking distance of each other, and like the Shuangmenlou is very much of the old school. The gardens

here are very pleasant. Rooms are cheaper than at the Hongqiao, but are slightly lacking in finesse. If such details don't concern you, you many like the Nanjing for its less stuffy atmosphere.

Inexpensive

Nanjing is unusual in that its university guesthouses (long a budget refuge throughout China for travelers in the know and with the right contacts) are open to all and sundry. The **Nanjing University Foreign Students Dormitory**, Shanghai Lu, is where

budget travelers inevitably end up, usually in double rooms with shared bathroom.

WHERE TO EAT

Nanjing is the perfect place to try Jiangsu cuisine at its best. The **Jiangsu Restaurant**, 26 Jiankang Lu, is famed for its Nanjing duck, which is totally unlike Beijing duck. Nanjing duck is pressed and salted, and if you are in any way a fan of duck it is a must-try while you are in town.

For something less pricey and a lot less local, the **Maxiangxing Restaurant**, on the Drum Tower traffic circle, does tasty inexpensive Moslem cuisine. Try the sliced cold beef.

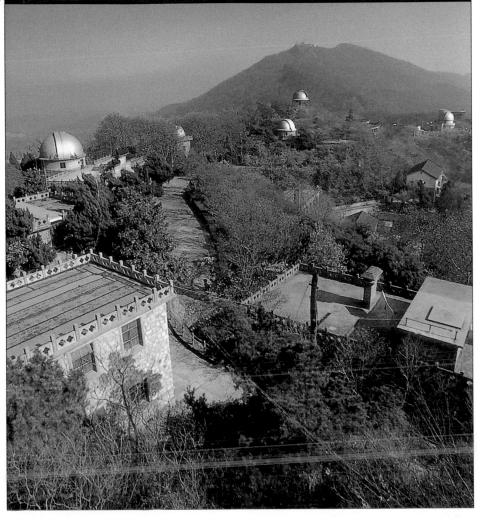

If you're hankering for something closer to home, hotels such as the Jinling do Western dishes; mind you, at a price. For Western favorites at budget rates and in a lively atmosphere, head down to the **Black Cat Café** on an alley just north of Hanzhong Lu (near Xinjiekou traffic circle). This place got its start doing simple meals for homesick foreign students at Nanjing University, and as time went by it grew and eventually moved from opposite the university to this more central location. Dishes include steaks, salads and pizzas.

The adventurous might take a stroll in the area south of Xinjiekou in the evening to seek out cheap eats in one of the many Chinese snack shops. The unadventurous might resort to one of the several branches of **KFC** or even **McDonald's**.

HOW TO GET THERE

Nanjing is connected by air with Hong Kong and with most other major domestic destinations. It's also a major port of call on the Yangtze River route west from Chongqing and east from Shanghai. Coming from Wuhan, this is the place to disembark for the trains on the Shanghai–Beijing–Xi'an route to Wuxi and Suzhou. The city also has a direct bus service to Hangzhou, a desti-

Nanjing — OPPOSITE: Majestic approach to Sun Yatsen Memorial, the key revolutionary landmark in the city. ABOVE: Zijinshan Observatory.

nation which otherwise can be reached only by train from Shanghai.

WUXI

On the eastward run to Shanghai, Wuxi is the first of the much touted Grand Canal cities. But, though it may once have been a picturesque place, nowadays it looks like most other Chinese cities in the region.

The real attraction is **Lake Tai** (Taihu), which in the summer is a-flutter with picturesque square-sailed fishing junks. The two viewing points for the lake are **Plum Garden** (Meiyuan) and **Turtle Head Island** (Guitouzhu). The time to be in the Plum garden is springtime, when, if you're lucky the plum trees will be in bloom. But even if the trees are bare of pink blossoms, the garden area provides good views of the lake. Turtle Head Island, which is strictly speaking a peninsula, is the traditional viewing area for the lake, and is also the place to get a ferry ride to the small Three Hills Island (*sanshan*).

If possible try to organize your itinerary to avoid an overnight in Wuxi. If you do have to stay here, it's a better to be beside the lake than in town. The **Taihu Hotel** ✆ (512) 676-7901 is not far south of the Plum Garden and is probably the best place to stay. It has upper mid-range rates.

SUZHOU

Suzhou is the undisputed pearl of the Yangtze delta and Grand Canal — vibrant, exciting, beautiful, historic — a place that once you settle in for a couple of days, you won't want to leave. Marco Polo was entranced by the city, and so too were many wealthy retired mandarins of the Ming and Qing dynasties who spent their last years there and are largely responsible for its greatest cultural drawing card — its famous villas and gardens.

Suzhou rose to prominence when the southern stretches of the Grand Canal were completed in the Sui dynasty 1,300 years ago. The city became an important trading and shipping link in the water transport chain, particularly for its most valued produce, silk. With its network of canals and waterways feeding off and into the Grand Canal, it was later hailed as the Venice of the East, a place of heaven on earth, the home of the most beautiful and accommodating women in China, a place of pleasure and sophistication, an ideal place, in fact, to spend one's waning days in the idyllic, meditative pursuit of higher thoughts and base instincts.

Not that it didn't have its upheavals. In the 1880s most of the city was destroyed and 70% of its population killed — and its silk industry devastated just as Japan was emerging as the major challenger to Chinese silk — by horrific fighting in the Taiping Rebellion. But Suzhou somehow survived the carnage and has since weathered the Japanese military occupation, the civil war, the 1949 revolution and the excesses of the Cul-

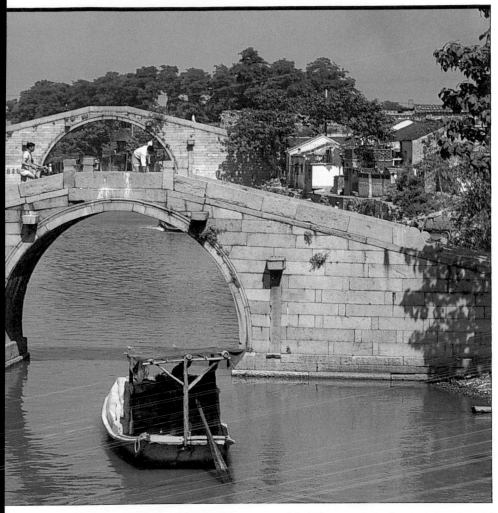

tural Revolution, not to mention its latter-day industrialization, to maintain much of its old-world refinement and charm.

GENERAL INFORMATION

Air bookings are handled by **China Eastern** ((512) 522-5758, 192 Renmin Lu, though Suzhou itself doesn't have an airport. The **Bank of China** is at 490 Renmin Lu. **CITS** ((512) 522-3175 is in the compound of the Suzhou Hotel, 115 Shiquan Jie.

GETTING AROUND

There's no better way to enjoy Suzhou than by bicycle; rentals are available from opposite the Suzhou Hotel. Taxis can be found

cruising the streets and swarming around the railway station and the better hotels.

WHAT TO SEE AND DO

Suzhou, like everywhere else in China, is modernizing with zeal, but it remains a pleasant city to cruise around in by bicycle. Buy an English-language tourist map and follow the city's spiderwork of canals through streets lined with beautiful old low-roofed white-washed housing, under the high cooling dome of dappled foliage of the huge plane trees, amidst great streams of bicycles, cars and buses, and alongside the raucous bellow and blaring horns and loudspeakers of

Softly rounded bridges in Suzhou, "garden city" of the Grand Canal.

the cargo boats and long convoys of barges on the canals.

The people of Suzhou are particularly relaxed and genial, especially the canal dwellers, and the first stop on any tour should be one of the bridges that cross the city's **Outer Moat** where you can stand for hours watching the concrete-hulled boats and barges cruise through hordes of sampans and moored craft. The **Renmin Bridge** to the south is a good spot, and there are other bridges, **Wannian**, **Wumen**, **Hongqi** and **Guangji** on the city's west side that offer interesting vantage points.

The main tourist hub is the **Guanqian Bazaar** area on Guanqian Jie, running east off the main north-south thoroughfare Renmin Lu. Part of the district has been closed off to traffic and turned into a pedestrian mall, and it's surrounded by arts and crafts and antique stores, bookshops, cinemas, confectionery stores and a number of famous old restaurants, most notably the 200-year-old Songhe Lou.

The **Suzhou Antique Store**, on Renmin Lu just up from the Lexiang Hotel and close to the new Friendship Store, is one of the best in all of China — crammed with ceramics, porcelain, scrolls, paintings, jewelry and other artwork. It has one floor of particularly refined porcelains and other art that's not for sale — it hasn't been given the government's wax seal of approval for export.

On the northern side of Guanqian Jie you'll find the Daoist **Xuanmiao (Temple of Mystery)**, a big wooden barn of a place with a main hall, **Sanqing**, supported by 60 pillars and a sweeping double roof with "winged" eaves. The temple was founded in the Jin dynasty, around 275 AD, but the main hall was built in 1181 after the original structure burned down. What makes the place more than just another temple is the bazaar that spreads through its courtyards and grounds — with so much buying and selling going on that the "religious" section, the altars and images, are roped off to prevent them being overrun by base commerce.

North of Guanqian along Renmin Lu, you can't help but notice the city's second most famous religious institution, **Bei Sita, (North Temple Pagoda)**, a soaring, beautifully deco-

rated nine-story pagoda. It's Suzhou's oldest Buddhist temple, built 1,700 years ago. The 72-m (236-ft)-high brick and wood pagoda of today dates from 1131 to 1136. Close by is another particularly well preserved temple, the **Avalokitesvara Hall**, built in the Ming reign, and to the southeast of the city center, just south of a small canal that runs alongside Ganjiang Lu, you'll find the elegant **Shuangtasi Shungta (Twin Pagodas)**, erected in the time of the Southern Song.

For a fascinating study of Suzhou's silk industry, CITS will arrange a visit to silk

farms and spinning mills, while the **Suzhou Silk Museum**, close to the North Temple Pagoda, has displays on sericulture and on the looms used to weave Suzhou's famous silk. **Suzhou Museum**, set in the former mansion of Prince Zhongwang, a leader of the violent and ill-fated Taiping Rebellion, has some very good exhibitions of sample silks, brocades and *kesi*, a combination silk and gold thread, of the Song, Ming and Qing ages. The raising of silkworms is one of the most remarkable processes known to man — a batch of 700,000 silkworms weighs only half a kilo at birth, and no less than five tons when they are fattened up on mulberry leaves and ready to spin their cocoons.

The Suzhou Gardens

These landscaped works of art, designed for harmony, meditation and tranquillity in the golden years of retired court officials, merchants and property owners, are the pride and joy of Suzhou. Many of them were built in the Ming reign, and at one stage there were about 100 of them scattered all over the city. Now there are only six, and thankfully they have been preserved for posterity. The one that's considered to be the most splendid is **Zhuozheng (Humble Administrator's) Garden**, to the north of

half a hectare (one and a quarter acres, its gardens, rocks, halls, pavilions and p have been artfully arranged to give the i sion of a far larger space.

Of the other gardens, the **Xiyuan (Wes Garden)** is perhaps the most interesting because it combines landscaping with temple architecture and Buddhist artwork. Situated to the northwest of the city beyond the Guangji Bridge, it includes the **Jiezhuanglu Temple**, originally called Guiyuan Si and built around 1271 in the Yuan dynasty. In the Ming reign it became the residence of a

the city adjacent to the Suzhou Museum. The name itself contains a tale: The garden was built by a Ming dynasty official who fell from imperial grace and was bundled off to Suzhou as a punishment. Among its most beautiful aspects are an ancient tea house, a large ornamental pool with a bridge that becomes crowded with visitors photographing each other, and beyond it **Mandarin Duck Hall**, a lovely pavilion that was once a small theater and has latticed windows with blue-glazed glass overlooking a smaller pond.

The most fascinating garden is **Wangshi (Garden of the Master of the Nets)**, which lies to the west of the Suzhou Hotel off Shiquan Jie. It is a very small place, less than

high court official named Xu Shitai and was given its present name. In 1860 it was destroyed in the Taiping Rebellion, but was restored in the latter years of the Qing dynasty.

The temple has several well preserved halls, including the **Hall of Celestial Kings, Main Shrine Hall, Avalokitesvara Hall** and the **Hall of the Arhats**, containing a striking display of 500 gilded clay statues of these immortals, along with several Buddha images and a statue of a guardian deity whose face is friendly on one side and severe on the other.

Elegant Song dynasty Twin Pagodas OPPOSITE and canalside houses ABOVE in Suzhou's southeast.

HERE TO STAY AND EAT

he best hotel you will find in Suzhou is the **Bamboo Grove** ((512) 520-5601 FAX (512) 520-8778, Zhuhui Lu, in the old section of town. The place is surprisingly opulent compared to other acomodation in town, and it also has a particularly good location close to the fascinating street life of the old quarter.

Not far away from the Bamboo Grove, also on Zhuhui Lu, the **Friendship Hotel**

The most famous restaurant in Suzhou is the **Songhelou Restaurant**, where the Emperor Qianlong is said to have eaten. It won't be the cheapest meal you'll have in China, but it does provide an opportunity to sample Suzhou's famous cuisine in atmospheric surroundings.

HOW TO GET THERE

Suzhou's nearest airport is in Shanghai, but lies on the Nanjing–Shanghai express rail route (Shanghai is a little over an hour away).

((512) 520-5218 FAX (512) 520-6221, is an excellent mid-range choice. The comfortable doubles are reasonably priced at around $30, and there's a good restaurant at the back of the hotel.

The **Lexiang Hotel** ((512) 522-2890 FAX (512) 524-4165, 18 Dajing Xi'ang, in the central tourist area on the edge of Guanqian Bazaar, has both budget and mid-range rooms, and is geared to the needs of Western travelers. There are some inexpensive Chinese restaurants in the vicinity with English menus.

Hangzhou Hotel ABOVE lies in idyllic setting on bank of West Lake while Pagoda of Six Harmonies OPPOSITE lies en route to Dragon Well Temple in Hangzhou.

It also has Grand Canal ferry services to and from Hangzhou. Tickets for the latter can be booked with CITS.

HANGZHOU

Like Suzhou, Hangzhou (capital of Zhejiang province) rose to prominence and flourished as a trading center, key food supplier and a hub of the rich silk industry of the region when the Grand Canal was built in the Sui reign. The canal began at Hangzhou, eventually to link this southern city with Beijing, and this imperial bonding was not by trade and commerce alone. The Song dynasty — pushed southward by the "barbarian" Liao and Jin dynasty challenges from beyond the

Great Wall—settled and established its capital in Hangzhou, and it was here that the most renowned age of refinement in China was born. It lasted until the Mongol armies of Kublai Khan marched south in 1276 to put Hangzhou to the sword and destroy it in the campaign to bring the whole of the country under their heel.

The industrious Ming emperors restored the city, and in the Manchu Qing reign it became a popular imperial summer retreat rivaling that of Shenyang in the northeast. Then the Taiping rebels marched in and

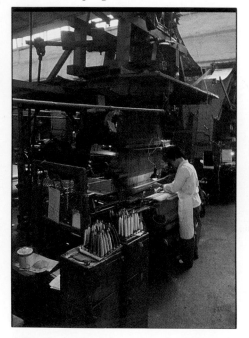

destroyed most of the city again in 1880, and much of its historic and cultural architecture and character went with it. But somehow it remains today one of the most renowned and beloved cities of China, famous for its balmy climate, its teas and silks, regarded as a place of romance and a mecca for honeymooning couples, still paid homage to in an old saying that has been applied to it, and its Grand Canal sister Suzhou, for many centuries: "Above there is heaven, below there is Suzhou and Hangzhou."

Today, as in the past, Hangzhou is famous for its nearby recreational resort, **West Lake**, formed in the eighth century when an emperor ordered the dredging and diking of a lagoon off the Qiantang River and land-

scaped and decorated with palaces, halls, temples, pavilions and gardens during the later dynastic reigns. It is now packed each summer with Chinese tour groups from Shanghai and the Yangtze cities and thousands of foreign visitors. Among its most distinguished contemporary visitors was the late President Richard Nixon in 1972. His sudden move to end years of Sino-American hostility was considered so momentous that the new airport 24 km (15 miles) from Hangzhou was built especially for his historic touchdown in Air Force One.

GENERAL INFORMATION

Dragonair ((571) 799-8833 is appropriately in the Dragon Hotel, Shuguang Lu, as is **Singapore Airlines** ((571) 798-5541. **CAAC** ((571) 515-2574 is at 390 Tiyuchang Lu.

The **Bank of China** is located at 320 Yan'an Beilu. **CITS** ((571) 798-0651 has an obscure location on the north shore of the lake at 231 Baoshu Lu.

WHAT TO SEE AND DO

Having been razed to the ground a couple of times, Hangzhou is pretty thin on historic monuments and relics. The big attraction is West Lake, which is always crowded with Chinese vacationers paddling boats, taking walks, clambering over rocks and so on. However, the city does have a remarkable temple, suitably named the **Lingyin Si (Temple of Inspired Seclusion)**, west of the lake. Originally built in 326, this temple has had a far rougher time than the city itself over the centuries: destroyed and rebuilt about 16 times through civil war, fires and other calamities.

It has managed to survive in a Qing dynasty renovated form with an impressive array of Buddhist relics — several large Buddha images, dominated by a 1956 camphor-wood carving of a Guatama Buddha, 26-m (85-ft) high, and about 150 smaller statues. There's a good vegetarian restaurant on the hillside near the temple. Also, on a hill facing the temple there's a cliff face filled with more than 300 Buddhist carvings going back as far as the year 951 and a huge sculpture of the Maitreya in the form of the rotund Laughing Buddha. Up in the hills you will also find the **Dragon Well** (with a temple), the namesake of China's most famous green tea, *longjing lucha*. Dragon Well Tea is cultivated on the terraced hills. You can wander through the tea bushes and in a tea house nearby you can taste this delicious brew. From here head southwards to the **Liuhe Ta (Six Harmonies Pagoda)** above the Qiantang River. On a hill above the pagoda you will find more Buddhist carvings. As for the pagoda itself, its main claim to fame is its historic role as a

ing the lake are usual chock-a-block with tour groups dutifully plodding along behind a uniformed guide with a bullhorn; the roads are more often than not packed bumper-to-bumper with tour buses.

WHERE TO STAY AND EAT

Hangzhou's top hotel is the **Shangri-La Hangzhou** ((571) 797-7951 FAX (571) 707-3545, 78 Beishan Lu. It has a superb setting, overlooking the northern section of the lake (rooms with a lake view cost extra), and is

religious force to try to tame the notorious Hangzhou Bore, a current which rushes up the Qiantang River each late summer and with such ferocity that local sailing junks and sampans were specially designed over many centuries to withstand the force of it and ride it out.

For the rest of the West Lake, you can walk around it and above it, paddle a boat on it, sit and contemplate it, visit its islands, bridges, dikes, pavilions and the mansions that formed part of the Summer Palace in Qing dynasty times. Unfortunately, it's unrealistic to expect any peace and quiet as you do so. Perhaps more than anywhere else in China, Hangzhou has become the focus of a local tourist boom, and the roads surround-

the perfect luxury base from which to explore Hangzhou and its surrounding attractions.

The **Dragon Hotel** ((571) 799-8833 FAX (571) 799-8090, Shuguang Lu, is another luxury option, and it soaks up a lot of the overseas Chinese tour groups. Its location in a dull part of town, however, is definitely not in its favor.

In the wooded, very rural area southwest of the lake are a couple of mid-range hotels that are relaxing, if somewhat remote places to unwind for a day or so. The **Zhejiang Hotel** ((571) 797-7988 FAX (571) 797-1904, 53 Longjing Lu, is particularly pleasant, set amid the

OPPOSITE: Hangzhou's historically most important product, silk, is still a key export. ABOVE: Hangzhou Railway Station.

tea plantations, a perfect area for late afternoon and early morning walks. Room rates range from around $40 up to $100. Another good mid-range hotel is the **Qingbo Hotel** ((571) 707-9988, Nanshan Lu, on the southeast corner of the lake. Although this area gets a lot of through traffic (mainly tour buses), it has a village-like atmosphere and once the tourist scoot off to dinner it is quite relaxing. The Qingbo is one of the better bargains in town, with rooms from around $40.

Hangzhou has virtually nothing that can be classed as budget accommodation.

The **Louwailou Restaurant** on Gushan Hill is Hangzhou's most famous dining establishment, but despite this is not particularly expensive. The sauteed eel slices and fresh shrimps with Dragon Well Tea are recommended.

For Chinese style cheap eats (you can dine at **KFC** beside the Shangri-La if your tastes run in that direction), Yan'an Lu, one street back from the northeast corner of the lake, is a good hunting ground.

HOW TO GET THERE

Hangzhou has international connections with Hong Kong and Singapore, and regular services to most major domestic destinations. Buses fan out across Zhejiang province, and there are long-distance buses to Shanghai from the long distance bus station on Hushu Nanlu. If you approach eastward down the Yangtze River, from Suzhou, say, traveling by train will force you to first go to Shanghai. Trains from Shanghai take around three hours.

HUANGSHAN

Though neither Buddhist nor Daoist, Huangshan is the most revered of all China's sacred mountains. To climb to its summit is to enter that peculiarly Chinese aesthetic of crags and peaks surrounded by swirling seas of clouds. For the Chinese this is the definitive mountain: climb it, the saying goes, and you will be done with climbing mountains. It's a sentiment that's hard to dispute, particularly when you're halfway up the seven-and-a-half-kilometer (four-and-a-half-mile) eastern

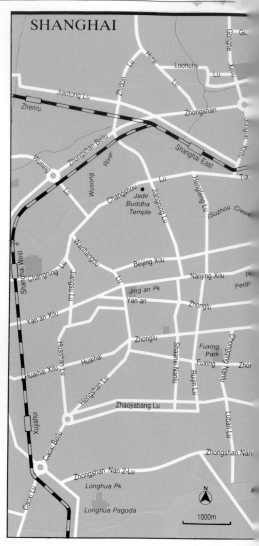

ascent, and ahead lies a dwindling ribbon of cut-stone steps disappearing into the clouds.

There are three approaches to the summit. The most difficult is the 15 km (nine mile) **western approach**. Unless you're in very good shape, consider *descending* via the western approach. It has some fabulous views — notably the precipitous stairway snaking up to the summit of the **Heavenly Capital Peak**, an optional detour of about an hour that is not recommended for those with a fear of heights, and the **Flying Rock**, which is at the summit, at the start of the descent. The western descent finishes at a **hot spring resort**, which has several hotels. The pick of them is the **Peach Blossom Hotel**

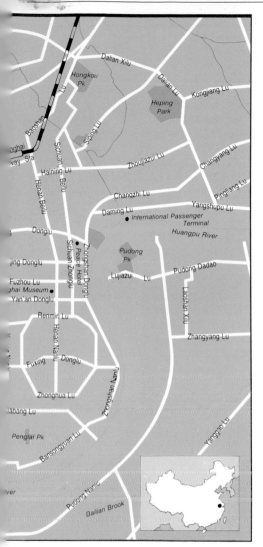

((559) 556-2196, where your room will have hot spring water piped into your bathtub — something your aching muscles will sorely appreciate.

The **eastern approach** to Huangshan is a vertiginous climb that takes around three to four hours, depending on your level of fitness. No matter how fit you are, it is unlikely you'll have much bounce left in your stride by the time you've reached the top. But if you simply can't face the downward trek, there's the **cable car**, which shadows the eastern approach, doing the journey in a brisk eight minutes.

Accommodation is available at the summit of Huangshan at the **Xihai Hotel** ((559)

256-2132, a beautiful place, but one that is not cheap. Several hotels can also be found on the western approach. The best of them is the **Jade Screen Tower Hotel** ((559) 556-2540, which sits at over 1,600 m (5,250 ft) and has a stunning prospect of the Heavenly Capital Peak.

HOW TO GET THERE

The easiest way to get to Huangshan is to fly there from Shanghai, though flights are also available from as far away as Beijing, Guanghzhou and Hong Kong, underlining what an important attraction the mountain is. Buses run direct from Shanghai to Huangshan, taking around 10 hours.

SHANGHAI

Shanghai is a booming, teeming time warp, a step back into a strange evocative combination of Manhattan, the Hong Kong waterfront and the Liverpool docks, circa 1930. Who knows, perhaps some of that art deco neon that glows at night along the antique skyline may have been there since the last Japanese Zero buzzed over the city more than 40 years ago.

In Shanghai the British and their European rivals, the French, Germans and Italians, and the Americans, gained not so much a toehold as a colonial throat-hold, backed by military force, on the Chinese economy and society — turning a small insignificant fishing town on the Huangpu River close to the Yangtze's wide estuary, into one of the richest, most frenetic, most desperate, most exciting, freewheeling and most wicked cities on earth.

In its heyday as the Treaty Port and International Settlement of China, it had a foreign population of 60,000. Huge trading and financial houses built out of the nefarious "foreign mud" of opium rose up on The Bund, over the wharves, smokestacks and derricks of the Huangpu waterfront alongside branches of some of the most respected, distinguished, and just as sharp, financial institutions of the West. Based on cotton textiles, an immense low-paid Chinese manufacturing workforce and its position as a natural Yangtze River conduit of trade goods from the interior of China, Shanghai reveled in its wealth, flamboyant materialism, snobbery, vice and a kind of swaggering modernity compared with the rest of the country while an epic power struggle took place around it between the nationalists, communists and the Japanese.

In the late 1930s, when the Japanese blitzkrieged their way down into the south of China, the entire Shanghai dream collapsed into a nightmare of military repression, starvation and atrocity that cannot be imagined unless one was there at the time, imprisoned, or takes the time today to read accounts like J.G. Ballard's disturbing *Empire of the Sun*, brilliantly portrayed in the 1987 movie by Steven Spielberg. When it was all over — World War II, the Japanese masterplan, the struggle for supremacy between Mao Zedong and Chiang Kaishek — it was as though only a city as wicked as Shanghai could have been punished with such suffering.

It is perhaps because of that legacy of suffering that one of the most crucial power struggles of the revolutionary years was played out chiefly in Shanghai — the city was the hotbed of radical socialism, the power base of the Gang of Four, the place where the barricades of the People's Commune went up in the violent and ill-fated campaign to head off the "rightist tendencies" in Chinese society who wanted to nudge the nation onto the capitalist path.

Shanghai has always been a place of ferment, and for many years the central government simply shut the place down. To visit Shanghai in the 1980s was to visit a city that was a pale shadow of its former self. All that changed in 1990, when Shanghai was given the go-ahead to exercise some open-door policies of its own. The results have been astounding. With over 13 million people toiling away, China's biggest city has turned itself into a powerhouse. It's impossible to visit Shanghai and not be impressed with how much has been achieved so quickly. This is a confident city with its eyes firmly set on a prosperous future, and for the foreign visitor it is the perfect place to start, or finish, the grand China tour (see WITNESS THE REAWAKENING OF A GREAT CITY in TOP SPOTS, page 15).

GENERAL INFORMATION

Airline carriers represented in Shanghai include: **Air China (** (21) 6327-6322, 600 Huashan Lu; **Air France (** (21) 6268-8817, Room 3223, New Terminal Building, Hongqiao International Airport; **Canadian Airlines (** (21) 6415-3091, New Jinjiang Tower, 161 Changle Lu; **China Eastern Airlines (** (21) 6247-5953, 200 Yan'an Xilu; **Dragonair (** (21) 6279-8099, West Tower, Shanghai Centre, 1376 Nanjing Xilu; **Lufthansa (** (21) 6248-1100, Shanghai Hilton Hotel, 250 Huashan Lu; **Northwest Airlines (** (21) 6279-8100, East Tower Shanghai Centre, 1376 Nanjing Xilu; **Qantas (** (21) 6279-8128, West Tower, Shanghai Centre, 1376 Nanjing Xilu; **Shanghai Airlines (** (21) 6268-8558, 2550 Hongqiao Lu; **Swissair (** (21) 6279-7381, West Tower, Shanghai Centre, 1376 Nanjing Xilu; **United Airlines (** (21) 6279-8009, West Tower, Shanghai Centre, 1376 Nanjing Xilu.

American Express ((21) 6279-8082 has an office in Room 206, Retail Plaza, Shanghai Centre, 1376 Nanjing Xilu.

The head office of the **Bank of China** is at 23 Zhongshan Dong 1 Lu.

CITS ((21) 6321-7200 is on the third floor of the Guangming Building, 2 Jinling Road, on The Bund. Essentially, it is a booking office for flights, trains and boats.

The following consulates are found in Shanghai: **Australia (** (21) 6433-4604, 17 Fuxing Xilu; **Austria (** (21) 6279-7197, West Tower, Shanghai Centre, 1376 Nanjing Xilu; **Canada (** (21) 6279-8400; West Tower, Shanghai Centre; **France (** (21) 6472-3631, Room 2008, Ruijing Building, Maoming Nanlu; **Germany (** (21) 6433-6953, 181 Yongfu Lu; **Great Britain (** (21) 6279-7650, Suite 301, Shanghai Centre; **United States (** (21) 6433-6880, 1469 Huaihai Zhonglu.

GETTING AROUND

Shanghai may be big, but it's one of the easier Chinese cities to get around. For starters it's fascinating to explore on foot. And when you tire of walking there's always a taxi (inexpensive and metered) or a subway stop nearby.

The public buses are best avoided unless you are an old China hand and used to the conditions in which ordinary Chinese travel. Just getting on the bus can be a battle, not to mention disembarking when your stop comes around.

Try to avoid having to be anywhere during the peak rush-hour periods, from 8 to 9:30 AM and from 4:30 to 7 PM. It can be hard to flag down a taxi at these times, and if you do get one you're likely to spend a lot of time sitting in the traffic.

WHAT TO SEE AND DO

With very little notable history beyond its Treaty Port days, Shanghai doesn't have much in the way of cultural attractions, but it is still a wonderful city to be in and to stroll around. It's the time warp that makes it interesting — the feeling that this is probably the last place in the world where you can actually get an impression of what a Victorian port looked like in the days of maritime power, what parts of Chicago may have looked like when Al Capone and his mobsters ruled supreme, what a Chinese city looked like in the days when Guomindang generals and Shanghai textile magnates packed and fled in the path of the Japanese war machine.

There are those who have a fetish about identifying every aspect of the **Shanghai International Settlement**, where the famous hotels, nightclubs, brothels, restaurants and great homes were. But such things are long gone. Besides, the Shanghai of today has 13 million walking, living, breathing realities that are far more relevant and interesting than all the ghosts of its past.

Every day, they crowd along **The Bund** and into the tiny **Huangpu Park**, overshadowed by the immense bulk of the Shanghai Mansions Hotel, strolling, chatting, picnicking, taking pictures of each other amid gardens that were once forbidden to all "dogs and Chinese." They pack the sidewalks down the long east-west shopping thoroughfare, Nanjing Lu, where you can find the **Shanghai Nº 1 Department Store**, countless fashion boutiques, bookstores, arts and crafts centers and, finally, everything you'd expect to find on the main shopping strip of a big cosmopolitan city.

Along Nanjing Lu you'll also find the **Shanghai Acrobatic Theatre**, an auditorium with nightly performances. Buy tickets at the ticket booth the day of the performance.

Huaihai Zhonglu is the emerging "Paris end" of Shanghai, with some of the city's best department stores and boutiques (virtually all the name brands are represented here). And this is appropriate; it was once the French concession, after all. In those days Huaihai Zhonglu was called Avenue Joffre.

South of this area, in what was once the Frenchtown of the Treaty Port days, the **Site**

of the **First National Congress of the Communist Party of China** commemorates the city's role in the revolutionary groundswell during the chaotic republican years. Shanghai was where the communist party was founded in July 1921. To the south of the commemorative hall, you'll find more of the former **residences of Sun Yatsen and Zhou Enlai**, and, on Fenyang Lu, a mansion housing the **Arts and Crafts Research Institute** and another where the **Conservatory of Music** is based.

On Renmin (People's) Square, the **Shanghai Museum** is now housed in an impressive new urn-shaped building, reopened in

Shanghai's commercial center, where architecture reflects the city's past as a Treaty Port.

October 1996. Probably the best museum in China, it shouldn't be missed. Whereas most Chinese museums are gloomy and poorly labeled, the Shanghai Museum is the wave of the future. It has a collection of over 120,000 cultural relics. The galleries for bronzes, ceramics and paintings, and calligraphy are the most highly rated.

Another Renmin Square attraction is **Great World**, an old and infamous entertainment center that has been resuscitated in a less raunchy version of its former self. Karaoke, acrobats, opera and music all share the same roof. There's even a haunted house ride and a Guinness Book of Records display.

On the religious side, Shanghai offers the **Jade Buddha Temple**, in the city's northwestern Putuo District, not very old — it was originally founded in 1882 — but featuring a good collection of gilded Buddha figures, scriptures and paintings representing the major dynasties going back to the time of the Northern Wei. The **Longhua Temple and Pagoda**, on the city's southern riverbank, goes back a little further, to 247 AD and has an *arhats* hall, bell and drum towers and several other interesting buildings—along with its vegetarian early luncheon restaurant.

For a tacky but fun Chinatown experience, go along to the **Yuyuan (Mandarin Garden)**, south of The Bund. The garden itself is a compact affair, covering only two hectares (five acres) and was built in the Ming reign. The shops and restaurants, all housed in mock Qing dynasty style, are the real attraction. The **Temple of the Town Gods** is a real temple; it failed to safeguard the gardens when Shanghai was attacked in the Opium War of 1842, and was again virtually destroyed by the French when it was used as a command base for the Taiping Rebellion. Yuyuan Gardens is a good place for lunch or dinner (see WHERE TO EAT, below).

Another pleasant outing is the three-and-a-half-hour, 60-km (37.2-mile) **Huangpu River Cruise**. Boats leave from an area north of the Shiliupu Wharf area, next to the huge Diamond Restaurant, and tickets can be bought before boarding. Weather permitting, there are two departures daily at 9 AM and at 2 PM. The cruise not only provides a wonderful vantage point from which to view that

famous shoreline, The Bund, but it also gives you a glimpse of the massive **Pudong New Area** development on the other side of the river, where history is in the making.

If you can't be bothered with the grand river tour, a short hop over to Pudong by ferry is the abridged alternative. Boats leave from opposite the Yanan Lu intersection on the Bund. It's a 10-minute ride, providing a view of the Bund's façade. After alighting, you can take a 15-minute walk to the bulbous **Oriental Pearl Tower**, which has an overpriced lookout platform. For a free aerial view of the waterfront and the busy **Suzhou Creek** back on the other side of the river, the best place is from the 18th floor of Shanghai Mansions.

Lastly, for a quick overview of Shanghai, take a red **Jin Jiang Tour Bus**. The buses leave every half hour or so from the side entrance of the Garden Hotel on Mao Ming Nan Lu. Tickets can be purchased when you board the bus.

WHERE TO STAY

Luxury

Shanghai has quite a number of hotels that slip easily into the luxury category, and making recommendations is no easy matter. Still, few if any will object to the inclusion of the **Portman Shangri-La Hotel (** (21) 6279-8888 FAX (21) 6279-8800, 1376 Nanjing Xilu. The Portman is part of the Shanghai Centre, which is where you will also find most of Shanghai's foreign airlines, consulates and business representatives. In short, it's a perfect executive hotel. Amenities include the usual: restaurants, swimming pool, business center, and extras include squash courts and a theater. The tastefully decorated interior, complete with objets d'art, sets a high tone that is sustained throughout.

The **Shanghai Hilton International (** (21) 6248-0000 FAX (21) 6248-3848, 250 Huashan Lu, has a good location not that far from the Shanghai Centre, and inside is a veritable city of delights, with 775 guestrooms, eight cafés, restaurants and bars, a highly rated health club, tennis and squash courts, and a business center. The atrium has a splendid garden-setting café that is a wonderful place to sit with a coffee and a newspaper.

The **Peace Hotel** ((21) 6321-6888 FAX (21) 6329-0300, 20 Nanjing Xilu, doesn't strictly speaking deserve a place in the luxury stakes, unless you stay in one of the suites. Even then, be warned: You are not at the Peace for its exemplary service standards or its outstanding amenities; you're there because it is a slice of history. Formerly known as **The Cathay**, it was one the four big names of the East: **The Peninsula** in Hong Kong, **Stanley Raffles** in Singapore and **The Taj** in Bombay. Everybody who was anybody stayed at The Cathay, and Noel Coward wrote *Private Lives* in one of the hotel's suites. Today, despite renovations, there's still a thirties ambiance about the place — note the revolving doors, the paneling, the deco windows, and pop into see the Jazz Bar in the evenings; the band members look to be venerable as the hotel.

Mid-Range

Shanghai has a large number of mid-range lodgings. The **Yan An Hotel** ((21) 6248-1111 FAX (21) 6247-7149, 1111 Yanan Lu, is a good, centrally located choice, opposite Jing An Park. This is definitely an upper mid-range hotel and a massive place with no less than 14 restaurants, representing most of the Chinese cuisines and a number of Western cuisines as well. Facilities include a business center, shopping center, gym, billiards, and garden. Room rates start at around $60.

The **Donghu Hotel** ((21) 6415-8158 FAX (21) 6415-7759, 70 Donghu Lu, is another downtown hotel, and though slightly cheaper is a very similar setup to the Yan An. Sporting restaurants, along with a business center, tennis, billiards, even a swimming pool — with rates starting at around $50 — it's not a bad deal.

For something cheaper still, the **Nanjing Hotel** ((21) 6322-1455 FAX (21) 6320-6520 is a tucked away secret on Shanxi Nanlu, very close to The Bund, with little in the way of amenities, that is popular with repeat visitors to Shanghai.

The **Ocean Hotel Shanghai** ((21) 6545-8888 FAX (21) 6545-8993, 1171 Dongdaming Lu, is an upper mid-range hotel (rates starting at an expensive $90) that actually has

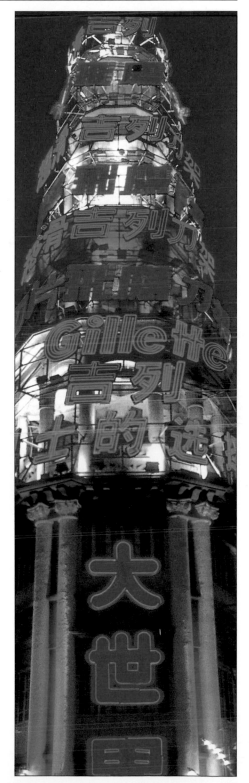

Shanghai's Great World Building is a cherished landmark that has been entertaining the masses for the better part of a century.

views of the Huangpu River. It has a good range of dining spots, including a 28th floor revolving restaurant.

Inexpensive

And now for the bad news. Shanghai is not a backpacker heaven. The old standby for more than a decade has been the **Pujiang Hotel** ((21) 6324-6388, 15 Huangpu Lu, which has dorm beds in clean, high-ceilinged rooms, some of which sport views of The Bund. The Pujiang is still going strong, and now also has very reasonable doubles at around $40. Given the location, it's one of the best deals in town.

The **Music Conservatory** ((21) 6437-2577, 20 Fenyang Lu, is a wonderful base if you can get a room. The refurbished doubles (formerly dorm rooms) are not bad at all, and at just $25 are very good value, particularly given that you are just a short walk from fashionable Huaihai Lu and the Shaanxi subway stop. The only catch is finding the rooms for rent in the conservatory — don't give up; they're in there.

The **Changyang Hotel** ((21) 6543-4890, 1800 Changyang Lu, should be considered as a last option. It's too far out of town to make being in Shanghai fun (remember the traffic). Bus Nº 22 takes about half an hour to get to it from the Bund. Rooms cost around $30.

Where to Eat

Shanghai is swarming with restaurants, and rates up there with Beijing, Guangzhou and Chengdu as one of the great culinary capitals of China. The local cuisine tends to get a lot of flak for being too heavy on the oil and sugar, but this probably reflects regional frictions as much as anything else — Shanghai will always be the new kid on the block in the Chinese world.

For the best in Shanghai cuisine, the relatively new **Folk Restaurant** ((21) 6372-9893, 57 Nanchang Lu, is one of the new breed of confident and adventurous restaurants that are springing up in Shanghai these days. The exotic animal parts displayed in the hall are optional.

For Shanghai cuisine in unusual, entertaining surroundings the **Magic Restaurant**, on Fuzhou Lu opposite the Metropole Hotel, lives up to its name not only with the food, but with real magic shows, held at lunchtime and at 6:15 PM.

If you're the adventurous type, head out for the **Yunnan Road Night Market**, found on the street of the same name, just off Nanjing Lu. Mingle here with the crowds, pick up some cheap eats (point at something that someone else is dining on, if you have to), and you are as close to the heart of Shanghai as you are likely to get.

Curiously, given that Xinjiang is so far away, Shanghai has some very good Chinese Moslem restaurants. The **Tianshan Hotel Uighur Restaurant** ((21) 6554-8366, 775 Quyang Lu, and the **Xinjiang Restaurant** ((21) 6350-6649, 81 Zhejiang Zhong Lu, both lie in what can only be called the heart of Shanghai's Moslem community. The Tianshan is the larger of the two. Both do authentic dishes from the far west — try the *yangrou paomo*.

For Sichuan cuisine, the best choices are mostly hotel restaurants, such as the **Bamboo Garden** ((21) 6415-1188, in the Jinjiang Tower, and the **Fu Rong Zhen** ((21) 6280-8888, in the Holiday Inn. One exception is a Sichuan hotpot restaurant, aptly named **Sichuan Hotpot**. It's next to Shanghai Mansions. Locals claim that this is the hottest hotpot in Shanghai.

Moving away from Chinese fare, **Frankie's Place Restaurant and Café** ((21) 6247-0886, 81 Tong Ren Lu, is a friendly Singaporean restaurant that has become popular with the foreign community. It's just across the Shanghai Centre. If you're the type who misses Indian food, the **Tandoor Indian Restaurant** ((21) 6258-2582, in the Jinjiang Hotel, is excellent. The lunchtime deals are worth stopping in for.

And just to prove that Shanghai is once again a thoroughly international, jiving city, the Americans have moved in, not just with the obvious chains like **McDonald's** and **KFC** (both of which are plentiful) but with their high-culture side kicks, the **Hard Rock Café** (6279-8888, Shanghai Centre, and **Tony Roma's**, with the same address and telephone number.

Shanghai's celebrated acrobatic troupe does the impossible on a daily basis.

Just around the corner from the Shanghai Centre is **Malone's**, 257 Tongren Lu, a Canadian-run sports bar that passes itself off as American. It pulls in the crowds, and the hamburgers are amongst the best in town.

If you need a decent pizza (and who doesn't from time to time), **Pasta Fresca Da Salvatore** ((21) 6270-4693, 6 Zunyi Nanlu, is said by local foreign residents to have the best in Shanghai.

Lastly, in the hope that it stays, **Paulaner Brauhaus** ((21) 6474-5700, 150 Fenyang Lu, is a brave adventure into the beerhall theme. It's in the heart of the old French concession, and the building used to be a music academy rehearsal hall. Expect live classical music, German sausages and microbrewed beer.

NIGHTLIFE

For conviviality and drinking, a few joints jostle for the coveted status of most popular expatriate bar. **Malone's** (WHERE TO EAT above) is a good sports bar around the corner from the Shanghai Centre. The **Long Bar** is in the Shanghai Centre, and has live jazz Tuesday nights and Sunday afternoons. At other times it's a good place for a quiet drink. **Shanghai Sally's** ((21) 6327-1859, 4 Xi'angshan Lu, is an English-style pub with darts, pool and so on.

O'Malley's Irish Pub is near the United States consulate on Taojiang Lu. For many foreigners living in Shanghai it is a home away from home. With Guinness on tap and countless corners in which to hide away with a book or friend, it is probably one of the best bars in China.

The **Blues & Jazz Bar**, at 44 Sinan Lu, is celebrated in Shanghai for its sound system and for its compact disc collection. There's usually live music on Saturday nights.

If you find yourself out late, there's **DD's**, 298 Xingfu Lu, a club with drinks, dancing, the lot, and which stays open until 6 AM.

Nominating the most popular dance club in town is never easy, but **New York New York** ((21) 6321-6097, 146 Huqiu Lu, has survived a couple of years of competition, and perhaps it will continue to do so. Housed in an old French theater not far from Suzhou Creek, near The Bund, it's a fascinating place to explore and well worth the cost of the entry.

HOW TO GET THERE

Getting to Shanghai is like getting to China. There are countless ways to do it. Most major airlines have international flights to Shanghai's Hongqiao Airport these days, and as for domestic flights Shanghai is connected with almost every town that has an airport in China.

CITS will sell you boat tickets to a number of destinations, including Yokohama and Osaka in Japan, and Hong Kong. There are also boats to Qingdao, and you can start the Yangtse River cruise here, if you don't mind spending many days on a boat.

It's best to buy train tickets either at CITS or at the Longmen Hotel ((21) 6317-0000 extension 576, which is next door to the main Shanghai railway station, at 777 Hengfeng Lu. Shanghai is on the new Kowloon–Beijing train line, but tickets on this service are generally booked up for weeks ahead.

Nanjing Road, China's most famous shopping street.

立陽飯店

Travelers' Tips

THE WAY TO CHINA

INDIVIDUAL TRAVEL

China has been allowing foreigners to come in and get around on their own wits and steam since about 1982, and if you have the courage to strike off into the unknown this is the most rewarding way to travel.

THE AERIAL ROUTE

As for getting to Hong Kong and China, you can choose from of a large variety of airlines flying to both destinations, and a selection of standard and special fares. It's generally cheaper to fly to Hong Kong than to China, and for more remote destinations it may well be cheaper to fly to Hong Kong, travel overland to Shenzhen or Guangzhou and fly from there. Book your ticket though through a travel agent as airline companies tend not to give discounts. For very cheap flights look in your local newspaper. But a word of warning: with any discounted fare there are bound to be restrictions so before committing yourself check the conditions thoroughly.

HONG KONG TO CHINA

By Train

The main route from Hong Kong to China is by rail from the Kowloon–Canton Railway's (KCR) Hung Hom terminus next to the Cross Harbour Tunnel's Kowloon exit. Trains depart for Lo Wu at the Hong Kong–China border from around 6 AM till 10 PM, every six to 12 minutes. From Lowu you walk across the border to Shenzhen and take a connecting train to Guangzhou. Direct to Guangzhou, the Hong Kong–Canton Express leaves five times a day between approximately 8:30 AM and 5 PM. It is now also possible to travel directly to Beijing, Shanghai and other destinations such as Hangzhou from Kowloon. Services leave every other day, and are usually booked up weeks in advance. (For train travel in China see RIDING THE RAILS, below.)

By Air

China Air (CAAC) (RESERVATIONS (852) 2840-1199, flies directly to most cities in China, and covers virtually the entire country from Guangzhou. You'll find them at two locations: Ticketing, Ground Floor, Gloucester Tower, The Landmark, 17 Queen's Road, Central; or 34th Floor, United Centre, Queensway, Central,

Dragonair (RESERVATIONS 2590-1188 FAX FOR RESERVATIONS AND RECONFIRMATION (852) 2590-1331 **(** TICKETING (852) 2868-6777, has direct services to Beijing, Changsa, Chengdu, Dalian, Guilin, Haikou, Hangzhou, Kunming, Nanjing, Ningbo, Shanghai, Tianjin, Xiamen and Xi'an. They are located on the

9th Floor, Worldwide House, 19 Des Vœux Road, Central.

By Bus

Air-conditioned bus excursions leave daily to Shenzhen, Dongguan and Guangzhou (separate services) from the Admiralty bus terminus on Queensway on Hong Kong Island and from the basement of China Hong Kong City, 33 Canton Road, Kowloon. For more information contact **CityBus (** (852) 2736-3888. The **CTS Express Bus (** (852) 2764-9803, only runs to Guangzhou, but does so 15 times a day from various Hong Kong locations.

By Boat

From the China Ferry Terminal, China Hong Kong City, 33 Canton Road, Kowloon, hoverferries make the passage seven times a day to Shekou, a China–Hong Kong trading and manufacturing enclave west of

Scenes on Lake Tai (Taihu) near Wuxi. Ducks OPPOSITE and picturesque square-sailed junk ABOVE.

Shenzhen and four times a day to Shenzhen International Airport.

There are regular sea services, many of them daily, to a variety destinations in Southern China such as Guangzhou, Nanhai, Haikou, Xiamen and Wuzhou. Steamers run two to four times a month to Shanghai and Ningbo, south of Shanghai. The trip to Shanghai takes 60 hours and to Ningbo 53 hours. Tickets can be purchased through CITS, CTS or a travel agent.

Also from the China Ferry Terminal, another interesting route to consider is going

by hydrofoil to Macau, the Portuguese-administered enclave and gambling playground across the mouth of the Pearl River, one hour away. Boats leave every half hour and can be booked through travel agents, CTS, CITS or at the Macau Ferry Terminal in the Shun Tak Centre, 200 Connaught Road Central — next to the Victoria Hotel, along Hong Kong Island's waterfront. (Hydrofoils also leave from the China Ferry Terminal.)

From Macau you can take a bus across the border to Gongbei in the Zhuhai Special Economic Zone and from there buses or minibuses to Guangzhou or elsewhere in Guangdong province.

VISAS

Tourist visas for one month are readily available at your nearest Chinese embassy or consulate, or through your travel agent. If you need longer, organize your visa in Hong Kong. From Hong Kong visas can be obtained from the Visa Section, 5th floor; Chinese Ministry of Foreign Affairs, 26 Harbour Road,

or from almost any travel agency in town. It's a simple and efficient process — just fill out the application form, leave one photo and your passport and 72 hours later (after your form and passport have been faxed to the Public Security office in Shenzhen for vetting and authorization), you have a visa. If you need a visa in a hurry, the price goes up. You can have one issued in a morning if you wish.

Although the Chinese authorities seem extremely tolerant of who visits China, it still pays to fill in your visa application conservatively: There's no point trumpeting, for example, the fact that you're an editor or a photographer or that you plan to visit Tibet.

GETTING AROUND

Travel inside China is surprisingly easy and efficient, largely because of the extensive air and rail networks.

DOMESTIC AIRLINES

While China Air operates the international flights into the country, domestic services are divided among some 100 large and small airlines, headed by **Air China** based in Beijing, **China Eastern** (Shanghai), **China Southern** (Guangzhou), **China Northern** (Shenyang), **China Southwest** (Chengdu) and **China Northwest** (Xi'an). There are also numerous smaller airlines. How safe they are is anyone's guess.

Most hotels with three-star ratings and upwards will have an airlines booking desk, thus making bookings very simple. Despite this, a large number of the old CAAC offices linger on in China.

Most domestic routes are far better served nowadays than they were half a decade ago, and it's rare that you have to wait to get on a flight. It always pays to book a few days in advance, but it's usually possible to book the day before providing you're not much concerned about what time you fly.

RIDING THE RAILS

If you have the time, the best way to get around China is by rail. It's the way to meet people. Even in the relatively pampered soft-sleeper class, you will find yourself in a compartment with three other strangers. But, as you will soon discover, the Chinese are not content to allow people around them to remain strangers for long. You'll probably be offered fruit and tea and generally drawn into the give-and-take of the Chinese world.

There are three classes of travel on the trains — soft-sleeper, hard-sleeper and hard-seat. Soft-sleeper is the top of the range, offering separate four-berth compartments, well serviced by the attendants, equipped with a table and lamp between the bunks, white

steamer. But they are comfortable, nonetheless. Be careful not to select a bottom bunk when you buy the ticket, as Chinese travelers will sit on the bottom bunks late into the night — eating peanuts, playing cards, slurping on jam jars full of tea — whether someone is asleep in the bed or not.

Essentials

Whatever class of train travel you choose, you need to carry snack food with you, especially on the long hauls. The dining cars get terribly overcrowded and the food they

nylon curtains and carpet slippers. It's the most comfortable form of travel and if you can afford it (usually it works out to be as expensive as flying) the perfect way to get around China.

Hard-seat is the other extreme — open carriages packed with simple vinyl-covered wooden seating, crammed with peasants, soldiers and workers and their luggage, and anything from crated television sets to factory spare parts. Such travel is only for the hardened, as conditions can be nothing short of horrifying on some runs.

Hard-sleeper is the compromise many travelers end up taking. These are carriages lined with open three-tiered sets of bunks, rather like steerage class on a migrant

offer is generally basic. The standard of cleanliness and hygiene in the dining cars can also be a rude shock. On most routes the trains stop long enough at main stations and junctions for you to stretch your legs on the platforms and buy hard-boiled eggs, buns, fruit and cigarettes.

The toilets, marked CESUO, at each end of the carriages are basic hole-in-the floor conveniences over which you squat and hold tightly to a rail, especially in the vicinity of the main stations where the drivers tend to brake the trains so abruptly that they sometimes actually skid to a halt.

OPPOSITE: Yangtze river ferries at Wuhan. ABOVE: Early industrial beauty and power still in action on China's extensive rail network.

There is one infernal problem on all the trains that Westerners find quaint and interesting at first, and then increasingly aggravating — a constant blare of travel information, public announcements, Chinese pop music and Beijing or Cantonese opera from public address speakers installed up and down every carriage. The racket begins at 7 AM (sometimes earlier) and does not stop until 10 PM, and while you can switch the speakers off in the soft-sleeper compartments there's nothing you can do about them in hard-sleeper or hard-seat areas. Some have very flimsy wiring, if you care to inspect them closely, but otherwise you just have to accept that nothing moves in China without a lot of commotion and noise to help it along.

Reservations

It used to be that CITS handled train bookings for foreigners. This is very rare nowadays. Most train bookings can be done at the front desk of your hotel. If you're staying in a tourist class hotel this will be a simple affair; if you're staying in a budget hotel you may need the help of a phrasebook or a friendly interpreter. Only go to the railway station and book your ticket yourself as a last resort. Once you see the "queues" you will realize why buying a railway ticket is not a chore that anyone in China relishes.

As for the struggle to get to the trains, you'll find that at most of the major stations right down the east of China there are special segregated waiting rooms with soft chairs and sometimes even a coffee bar and souvenir counter for anyone traveling soft-sleeper. In some stations the alternative is very unpleasant. More often than not you are pitched in with everyone else, and even with the station police and attendants controlling the crowds, you can expect a rough free-for-all getting through the ticket barriers.

BUSES

With a rapidly improving road infrastructure, long-distance buses are gaining in popularity. The latest arrival is the overnight sleeper bus. These are mixed blessing. All berths are allocated by number (so there's no overcrowding), but unless you are traveling as a couple you will probably end up reclining in a space the size of a single bed with a complete stranger.

If it's possible to avoid traveling by bus, do so. They're generally slow, crowded, dirty and sometimes dangerous. In certain parts of China you will have no choice. A travel companion makes long bus journeys far more bearable.

TAXIS

All major Chinese cities are well supplied with taxis nowadays, and you rarely have to wait more than a couple of minutes before one happens past. Communication is often a problem, even for foreigners who have studied some Chinese (accents vary greatly from region to region, and most foreigners have problems with tones that make uncontextualized place names difficult for Chinese to understand). Rates are reasonable by Western standards: In most cities you can cover a lot of ground for around $3. As a general rule, avoid taxi drivers who loiter around bus and railway stations — they are usually waiting for a big payoff by an out-of-towner.

PEDAL POWER

The most convenient and enjoyable form of transport in any city is the Chinese answer to the Western family car, the bicycle. Previously the bikes were the standard proletarian Chinese models, all of them based on the design of the old British workhorse, the Raleigh, equipped with just two accessories, a security lock and a bell. Today, you'll see all kinds of bikes on the streets, with a basic road version of the mountain bike being the most popular. Out in rural China of course, the old Flying Pigeon still rules supreme.

You can rent a bicycle by the hour or full day, paying an average ¥20 for eight hours, with orders to be back by nightfall. You pay in advance and will usually be required to provide ¥400 as a refundable deposit. You also need to check the bicycle over first for loose components or tire leaks and make sure that the saddle is at a comfortable height. You then wheel out into the streets and find that biking in China is initially like venturing in a rented car into the Los Angeles freeway system. It takes some nerve and eyes in the back of your head to learn to flow along smoothly in the creaking, jingling floods of chrome, steel and rubber. You need a good English-language street-map showing you how to get to the main tourist attractions, and you can find one at any hotel Friendship desk. From there, Chinese society is yours.

WHEN TO GO

The peak season for organzied tour groups is April to October, and during this period there is a veritable conveyor belt of tour groups coming and going — and the inevitable mêlée at major attractions and shopping spots. With the rapid growth of hotel accommodation, individual travelers can now make their way through all this high-season clamor with a reasonable guarantee of a hotel room — an improvement on the mid-80s when many found themselves virtually camping in guesthouse and hotel lobbies and corridors waiting for a bed.

Though summer is by far the best time to go, for reduced hotel rates and an assured berth on the train, travel in the off-season, from November to March, is not a bad idea. It means traveling through the northern areas of China in the grip of winter, when Arctic winds blowing from the Gobi Desert can chill you to the bone. You need to be heavily dressed, with several layers of clothing over long woolen underwear, to feel comfortable. Monsoonal cold fronts sweep right down through China at this time and in the southern provinces it can be quite chilly, but between the fronts, when the weather is from the south, it can be comparatively warm, even balmy.

WHAT TO WEAR

In summer, wear the lightest clothing possible, obviously. Drip-dry garments that can be rinsed through and dried overnight are preferable, though most hotels offer inexpensive same-day laundry services. In winter, long thermal underwear, thick socks, a Chinese-style hat with earflaps and good gloves are a must if you're going north. In all seasons, dress for comfort rather than fashion

— soft-soled walking shoes, jogging shoes or hiking boots rather than high-heels, for example. If you plan to tour Tibet in the summer, take warm clothing and a lightweight sleeping bag — there have been many instances of trekkers caught without adequate protection on mountains where the temperature plunges to freezing point at night.

WHAT TO TAKE

Individual travelers should travel as lightly as possible if they want to keep their trip from

becoming an endurance test. One large but comfortable backpack, and preferably not the type with a bulky aluminum frame — they're cumbersome in crowded situations, and they get snagged in train and bus doorways. Add one other soft hold-all and a camera case — but no more than that; you'd be surprised how grueling it is to negotiate the length of an average Chinese railway platform after a long journey, if you're loaded down with heavy luggage. Other basic necessities that should be taken along are as follows:

Chapstick: In winter, particularly, the climate in the north and in Tibet is harshly dry.

Coffee: This is readily available in sachets at Chinese department stores, but rarely served in any place other than luxury hotels.

Vitamin pills: Definitely of supplementary value in Tibet and in the northern provinces in winter.

Swiss Army knife: You never know.

Batteries: The Chinese ones are so weak that

Trolley buses and bicycles are the main forms of transport on a frigid Beijing morning.

if you don't have your own you'll have to kick-start your Walkman.

Flashlight: Optional, but comes in handy in the dead of night on the way to toilets in Tibet.

Chopsticks: Optional, but certainly cuts down on health hazards when eating communally.

CURRENCY

The standard Chinese currency is the *renminbi* (people's currency) or RMB, known officially as *yuan* but popularly called *kuai*. The highest denomination is the 100-yuan note (¥100).

Exchange rates for major currencies at press time are:

US$1 = ¥8.28
J¥100 = ¥6.49
UK1 = ¥13.62
DM1 = ¥4.53
HK$1 = ¥1.07

The yuan is divided into 10 *jiao*, more popularly known as *mao*, and there are 10 *fen* to the jiao. Fen are seldom seen these days, which is just as well because they had a tendency to fill your wallet up.

At first, the currency can be confusing, but it follows two simple, if illogical, rules: Wherever renminbi is written, it's called yuan and jiao; when you're actually buying something with it, it's kuai and mao.

The following credit cards are accepted: Visa, MasterCard, Federal Card, Million, JCB, American Express and Diners Club — but only in the major cities, and only by a handful of the budget-category hotels.

CUSTOMS

The usual customs rules apply. China no longer requires that you fill out a form listing all your valuables and how much money you have on you. Two liters of alcoholic beverages and 600 (!) cigarettes is the legal limit. Officially you shouldn't bring in more than 72 rolls of still film, but no one seems to be counting.

HEALTH

You don't need to show a vaccination certificate on arrival in China unless you've traveled from or through an area where there's been a recent outbreak of smallpox, cholera or yellow fever. Inside China you'll probably come down with colds, chest and sinus congestion and a persistent cough if you stay any real length of time, largely from a combination of damp and industrial pollution in the bigger cities. You'll also suffer a bout or two of stomach trouble from the change of diet, and so should take along a supply of Lomotil or any similar anti-diarrheal medicine. In the event of non-serious illness don't be shy about visiting a Chinese clinic armed with a phrasebook. Some of the Chinese herbal rem-

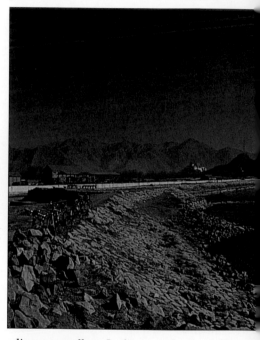

edies are excellent. In the case of serious illness or an accident, get to Hong Kong.

Hepatitis is the main illness to worry about, because of the general lack of hygiene at eating houses, noodle and soup stalls and even some of the hotel kitchens. It's advisable to have a gamma-globulin shot before you go to China. Once there, always be careful of where and what you eat on the streets, use your own chopsticks wherever you can, always drink only the boiled water supplied in the hotels and on the trains for tea, and if you're unlucky enough to come down with extreme lethargy, nausea, fever, loss of appetite and a yellowing of the whites of the eyes, get right out of China, fast. Go to Hong Kong, and straight to hospital.

LANGUAGE

Mandarin, or Putonghua, is the official language of China. Mutually unintelligible dialects are legion: Cantonese, for example, is the dialect in Guangdong and Hong Kong, though Chaozhou is spoken in the north of Guangdong, and north of here again the locals speak Minnan (Hokkien). To complicate things even further, there are the Turkic tongues of the Moslem northwest and Tibetan in Tibet.

on the whole very patient with non-Mandarin speakers. Be sure too that your reference is in Pinyin, the new Romanized form of Chinese, as distinct from the old Wade-Giles system. It is Pinyin that has changed Peking to Beijing, Mao Tse-tung to Mao Zedong, Soochow to Suzhou and Chungking to Chongqing. From the tourist's point of view, the Pinyin is rendered indecipherable by five letter combinations, which will draw a blank if they're not pronounced properly:

"x" — pronounced "s" (but slightly more slurred than in English).

Although Mandarin is grammatically a very simple language, its written form is probably the most difficult in the world to learn, and as a spoken language it is made difficult for foreigners by its tonal aspect. There are four tones, and depending on which tone you use, a sound can mean any of four things. Thus, famously, the sound *ma* can mean variously "mother," "hemp," "horse" or "scold." The possibilities for miscommunication should be immediately apparent.

The best advice is to get yourself a Mandarin phrasebook that includes the written Chinese for everything you need to say. At least you can then point your meaning out and be understood. You will find the Chinese

"q" — pronounced "ch" (but harder than in English).

"c" — pronounced "ts," as in "it's."

"zh" — pronounced "j," as in "Joe."

"j" — pronounced "ds," as in "fads."

There are two phrases that you will find useful just about wherever you go, "Ni hao" (pronounced "nee how"), which means "Hello. How are you?" and "xiexie" (pronounced "seeyuh, seeyuh"), which means "thank you."

The polite way to get things done in China is to preface your request with the expression "mafan ni," or literally "bother you."

Framed by dry foothills and rocky banks, the Lhasa River in remote Tibet, receives the day's first welcome rays of sunlight.

Once you've said that you can say "wo yao…", meaning "I want…". But this is hardly the place for a crash course in Mandarin. With a phrasebook and some perseverance, you should have a repertoire of basic phrases together within a short time.

The followings are some terms frequently used in this book:

lu, dao, jie — road, street
da — big, major, great
dajie, dadao — main street or avenue
dong — east
xi — west

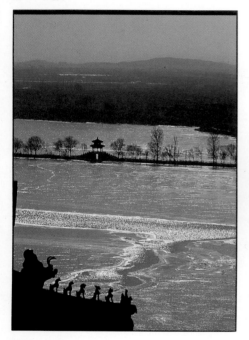

bei — north
nan — south
Beijing *Nanlu* — Southern Beijing Road
hu — lake
si, miao, yuan — temple or monastery
shan — mountain
ta — pagoda
gongyuan — park
yuan — garden
cun — village
qu — district

PHOTOGRAPHY

You can take photographs just about anywhere in China except in the vicinity of military installations or some administrative compounds and at some major tourist attractions, like the Mogao Buddhist Grottoes at Dunhuang and the terracotta warriors in Xi'an, for example, where there are signs saying "No Photographs."

Though to Westerners, this rule may seem like forbidding photography at the Lincoln Memorial or Nelson's Column, it is an understandable response from a country that has seen much of its cultural treasures plundered in the past.

Amongst the people themselves, the Chinese are like any other nationality — they do not like cameras poking at them. However, they often enjoy having their children photographed, and they will relax if you spend time around them blending in with their environment; this is where a bicycle really comes in handy.

The Chinese love photographing each other, however, and twist themselves into remarkable contortions with the latest instamatics. If you're quick-witted but discreet you can often piggyback a good group or human interest shot by simply shooting what they're lining up. Sometimes all it takes is a friendly but bold request, and they'll pose willingly for you.

As for film, Kodak and Fuji print film is widely available. The only slide film available in most places is Ektachrome; for anything else you'll have to do your shopping in Hong Kong or at home.

COMMUNICATIONS

POST

Every reasonable hotel in China has its own mailing desk for postcards and letters. Mailing costs vary from place to place, but are always reasonable. Most hotels provide stationery too, but the envelopes have no adhesive on them and must be stuck down with glue at the mail desk. All cities and larger towns have a centrally located post office as well, where you can mail postcards, letters and parcels.

TELEPHONES

Most hotels, even budget ones nowadays, have telephones in the rooms with International Direct Dial lines. Local calls are not free but should cost next to nothing, and if your hotel doesn't have IDD for international calls, you can go telephone via an operator or fill out a booking form at the desk. Bear in mind, however, that it will be around 30% cheaper to dial from the central telecommunications office (usually in the same building as the general post office) than from the hotel.

TELEGRAMS, FAXES AND E-MAIL

The telecommunications office at the post office is the place for telegrams and theoretically for faxes too. In practice, important faxes should be done at a hotel business center where you can watch them go through and receive a slip confirming they reached their destination. On the e-mail front, China is not exactly "wired," but the situation is improving fast. Check whether your server has a "roaming account" with China access numbers. The big servers like Compuserve and America Online have local China numbers.

BASICS

SECURITY

Crime is on the rise, especially in the big cities, where poorer rural people are flocking to find work. While you could safely leave your hotel door open and not worry about your possessions being stolen during the revolutionary years, there have since been increasing reports of foreigners being robbed on trains and buses, and even in the new international hotels. Nowadays, never leave anything valuable in your rooms or otherwise unattended.

The safest way to conduct yourself in China is the way you'd do it in any country or city — don't flash large amounts of money around, don't take in too much in the way of valuables, and consign those that you buy along the way to your hotel safe deposit.

ELECTRICITY

Electrical current is 220 volts all over China, and the sockets are mostly two-pin. It's best to take battery-operated shavers, hair dryers and other gadgets.

TIME

Despite the size of the country, there are no time zones. When it's noon in Beijing it's noon everywhere else in China.

ACCESS

Just about every area of tourist interest is now open to organized tours and individual travel, though two regions bear watching for political and social unrest and the possibil-

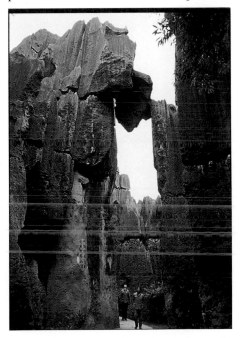

ity of travel restrictions. Tibet is obviously one of them. In the sudden upsurge of anti-Chinese demonstrations and riots in the late 1980s, student backpackers from the West actively encouraged and even helped organize Tibetan resistance. Whatever the merits of their involvement, it convinced the authorities that they'd better keep much stricter control on foreign travel into the country — hence the restrictions that have gone into place since.

Another troubled region is Xinjiang in the northwest, where in the wake of the

OPPOSITE: Winter ice glistens on Kunming Lake, the landscaped centerpiece of the Summer Palace in Beijing. ABOVE: A rock hangs precariously, forming an arch in the Stone Forest.

breakup of the neighboring Soviet Union, and a rise in Islamic activism throughout Central Asia, China's Muslim minorities have started flexing their political muscle. From X'ian to Kashgar, the signs of a possible Islamic independence movement, and the prospect of a Chinese crackdown, have been evident for some time; anyone planning to travel the old Silk Road route, for example, would be well advised to check on safety and security first. There are good reasons to avoid certain other areas. Some have cultural attractions but are just not

221-8681 or (65) 221-8682 FAX (65) 221-9267, 1 Shenton Way, 17-05 Robina House, 01106. **Spain (** (34 1) 548-0011 FAX (34 1) 548-0597, Gran Via 88, Grupo 2, Planta 16, 28013 Madrid. **United Kingdom (** (44171) 935-9787 FAX (44 171) 487-5842, 4 Glentworth Street, London NW1. **United States**: New York **(** (1 212) 760-9700 FAX (1 212) 760-8809, 350 Fifth Avenue, Suite 6413, Empire State Building, NY 10118; Los Angeles **(** (1 818) 250-8906 FAX (1 818) 545-7506, 333 West Broadway, Suite 201, Glendale, Los Angeles, CA 912204.

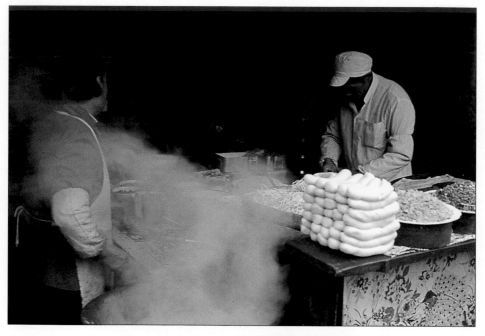

worth the expense and trouble it can take to get through to them. As I've already stated, the paramount consideration that should be given to any itinerary or travel plan in China is the question of enjoyment versus endurance.

CHINA NATIONAL TOURIST OFFICES (CNTO)

Australia ((61 2) 9299-4057 FAX (61 2) 9290-1958, 19th Floor, 44 Market Street, Sydney, 2000. **France (** (33 1) 44 21 82 82 FAX (33 1) 44 21 81 00, 116, avenue des Champs Élysées, 75008 Paris. **Germany (** (49 69) 520135 FAX (49 69) 528490, Ilkenhanstrasse 6, D-60433, Frankfurt am Main. **Singapore (** (65)

CHINESE EMBASSIES AND CONSULATES

Australia ((6) 273-4780, 15 Coronation Drive, Yarralumla, Canberra, ACT 2600. **Austria (** (1) 713-7606 Metternichgasse 4, A-1030, Vienna. **Belgium (** (2) 640-4006, 21, boulevard Gen. Jacques, 1050 Brussels. **Canada (** (1 613) 234-2706 FAX (1 613) 230-9794, 515 St. Patrick Street, Ottawa, ON KIN 5H3. **Denmark (** 31611013, Oregaards Alle 25, DK 2900, Hellerup, Copenhagen 2900. **France (** (1) 47 20 86 82, 21, rue de l'Admiral Destaing, 75016 Paris. **Germany (** (228) 353654, Friedrich-Ebert Strasse 59, 53177 Bonn. **Italy (** (6) 3630-8534, 613 Via Della Camilluccia, Rome 00135. **Japan (** (3) 3403-3381, 3-4-33, Moto-Azabu,

Minato-ku, Tokyo. **Netherlands** ((70) 355-1515, Adriaan Goekooplaan 7, 2517 JX DEN, The Hague. **New Zealand** ((4) 587-0407, 104A Korokoro Road, Petone, Wellington. **Spain** ((341) 413-5892, C/Arturo Soria, 113, 28043 Madrid. **Sweden** ((8) 767-8740, Ringvagen 56, 18134 Lidings. **Switzerland** ((31) 951-1401, 7 JV Widmannstrasse, 3074 Muri Berne. **United Kingdom** ((171) 631-1430, Cleveland Court, 1–3 Leinster House, London W2 (visas 31 Portland Place, London W1). **United States** ((202) 328-2500, 2300 Connecticut Ave. NW, Washington DC 20008.

NICHOLAS D. KRISTOF, SHERYL WUDUNN, *China Wakes: The Struggle for the Soul of a Rising Power*, Vintage Books, 1995.

ANTHONY LAWRENCE, *China: The Long March*, London, Merehurst Press, 1986.

LYNN PAN, *The New Chinese Revolution*, London, Hamish Hamilton, 1987.

DANIEL P. REID, *Chinese Herbal Medicine*, Hong Kong, CFW Publications Ltd., 1987.

K.G. ROBERT, *China: Land of Discovery and Invention*, Weldingborough, (UK), Patrick Stephens, 1986.

HARRISON E. SALISBURY, *China: 100 years of*

Recommended Reading

BLUNDEN & ELVIN, *Cultural Atlas of China*, Phaidon Publications, 1983.

RICHARD BAUM, *Burying Mao: Chinese Politics in the Age of Deng Xiaoping*, Princeton, 1994.

DAVID BONAVIA, *The Chinese: A Portrait*, Penguin, 1987.

JOHN KING FAIRBANK, *China: A New History*, Harvard University Press, 1994.

JACQUES GERNET, *A History of Chinese Civilization*, Cambridge, Cambridge University Press, 1986.

PETER HOPKIRK, *Foreign Devils on the Silk Road.*

PETER HOPKIRK, *The Great Game.*

ZHU JIAJIN, *Treasures of the Forbidden City*, Viking Press, 1986.

Revolution, André Deutsch, 1983.

HARRISON E. SALISBURY, *The Long March*, Pan, 1986.

STERLING SEAGRAVE, *The Soong Dynasty*, Sidgwick & Jackson, 1985.

PAUL THEROUX, *Riding the Iron Rooster: By Train Through China*, Penguin, 1989.

COLIN THUBRON, *Behind the Wall: A Journey Through China*, Penguin, 1987.

OPPOSITE: Steamed bread and noodles, the staples of northern cuisine, on a food stall in Beijing. ABOVE: Young Kazekhs from northwestern China ride horseback in traditional costume.

Quick Reference A–Z Guide to Places and Topics of Interest with Listed Accommodation, Restaurants and Useful Telephone Numbers

Picture Credits

Adina Amsel: page 108. **Airphoto International (Profile Photo Library):** page 55. **Adrian Bradshaw:** *cover*, and pages 3, 4, 5 *right*, 6 *left*, 7 *left and right*, 13, 15 *top*, 25 *top*, 34, 68, 70, 74, 82, 84, 87, 95, 97, 101, 105, 137, 142, 143, 149, 150, 164, 165, 168, 171, 177, 184, 185, 186, 187 *right*, 188, 189, 193, 194, 195 *top and bottom*, 197, 198, 199, 212, 213, 222, 223, 225, 227 *top and bottom*, 229, 231, 233, 236, 237, 242, 249, 250, 251, 255 *top and bottom*, 265, 266, 268, 270, 271, 272, 273, 275, 280, 285, 289, 296, 297, 300, 303, 305, 307. **Rex A. Butler (Profile Photo Library):** page 120. **Peter Danford:** pages 31, 42, 123. **Alain Evrard:** page 71. **Hong Kong Museum of History, Urban Council:** page 114. **HKTA:** pages 53, 129 **Derek Maitland:** pages 85, 109, 139, 141 *left and right*, 147, 162, 163, 167, 178, 181, 183, 187 left, 196, 201, 243, 247, 269. **Yann Layma:** pages 11, 79, 83, 103, 134. **Hans Lindberg (Profile Photo Library):** page 132. **Fiona Nichols:** pages 32, 33, 39, 41, 45, 46, 57, 235, 293. **Novo Editions:** page 59. **Chris Stowers:** pages 136, 157. **Chris Taylor:** pages 14, 18, 19, 29, 47, 151, 157, 160, 200, 291. **Paul Thompson (Profile Photo Library):** page 64. **Graham Uden:** pages 21, 23, 24, 25 *bottom*, 27, 49, 50, 61, 63, 67, 73, 89, 111, 172, 209, 228, 241, 256, 257, 258, 260, 277. **Nik Wheeler:** pages 5 *left*, 6 *right*, 10, 15 *bottom*, 17, 35, 37, 69, 76, 75, 77, 78, 80, 90, 91, 96, 117, 119, 121, 124, 127, 131, 145, 153, 154, 155, 159, 202, 206, 207, 215 *top and bottom*, 217, 219 *top and bottom*, 220, 221, 226, 238, 239, 264, 276, 279, 281, 282, 283, 284, 295, 298, 299, 301, 306, 308, 309.